UNREAL ENGINE 5 I
Volume I: BASICS, COMBAT, AND VFX
Second Edition

Dr. CHIHMING CHIU

MW01286346

Cover Design: Christina Lee Chiu

ISBN: 978-1-9992127-0-4 (Paperback)

Imprint: Independently published

Dedication

To Shih-Kuo Chiu (1940-2018) for your love and inspiration

C. C.

Contents

Dedication iii

Foreword xi

Preface xiii

CHAPTER 1   Unreal Engine 5 and Visual Studio 1

1.1 Unreal Engine 5 Installation and Migration Guide 2

    1.1.1   Installing Unreal Engine 5 2

    1.1.2   What's New and Migration Guide 5

1.2 Visual Studio Installation and Setup 11

1.3 Unreal Editor and the New Interface 13

    1.3.1   Creating UE5 Game Projects 13

    1.3.2   UE5 Editor Windows 14

    1.3.3   Unreal Editor Toolbars 18

1.4 Visual Studio IDE 20

    1.4.1   Creating C++ Projects 20

    1.4.2   Creating C++ Source Files 22

    1.4.3   Visual Studio Windows 23

    1.4.4   Visual Studio Toolbar 25

    1.4.5   How C++ Works in Visual Studio 26

    1.4.6   Debugging C++ Projects 28

1.5 Summary 30

Exercises 31

CHAPTER 2   Modern C++ Primer 33

2.1 C++ Fundamental Data Types, Variables, and Arrays 34

    2.1.1   C++ Fundamental Data Types 34

    2.1.2   User-Defined Data Types 35

2.1.3   Enumeration Data Types 36

2.1.4   Conversion between Data Types 37

2.1.5   C++ Variables 37

2.1.6   Constants 39

2.1.7   Arrays 39

2.1.8   Strings 40

2.2 C++ Operators **41**

2.2.1   Arithmetic Operators 41

2.2.2   Assignment Operators 42

2.2.3   Comparison Operators 42

2.2.4   Logical Operators 43

2.2.5   Bitwise Operators 43

2.2.6   Operator Precedence 44

2.3 Functions **45**

2.4 C++ Statements **46**

2.4.1   Selection Statements 46

2.4.2   Iteration Statements 48

2.5 Pointers **50**

2.5.1   Call by Reference 52

2.5.2   Pointer Arithmetic and Arrays 54

2.6 Macros **55**

2.7 Templates **57**

2.8 Summary **59**

Exercises **59**

CHAPTER 3   C++ Object-Oriented Programming **61**

3.1 Classes and Objects **62**

3.1.1   Declaration of Classes 62

3.1.2   Constructors and Destructors 63

3.1.3   Inheritance 66

3.1.4   Encapsulation 67

3.1.5   Polymorphism 71

3.1.6   Abstract Classes 78

3.2 Interfaces **80**

3.3 Exceptions **84**

3.4 Multithreading Programming **88**

3.4.1   Threads 88

3.4.2   The `async` Function Template 90

3.5 Data Structures in Modern C++ **92**

3.5.1   The `vector` Class 92

3.5.2   The `list` Class 94

3.5.3   The `queue` Class 95

3.5.4   The `stack` Class 97

3.5.5   The `map` Class 98

3.6 Summary **100**

Exercises **100**

CHAPTER 4   Introduction to UE5 Game Programming **103**

4.1 UE5 Game Programming Quick Start **104**

4.1.1   Required Setup 104

4.1.2   Creating a New C++ Class 105

4.1.3   Editing Your C++ Class 107

4.1.4   Compiling and Testing Your C++ Code 109

4.1.5   Creating Blueprints from the C++ Class 112

4.2 Introduction to Programming in UE5 .... **117**

4.2.1   C++ and Blueprint 117

4.2.2   Hot Reloading and Live Coding 126

4.3 UE5 Class Libraries **129**

4.3.1   Gameplay Classes: Objects, Actors, and Components 129

4.3.2   Math Class Libraries in UE5 133

4.3.3   UE5 Numeric Types, Strings, and Containers 137

4.4 Memory Management and Garbage Collection **141**

4.4.1   UObjects and Garbage Collection 141

4.4.2   Actors and Garbage Collection 142

4.4.3 UStructs and Non-UObject References 143

4.5 Summary **144**

Exercises **144**

CHAPTER 5   Combat for Action RPGs **145**

5.1 Creating Art Assets for RPGs **146**

    5.1.1   Creating the C++ RPG Project 146

    5.1.2   Creating an Open World Level 147

    5.1.3   Player Characters 195

    5.1.4   Enemy Characters and Trees 198

    5.1.5   The Great Sword Weapon 202

    5.1.6   Animation Sequences 205

    5.1.7   ARPG Root Motions 209

5.2 Blend Spaces **216**

    5.2.1   Creating Blend Spaces for Warriors 216

    5.2.2   Creating Blend Spaces for Wolves 220

5.3 The Character and Camera Controls **222**

    5.3.1   The Character Controller 222

    5.3.2   Animation Classes and Blueprints 231

    5.3.3   The ARPG Third-Person Camera Controller 256

    5.3.4   Maps and GameMode 263

    5.3.5   Double and Multiple Jump 268

5.4 Stats in RPGs **270**

    5.4.1   What Is a Stat? 270

    5.4.2   Why Have Stats at All? 272

    5.4.3   Implementing Stats 273

    5.4.4   Implementing the Stamina System 280

5.5 Action RPG Combat **298**

    5.5.1   Character Health and GUI Design 299

    5.5.2   Animation Montages 304

    5.5.3   Combos in ARPGs 315

    5.5.4   Damage Rolls 326

5.5.5   Weapon Classes 331

5.5.6   Enemy Classes and Animation Setup 346

5.5.7   Melee Weapon Loading Setup 362

5.5.8   Automatic Enemy Locking 377

5.5.9   Damage Texts 385

5.6 Integrating Animation and Sound Effects........................ **393**

5.6.1   Importing Sound Clips 393

5.6.2   Physical Materials 394

5.6.3   Playing Footstep Sound Effects 398

5.7 Horse Riding System **403**

5.7.1   Horse Skeletal Mesh and Animations 403

5.7.2   Horse Characters 409

5.7.3   Horse Full-Body IK 441

5.8 Summary.. **460**

Exercises **460**

CHAPTER 6   Visual Effects Design... **463**

6.1 Niagara VFX System **464**

6.1.1   Niagara Overview 464

6.1.2   Niagara VFX Workflow 466

6.2 Niagara Quick Start.. **467**

6.2.1   Project Setup..467

6.2.2   Creating the Effect...472

6.2.3   Editing Module Settings..477

6.2.4   Attaching Niagara Effects to the Character 484

6.3 Special Effects for Action RPGs **488**

6.3.1   Sword Trails 488

6.3.2   The Impact Effect and Shockwaves 511

6.3.3   Fireballs...534

6.3.4   The Mesh Disintegration Effect 552

6.3.5   Mesh Disintegration in C++...575

6.3.6   Enemy Destruction and Resurrection 583

6.3.7   Fireball Projectiles..587

6.4 Summary **599**

Exercises..**599**

Appendix...**602**

A.1 How to Avoid Crashing the Unreal Editor **602**

A.2 Online References and Resources **602**

A.2.1   Video Tutorials..603

A.2.2   Modern C++ in Visual Studio 604

A.2.3   UE5 Online Document 604

A.2.4   Unreal Engine Forums 604

A.3 Online Art Assets and Tools **605**

A.3.1   Online Free Assets 605

A.3.2   Free Art Creation Tools..605

Index...**606**

Foreword

I still remember the first time I met Dr. Chiu at the Taipei World Trade Center, the annual new generation design exhibition venue ten years ago, when his students showed the award-winning online game – Chaos Era Online. I was surprised at how a team of several college students developed a game comparable to the industry quality. Later I learned that Dr. Chiu is already the founder and CEO of a mobile game developer which was also the content provider for Chunghwa Telecom, the largest Taiwanese telecommunications company. At that time, I was looking for industry faculty for our department and decided to invite Dr. Chiu to join the Digital Media Design Department at Yunlin University of Science and Technology as a faculty member. During his tenure in this department, his game design courses including Game Planning and Game Programming were well received by students.

In the academic field, Dr. Chiu has also made great achievements. His doctoral dissertation – A Game Engine Framework featuring Natural Interaction (GENI) was one of the few academic papers that discussed the design of an interactive online game engine. He also published journal papers in Virtual Reality and Artificial Intelligence for games. When Dr. Chiu informed me that he would author a book series about how to design and program an Action RPG (ARPG) using the latest Unreal Engine 5 (UE5) and invited me to write a foreword. I was delighted! Because UE5 has recently become the industry standard for developing AAA games, and with the Chaos Era Online ported to UE5, I believe the new book series will be the best resource to learn to program in Unreal C++ and implement an ARPG.

Whether you are a college student or a game programmer who wants to understand how to program an ARPG in Unreal C++ and Blueprint, I highly recommend this book – Unreal Engine 5 RPG Development with C++ and Blueprint – by Dr. Chihming Chiu.

Chairman, Taiwan Association of Digital Media Design and
Professor, College of Design, National Yunlin University of Science and Technology

Kuo-Kuang Fan

Preface

With the Unreal Engine 5 (UE5) officially released, it has been well received and has become the industry standard for developing AAA titles according to the announcement made by many game studios including CD Projekt Red and Crystal Dynamics.

Since UE5 first launched in Early Access unveiled in 2020, I decided to port our award-winning ARPG, Chaos Era Online (COA online), developed using the **Torque** Game Engine and C++, to UE5. This is because my co-workers at the Southern Taiwan University of Science and Technology (STUST) always asked whether I could port the game over using the Unreal Engine, which was already powerful and popular in the past. After about one year of porting it over to UE5, the progress was smooth, and I decided to author a new book series to share the experience of using Unreal C++ and Blueprint to develop an online Action RPG.

This book is the first volume of the series and will cover basics, combat systems, and visual effects (VFX). In the series, we aim to not only explore how a commercial ARPG can be made using UE5 in C++ and Blueprint but also discuss the theory behind the RPG design. The reason why it can be presented in this way is based on my work over a decade as both a professional game developer and a lecturer of multimedia and game development at several universities in Taiwan, including the Department of Multimedia and Entertainment Science department at the Southern Taiwan University of Science and Technology and the Department of Digital Media Design at the National Yunlin University of Science and Technology. Over the years, our team has accumulated experience and achievements in making online games and obtained good results in related online game design competitions.

With the accompanying exercises in each chapter, this book is also suitable as a textbook for a one-semester course in game programming for Juniors or Seniors in a four-year college. The teaching materials will be available soon by request after this book is published.

About the Author

Dr. Chiu earned his Ph.D. in Interactive Game Engine Technology from National Chung Cheng University in Taiwan in 2015 and a Master of Computer Science degree in Computer Graphics from Arizona State University at Tempe in 1993. Before immigrating to Canada, he was the founder and CEO of the Powernet mobile business cooperation, a mobile game content provider for the largest Telecom company in Taiwan, Chunghwa Telecom. He has also taught game design and development classes for top-ranked universities including the National Yunlin University of Science and Technology and Southern Taiwan University of Science and Technology (STUST), where he helped found the first graduate school in multimedia and entertainment science. While in STUST, his team created the online game Chaos Era, which won the Jury Award in the 2009 Chinese Gamer online game design competition. Dr. Chiu currently is an author and tutor living in BC, Canada.

Who This Book Is For

If you have some experience in any programming language, are even a beginner, and want to know how to implement an action RPG using UE5, this book is perfect for you. The first part of this book covers the essentials of the C++ programming language, followed by exploring the modern C++ Object-Oriented Programming techniques required in the later chapters. After you become familiar with programming in C++, further examples are provided in the rest of this book to guide you in building an ARPG using Unreal C++ and Blueprint.

If you are an experienced UE game developer who is interested in ARPG development using the latest UE5, this book is also useful. Through the provided working examples, you'll not only understand the details of implementing a future online ARPG but also apply the techniques presented in this book to the other game engines.

Conventions Used in This Book

Several writing conventions are used in this book to distinguish between different sorts of information. Examples of these conventions and the explanation of their meaning are as follows.

The code is written in a monospaced font (Cascadia Mono) and the following is an example:

```
int total = 0;
for(int n = 1; n <= 100; n++)
{
  total = total + n;

  if (total > 10000)
    break;
}
```

Some code blocks will expand the code you have written or already exist in the C++ file. Then the old lines will be at the normal weight, but the new lines will be shown in **bold**.

Besides, when the author wants to draw your attention to a certain part of a code block, the relevant items or lines are also displayed in **bold** as follows:

```
private void Update()
{
  if(aNumber == 0)
    printf("aNumber = 0");
}
```

The code words are set in regular paragraph text: "The isGrounded variable is a flag." Important words and new terms are displayed in **bold**, and the words that you see on the UI will be as follows: "Enter a message…".

The Companion Website and YouTube Channel

You can find further information and assets for this book at the accompanying author website at **www.mmoprogramming.net**, including the book's source code, art assets, and the errata.

If you are a teacher or professor who needs the teaching materials, we provide PowerPoint slides in different languages by request as well. For solutions to the exercises in each chapter, please contact the author using the form on this website.

Any suggestion or correction is also welcome including the errors you discovered, and you can use the form provided on the website to give the feedback. The author also has a YouTube channel dedicated to providing additional supplementary tutorials for the book. You can find the link on the website as well.

Download the Color Images

You can also find a PDF file that contains all color images of the screenshots and diagrams used in this book from the author's website.

Acknowledgments

First, I would like to think my wife, Ruby, has been supportive and understanding during the times I'm writing code furiously to meet deadlines. I also want to thank my family, Danny, and Christina, they have been a massive support for this book, and their partnership in testing all the examples and the game is invaluable.

I would also like to thank all the educators who have taught me and worked as my colleagues. Special thanks go to Dr. Jyh-Jong Tsay and Dr. Ding-Yue Hung. Though I had worked as a lecturer and game designer before meeting them, they each profoundly affected my understanding of machine learning and game AI. I also owe tremendous thanks to Dr. Kuo-Kuang Fan, who was a friend and mentor to me during the years I taught at the National Yulin University of Science and Technology Digital Media

Design Department. Many other brilliant faculty and friends at STUST College of Digital Design helped me make the award-winning online game, Chaos Era Online, which inspired me to author this book, including Dr. Ming-Yuhe Chang, Dr. Hua-Cheng Chang, Dr. Chih-Cheng Sun, and Dr. Her-Tyan Yeh.

Thanks as well to all the fantastic students, including Wei-Xiang Chen, Ron-Tai Xie, Shi-Yu Liu, and Feng-Yue Gao whom I have taught over the past decade. You convinced me that a practice oriented online ARPG game programming textbook is important and inspired me to author this book.

I also acknowledge Epic Games for the fantastic game engine and wish together with the content of this book, new generations of students and game programmers can understand the design theory and the details of implementing an ARPG. I also greatly appreciate all members of the Unreal Engine community who regularly contribute to the forums, several important ideas, and the code in this book were inspired by this invaluable knowledge base.

Finally, I would like to thank you for purchasing this book, and I hope that it helps you fulfill the dream of making an ARPG using UE5. Looking forward to seeing and playing your ARPGs in the future.

CHAPTER

1

Unreal Engine 5 and Visual Studio

In the first chapter of this book, we are going to introduce the installation of Unreal Engine 5 (UE5) which is required for this book, and the installation and setup of the Visual Studio integrated development environment (IDE).

After the installation and setup for the UE5 and Visual Studio are ready, we'll introduce UE5's new features and discuss how to migrate your old UE4 game projects to the new version. Lastly, we are going to introduce how C++ works in Visual Studio and how to create the C++ project required for the following chapters.

1.1 Unreal Engine 5 Installation and Migration Guide

This first section discusses the installation of the UE5 and then introduces migrating your old UE4 game projects over to the new version of the game engine.

1.1.1 Installing Unreal Engine 5

To download and install UE5, you need to:

1. Download and install the **Epic Games Launcher**.
2. Sign up for an Epic Games account if you don't have one.
3. Sign into the Epic Games Launcher.
4. Install Unreal Engine.

Download and Install the Epic Games Launcher

To download and install the Launcher, follow the following steps:

1. Access the **Download Unreal Engine** page[1] and scroll down until you see the **DOWNLOAD LAUNCHER** button as shown below:

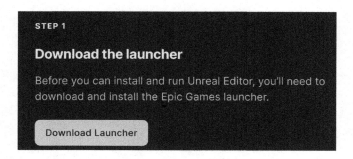

---

[1] **Download Unreal Engine**, https://www.unrealengine.com/en-US/download.

2. Click the button and the Launcher installer will be downloaded to your computer. Depending on your operating system settings, you might be asked to select a save location or approve a security prompt before the download can start.
3. After the download finishes, run the installer and wait for it to complete.

Note: In addition to the Launcher, this may also install other programs you require to run Unreal Engine, such as DirectX.

Creating an Epic Games Account

After the setup program installs the Epic Games Launcher on your machine, you will be prompted to sign in with your Epic Games account as follows:

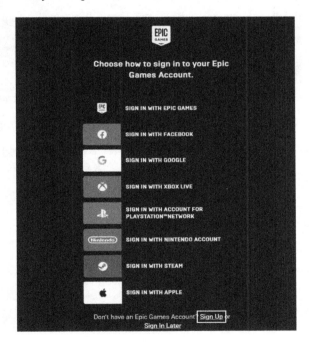

If you have an account, sign into the Launcher and continue to the next section. If you don't have an account, click **Sign Up** to create one. You can sign up for an Epic Games account with your email or a supported social media or gaming platform account. You can also proceed without creating an account by clicking **Sign In Later**. However, you will not be able to download or use Unreal Engine without an account. After you've created your account, **Sign In** to the Launcher.

Installing Unreal Engine 5

Now that you've **signed in**to the Epic Games Launcher, you're ready to install UE5, and the steps are as follows:

1. Click the **Unreal Engine** tab inside the Epic Games Launcher, then click the **Install Engine** button as shown below:

2. (Optional) Click the **Browse** button, as shown below, to change the install path.

3. Click the **Install** button and wait for the installation to complete. Depending on your system specifications and Internet connection speed, downloading and installing Unreal Engine 5 can take between 10 to 40 minutes, sometimes longer.

Launching Unreal Engine

After the installation is complete, press the **Library** tab and you will see all of the different engine installations on our computer. Choose one of the versions and click the **Launch** button, as shown below, to open the UE5.

Congratulations! You are now ready to start using UE5. In the next section, we are going to explore what's new in the UE5 and provide a migration guide for UE4 developers.

1.1.2 What's New and Migration Guide

This section will outline what's new in UE5 and the migration guide for UE4 developers to migrate their game projects over.

What's new in UE5

UE5 enables game developers and creators across industries to realize **next-generation** real-time 3D content and experiences with greater freedom, fidelity, and flexibility than ever before. UE5 also empowers big and small teams to push the boundaries of what's possible, visually and interactively, with the ability to:

❖ **Leverage game-changing fidelity**: Bring incredibly immersive and realistic interactive experiences to life with groundbreaking new features like **Nanite** and **Lumen** that provide a generational leap in visual fidelity and enable worlds to be fully dynamic.

❖ **Build bigger worlds:** Think big, really big. UE5 provides the tools and assets you need to create truly expansive worlds for your players to explore, using content that scales.

❖ **Animate and model in context:** New artist-friendly animation authoring, retargeting, and runtime tools—together with a significantly expanded modeling toolset—reduce iteration and eliminate round-tripping, speeding up the creative process.

❖ **Get up to speed faster:** With a modern, flexible UI that offers an enhanced user experience and increased efficiency; updated industry-specific templates that act as more useful starting points; and migration guides that provide a smooth transition from previous versions for existing users, UE5 is easier to adapt and learn than ever before.

Lumen Global Illumination and Reflections

Lumen is a fully dynamic **global illumination** and **reflection** solution that immediately reacts to scene and light changes, allowing artists and designers to create more dynamic scenes with greater realism. Changing the angle of the sun, turning on a flashlight, opening an exterior door, or even blowing up a wall will cause a change to indirect lighting and reflections.

The system renders diffuse interreflection with **infinite** bounces and **indirect** specular reflections, highlighting even the most minute details within expansive, elaborate environments. Artists and designers are no longer tied to static scenes with precomputed lighting baked into textures — a huge timesaving when you can see the results of changes in the editor without needing to rebuild lighting or set up lightmap UVs for individual Static Meshes.

Nanite Virtualized Geometry

Nanite's virtualized micro polygon geometry system enables developers to create games with massive amounts of geometric detail. You can directly import film-quality source art composed of millions of polygons — anything from **ZBrush** sculpts to photogrammetry scans — and place them millions of times, all while maintaining a real-time frame rate, and without any noticeable loss of fidelity.

Nanite intelligently streams and processes only the detail you can perceive, largely removing triangle count and draw call constraints. It eliminates time-consuming work, such as baking details to normal maps and manually authoring levels of detail, freeing you to concentrate on creativity.

World Partition for Large, Open Environments

World Partition is an **automatic** data management and streaming system used both in the Editor and at runtime, which completely removes the need to manually divide the world into countless sublevels to manage streaming and reduce data contention.

Using World Partition, the world exists as a single persistent level. In Editor, the world is split using a 2D grid, and data is partially loaded based on your area of interest using the World Partition editor window. This makes it possible to handle massive worlds that would otherwise not fit in memory or take a long time to load. When cooking or launching PIE, the world is divided into **grid cells** optimized for runtime streaming, which becomes individual streaming levels.

World Partition is enabled **by default** when using many of the New Project templates designed for Games and the **Open World** and Open World Empty map types.

Data Layers for World Partition

Data Layers for World Partition is a system designed to **conditionally** load world data by activating and deactivating layers in the editor and at runtime. Data Layers are an excellent way to organize your world in the editor. You can also use it to handle different scenarios in your game and create different variations of the same World. This is great for different setups for night and day or changes to the world after completing quests.

Updated User Interface

The **User Interface (UI)** has been updated for UE 5 to provide a consistent and streamlined experience. The default colors have been adjusted for a darker default theme. Users can also set up their **Themes** in the **Editor Preferences**, to customize the editor to their own erred style. Updated icons provide compact and consistent visual cues.

New features such as the **Content Drawer**, sidebar **Tabs,** and the **Create Menu** provide easy access to the tools you need while allowing maximum viewport space.

Content Drawer

The **Content Drawer** is a new feature that allows you to summon a **Content Browser** overlay. This gives you rapid asset access without having to reserve space for a docked panel. You can summon the Content Drawer using **Ctrl + Spacebar**. Alternatively, you can click on the Content Drawer tab name to expand the drawer. The Content Drawer can also be docked within the Editor layout or used in conjunction with the traditional Content Browser.

Sidebar Tabs

Users can now dock a Panel into a **Sidebar Tab** on either side of the Editor. By docking a Tab, you can keep frequently used Panels accessible, without the need to sacrifice screen real estate.

Quixel Bridge Integration

Quixel **Bridge** is now integrated directly into Unreal Editor. You can dock Quixel Bridge in the Editor layout, then drag Assets directly into your Level. The Quixel Bridge panel can be accessed from the main menu **Window > Quixel Bridge**.

Note: If you previously installed the UE5 Preview versions, you need to update Quixel Bridge to the **latest** version before use. You can update the plugin in the Epic Games Launcher.

For all details of the UE5 new features, please refer to the online **Unreal Engine 5.0 Release Notes**.

UE5 Migration Guide

This guide describes how to upgrade your UE4 projects to UE5. **UE5** introduces a series of changes, upgrades, and new features to the systems that make up Unreal Engine 4 (UE4). Although there have been significant changes to the engine, the built-in conversion process handles most of the migration work without requiring user action.

To begin, open UE5 from the Epic Games Launcher, and press the **Browse...** button on the bottom of the **Unreal Project Browser** window. If UE5 is already running, click **File > Open Project** from the main menu, select the project you want to upgrade, and click **Open**.

Then the following **Convert Project** window will appear, click the **Open a Copy** button, as shown below, to upgrade a separate copy of your project, leaving the original **unchanged**.

If you click **More Options** on this dialog, you can choose either:

- ❖ **Skip the conversion**, which attempts to open the project as-is.
- ❖ **Convert in-place**, which attempts to convert the existing project rather than make a copy of it.

Note: When you convert a project to UE5, we highly recommend using the **Open a Copy** workflow described above. The **Convert in-place** and **Skip conversion** options

may not work as expected and may lead to data corruption and data loss. Besides, once you update a project to a newer version of Unreal Engine, you won't be able to open it in an older version. Attempting to do so will fail.

Once the conversion process is complete, most projects will be ready to build and run in UE5 without further action. However, certain new or upgraded features benefit from, or even require, some manual updates to operate properly in UE5 and take advantage of its full capabilities. Among the largest systemic changes are **Nanite**, **Lumen**, and **Chaos**. Nanite and Lumen will require some work to get graphics-centric projects to look the same as they did in UE4, and heavily physics-based projects that have not already switched to Chaos will need configuration and Asset modification.

Version-Specific Conversion Notes

Refer to the table below to understand how your project will convert depending on the Unreal Engine version it was created with.

Project Created with Version	Conversion Notes
Unreal Engine 4.0 to 4.26	Your project will load in any version of Unreal Engine that is the same or newer than the version with which it was created. **Note**: The Unreal Engine API has changed over time, which means some projects created with much older versions may not load correctly. For example, Blueprints saved back in 4.0 might call functions that were deprecated in 4.10 and no longer exist in 5.0. However, the project should still load and let you fix up the references that were **deprecated** or **removed**.
Unreal Engine 4.27	Your project will load in Unreal Engine 4.27, 5.0, and newer versions. Note that your project will **not** load in Unreal Engine 5.0 **Early Access**.
Unreal Engine 5.0	Your project will load in Unreal Engine 5.0 and newer versions.
Unreal Engine 5.1 and newer versions	Your project will load in any version of Unreal Engine that is the same or newer than the version with which it was created.

Asset Compatibility

Assets saved in an older version of Unreal Engine can be opened in a **newer** version. For example, if you save an Asset in Unreal Engine 4.26, you can open it with Unreal Engine 5.0.

Assets saved in a **newer** version of Unreal Engine **cannot** be opened in an older version. For example, if you saved an Asset in Unreal Engine 5.0, you will not be able to open it in Unreal Engine 4.26.

Development Platform Changes

UE5 does not support Visual Studio 2017 or Visual Studio 2015. So, if you write C++ code in Visual Studio, you must switch to Visual Studio **2019** or **newer** versions if you are not already using it. Besides, UE5 does not support 32-bit platforms, and there are no plans to add 32-bit platform support in the future.

What's New in the Second Edition

A major feature now is deprecated namely the Input System since the release of UE**5.1**. In this new edition, we will use the **Enhanced Input Actions and Input Mapping Contexts** to re-implement the mechanism for user interaction. Some built-in function calls also have been deprecated, and in this edition, they are replaced with new ones.

Besides, because the second volume is on the way and to be better connected with the volume II, in this edition serval classes, especially the **Equipment-related** component classes are added for the future **Inventory** system.

Some reviews from Amazon.com mentioned about the readability of the pictures and the words in them because of the default **Dark** theme used in the Unreal Editor. Therefore, in this new edition, to improve readability of diagrams and the words inside, a new **Light Grey** theme is used instead of the default one.

On the other hand, to make the words in the pictures become larger, we adjust the **Application Scale** in the UE5 Editor's **Widget Reflector** to achieve this purpose. So, in this new edition, almost all the diagrams have been replaced, with the new theme applied and readability of the words inside should be greatly improved.

Lastly, for the readers of the first edition, the author will provide a migration guide in the near future for how to migrate from the previous edition. Please refer to the author's website to download the guide.

1.2 Visual Studio Installation and Setup

This section will introduce the installation and setup of the free Visual Studio IDE. Please access the free **Visual Studio Community** page[2], scroll down the page until you see the **Free download** button as shown below:

After pressing the button, the **Visual Studio Setup** executable will be downloaded to your computer.

When the download is complete, run the downloaded installer file and the **Visual Studio Installer** will appear as shown below:

After pressing the **Continue** button, Visual Studio Installer will show the window for selecting **Workloads** as shown below. First, find and tick the checkboxes to the **right** of the **.NET desktop development** and **Desktop development with C++**.

---

[2] **Visual Studio Community**, https://visualstudio.microsoft.com/free-developer-offers/.

Continue to tick the checkbox on the right of **Game Development with C++** as shown below:

Finally, press the **Install** button and wait for the installation to complete, the screen is as shown below. If you need to add or remove individual components, you can press the **Modify** button to open the installation window again.

1.3 Unreal Editor and the New Interface

This section will introduce the Unreal Editor and describe the most common elements of the Unreal Engine 5 interface and what they do.

1.3.1 Creating UE5 Game Projects

To create a UE5 game project, please launch the UE5 and the following **Unreal Project Browser** window will appear:

After clicking the **GAMES** on the left panel and selecting the **Third Person** Template, as shown above, on the right panel, click the **C++** tab which means we are going to create a C++ project. UE5 provides several game templates and the **Starter Content** for us to prototype our games quickly.

Then press the **Create** button to create the game project and open the **Unreal Editor** as shown below:

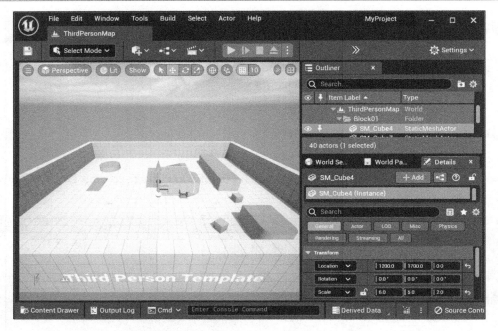

Because this is also a C++ UE5 project, the Visual Studio will be opened as well.

1.3.2 UE5 Editor Windows

This subsection provides a detailed tour of the most common editor windows and how to use them fully.

Level Viewport

The **Level Viewport** displays the contents of the Level that is currently open. When you open a project in Unreal Engine, the project's **default** Level opens in the Level Viewport by default. This is where you can view and edit the contents of your active Level, whether it's a game environment, a product visualization app, or something else.

The Level Viewport can generally display the contents of the Level in two different ways:

❖ **Perspective**, which is a 3D view you can navigate to see the contents of the viewport from different angles.

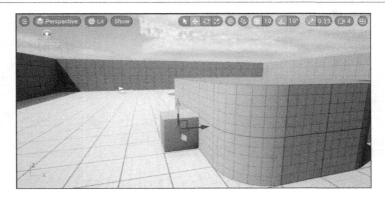

❖ **Orthographic**, which is a **2D** view that looks down one of the main axes (X, Y, or Z).

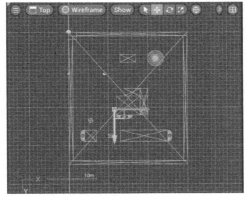

The Level Viewport displays the current Level **Camera's** orientation and allows you to quickly toggle **Perspective** on and off. You can get back to the **Perspective** view by clicking the **Perspective** drop-down.

Besides, in the **Perspective** view, you can use the **Arrow Keys** to move around the level as "**walking**" or "**flying**" through it depending on the current Level **Camera Speed** or **orbit** the Camera around the current pivot point by **left clicking** on the Level and **dragging**. Finally, you can also **zoom in/of out** the Level view by moving the mouse wheel in the Level.

Content Drawer / Content Browser

The **Content Browser** window, similar to Windows Explorer, displays all of the Assets, Blueprints, and other files in your project. You can use it to browse through your content, drag Assets into the Level, migrate Assets between projects, and more.

There are several commonly used folders, which are described below:

❖ **Content**

All game assets accessed through the code should be stored in this folder, which we will use in later chapters.

❖ **StarterContent**

The **StarterContent** folder stores the assets including **Textures** and **Materials** that help us to quickly prototype our games and will be used in later chapters as well.

❖ **C++ Classes**

All the C++ classes generated by UE5 will be stored in this folder.

❖ **Engine**

This folder stores all the Engine-related assets including the C++ code and the content of the **Plugins**.

The **Content Drawer** button, located in the **bottom-left** corner of the Unreal Editor, opens a special instance of the **Content Browser** that **automatically minimizes** when it loses focus (that is, when you click away from it). To keep it open, click the **Dock in Layout** button in the top-right corner of the Content Drawer. This creates a new instance of the Content Browser, but you can still open a new Content Drawer.

Outliner

The **Outliner** panel (formerly known as World Outliner) displays a hierarchical view of all content on your Level. By default, it is located in the upper-right corner of the Unreal Editor window.

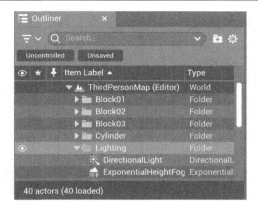

You can also use the Outliner panel to:

❖ Quickly hide or reveal Actors by clicking their associated **Eye** button.
❖ Access an Actor's **context menu** by right clicking that Actor. You can then perform additional, Actor-specific operations from that menu.
❖ Create, move, and delete content folders.

Details Panel

When you select an Actor in the Level Viewport, the **Details** panel will show the settings and properties that affect the Actor you selected. By default, it is located on the right side of the Unreal Editor window, under the **World Outliner** panel.

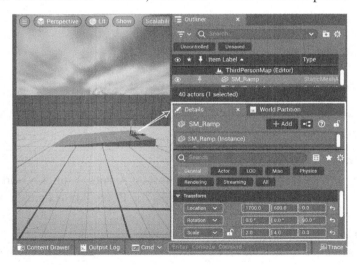

With the **SM_Ramp** Static Mesh selected, as shown above, the **Details Panel** appears docked to the right-hand side of the Unreal Editor.

1.3.3 Unreal Editor Toolbars

In this subsection, we'll explore the Toolbars in the Unreal Editor and outline the functionalities of the tools in them.

Main Toolbar

The **Main Toolbar** contains shortcuts to some of the most used tools and commands in Unreal Editor. It is divided into the following areas:

1. **Save Button**

   Click this button to save the Level that is currently open.

2. **Mode Selection**

   Contains shortcuts for quickly switching between different modes to edit content within your Level:

   ❖ **Select** Editing
   ❖ **Landscape** Editing
   ❖ **Foliage** Editing
   ❖ **Mesh** Painting
   ❖ **Fracture** Editing
   ❖ **Brush** Editing
   ❖ **Animation** Editing

3. **Content Shortcuts**

   Contains shortcuts for adding and opening common types of content within the Level Editor.

Shortcut	Description
Create	Choose from a list of common Assets to quickly add to your Level. You can also access the **Place Actors** panels from this menu.
Blueprints	Create and access Blueprints.
Cinematics	Create a Level Sequence or Master Sequence cinematic.

4. **Play Mode Controls**

Contains shortcut buttons (**Play**, **Skip**, **Stop**, and **Eject**) for running your game in the Editor.

5. **Platforms Menu**

   Contains a series of options you can use to configure, prepare, and deploy your project to different platforms, such as desktop, mobile, or consoles.

6. **Settings**

   Contains various settings for the Unreal Editor, Level Editor Viewport, and game behavior.

Bottom Toolbar

The **Bottom Toolbar** contains shortcuts to the **Command Console**, **Output Log**, **Trace Insights Widget**, and **Derived Data** functionality. It has the following main areas:

Number	Name	Description
1	**Content Drawer**	Opens the **Content Drawer** / **Content Browser** window.
2	**Output Log**	The debugging tool that prints out useful information while your application is running.
3	**Command Console**	Behaves as any other command-line interface: enter console commands to trigger specific editor behaviors. **TIP**: Type **help** and press **Enter** to open a list of available console commands in your browser.
4	**Tracing to**	The **Trace Insights Widget** provides a way to control and manage your **Trace Data** using an Editor interface.
5	**Derived Data**	Provides Derived Data functionality.
6	**Recompiles and reloads C++ code**	Recompiles and reloads C++ code for game systems on the fly using **Live Coding**.

		TIP: You can **disable** the Live Coding using the **Compile options menu** on the right of this area.

1.4 Visual Studio IDE

This section will introduce the Visual Studio IDE and discuss how to use it for creating C++ projects and how C++ works in Visual Studio.

1.4.1 Creating C++ Projects

Launch Visual Studio and the following Startup window will appear:

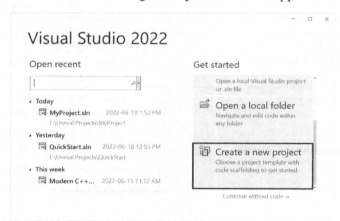

Press the **Create a new project** in the **Get started** panel to continue, and in the next step, after selecting the **C++** from the drop-down menu, make sure that the **Empty Project** template is selected as shown below, then press the **Next** button.

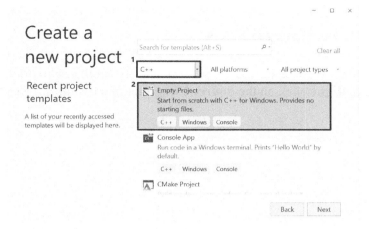

Next, enter "**HelloWorld**" in the **Project name** field as shown below, and after choosing the **location** to store the generated C++ project, press the **Create** button.

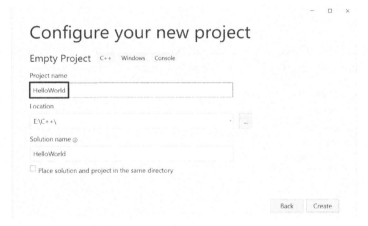

After a while, the Visual Studio IDE will show up as shown below:

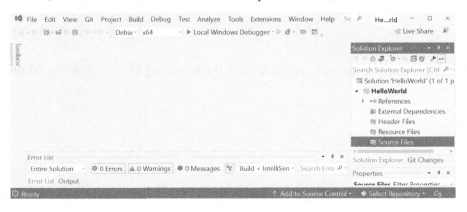

1.4.2 Creating C++ Source Files

In this subsection, we'll create the C++ code using Visual Studio to print out a message to the console. **Right**-click on the **Source Files** filter in the **Solution Explorer** panel as shown below:

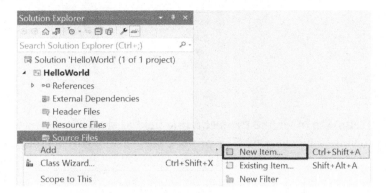

Choose **Add** > **New Item...** from the context menu, and in the next step, press the Add button after changing the C++ file name to Main.cpp as shown below.

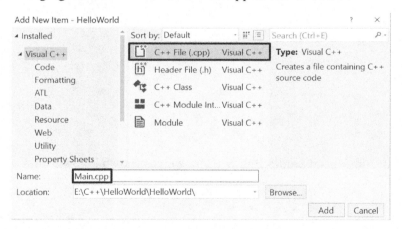

Then the **Source Editor** will open and enter the following C++ code in the **Main.cpp** tab as shown below:

Next, right-click on the **HelloWorld** project and click **Build** on the context menu to build the project. In the meantime, the messages about the build will appear in the **Output** window as shown below:

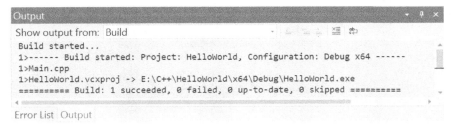

As you can see from the messages, a **HelloWorld.exe** executable file was created, under the project's path, in the "\x64\Debug" folder.

Finally, press the **Local Windows Debugger** button on the **Tollbar** as shown below to **run** the program.

The result is shown below and a "Hello World!" message is printed out to the **console** window.

1.4.3 Visual Studio Windows

This section will introduce the common windows UI in Visual Studio IDE.

The Code Editor

Each opened C++ file will be displayed on a separate page with its tab in the **Code Editor**. Users can click on the **left** margin of the window to set the **breakpoint(s)**, as shown below:

The Solution Explorer

The Solution Explorer allows you to view, navigate, and manage the current C++ project(s) as shown in the following figure:

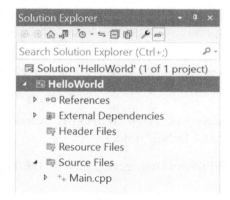

Note: You can put **more than** one project into a solution.

The Options Window

Developers can select the **Tools(T) > Options(O)** from the main menu to open the **Options** window and use this window to set the Visual Studio IDE, such as setting the font and font color under the **Environment > Fonts and Colors** settings. Besides, through the **Line Number(L)** option under the **Text Editor > C/C++** settings, the developer can switch whether to display the line numbers to the left of the Code Editor, as shown below:

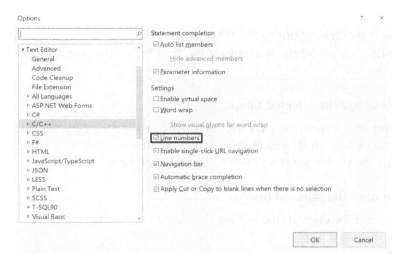

1.4.4 Visual Studio Toolbar

The Visual Studio **Toolbar** displays the tools commonly used in the IDE, as shown in the following figure.

The most commonly used tools in the Toolbar, from left to right as shown in the figure above, are described respectively as follows.

1. **Create a new project**

    Press this icon to open the **Create a new project** window. You can use the project template in this window to create different kinds of applications, including **Console** applications and **Class Libraries**. A template contains the basic files and settings needed for a given project type.

2. **Save the current file**

    Press this icon to save the current modified and unsaved C++ file.

3. **Save all files**

    Press this icon to save all the modified and unsaved C++ files.

4. **Local Windows Debugger**

After pressing this button, Visual Studio will start **compiling** your C++ source files, then enter the **debugging** mode. If you have already set the breakpoint(s) in the source file, Visual Studio will **stop** at the **first** breakpoint encountered during its execution.

5. **Comment out the selected line(s)**

   Press this icon to turn the **current line** of code where the cursor is located into a comment or turn all the **selected** code into comments, after which the code that becomes the comment(s) will **not** be compiled and run.

6. **Uncomment the selected line(s)**

   Uncomment the current line or turn all selected comments into code.

1.4.5 How C++ Works in Visual Studio

This section will introduce how C++ works, the compiling process, and also explore the debugging tools in Visual Studio.

How C++ Works

To understand how C++ works, let's go back to the **HelloWorld** application's code as follows that we wrote in the previous section, which is a considerably basic program that we are going to explore in this subsection.

```
#include <iostream>

int main()
{
    // Print out the string "Hello World!" to the console
    printf("Hello World!");
    system("pause>0");  // Get rid of the system message
}
```

At the beginning of the code, we have the #include <iostream> statement, called a **preprocessor** statement. In C++, any line of code that begins with a **hash (#)** is a preprocessor statement. The first thing a compiler does when it gets a source file is to preprocess all of the preprocessor statements. This happens just before the actual compilation. In this case, it's called **include**.

What an **include** will do is **find a file**, so in this case, we're looking for the file called **iostream** and take all of the contents of that file and just paste it into this current file. All of the included files are typically called **header** files or just headers. The reason that we have to include the `iostream` header here is that we need the **declaration** for the C++ **built-in function** called `printf`, which prints **formatted output** to the standard output stream here is the **console** window.

Next, we have the `main()` function which is important and special, and it's the **entry point** for our application. When we run the application, the computer starts executing code from the first line in this function. As the program is running, the computer will execute the lines of code **in order** in the `main()` function.

At beginning of the `main()` function, we call the built-in `printf()` function, which requires a **string** parameter, to print out the "Hello World!" string. Finally, we use a special statement `system("pause>0")` to get rid of the Visual Studio system message appended to the printouts after the program is running. Now if you **comment out** this line and press **F5** to run the program, you'll see the output as follows instead of the screen in the previous section.

The C++ Build Process in Visual Studio

In the previous section, we built the **HelloWorld** C++ project in Visual Studio and created an executable file called **HelloWorld.exe** in the project's folder. Behind the scenes, there are **three** main steps involved in the whole process. The process is illustrated in the following figure:

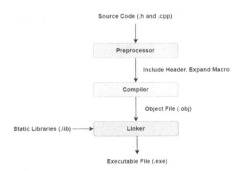

The first step is called **Pre-processing** in which the C++ preprocessor transforms all the **#directives** and **macro** definitions in each source file. This creates a **translation unit**. The second step is **Compiling**, the C++ compiler compiles each translation unit into **object** files (.obj), applying whatever compiler options have been set. The third step is **Linking,** and the linker merges the object files, applying the linker options that have been set, and finally links the standard C++ library/dependencies with the object file into a single executable.

1.4.6 Debugging C++ Projects

In this final section, we'll trace the above HelloWorld C++ code in Visual Studio as an example to illustrate the debugging process. First, click on the far-left **margin** of the code editor to set a breakpoint, that is, making the program pause execution at this line as shown below:

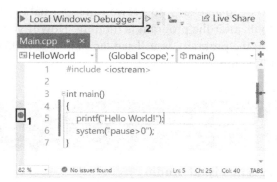

Then press the **Local Windows Debugger** button, and the Visual Studio debugger will launch and enter the **debugging** mode. After a while, the focus will return to the Visual Studio code editor, and the program will **stop** at the line of code with the breakpoint, as shown below, a **yellow arrow** appears on the breakpoint.

Visual Studio Debugging Toolbar

The commonly used tools in the Visual Studio debugging toolbar, after the debugger is running, are shown above from left to right, and are described as follows:

1. **Continue**

   Press the **Continue** button to continue the execution of the program and if you have other breakpoints, the debugger will stop at the next breakpoint.

2. **Stop Debugging**

   Press this icon or **Shift + F5** on the keyboard to stop debugging and return to Visual Studio.

3. **Step Into**

   After pressing this icon or the **F11** key on the keyboard, the debugger will advance the program execution one statement at a time. If you press the **Step Into** button on the line that calls the **user-defined** function, the Visual Studio debugger will enter the function and stop at the **first** line within the function.

4. **Step Over**

   Step Over or **F10** advances the debugger **without** stepping into functions or methods in your code. By pressing this icon, you can skip over code that you're not interested in, that is, you can quickly get to code that you're more interested in.

5. **Step Out**

   Press this icon or **Shift + F11** to continue your debugging session but advance the debugger through the current function.

Now, let's continue the above debugging example, press the **F11** key once and the execution will advance to the next statement as shown below:

Switch to the console window, you'll see the "Hello World!" message inside. Finally, click the **Stop** button on the toolbar, and the debugger will stop and return to Visual Studio.

Error List and Output Window

Visual Studio presents errors in mainly **two** ways; one of which is the **Error List,** and another is inside the **Output** window. For example, if you made some kind of **syntax** error like **forgetting a semicolon** as shown below:

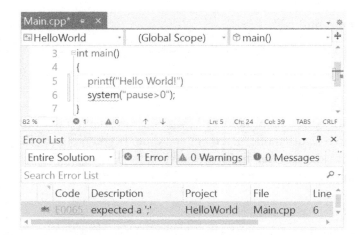

You'll see the error appears in the **Error List** window and the line number. **After** building the project, the details about this error will show up in the **Output** window as shown below:

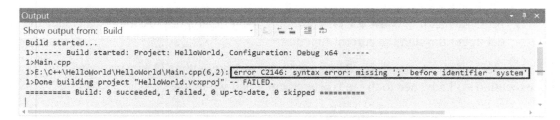

Note: Compared with the Error List, the **Output** window will give you more details about the errors during the Build. So **always** remember to check the **Output** window if some errors happened that are not displayed in the Error List!

1.5 Summary

The installation and setup of UE5 and Visual Studio IDE were introduced in this chapter. We also covered new features of the UE5 and provided a migration guide for the UE4 developers who want to migrate their game projects over. Besides, before the end of this chapter, we explored how C++ works and debugging tools in Visual Studio IDE. In the next chapter, we'll give the reader a primer introduction to the modern C++ programming language.

Exercises

1.1 Visit the **Unreal Engine 5.0 Release Notes** page at https://docs.unrealengine.com/5.0/en-US/unreal-engine-5-0-release-notes/ and explore the new features in UE5.

1.2 In the **HelloWorld** C++ code, we used the `printf()` function to print out a string to the console. That's because UE5 also uses it to format an output string. In modern C++, the HelloWorld example usually uses the **cout** (standard output stream) object to print out strings. So, modify the HelloWorld C++ code in this chapter to use the **cout** to print out the "Hello World!" message.

CHAPTER

2

Modern C++ Primer

Modern C++, like Java, is a programming language with complete OOP (Object-Oriented Programming) support, including class inheritance, polymorphism, and interface. Details about C++ Object-Oriented Programming will be discussed in-depth in the next chapter.

2.1 C++ Fundamental Data Types, Variables, and Arrays

This section will introduce the topics related to the C++ language foundations, such as the simple data types, variables, and arrays.

2.1.1 C++ Fundamental Data Types

The C++ fundamental data types can be divided into the following categories:

Numeric Types - Integral Types

The C++ integer types include **char** (8-bit), **short** (16-bit), **int** (32-bit), and **long** (32-bit). The range of each integral type is shown in the following table:

C++ Integral Type	Range
char	-128 to 127
short	-32,678 to 32,767
int	-2,147,483,648 to 2,147,483,647
long	–2,147,483,648 to 2,147,483,647

The keyword **short** is equivalent to **short int**, and **short** is used most often. The integer type, **long**, which can also be written as **long int**, has the **same range** as the type **int** in Visual C++.

Note: In other C++ compilers, the type **long** may not be the same as the type **int**, so if you expect your programs to be compiled in other environments, don't assume that **long** and **int** are equivalent types. In chapter four, we are going to introduce UE5 Numerical Types.

Integer Type Modifiers

The above integral types store **signed** integer values by default, so you can use these types to store either positive or negative values. This is because these types by default are assumed to have the type modifier **signed**. So, wherever you wrote **short** or **int**, meaning that **signed** **short** or **signed** **int**, respectively.

You can add the **unsigned** modifier keyword in front of these types and the range of each **unsigned** integral type is shown in the following table:

C++ Integral Type	Range
unsigned char	0 to 255
unsigned short	0 to 65,535
unsigned int	0 to 4,294,967,295
unsigned long	0 to 4,294,967,295

Numeric types - Floating-Point Types

The floating-point types include **float** (32-bit) and **double** (64-bit). The range of each type is as follows:

C++ Floating-Point Type	Approximate Range
float	3.4E +/- 38 (7 digits)
double	1.7E +/- 308 (15 digits)

Note: Since the integer operations are faster than the operations with floating-point numbers, if you don't need the precision of the floating-point numbers, the integral data types should be used to declare the variables.

The Boolean Type

The Boolean data type in C++, or the **bool** type, refers to an **8**-bit value that is regarded as an integer type, and its content must be **true** or **false**.

Character Data Types

The **char** data type serves a dual purpose. It occupies a single byte that you can use to store integers within a given range or to store the code for a single **ASCII character**.

The type **wchar_t** (wide-character type) is similar to the **char** data type, and it stores **2**-byte character codes with values in the range from 0 to **65,535**.

2.1.2 User-Defined Data Types

You can combine different data types into a new type called the **user-defined** type. The benefit of using this type is that you can make a single variable hold related data of various types. For example, if you want to declare a `Student` type that contains the name and age of a student, the following code demonstrates how to use the **struct** keyword to declare such a type.

```
struct Student
{
    // Declare the members of this type
    string name;      // Student's name
    short  age;       // Student's age
};
```

The above `Student` is a user-defined type, you can use it to declare a variable in the `main()` function as follows:

```
Student aStudent;
```

With the variable name, you can access its member values using the **dot** (.) token as follows:

```
aStudent.name = "Danny";
aStudent.age = 18;
```

We'll discuss how to declare variables and the `string` type in the following sections.

2.1.3 Enumeration Data Types

The **enumeration** (or **enum**) type is a special **numerical** type. Its purpose is to replace the values in a certain range with specific strings. The type must be declared using the **enum** keyword. Please refer to the following example:

```
enum Seasons
{
  Spring,
  Summer,
  Autumn,
  Winter
};
```

The above is a declaration of the `enum` type indicating that there are **four seasons** in a year, which lists the names of the four seasons. In the system, each member of it represents an **integral** constant, so the following code will get the value it represents.

```
int s1 = Summer;    // s1 = 1
```

The variable `s1` is **1**, representing the **index** value of the `Summer` in the `Seasons` enum type (starting from **zero**).

2.1.4 Conversion between Data Types

During program execution, you might need to copy a value into another type's variable or function parameter. These kinds of operations are called **type conversions**. In C++, you can perform two kinds of conversions: **implicit** conversions and **explicit** type conversions (casts).

Implicit conversion does not require special syntax because the conversion is type-safe and no data will be lost, such as in the following syntax.

```
int i;
float f;

i = 666;
f = i;
```

C++ implicitly converts the integer variable **i** into a **float** and then assigns it to the variable **f**. The above implicit conversion is type-safe because we are converting from the smaller integral type to the **larger** floating-point type.

Explicit conversions require the **cast** operator **()** and the keyword of a data type. In the following syntax, the above float variable, **f**, is first converted to an **integer** and then assigned to the variable **i**.

```
i = (int)f;
```

We can also use the explicit conversion syntax to obtain a specific interface implemented by an object, as further explained in the following chapter.

2.1.5 C++ Variables

C++ uses variables to store the data required for program execution like other programming languages. A variable must have a name and be declared with a type.

Naming C++ Variables

The C++ variable names must meet the following conditions:

1. Must start with a **character**, such as a letter.
2. They can only contain characters, integral numbers, or underscore characters (_).
3. C++ keywords **cannot** be used as variable names.
4. The length of a variable name **cannot** exceed 255 characters.
5. Within the scope to which the variables can be accessed, such as in the same function or class, they must be **unique**.

Note: It is recommended to use a meaningful name for naming the variable. For example, use `lastName` to represent a person's last name to declare the variable.

Unreal C++ Variable Declaration

In C++, you must use a type keyword to declare the variable before using it. In object-oriented programming, the access modifiers like **public**, **private**, or **static** are also used to specify the accessibility of a variable when you declare it.

In **Unreal** C++, the following types can be used to declare variables:

1. The basic types, such as **int** or **string**.
2. User-defined data types.
3. The Unreal Engine's **built-in** classes include **FText** or **AActor**.

In C++, it is allowed to declare **multiple** variables of the same type in the same line without repeatedly declaring their data types, such as:

```
int a, b, c;   // a,b,c are all integers
```

You can also assign an **initial** value to the variable while declaring it, for example:

```
float x = 88.99f;
```

In the above assignment operation, the letter '**f**' after the number 88.99 represents that the value is a **32**-bit decimal instead of a **double** numeric type.

Note: You should **avoid** using the `auto` keyword in C++ code, although a few exceptions exist. Always be explicit about the type you're initializing. This means that the type must be visible to the reader.

C++ Variable Scope

The visibility scope of a variable can be divided into the following:

1. **Block** scope: only in the block of code in which it is declared.
2. **Procedure** scope: only in the function or method where it is declared.
3. **Module** scope: only in the class or struct in which it is declared.

We'll introduce the Block scope in this subsection first. A so-called code block refers to the code that starts with the **left** curly bracket (**{**) and ends with the **right** curly bracket (**}**). The variables declared inside a block can only be used in the block. For example, in the following code fragment, the visibility scope of the variable `PlusOne` is limited to the block in which it is declared, and the code **outside** the block will **not** be able to access the variable.

```
bool addOne = false;
```

```
if(addOne)
{
  int PlusOne = 0;
  PlusOne += 1;
}
PlusOne += 1;  // Cause an error
```

2.1.6 Constants

You can use the **const** keyword to declare constants that are **immutable** values or strings that **do not change** for the program's life. Below are some examples of declarations of constants:

```
// Declare the mathematical constant Pi
const float Pi = 3.14159f;
// Declare a string constant
const string myName = "Danny";
// Declare an integer constant
const int myAge = 18;
```

Using constants increases the program's readability and flexibility of programming. Because if it's required to modify the value of a constant in a program, all you need to do is to modify the **declaration** of the constant but don't have to modify all the code that uses the constant.

2.1.7 Arrays

Arrays allow you to declare multiple variables of the **same type** and the **same name** at the same time. After an array is created, its elements can be accessed by using the **index** number which is a number placed inside square brackets that follow the array name.

For example, to declare a variable for storing bank account balances in 12 months, You can declare an array variable named `balance` with 12 elements as follows, and don't require to declare the 12 individual variables with different names.

```
// Declare 12 decimal variables with the same name
float balance[12];
```

By using the index number, values can be specified to the individual variables as follows:

```
// The index number starts with 0
balance[0] = 1000;
balance[11] = 110000;
```

Note: The **lower** bound of the array index number in C++ is **zero**, starting from zero.

2.1.8 Strings

In C++, a string consists of an array of characters. You can declare a character array and initialize it with a **string literal**. For example:

```
// "Hello world!" is a string literal
char string1[13] = "Hello World!";  // The array size is 13, not 12
```

Note that here the size of the array is **13, not 12**, that's because a special terminating '\0' character is supplied automatically by the compiler and appended to indicate the **end** of the string. The **escape sequence** '\0' is sometimes referred to as a **null** character, being a byte with all bits as zero. A string of this form is also known as a **C-style** string because defining a string like this was introduced in the C language.

Besides, we can let the compiler work out the length of an initialized array for us and the following is another example:

```
char string2[] = "Good Bye!";
```

Because the array size is unspecified, the compiler allocates space for enough elements to hold the initializing string, **plus** the terminating null character. In this case, it allocates **10** elements for the array string2.

Modern C++ provides the **string** type, which is a **class**, for us to store strings and the type is defined in the **string** header. This means that before declaring string variables, you have to include the header as follows:

```
#include <string>
```

To print out a string variable to the console, please refer to the following example:

```
#include <iostream>
#include <string>

int main()
{
  using namespace std;

  string hello = "Hello";  // Or std::string hello = "Hello";
  // We have to call the c_str() function to convert the string
  // variable to a C-style string before printing it out!
  printf(hello.c_str());
}
```

In the above code, because the printf() function **requires** a **C-style** string parameter, here we **have to** call the **c_str()** function of the string variable hello to convert it to a C-style string and then print out the string.

Note: The **string** class also belongs to the **std namespace**, which is used to organize code into logical groups and to prevent name collisions. Here we use a **using** Directive (`using namespace std;`) for all the identifiers in the std namespace **before** using the **string** type. If omitting the **using** statement, you have to use the **fully qualified name** for each identifier, for example, **std::string** to declare the above `hello` variable.

String Concatenation

To concatenate two strings into a single string, the **string** type has **overridden** the + operator for us to do string concatenation. Refer to the following revised example:

```
int main()
{
  using namespace std;

  string hello = "Hello";
  // The " World!" is a C-style string!
  string helloworld = hello + " World!";
  printf(helloworld.c_str());   // "Hello World!"
}
```

In the above revised code, we declare another string variable `helloworld`, and use the + operator to concatenate the strings. Note that the compiler **implicitly** converts the C-style string " World!" to a **string** and then performs the concatenation.

2.2 C++ Operators

The C++ operators can be divided into the following categories: **Arithmetic** operators, **Assignment** operators, **Comparison** operators, **Logical** operators, and **Bitwise** operators.

2.2.1 Arithmetic Operators

The C++ arithmetic operators and their usage are outlined in the following table:

Operator	Description	Example
+	Addition	`int intValue = 2 + 3;     // intValue = 5`
−	Subtraction	`int intValue = 2 - 3;     // intValue = -1`
*	Multiplication	`int intValue = 2 * 3;     // intValue = 6`
/	**Division**	`float fValue = 10 / 3.0; // fValue = 3.333333`

%	**Remainder**	`int intValue = 12 % 5;   // intValue = 2`

2.2.2 Assignment Operators

The C++ assignment operators and their descriptions are outlined in the following table:

Operator	Description
=	Assignment
/=	Division Assignment
+=	Addition Assignment
-=	Subtraction Assignment
*=	Multiplication Assignment

In addition to the assignment operator, the purpose of the rest operators is to **combine** arithmetic operations and assignments, which can save you the time to write the expression. For example, to add 2 to the content of a variable a, you can use the following syntax:

```
a += 2;
```

Note: You can also use the += operator for delegate assignments in the later chapter.

2.2.3 Comparison Operators

C++ comparison, also known as **relational**, operators compare their operands, and the results are Boolean values. The operators and their usage are outlined in the following table:

Operator	Description	Example
<	Less than	`bool result = 2 < 3;   // result = true`
<=	Less than or equal	`bool result = 3 <= 2;   // result = false`
>	Greater than	`bool result = 10 > 3;   // result = true`
>=	Greater than or equal	`bool result = 3 >= 10; // result = false`
==	Equal	`bool result = 45 == 45;// result = true`
!=	Not Equal	`bool result = 2 != 3;   // result = true`

2.2.4 Logical Operators

The C++ logical operators are used to perform **logical** operations with **bool** operands, and the results are also **bool** values.

Conditional Logical AND Operator - &&

The **&&** operator computes the logical **AND** of its operands, the result is **true** when both operands evaluate to **true**, otherwise, the result is **false**. Please refer to the following example.

```
int a = 5, b = 7;
bool result1, result2;
result1 = a > 3 && b < 8;      // result1 = true
result2 = 5 > 3 && 7 > 8;      // result2 = false
```

Conditional Logical OR Operator - ||

The || operator computes the logical **OR** of its operands, the result is **true** when either one of the operands evaluates to true, otherwise, the result is **false**. If the first operand evaluates to true, then the second operand is **not** evaluated. The above example continues as follows:

```
result1 = a > 3 || b > 8;      // result1 = true
result2 = 3 > 5 || 7 > 8;      // result2 = false
```

Logical Exclusive OR Operator - ^

The ^ operator computes the exclusive **OR** of its operands, the result is **false** when both operands evaluate to **true** or **false**, otherwise, the result is **true**. The above example continues as follows:

```
result1 = a > 3 ^ b > 8;       // result1 = true
result2 = 5 > 3 ^ 8 > 7;       // result2 = false
```

Logical Negation Operator - !

The unary prefix ! operator computes the logical negation of its operand. If the operand evaluates to **false** then the result is **true**, otherwise, the result is **false**, if the operand evaluates to **true**. The above example continues as follows:

```
result1 = !(a > 3);            // result1 = false
result2 = !(3 > 5);            // result2 = true
```

2.2.5 Bitwise Operators

The C++ bitwise operators perform bitwise or shift operations with operands of the integral numeric or type.

Logical AND Operator - &

The **&** operator computes the **bitwise** logical **AND** of its operands. Please refer to the following example.

```
char a = 0b00000011;       // a = 3
char b = 0b00000110;       // b = 6
char result = (char)(a & b); // result = 2 (0b00000010)
```

Logical OR Operator - |

The **|** operator computes the **bitwise** logical **OR** of its operands. The above example continues as follows:

```
result = (char)(a | b);      // result = 7 (0b00000111)
```

Logical Exclusive OR Operator - ^

The **^** operator computes the **bitwise** logical exclusive **OR** of its operands. The above example continues as follows:

```
result = (char)(a ^ b);      // result = 5 (0b00000101)
```

Left-Shift Operator - <<

The **<<** operator shifts its **left-hand** operand left by the number of bits defined by its right-hand operand. The left-shift operation **discards** the **high-order** bits that are outside the range of the result type and sets the low-order empty bit positions to **zero**, The above example continues as follows:

```
result = (char)(a << 1);     // result = 6 (0b00000110)
```

Bitwise Complement Operator - ~

The **~** operator produces a **bitwise complement** of its operand by reversing each bit. The following is an example:

```
unsigned char result3 = (unsigned char)~a;  // result = 252 (0b11111100)
```

2.2.6 Operator Precedence

The following list orders C++ operators starting from the highest precedence to the lowest:

1. **Arithmetic** operators: ^, – **(negative)**, * or / , \, %, + or –

2. **Bitwise** operators: ~, &, ^, | or <<
3. **Concatenation** operator for strings: +
4. **Comparison** operators: ==, !=, <, >, <=, >= (They all have the same precedence, that is, compute from **left** to **right** in the order in which they appear.)
5. **Logical** operators: !, && or || or ^

2.3 Functions

In C++, every executed instruction is performed in the context of a **function** (or **method** in OOP), a code block containing a series of statements. A program causes the statements to be executed by calling the function and specifying any required function arguments. The function declaration syntax is as follows:

```
<Access_modifier> <Return_type> <Function_name>([<param_list>])
{
    [Statements]
}
```

Functions are declared in a **class** or **struct** by specifying the access level using the **access modifiers**, such as `public`, `private`, or `protected`, the return type, the name of the function, and any function parameters. These parts together are the signature of the function.

Function parameters are enclosed in parentheses and separated by commas. Empty parentheses indicate that the method requires **no** parameters. The parameter declaration syntax is as follows:

```
<Type> <Parameter_name>
```

In C++, arguments can be passed to parameters either by **value** or by **reference**. To pass a parameter by reference to change the value, you have to use the **pointers**, which will be discussed in the later section.

Below is an example of declaring a function for calculating sales tax:

```
void ComputeSalesTax(double salesAmount)
{
    double salesTax = salesAmount * 0.12;
}
```

The **void** keyword used in the function declaration above indicates that the method has **no return value**. After declaring the method **above** the `main()` function, you can call it and pass in the sales amount to perform the calculations as follows:

```
int main()
{
    // Call the ComputeSalesTax() method,
    // and pass the value, 1,000, to the salesAmount parameter
    ComputeSalesTax(1000);
}
```

A function can have a return value and you must return it to the calling method via the **return** keyword. For example, the following is a function that performs multiplication.

```
int Multiple(int value1, int value2)
{
    return value1 * value2;
}
```

You can call the above `Multiple()` function and assign its return value to a variable as follows:

```
int main()
{
    int result4 = Multiple(2, 5);      // result4 = 2 * 5 = 10
}
```

2.4 C++ Statements

C++ supports several different kinds of statements within a code block. A block consists of a list of statements written between the delimiters **{** and **}**.

2.4.1 Selection Statements

During program execution, we may need to execute a piece of code according to whether the condition is true or not. These are called decision-making structures, and they contain two main types of statements namely the **if** statement and the **switch** statement.

The if Statement

`if` statement determines whether to execute a certain piece of code based on the value of a **Boolean** expression. The syntax is as follows:

```
if(condition_1) {
    [Code Block]
}
```

```
[else [if(condition_2)] {
  [Code Block]
 }
 ]
```

Below is an example using a single `if` statement:

```
int value = 1;
// If the value is greater than 0 then add one to the variable
if(value > 0) { value = value + 1; }
```

Multiple `if` statements can become **nested** structures, please refer to the following example:

```
if(value > 0)
{
  printf("value > 0");
} else if( value == 0)
{
  printf("value = 0");
} else
{
  printf("value < 0");
}
```

The `switch` Statement

The `switch` statement executes a section of code based on the **value** of an expression. Its syntax is:

```
switch(expr)
{
    [case value_1:
          [[Code Block]
          [break;]]
    ]
    [case value_2:
          [[Code Block]
          [break;]]
    ]
    ...
    [default:
          [[Code Block]
          [break]];
    ]
}
```

The match expression is a required item and its value **must be** one of the **primitive** types. The **break** keyword is used to exit the `switch` structure. If there is no code in a **case** label section, you can omit the `break` keyword, which means that the program will continue to execute the next case label block. If no `case` label pattern matches the match expression, control is transferred to the optional section with the **default** case label, if there's one. Note here that the **last** `break` keyword **cannot** be omitted. Below is a typical example of using the `switch` structure:

```
switch (value)
{
  case 1:
    printf("Case 1...");
    break;
  case 2:                    // Continue to the next case label block
  case 3:
    printf("... and/or Case 2");
    break;              // Exit the switch structure
  default:
    printf("Default value...");
    break;
}
```

2.4.2 Iteration Statements

At some point, we'll need to execute a piece of code **repeatedly**, C++ provides the **Iteration** statements or **Loop** controls to complete this kind of task.

The `for` Statement

The `for` loop allows you to repeatedly execute a certain piece of code several times, and then jump out of this loop while a specified Boolean expression evaluates to **false**. The syntax is as follows:

```
for([initializer];[condition];[iterator])
{
  [Code Block]
  [break;]
}
```

The `for` loop usually uses a **counter** variable, after the **initializer** sets its initial value, the control enters the **condition** section for execution. When the condition evaluates to `true`, the control continues to execute the body of the loop. After finishing executing the loop body, it enters the **iterator** for execution, updates the value of the counter, and then evaluates the condition again. The loop continues until the condition evaluates to `false` and exits.

The `for` loop is usually used when you know the **number of times** the loop body is to be executed repeatedly. If you don't know the number of executions in advance, the following `while` loop is more suitable. During program execution, you can use the `break` keyword to exit the `for` loop. Below is an example of using the `for` loop to calculate the sum of the integer numbers from 1 to 100:

```
int total = 0;
for (int n = 1; n <= 100; n++)
{
   total = total + n;
}
// Print out the total in the format specified by the format string %d
printf("1+2+3+...+100 = %d", total);
```

Note: The **%d**, inside the above string, is called the **format string**, which is used to specify the **output format** of the number `total`. The **type character** 'd' here means to print out the `total` as a `short` integer type. You can add more than one format string in the format control.

Another type of `for` statement called the **for-each** loop is similar to the `for` loop, but it repeatedly executes the code in the loop body for each element in the array or vector instead of executing a specific number of times. The syntax is as follows:

```
for(type element : array/vector)
{
   [Code Block]
   [break;]
}
```

When using the `for-each` loop, you may not know exactly where each element is in the array/vector, so if the code in the loop needs to be executed in a specific order, using the `for-each` loop may not achieve the desired result, unless you know the contents of all the elements in the array/vector.

Below is an example that sequentially print the value of each member in an array:

```
int array[] = { 1,2,3,4,5 };
printf("The elements are: ");
for (int i : array)
{
   printf("%d ", i);
}
```

The `while` Statement

The `while` statement executes a statement or a block of statements while a specified Boolean expression evaluates to `true`.

```
while(condition)
{
   [Code Block]
```

```
    [break;]
}
```

When entering the `while` loop, it first evaluates the condition. If the condition is `true`, the loop body will be executed repeatedly until the condition becomes `false`. Because condition expression is evaluated before each execution of the loop, a `while` loop executes zero or more times. This differs from the **do** loop below, which executes **one or more** times. You also can use the `break` keyword to exit the `while` loop. Below is an example using the `while` loop.

```
int number = 10;
while (number > 0)
  number = number - 1;
```

The do Statement

The `do` statement is similar to the `while` statement. The difference is that the `do` loop will execute the loop body **before** checking the condition. The syntax is as follows:

```
do {
  [Code Block]
  [break;]
} while(condition);
```

Continue to modify the previous example of using the **do** loop as follows:

```
do
{
  number--;
} while(number > 0);
```

In the above code, within the `do` loop, the value of the `number` variable is subtracted by 1 before checking whether it is greater than 0. If the condition is `false`, it exits the loop.

2.5 Pointers

A pointer is a variable that stores the **memory address** of an object. Pointers are used extensively in both C and C++ for three main purposes:

1. To allocate new objects on the **heap**.
2. To pass functions to other functions.
3. To iterate over elements in arrays or other data structures.

Declaring pointers

The declaration of pointers follows this syntax:

```
<type> * <name>;
```

where **type** is the data type pointed to by the pointer. This type is **not** the type of the pointer itself, but the **type of data** the pointer points to. For example:

```
int * number;
char * character;
float * floats;
```

A pointer can be assigned the **address** of another non-pointer variable with the **address-of** operator (**&**), or it can be assigned a value of **nullptr**.

Note: A pointer that hasn't been assigned a value contains **random** data.

A pointer can also be **dereferenced** to retrieve the **value** of the object that it points at using the **dereference operator** which is also written with an **asterisk** (*****). Please refer to the following example :

```
#include <iostream>

int main()
{
    // Declare a pointer and initialize it
    // so that it doesn't store a random address
    int* p = nullptr;

    int i = 5;
    p = &i; // Assign pointer to address of object
    printf("The address of variable i in memory is: %p\n", p);

    int j = *p; // Dereference p to retrieve the value at its address
    printf("The value pointed to by p is: %d which is also the value of
                                                    i\n", j);

    system("pause>0");
}
```

In the main program, we declare a **pointer** variable p and initialize it to **nullptr** so that it **doesn't** store a random address. Next, the **address** of the object i is assigned to the pointer with the & operator, and then the address is printed out to the console. To print out the content of a pointer, here we use the **%p** format string. Finally, we **dereference** p using the * operator to retrieve the **value** at its address. The results of the above program are as follows:

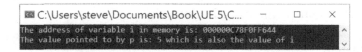

So far you should have a basic understanding of what the pointer is and how to use it in C++. In the next section, we are going to explore an important feature in programming languages called **Call by Reference**.

2.5.1 Call by Reference

As demonstrated in the **Functions** section, we can define functions with parameters. When calling the functions, we can also pass values into the parameters. In C++, such a mechanism is called **Call by Value**, which means we pass the **value(s)** into the parameter(s) which are stored in a special memory in a computer called **Stack**.

You can pass arguments to a function through Call **by Value** or Call by **Reference** (Call by **Address**). Before the discussion, let's see the result of the following example to **swap** two integer variables:

```
#include <iostream>

// Function to swap two integer variables
void Swap(int a, int b)
{
    int temp = a;
    a = b;
    b = temp;
};

int main()
{
    int a = 5, b = 3;

    printf("Before swapping: a = %d, b = %d\n", a, b);
    Swap(a, b);  // Call the Swap() to swap the values of a and b
    printf("After swapping: a = %d, b = %d\n", a, b);

    system("pause>0");
}
```

Here we define a function named **Swap** with two integer parameters to swap the values of the incoming parameters. In the main program, after declaring two integer variables namely **a** and **b**, their values are printed out to the console before the swapping. Then after calling the Swap() function and passing in the two variables, the values of a and b are printed out again to the console after the swap. The result is as shown below:

As you can see from the result, before and after the swap, the values of a and b are the same which means calling the Swap() function does nothing to the variables. This is because in the main program when the Swap() is called, the **copies** of the values of the variables a and b are passed into the function's formal parameters. So even if there is any change in the values inside the function, it will **not** reflect that change in the actual values. Besides, the parameters of the function are stored in the **stack** memory, so after the return of the Swap() function, both memory that the a and b parameters occupied will be returned to the OS.

To let the swap in the function reflects the changes in the main program, we can pass the **addresses** of variables a and b to the parameters as shown in the following revised example:

```cpp
#include <iostream>

void Swap(int *a, int *b)
{
    // Store the dereferenced value at a's address to a temp variable
    int temp = *a;
    // Dereference b and store the value to the heap memory pointed by a
    *a = *b;
    // Store the temp value to the heap memory pointed by b
    *b = temp;
};

int main()
{
    int a = 5, b = 3;

    printf("Before swapping: a = %d, b = %d\n", a, b);
    Swap(&a, &b);    // Pass in the addresses of the variables
    printf("After swapping: a = %d, b = %d\n", a, b);

    system("pause>0");
}
```

Here we re-declare the Swap() function with two **pointer** parameters and in the function, after **dereferencing** the values from the addresses of the original variables, we perform the swap. Then in the main program, the **addresses** of the variables are passed into the function. The result of the above-revised example is shown below:

Now you can see the new Swap() function swaps the values of the two variables after it returns. This is because, in the revised function, we can **deference** the values from the original **heap** memory and store the values back in the memory by the pointers.

2.5.2 Pointer Arithmetic and Arrays

Pointers and arrays are closely related. When an array is passed by value to a function, it's passed as a **pointer** to the **first** element. Please refer to the following example:

```cpp
#include <iostream>

void PrintArrayByValue(int arr[], int length)
{
    printf("The array members are: ");

    for (int i = 0; i < length; ++i)
    {
        printf("%d ", arr[i]);
    }

    printf("\n");
};

void PrintArrayByReference(int* arr, int length)
{
    printf("The array members are: ");

    for (int i = 0; i < length; ++i)
    {
        // Deference arr and print out its value,
        // then the arr pointer is incremented and continue
        printf("%d ", *(arr++));
    }

    printf("\n");
};

int main()
{
    int i[5]{ 1,2,3,4,5 };
    // Divide total bytes by the size of one element to determine
    // the number of elements and sizeof(i) = total bytes
    int j = sizeof(i) / sizeof(i[0]);
    // Call the functions respectively and pass in the array and its
    // length
    PrintArrayByValue(i, j);
```

```
    PrintArrayByReference(i, j);

    system("pause>0");
}
```

The above example demonstrates the following important properties of pointers and arrays:

- ❖ The **sizeof** operator returns the **total size** in **bytes** of an array.
- ❖ To determine the number of elements, **divide** the total bytes by the **size** of **one** element.
- ❖ When an array is passed to a function, it **decays** to a **pointer** type.
- ❖ When the **sizeof** operator is applied to a pointer, it returns the **pointer** size, for example, **4** bytes on **x86** or **8** bytes on **x64**.

In the **PrintArrayByValue()** function, the array is passed in by **value** and it **decays** to a pointer type. Then an index is used to retrieve the elements in the array and their values are printed out.

In the **PrintArrayByReference()** function, the array is passed in by **reference**. Then after **dereferencing** the **arr** pointer and printing out its value, the pointer is **incremented** and continues the loop.

Certain arithmetic operations can be used on non-const pointers to make their point to another memory location. Pointers are incremented and decremented using the ++, +=, – =, and -- operators. This technique can be used in arrays and is especially useful in buffers of untyped data. A **void*** gets incremented by the size of **a char** (**1 byte**). A typed pointer gets incremented by the **size of the type** it points to.

The output of the above example is shown below, and you can see the results are the same for calling both functions.

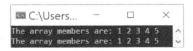

2.6 Macros

The **preprocessor** expands macros in all lines except preprocessor directives, lines that have a **#** as the first non-white-space character. It expands macros in parts of some directives that aren't skipped as part of a conditional compilation. **Conditional** compilation directives allow you to suppress the compilation of parts of a source file.

They test a constant expression or identifier to determine which text blocks to pass on to the compiler, and which ones to remove from the source file during preprocessing.

#define Directives

The #define directives define the identifier as **macro**, which instruct the compiler to replace all successive occurrences of identifier with replacement-list, which can be optionally additionally processed. If the identifier is already defined as any type of macro, the program is ill-formed unless the definitions are identical.

In practical terms, there are two types of macros. **Object-like** macros take no arguments. **Function-like** macros can be defined to accept arguments so that they look and act like function calls.

The syntax of a function-like macro invocation is similar to the syntax of a function call, each instance of the macro name followed by an (as the next preprocessing token introduces the sequence of tokens that is replaced by the replacement-list. The sequence is terminated by the matching) token, skipping intervening matched pairs of left and right parentheses.

Because macros don't generate actual function calls, you can sometimes make programs run faster by replacing function calls with macros. (In C++, inline functions are often a preferred method.) However, macros can create problems if you don't define and use them with care. You may have to use parentheses in macro definitions with arguments to preserve the proper precedence in an expression. Also, macros may not correctly handle expressions with side effects.

The **#undef** directive **removes** the definition of a macro. Once you've removed the definition, you can redefine the macro to a different value.

Note: Once you've defined a macro and if you redefine it to a different value without first removing the original definition, a **warning** message saying **macro redefinition** will appear in the **Error List**. However, you can redefine the macro with the same definition after removing it. Thus, the same definition may appear more than once in a program.

Please refer to the following example, in which we define two Macros, one is Object-like, and another is Function-like.

```
#include <iostream>

// Define the value of the PI
#define PI 3.14159
// A function-like macro to determine the minimum of two numbers
#define MIN(lhs, rhs) lhs < rhs ? lhs : rhs
// Remove the macro
```

```
#undef PI
// Redefine the Macro to a different value
#define PI 3.14

int main()
{
  printf("The minimum of 3 and 5 is: %d\n", MIN(3, 5));
  printf("The minimum of 3.0 and 5.0 is: %f\n", MIN(3.0, 5.0));
  printf("The value of PI is: %f\n", PI);

  system("pause>0");
}
```

In the above code, we define a macro to replace the identifier `PI` to **3.14159** and the `MIN()` macro with two parameters. In the body of the `MIN()` macro, we use the **ternary operator**, which is a short-hand of the `if-else` statement with **three** operators, to return the **minimum** of two numbers.

Then after using the `#undefine` directives to **remove** the definition of PI, it is **redefined** to **3.14**. In the main program, we call the `MIN()` macro **twice** to get the minimum of two integers and floats, respectively. After their values are printed out, the redefined PI value is printed out to the console. The results of the above example are shown below:

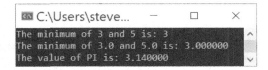

2.7 Templates

Templates are the basis for **generic** programming in C++. As a **strongly** typed language, C++ requires all variables to have a **specific type**, either explicitly declared by the programmer or deduced by the compiler. However, many data structures and algorithms look the same no matter what type they are operating on. Templates enable you to define the operations of a class or function and let the user specify what concrete types those operations should work on.

Defining and Using Templates

A template is a construct that generates an ordinary type or function at **compile**-time based on **arguments** the user supplies for the template parameters. For example, you can re-define the `MIN()` macro from the previous section to a **function template** using the `template` keyword like this:

```
template <typename T>
T MIN(const T& lhs, const T& rhs)
{
    return lhs < rhs ? lhs : rhs;
}
```

The above code describes a template for a generic function with a single type parameter T, whose return value and call parameters (lhs and rhs) are all of this type. You can name a type parameter anything you like, but by convention single upper-case letters are most commonly used. T is a template **parameter**; the **typename** keyword says that this parameter is a **placeholder** for a type. When the function is called, the compiler will replace every instance of T with the concrete type argument that is either specified by the user or deduced by the compiler. The process in which the compiler generates a class or function from a template is referred to as **template instantiation**; MIN<float> is an instantiation of the template MIN<T>. So, refer to the following example:

```
#include <iostream>

template <typename T>
T MIN(const T& lhs, const T& rhs)
{
    return lhs < rhs ? lhs : rhs;
}

int main()
{
  // Call MIN() just like an ordinary function
  printf("The minimum of 3 and 5 is: %d\n", MIN(3, 5));
  // Compiler will generate a new function in which every occurrence
  // of T in the template is replaced with float
  printf("The minimum of 3.0 and 5.0 is: %f\n", MIN<float>(3.0f, 5.0f));

  system("pause>0");
}
```

The output of the above example is the same as the example in the Macros section. However, because the MIN() here is a function template and the compiler can deduce the type of T from the arguments, you can call it just like an ordinary function as shown in the **first** printf().

When the compiler encounters the **second** MIN() statement, that is the MIN<float>(3.0, 5.0), it generates a new function in which every occurrence of T in the template is replaced with **float**:

```
float MIN(const float& lhs, const float& rhs)
{
    return lhs < rhs ? lhs : rhs;
}
```

2.8 Summary

C++ currently is the most popular programming language for writing game engines including the Unreal Engine, therefore for those who are not using this language for development, this chapter provides a primer for the modern C++ essential features that can get you started to use it for further game programming. The modern C++ Object-Oriented Programming features will be discussed in detail in the next chapter.

Exercises

2.1 Write a C++ code that multiplies an integer by 2 using the **left shift** operator. What happens when you shift a number to the right?

2.2 Write a C++ code that calculates the following summation using a **for** loop.

$$\sum_{n=1}^{10} n^2$$

2.3 Create a C++ Console application in Visual Studio and use the **while** statement to make an **infinite** loop, meaning that it will execute forever. Then, in the loop, add a **switch** statement that exits the program when the user enters the character 'Q' in the Console window.

C++ Object-Oriented Programming

The main difference between object-oriented programming and traditional structured programming is that the former combines data and methods for processing the data into a single data structure, and therefore also solves many problems in traditional programming methods. Besides, object-oriented design is closer to the concept of objects in the real world because each object has its inherent attributes and behaviors. For example, in addition to attributes such as height and weight, humans also have behaviors such as speaking or walking.

3.1 Classes and Objects

Class is the most important data structure in object-oriented programming. It also defines a data type, and the so-called **object** refers to the variable declared using a **class** type. After a class is defined, you can declare the required object variables using the class.

3.1.1 Declaration of Classes

The declaration of a class is similar to the **Struct** discussed in the previous chapter but begins with the **class** keyword. You can declare **data** members (**properties**), member **functions (methods)**, and **events** in the class body. **Access modifiers** are used to specify the access range of the class members, and the keywords for access modifiers are **public**, **protected**, and **private**. Classes and Structs are identical in C++ except that in structs the default accessibility is **public**, whereas in classes the default is **private**.

Here is an example of a class declaration:

```
class Box
{
public:
    // Data members
    float length, width, height;
    // Member functions (methods)
    float GetVolume()
    {
        return length * height * width;
    }
};
```

In the above program, a **Box** class is declared, which includes the declaration of the three Box's attributes, `length`, `width`, `height`, and a member function `GetVolume()` to get the **volume** of a box. As mentioned at the beginning of this chapter, data and access methods are integrated into classes, which is unique to object-oriented design. After the class is declared, you can use it to declare the required object variables in the `main()` function as follows:

```
Box aBox;
Box* pBox = new Box(); // Allocate object on the heap
```

We declared a box object variable in the above and, at the same time, also use the **new** keyword to create another instance of the class on the **heap** memory.

Next, you can use the dot (.) syntax to assign the values to the `length`, `width`, and `height` of the `Box` variable and then call the `GetVolume()` method of the `Box` to calculate its volume as follows:

```
aBox.length = 1000;
aBox.width = 100;
aBox.height = 10;
aBox.GetVolume();  // Return the volume of the box
```

Then we use the **member access** operator (->) with the `pBox` pointer to assign values to the three properties of the `Box` object, and print out its volume to the console as follows:

```
pBox->length = 10;
pBox->width = 10;
pBox->height = 10;

printf("The volume of the box is: %f", pBox->GetVolume());
```

Finally, don't forget to use the **delete** keyword to **delete** the object from the heap as follows before the end of the program.

```
delete pBox;        // Delete object (please don't forget!)
```

Note: The `pBox` here is a **raw pointer**, which is a pointer whose lifetime isn't controlled by an encapsulating object, such as a **smart pointer**. Memory allocated using `new` for a raw pointer must be freed by using `delete` (or `delete[]`), Failure to free the memory results in a **memory leak**, and renders that memory location unavailable to any other program on the machine.

3.1.2 Constructors and Destructors

Each class has a special method called the **constructor**, which is used to **initialize** objects. C++ uses the **name** of a class as the name of its constructor. When we use the `new` operator to create an object, its constructor will be called. C++ will create one **by default** that instantiates the object and sets member variables to the default values if you **don't provide** a constructor for a class.

In C++, a class usually also has a method called **destructor**, which is used to perform any necessary final **clean-up**, such as deleting all raw pointers.

Note: The **Garbage Collector (GC)** implemented in **UE5** can **automatically** collect and release unused system resources, so we usually do **not** use the destructor for the final clean-up in Unreal Engine.

Implementing Constructors

Now press **File** > **Add** > **New Project…** from the main menu in Visual Studio to add a new **Empty** C++ project named **BoxVolume** in the Solution Explorer. Then right-click on the **Source Files** filter and add a C++ file called **BoxVolume.cpp**, then add the C++ code of the Box class above **before** the main() function, but this time we **add** a constructor for it and specify the default values of the class members in the constructor as follows:

```cpp
#include <iostream>

class Box
{
public:
    float length, width, height;
    // Constructor
    Box()
    {
      length = 100;
      width = 100;
      height = 1;
    }

    float GetVolume()
    {
        return length * height * width;
    }
};

int main()
{
  Box* pBox = new Box();// The constructor will be called
    printf("The volume of the box is: %f", pBox->GetVolume());

    delete pBox;
}
```

The output of running the above program is shown below:

From the above result, it can be confirmed that the volume of the box is 10000, which is equal to the length times the width, and then times the height, the three member's values are set in the constructor. In the main() function, the value is output to the console by the built-in printf() function using the format string "**%f**", which means to print out the volume as a float.

Using Parameterized Constructors

In the above example, the initial values of the data members are set in the constructor. Because the constructor can have parameters, the script can be rewritten as follows:

```cpp
#include <iostream>

class Box
{
public:
    float length, width, height;
    // Constructor
    Box()
    {
        length = 100;
        width = 100;
        height = 1;
    }

    // Parameterized constructor
    Box(float length, float width, float height)
    {
        this->length = length;
        this->width = width;
        this->height = height;
    }

    float GetVolume()
    {
        return length * height * width;
    }
};

int main()
{
    // Create the Box object with parameters
    Box* pBox = new Box(100, 100, 1);

    printf("The volume of the box is: %f", pBox->GetVolume());

    delete pBox;
}
```

A new constructor with three parameters has been added to the revised program. This time in the main() function we use this new constructor to create an object and pass initial values into it. The result of the new script is the same as before, but the use of parameterized constructors does make the program more flexible, you will see this usage again in subsequent examples.

Besides, you may have noticed that when assigning parameter values to data members, **this** keyword is used mainly because the parameter names of the new constructor are the same as the data member names. To distinguish them, we have to use **this**, which refers to the current instance of the class when accessing the data members.

3.1.3 Inheritance

We made a basic introduction to C++ classes in the previous subsection and believe that you already have a concept of the definition and application of classes. The concept of classes in object-oriented design is consistent with the concept of object classification in nature. More specifically, the idea of object-oriented design in software is to provide a more accurate way to represent object models in the real world, and the specific method is to integrate data and procedures for processing these data also known as methods to become a single data structure which is called a class. With the definition of a class, you can use it to create the instances of the class called objects.

In addition to the classification of species in the real world, a more important phenomenon is the concept of inheritance. For example, the descendants of a species must inherit certain characteristics of the parent or completely replicate all the behaviors of the parent. In addition to inheriting the attributes and behaviors from the parent, some children have evolved their unique characteristics and behaviors. These features all can be implemented in an object-oriented language like C++.

Class inheritance is one of the most important features of object-oriented languages. If a language does not have the function of class inheritance, it is usually not called an object-oriented programming language. In C++, the inheritance of a class must use the : symbol, followed by the name of the parent class to be inherited. Refer to the following inheritance example, a `Monster` class is declared first as follows:

```
class Monster
{
public:
    string name;

    void Move()
    {
    }
};
```

In the `Monster` class, we declare a property, `name`, and a `Move()` method, because each monster must have a name and it will move. Next, a `Dragon` class is declared and because it's a `monster`, it will have all the attributes of the above `Monster` class, so the declaration is as follows:

```
class Dragon : public Monster
{
public:
    string color;
};
```

In the above class declaration, the inheritance operator (`:`) is followed by a class name for the `Dragon` class to inherit the properties and methods of the `Monster` class. By default, the members declared as **public** in a class can be inherited. Therefore, the `Dragon` class also has a `name` property and a `Move()` method. It also declares a `color` property belonging to the `Dragon` class to represent the color of each dragon.

As you can see, the first advantage of using an object-oriented programming language has emerged: class inheritance can greatly **reduce** the length of the code. It's immensely helpful for large GUI-based systems that often need hundreds of thousands of lines of source code in other programming languages.

3.1.4 Encapsulation

We have mentioned before that the members of a class can be declared `private` to **prevent** inappropriate access. In fact, in each object-oriented language, appropriate mechanisms are used to protect access to data members and methods within the class. Restriction on class inheritance is also another important feature. By appropriately **hiding** the internal implementation details of an object, its internal members can only be accessed through the interface exposed by the object is called the **Encapsulation** of the class.

C++ Access Modifiers

The so-called access modifier is to specify the accessibility level of members in a class that can be accessed and inherited through the declaration of certain keywords. The three access modifiers in C++ are **public**, **protected**, and **private**. The list of accessible and inheritable ranges of the access modifiers is as follows:

Access Modifier	Inheritable?	Accessible from the object?
`public`	Yes	Yes
`protected`	Yes	**No**
`private`	**No**	**No**

From the table above, we can see that the restriction of the `public` modifier is the most lenient, while the `private` is the strictest access modifier. The principle of using the three modifiers is to use the stricter modifier as possible, such as the `protected` or `private` to declare class members, because this can effectively avoid the situation of improper access to the members, which is especially important for the development of a large game project.

Let's look at a typical example first, please add a C++ **Console** project named **AccessModifier** to the Visual Studio Solution. Then **right**-click on the project and choose **Set as Startup Project** from the Context Menu. **Modify** the generated code as follows:

```cpp
#include <iostream>

using namespace std;

class Animal
{
protected:
    string name;

public:
    Animal(string name)
    {
        printf("The constructor of the Animal class is called!\n");
        this->name = name;
    }

    void Move()
    {
    }
};

class Dog : public Animal
{
protected:
    bool hasTail;
public:
    string color;

    // Call the constructor of the parent class to initialize
    // the name property
    Dog(bool hasTail, string name) : Animal(name)
    {
        this->hasTail = hasTail;
    }

    string Name()
```

```
        {
            return name;
        }
    };

    int main()
    {
        Dog* aDog = new Dog(true, "Bella");
        printf("The name of the dog is: %s", aDog->Name().c_str());
        delete aDog;
        system("pause>0");
    }
```

In the above code, a new class named `Animal` is declared. This time, we declare its `name` member as **protected** to **prevent** it from being directly accessed, then add a constructor and a `Move()` method for the class. Here the constructor is declared as **public,** and this is to consider the need to inherit and create instances of the class. C++ will use the **private** modifier if the `public` keyword is omitted by default.

Next, the `Dog` class is declared that inherits the `Animal` class. In the class, a Boolean type member, `hasTail`, is used to represent whether a dog has a tail, and its access range is set to **protected** so that it cannot be directly accessed by the object. Finally, a `Name()` method is declared to get the value of the protected `name` member.

Also worth mentioning is the constructor of the `Dog` class. In this example, the `Dog` class also inherits the constructor of the `Animal` class. Therefore, when the constructor is declared for the derived `Dog` class, you can call the constructor of the `Animal` parent class through its **class name**. The value of the passed `name` parameter is assigned to the inherited `name` member. Next, we set the initial value of the new member `hasTail` in this class and use the keyword `this` to refer to the `Dog` class itself.

Note: You can use the **this** keyword in a derived class to access any members of the parent class that are **not private**.

The output of the above example is as follows:

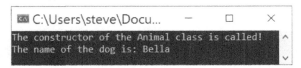

Static Members

The static members of a class refer to those properties or methods that belong to the class itself and can be accessed **without** through its objects and must be declared using the keyword **static** in C++. Normally all members of a class object will be allocated new memory space when it is created, but when a class member is declared **static**, no matter how many class objects are generated, the member will only be **initialized once** when the **first** object is instanced, the result is that all instanced objects will **share** the content of the static class member.

Please refer to a typical example of using static members below, and the name of the C++ project is **StaticMembers**.

```cpp
#include <iostream>

using namespace std;

class LoginUser
{
public:
  // Static member to accumulate the current number of logins
  static int userCount;

  LoginUser()
  {
    // Cumulative number of logins
    userCount += 1;
  }

  int UserCount()
  {
    return userCount;
  }
};

class Message
{
public:
  static void show(string aMessage)
  {
    printf(aMessage.c_str());
  }
};

// Initialize the static member before the main()
int LoginUser::userCount = 0;

int main()
{
  LoginUser* user[100];

  for (int i = 0; i <= 99; i++)
    user[i] = new LoginUser();

  // The UserCount of each object is the current cumulative number
  printf("The current number of logins: %d\n", user[0]->UserCount());
  // Message::show is the fully qualified name of the static method
```

```
    Message::show("Note: You can directly access static members of
                            a class without using its object.");

    for (int i = 0; i <= 99; i++) delete user[i];
    system("pause>0");
}
```

First, we declare a **LoginUser** class that contains the **static** member **userCount**, which will be **accumulated** in the constructor of this class. That is, every time a new **LoginUser** object is created will increase the value of the **static** member **userCount** by **1**, so the output of the **userCount** value of **any** object can always get the total number of all dynamically generated objects.

Of course, you can also use the same mechanism to limit the number of objects that can be generated. For example, the number of people who can log in to the system. You may have another way to achieve the same function without using the global static member. It will increase the complexity of program maintenance and make your algorithm more difficult to understand.

An additional benefit of using static members is that you can directly call or access static members of a class **without** using its object. As in the above example, the **show()** method of the **Message** class is called directly without through a **Message** object. The result of the above example is as follows:

Note: You have to **initialize** the static member using its **fully qualified** name **before** the **main()** function; otherwise, a **linking error** (unresolved external symbol) will occur!

3.1.5 Polymorphism

At the beginning of this chapter, we mentioned the inheritance phenomenon in nature. In addition to inheriting the characteristics of the parent, children may evolve their unique attributes and behaviors. This mechanism is called **Polymorphism** in object-oriented languages, which includes the **overriding** and **overloading** of the class methods.

Class member overriding means that when a subclass inherits a method of the parent class, it can have its new implementation code, that is, the subclass can **reimplement** the method, however, its name and parameter declaration are the same as those of the parent class method. In C++, the overriding of a class method must use the **override** keyword to **re-declare** the method in the **header** file and **re-implement** the **inherited** method in the **.cpp** file.

The following example first implements the `Move()` method of the previous `Animal` class with the **Virtual** keyword, then in the `Dog` subclass, we re-implement the `Move()` method. Besides, a new subclass `Fish` that inherits from `Animal` is also declared as follows:

```cpp
#include <iostream>

using namespace std;

class Animal
{
protected:
    string name;

public:
    Animal(string name)
    {
        this->name = name;
    }

    virtual void Move()
    {
        printf("Animals move!\n");
    }
};

class Dog : public Animal
{
protected:
    bool hasTail;
public:
    string color;

    // Call the constructor of the parent class to initialize the name
    // member
    Dog(bool hasTail, string name) : Animal(name)
    {
        this->hasTail = hasTail;
    }

    string Name()
    {
        return name;
    }

    // Override the parent's Move() method
    void Move()
    {
        printf("The way the dog moves is: run\n");
```

```
        }
};

class Fish : public Animal
{
public:
    Fish() : Animal("Fish")
    {
    }

  // Override the parent's Move() method
    void Move()
    {
        printf("The way the fish moves is: swim\n");
    }
};

int main()
{
    Animal* aAnimal = new Animal("Animal");
    Dog* aDog = new Dog(true, "Lucy");
    Fish* aFish = new Fish();

    // Call the Move() method of the Animal
    aAnimal->Move();
    // Call the Move() method of the Dog
    dynamic_cast<Animal*>(aDog)->Move();
    // Call the Move() method of the Fish
    dynamic_cast<Animal*>(aFish)->Move();

    delete aAnimal; delete aDog; delete aFish;
    system("pause>0");
}
```

Please note that the methods of a class in C++ are default **not** to be overridable, so the
Move() method of the Animal class must be declared as **virtual** to let it be **overridable**.
Next, in the derived Dog class, we re-implement the Move() method that belongs to it,
and also note that the **override** keyword is **optional** in the **.cpp** file but is **required** in
the **header** file.

There is a limitation that needs to pay special attention to here is that **both** the override
method in the derived class and the method in the parent class to be overridden must
have the **same** access scope; that is, must be both **public** or both **protected**; otherwise,
an error will occur during compilation. Also, the Fish subclass is added, and its Move()
method is implemented in the same way.

Finally, in the main() function, after creating objects of the three classes and then their
Move() methods are called, respectively. Here, to **verify** that the overrides are

successful, we use the **dynamic_cast** operator to convert the objects of the Dog and Fish to **Animal** objects before calling the Move().

The output of the above program is as follows:

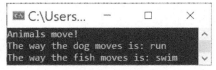

The results above show that although the Dog and Fish subclasses inherit from the Animal class, they can re-implement the inherited Move() method and have their unique behaviors.

Method Overloading

The **overloading** of a class method means that you can declare **multiple** methods with the **same name** but a **different** number of **parameters** or different parameter **types** in a class. Please refer to the example of **constructor overloading** below. We modify the Dog subclass in the previous example to add **another** constructor with only one parameter as follows:

```cpp
#include <iostream>

using namespace std;

class Animal
{
protected:
    string name;

public:
    Animal(string name)
    {
        this->name = name;
    }

    virtual void Move()
    {
        printf("Animals move!\n");
    }
};

class Dog : public Animal
{
protected:
    bool hasTail;
public:
    string color;

    // Call the constructor of the parent class to initialize the name
```

```
    // member
    Dog(bool hasTail, string name) : Animal(name)
    {
        this->hasTail = hasTail;
    }

    // An overloaded constructor
    Dog(bool hasTail) : Animal("Lucy")
    {
        this->hasTail = hasTail;
    }

    string Name()
    {
        return name;
    }

    void Move()
    {
        printf("The way the dog moves is: run\n");
    }
};

class Fish : public Animal
{
public:
    Fish() : Animal("Fish")
    {
    }

    void Move()
    {
        printf("The way the fish moves is: swim\n");
    }
};

int main()
{
    Dog* aNamedDog = new Dog(true, "Max");
    Dog* aDog = new Dog(false);

    printf("Assigned name: %s\n", aNamedDog->Name().c_str());
    printf("Default name: %s\n", aDog->Name().c_str());

    delete aNamedDog; delete aDog;
    system("pause>0");
}
```

Based on the **number** of parameters of the two constructors or the **types** of declared parameters, the C++ compiler can determine which constructor to use at **compile** time. Finally, when the **new** keyword is used to create the objects of the class in the main program, Visual Studio will automatically list all **overloaded** constructors for us to choose, as shown below:

```
Dog* aNamedDog = new Dog(true, "Max");
Dog* aDog = new Dog(false);
```

▲ 1 of 4 ▼ Dog(**bool** hasTail)

If you have typed the sample program in this chapter yourself, you may already be familiar with this screen. The result of the above example is as shown below:

```
⊡ Select C:\...    —    □    ✕
Assigned name: Max
Default name: Lucy
```

The first line is the result of using the constructor with the name parameter and the second line is the output of the constructor **without** the parameter.

Next, let's look at an example of overloading the methods of the class. First, modify the declaration of the Move() method in the **Animal** class as **private** to avoid inheritance. Next, modify the Dog subclass to add two **overloaded** Move() methods to it. The first Move() method contains one **string** type parameter method, and the second Move() method has an integral type parameter speed. The modified code is as follows:

```cpp
#include <iostream>

using namespace std;

class Animal
{
protected:
    string name;

public:
    Animal(string name)
    {
        this->name = name;
    }

private:
    virtual void Move()
    {
        printf("Animals move!\n");
    }
};

class Dog : public Animal
{
protected:
    bool hasTail;
public:
```

```cpp
    string color;

    // Call the constructor of the parent class
    Dog(bool hasTail, string name) : Animal(name)
    {
        this->hasTail = hasTail;
    }
    // An overloaded constructor
    Dog(bool hasTail) : Animal("Lucy")
    {
        this->hasTail = hasTail;
    }

    string Name()
    {
        return name;
    }

    // An overloaded method with a string type parameter
    void Move(string method)
    {
        printf("The way the dog moves is: %s\n", method.c_str());
    }

    void Move(int speed)
    {
        printf("The speed of the dog is: %d km/h\n", speed);
    }
};

class Fish : public Animal
{
public:
    Fish() : Animal("Fish")
    {
    }

    void Move()
    {
        printf("The way the fish moves is: swim\n");
    }
};

int main()
{
    Dog* aDog = new Dog(true, "Max");

    // Call the Move() methods of the Dog respectively
    aDog->Move("run");
    aDog->Move(1);

    delete aDog; system("pause>0");
```

```
}
```

The Dog object's two Move() methods are called respectively in the main program. In runtime, C++ will determine which Move() method to call according to the **types** of the passed parameters. The result is as follows:

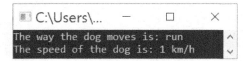

Finally, please note that the following situations are unable to distinguish two overloaded methods, that is, the following conditions are **invalid** C++ overloads:

❖   The two overloaded methods only use different **access modifiers**.
❖   The two overloaded methods only use different parameter **names**.
❖   The two overloaded methods are only different in their **return types**.

3.1.6 Abstract Classes

The abstract classes in C++ refer to the classes that contain at least one **pure virtual** member function. That's a **virtual** function declared by using the **pure** specifier (= 0) syntax. Classes derived from the abstract class must implement the pure virtual function or they, too, are abstract classes. So, the abstract classes are mainly used to be inherited, which define general concepts. For the Animal class in the previous example, it is mainly used to describe the **general concept** of species classification in nature, so it is best suited to be declared as an **abstract** class, as shown in the following revised code:

```
#include <iostream>

using namespace std;

// The Animal is an abstract class
class Animal
{
protected:
    string name;

public:
    Animal(string name)
    {
        this->name = name;
    }

    // Pure virtual methods do not have any implementation code!
    virtual void Move() = 0;
```

```cpp
};

class Dog : public Animal
{
protected:
    bool hasTail;
public:
    string color;

    // Call the constructor of the parent class to initialize the name
    // member
    Dog(bool hasTail, string name) : Animal(name)
    {
        this->hasTail = hasTail;
    }

    string Name()
    {
        return name;
    }

    void Move()
    {
        printf("The way the dog moves is: run\n");
    }
};

class Fish : public Animal
{
public:
    Fish() : Animal("Fish")
    {
    }

    virtual void Move()
    {
        printf("The way the fish moves is: swim\n");
    }
};

int main()
{
    // Because we cannot create objects of an abstract class,
    // the following line will cause a compile error!
    // Animal* aAnimal = new Animal("Animal");
    Dog* aDog = new Dog(true, "Lucy");
    Fish* aFish = new Fish();

    // Call the Move() method of the Dog
    aDog->Move();
    // Call the Move() method of the Fish
    aFish->Move();
```

```
        delete aDog; delete aFish;
        system("pause>0");
}
```

First, the `Move()` method of the `Animal` class is redeclared using the **pure** specifier (= 0). Besides, please note that there **cannot** be any implementation code here. The inherited `Dog` and `Fish` subclasses must provide their implementation of the `Move()` method in which the code is the same as in the previous example. Finally, also note that the `Animal` class **cannot** be used to create objects in the main program because the `Animal` class has been declared as an abstract class.

3.2 Interfaces

The C++ interface classes are similar to the abstract classes, but all the methods in an interface class **must** be **Pure virtual** functions. Any class that implements an interface must provide an **implementation** of the members defined in the interface. Its other purpose is to **avoid** using the **Multiple Inheritance** mechanism in C++.

Please add a new C++ **Console** project named **Interfaces** in the Solution Explorer. Then right-click on the **Source Files** filter and select **Add > New Item...** from the context menu to open the **Add New Item** window as follows:

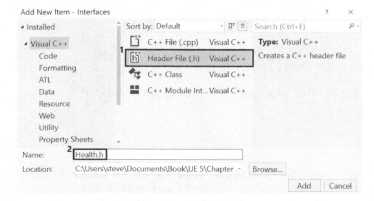

After selecting the **Header File (.h)** in the templates, modify the header name to **Health.h**, as shown above, then press the **Add** button to create the header file in the project as shown below:

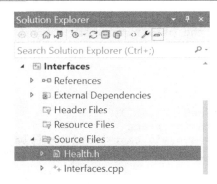

Next, in the code editor, enter the following code:

```
class IHealth
{
public:
    virtual void AddHealth(int points) = 0;
    virtual int GetHealth() = 0;
};
```

The IHealth class is an **Interface** because all of the member methods are **pure virtual** functions.

With the above interface declared in the header, we can write the code for the class that implements the IHealth interface in the **Interfaces.cpp** file. Modify the generated code in the file as follows:

```
#include <iostream>
#include "Health.h"

class Player : public IHealth
{
protected:
    int health;
public:
    // Implement the methods from the IHealth interface class
    void AddHealth(int points)
    {
        health += points;

        printf("The new health is: %d\n", health);
    }

    int GetHealth()
    {
        return health;
    }

    void Move()
```

```
    {
        printf("Move the player...\n");
    }
};

int main()
{
    Player* player = new Player();
    // Get the IHealth interface
    IHealth* health = dynamic_cast<IHealth*>(player);
    // If the player implements the IHealth interface
    if (health)
    {
        // Call the AddHealth() method through the interface
        health->AddHealth(100);
    }

    delete player;
    system("pause>0");
}
```

At beginning of the code, because the IHealth interface is declared in the user-defined **Health.h** header, we have to add a line **#include "Health.h"** to include the header.

The Player class inherits the members of the IHealth interface, and within the class, there are two methods to implement the functions defined in the interface. Note that in the declarations of the two methods, their names must be **the same** as the interface members.

In the main program, after creating a Player object, we **explicitly** cast the object pointer to an IHealth interface pointer. Then, if the pointer is not **nullptr**, which means that the player implements the IHealth interface, we call the implemented **AddHealth()** method, and the output is as follows:

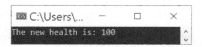

Note: A class must implement **all** member functions defined in the **interface**, otherwise an error will occur during compilation!

At the beginning of this section, we mentioned that another purpose of the interface is to replace Multiple Inheritance, which is a powerful feature in the C++ programming language. It allows a subclass to inherit **multiple** parent classes at the same time, but Multiple Inheritance is a complex design that requires more programming skills.

Instead, we can let a class implement **multiple** interfaces. Please refer to the following revised example of the above Player class that implements multiple interfaces:

```cpp
#include <iostream>
#include "Health.h"

// Another interface class to lock the player
class ILock
{
public:
    virtual void Lock() = 0;
};

class Player : public IHealth, public ILock
{
protected:
    int health;
public:
    // Implement the methods from the IHealth interface class
    void AddHealth(int points)
    {
        health += points;

        printf("The new health is: %d\n", health);
    }

    int GetHealth()
    {
        return health;
    }

    // Implement the method from the ILock interface class
    void Lock()
    {
        printf("You are locked!\n");
    }

    void Move()
    {
        printf("Move the player...\n");
    }
};

int main()
{
    Player* player = new Player();
    // Get the ILock interface
    ILock* lock = dynamic_cast<ILock*>(player);
    // If the player implements the ILock interface
    if (lock)
    {
        // Call the Lock() method through the interface
        lock->Lock();
    }
```

```
   delete player;
     system("pause>0");
 }
```

In the above code, another interface class called **ILock** is declared to **lock** the player. Then we modify the **Player** class to implement the **ILock** interface as well. Finally, in the main program, after obtaining the new **ILock** interface from the **player** object, we can call the **Lock()** method through the interface, and the result is as follows:

How to Use Abstract Classes and Interfaces

It is sometimes difficult to determine when to use the abstract classes or interfaces because both are often used as a template and contract in object-oriented design because if choosing to inherit an abstract class, you must implement its methods; otherwise, if choosing to implement an interface, you must also implement all the methods defined in it, which means that regardless of which way you choose, you must be bound by the abstract class or interface.

The author here provides a simple rule commonly used in object-oriented design for your reference: the so-called "**Is-A**" and "**Has-A**" relationships. For example, in the above example, Dog **is an** animal, so the **Dog** class should inherit the properties and methods of the **Animal** class, and every player **has a** health Stat, so the **Player** class should implement all the methods defined in the **IHealth** interface.

3.3 Exceptions

Modern C++ provides **try** and **catch** keywords for exception handling which allows a program to use a syntax like the **select** statement that can handle different types of exceptions. That is such a mechanism that allows us to easily write robust error-handling code, the syntax of the **try** statement is as follows:

```
try
{
    // The statements that might throw exceptions
}
catch ([…])
{
    // Exception handler
}
[catch([…])]
```

The statements in the `try` block above are the code that might throw exceptions. When any statement in the `try` block causes an exception, the flow of the control will jump to the first associated exception handler. In C++, the `catch` keyword is used to define an exception handler.

Note: You can use **multiple `catch`** blocks to handle different exceptions.

Let's look at a simple example as follows:

```
#include <iostream>
#include <exception>

using namespace std;

int main()
{
    int x = 1, y = 0;
    float z;

    // Put the code that may throw the exception in the try block
    try
    {
      // If the denominator is Zero throw runtime_error
      if (y == 0) {
          throw runtime_error("Attempted to divide by Zero\n");
      }

      z = x / y;
    }
    // If any runtime exception is thrown, it's stored in the exception
    // variable e
    catch (runtime_error& e)
    {
      printf("A runtime error occurred! The error message is as
                                                  follows:\n");
      // Display the message of the exception
      printf("%s\n", e.what());
      printf("%s\n", "Run error handling code...");
      // The following is the error handling code
      y = 2;
      z = x / (float)y;
      printf("The correct calculation result is: %d /  %d = %f\n",
                                                  x, y, z);
    }
}
```

First, put the code that may throw the exception in the `try` block and then use a `catch` block to get any exception thrown by the system and it's stored in the **exception** variable e. In the `catch` block, the message of the exception is displayed first. Here we call the

What() method of the **runtime_error** variable e to get the **error message** followed by the relevant exception handling code. The result of the above example is as follows:

```
C:\Users\steve\Documents\Book...    —    □    ×
A runtime error occurred! The error message is as follows :
Attempted to divide by Zero

Run error handling code...
The correct calculation result is: 1 / 2 = 0.500000
```

After the previous example, you should have some understanding of the structured exception handling syntax. Let's continue to see the following revised example to add the exception handling features by using a **custom exception** class.

```cpp
#include <iostream>
#include "Health.h"
#include <exception>

using namespace std;

// The user-defined exception class that inherits the runtime_error
// built-in class
class InterfaceException : public runtime_error {
public:
    // Defining constructor of class Exception
    // that passes a string message to the runtime_error class
    InterfaceException(string error) : runtime_error(error)
    {
    }
};

class ILock
{
public:
    virtual void Lock() = 0;
};

class Player : public IHealth
{
protected:
    int health;
public:
    // Implement the methods from IHealth interface class
    void AddHealth(int points)
    {
        health += points;

        printf("The new health is: %d\n", health);
    }

    int GetHealth()
    {
```

```
            return health;
        }

        void Move()
        {
            printf("Move the player...\n");
        }
    };

    int main()
    {
        Player* player = new Player();

        try {
            // Get the ILock interface
            ILock* lock = dynamic_cast<ILock*>(player);
            // If the player does not implement the ILock interface, throw
            // an exception
            if (lock == nullptr)
                throw InterfaceException("The ILock interface is not
                                                    implemented!\n");
        }
        catch (InterfaceException& e) {

            // Print out an exception that occurred and call the what()
            // function of the incoming custom exception object e
            printf("An exception occurred and the error is:\n%s", e.what());
        }

        delete player;
        system("pause>0");
    }
```

The above example mainly modifies from the previous **multiple interfaces** example, but the Player class in this example **only** implements the **IHealth** interface. Besides, we declare a **custom** exception class, **InterfaceException**, that inherits the C++ **runtime_error** class and has a constructor that calls the constructor of the parent class to initialize the error message. The main purpose of this constructor is to assign a **custom** error message.

At the beginning of the main program, a try block is used, and an attempt is made to obtain an **unimplemented** interface. Therefore, an exception will occur. We use a throw keyword to **explicitly** generate a custom exception for the **catch** block to process. Please note that the throw keyword must be followed by an **Exception** object, and we pass in the custom error message.

Then in the catch block, the code will handle the custom exception generated, and here we output the error message to the console. The results are shown below:

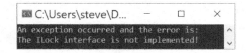

3.4 Multithreading Programming

With the popularity of the multi-core CPU, multithreaded programming has become an important topic in game development. We will introduce the essentials of multithreaded programming in this section.

3.4.1 Threads

C++ provides the **thread** class to define an object that's used to observe and manage a thread of execution within an application. Please refer to the following modified example from the **Pointers** section in the previous chapter.

```
#include <iostream>
#include <thread>

using namespace std;

// The num parameter is to represent the running thread's number
void Swap(int* a, int* b, int num)
{
  printf("Thread %d is running and ", num);
  int temp = *a;
  *a = *b;
  *b = temp;
  printf("after swapping: a = %d, b = %d\n", *a, *b);
}

int main()
{
  int a = 3, b = 5;
  // create two threads and pass in the parameters
  thread swap1(Swap, &a, &b, 1);
  thread swap2(Swap, &a, &b, 2);
  swap1.join();
  swap2.join();

  system("pause>0");
}
```

Because the **thread** class is defined in the **thread** header, we have to include the header at beginning of the example. Then we modify the Swap() function to add an **integer** parameter **num** to represent the number of the running thread.

In the main program, two `thread` objects are created and run. Here the `Swap()` **function's pointer**, the **addresses** of the variables a and b, and the thread number are passed in when creating the objects. Finally, we call the `join()` method of the two thread objects respectively to wait for them to finish.

Before running the program, create a **breakpoint** at the **first** `printf()` in the `Swap()` function, and then press **F5** to run the example. After the program is running, press **F10** (Step Over) and you'll see the program stops with a different icon on the break bar as shown below:

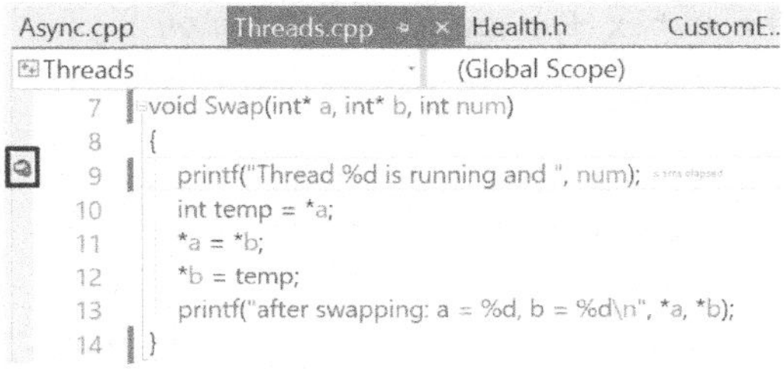

```
Async.cpp        Threads.cpp  • ×  Health.h        CustomE..
▣ Threads                      ·  (Global Scope)
      7  ⊟void Swap(int* a, int* b, int num)
      8   {
  ◉   9  |      printf("Thread %d is running and ", num);
     10         int temp = *a;
     11         *a = *b;
     12         *b = temp;
     13         printf("after swapping: a = %d, b = %d\n", *a, *b);
     14  |}
```

That means the `Swap()` function is running in **another thread**. Next, press on the breakpoint again to **clear** the breakpoint, and then press the **Continue** button **twice** on the Toolbar to run the program. The result is as shown below:

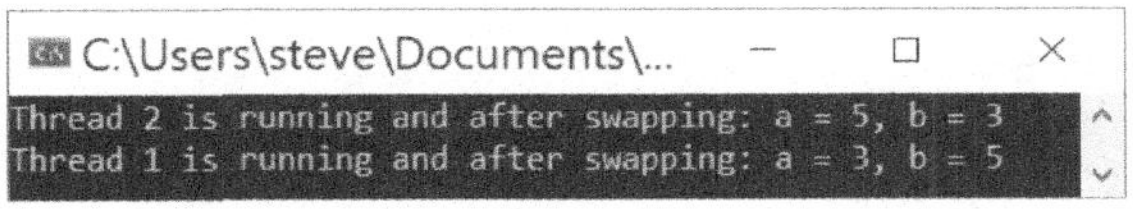

```
⬛ C:\Users\steve\Documents\...    —    □    ×
Thread 2 is running and after swapping: a = 5, b = 3
Thread 1 is running and after swapping: a = 3, b = 5
```

From the above result, you'll see that thread **2** is running **before** thread 1 is running, which represents they are running in different threads and thus the **order** may be different.

Continue to run the program several times, one of the results is shown below:

```
⬛ C:\Users\steve\Documents\Book\UE 5\Chapter ...   —   □   ×
Thread 1 is running and Thread 2 is running and after swapping: a = 3, b = 5
after swapping: a = 5, b = 3
```

This time the **first** swap does **not** work because the result should be: a = 5, b = 3, and why this is happing? That's because both threads are swapping the two variables **simultaneously** and thus **the order is mixed up**. This is not what we want! To solve this issue, modern C++ provides the `mutex` class to **synchronize** the execution of two threads.

Thread Synchronization

The mutex class in C++ provides the lock() method to protect certain blocks of code from being run by more than one thread; in other words, all threads are **synchronized** to access the code in that block. To use the mutex is simple, let's revise the above example as follows:

```
#include <iostream>
#include <thread>
#include <mutex>

using namespace std;

mutex mtx;   // The mutex for critical section

void Swap(int* a, int* b, int num)
{
  mtx.lock();
  printf("Thread %d is running and ", num);
  int temp = *a;
  *a = *b;
  *b = temp;
  printf("after swapping: a = %d, b = %d\n", *a, *b);
  mtx.unlock();
}

int main()
{
  int a = 3, b = 5;
  thread swap1(Swap, &a, &b, 1);
  thread swap2(Swap, &a, &b, 2);
  swap1.join();
  swap2.join();

  system("pause>0");
}
```

At the beginning of the revised code, we have to include the **mutex** header. Then we declare a mutex class object **mtx**, and in the Swap() function, the lock() method of the mtx is called to **lock** the next **five** lines of code from other threads to execute the code, until the unlock() method is called at the end of the function, which allows the other thread to run the code again. Now run the revised program **several times**, and you'll notice that the synchronization issue is never happening again.

3.4.2 The async Function Template

The function template **async** runs a function or the class method **asynchronously** and returns a **std::future** that will eventually hold the result of that function call. Let's see a typical example to run the AI method **asynchronously** using the async template as follows:

```cpp
#include <iostream>
#include <future>

using namespace std;

// The atomic Boolean flag to stop the AI async task
static atomic<bool> sAsyncTaskFinished = false;

class AsyncTask
{
public:
  void run() {
    while (!sAsyncTaskFinished)
    {
      printf("AI is thinking...\n");
      // Sleep for 1 second
      this_thread::sleep_for(1s);
    }
  }
};

int main()
{
  AsyncTask aiTask;
  // Note: The variable to get the return of the async task is required!
  //       Otherwise, it will not return the control to the main thread.
  auto fut = async(launch::async, &AsyncTask::run, &aiTask);
  cin.get();    // Wait for the Enter key to be pressed
  sAsyncTaskFinished = true;    // Stop the AI async task

  printf("Finished.\n");
  system("pause>null");
}
```

Because the **async** template is defined in the **future** header, we have to include the header at beginning of the example. Then an **atomic** Boolean flag **sAsyncTaskFinished** is declared to **stop** the AI async task. The **atomic** template is used to declare variables that avoid the **race condition** in multithreading programming, which means all threads that access the **atomic** variables will be **synchronized**.

Next, a class called **AsyncTask** with a public method **run()** is declared, and in the method, we use an **infinite** loop to simulate the AI until the **flag** becomes **true**. To avoid occupying all the CPU core computing resources, the **this_thread::sleep_for()**

method is called, and we pass in **1s**, which means 1 **second**, as the parameter to let the thread sleep for 1 second.

In the main program, after declaring an `AsyncTask` object, we call the `async` function template and pass in three parameters. The **first** one is called the **launch policy**, here the `launch::async` is used, which means the task will start right the way **asynchronously**. The second and third parameters are the **class method** to run and the **class object**, both are passed in **by reference**. Also, note that here we have to declare an `auto` variable to store the result of the function template; otherwise, the `async` function will **not yield** to the main thread, which means the next statement, namely the `cin.get()`, will never be executed.

Next, the `cin.get()` function will **stop** the program and wait for the user to press the **Enter** key in the console. After pressing the Enter, the `sAsyncTaskFinished` flag will be set to **true**, and the `printf()` method in the infinite loop of the `AsyncTask` object will be **stopped** and returned to the main thread. Finally, the "Finished." message will be printed out to the console. After the above example is running, move the mouse cursor into the **Console** window and then press the **Enter** key, the results are as shown below:

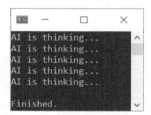

The **AI is thinking...** message will be printed out **per second** and after the Enter is pressed, the "**Finished.**" string is printed out.

3.5 Data Structures in Modern C++

Modern C++ provides useful **template**-based data structure classes in the `std` namespace to store data, including the `vector` and `map` classes.

3.5.1 The `vector` Class

The C++ Standard Library `vector` class is a **class template** for **sequence** containers also known as the **dynamic** array that can change in size. A `vector` stores elements of a given type in a linear arrangement and allows fast random access to any element. A vector is the preferred container for a sequence when random-access performance is at a premium.

Vectors allow constant-time insertions and deletions at the end of the sequence. Inserting or deleting elements in the middle of a vector requires linear time. Vector reallocation occurs when a member function must increase the sequence contained in the vector object beyond its current storage capacity. Other insertions and erasures may alter various storage addresses within the sequence. In all such cases, iterators or references that point at altered portions of the sequence become **invalid**. If no reallocation happens, only iterators and references **before** the insertion/deletion point remain valid.

Compared to the other dynamic sequence containers, for example, the list, vectors are very efficient in accessing their elements (just like arrays) and efficient in adding or removing elements from their end.

Refer to the following example for declaring an object of the vector class and populating its elements as follows:

```
#include <iostream>
#include <vector>

using namespace std;

int main()
{
    vector<int> v1;
    // Add two elements to the end of the vector
    v1.push_back(1);
    v1.push_back(2);
    // Get the second element in the vector
    int i = v1[1];
    printf("The second integer of v1 is %d\n", i);
    system("pause>null");
}
```

Because the vector class is defined in the vector header, we have to include the header at beginning of the example. In the main program, after declaring a vector object **v1**, the push_back() method of the **v1** is called twice to add two integers to the end of the vector, respectively. Finally, we get the **second** element in the vector using an index just like an array.

The commonly used methods (functions) of the vector class are outlined in the following table:

Name	Description
at	Returns a reference to the element at a specified location in the vector.

back	Returns a reference to the last element of the vector.
clear	Erases the elements of the vector.
empty	Tests if the vector container is empty.
erase	Removes an element or a range of elements in a vector from specified positions.
front	Returns a reference to the first element in a vector.
insert	Inserts an element or many elements into the vector at a specified position.
pop_back	Deletes the element at the end of the vector.
Push_back	Adds an element to the end of the vector.
size	Returns the number of elements in the vector.

3.5.2 The list Class

The C++ list class is a class template of sequence containers that maintain their elements in a **linear** arrangement and allow efficient insertions and deletions at any location within the sequence. The sequence is stored as a **bidirectional linked list** of elements, each containing a member of some type.

List reallocation occurs when a member function must insert or erase elements of the list. In all such cases, only iterators or references that point at erased portions of the controlled sequence become invalid.

The list class has many common methods that are the same as in the vector class, for those which are **different** are outlined in the following table:

Name	Description
pop_front	Deletes the element at the beginning of a list.
push_front	Adds an element to the beginning of a list.
remove	Erases elements in a list that match a specified value.
reverse	Reverses the order in which the elements occur in a list.
sort	Arranges the elements of a list in ascending order or concerning some other order relation.

Refer to the following example for populating the list class object and **sorting** the elements:

```cpp
#include <iostream>
#include <list>

using namespace std;
```

```cpp
int main()
{
    list<int> l1;
    // Add three elements to the end of the list
    l1.push_back(3);
    l1.push_back(2);
    l1.push_back(1);
    // Arrange the elements of the list in ascending order
    l1.sort();

    printf("After sorting the list: ");
    // Use the for-each loop to print out the elements
    for (int i : l1)
    {
        printf("%d ", i);
    }
    printf("\n");
    // Remove the integer three in the list
    l1.remove(3);
    printf("After removing the 3: ");
    for (int i : l1)
    {
        printf("%d ", i);
    }

    system("pause>null");
}
```

Because the list class is defined in the **list** header, we have to include the header at beginning of the example. In the main program, after creating the list object and adding three elements to the **end** of the list using the **push_back()** method, we call the **sort()** method to arrange the elements of the list in **ascending** order.

After sorting the elements in the list, because the list class does **not** overload the **[]** operator, here we use the **for-each** loop to output the result to the console. Finally, we call the **remove()** method and pass in integer **three** to **remove** the integer from the list. The result of the above example is shown below:

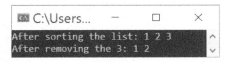

3.5.3 The queue Class

The queue class supports a **first-in**, **first-out** (**FIFO**) data structure. Elements can be added at the **back** or removed from the **front**, and elements can be inspected at **either end** of the queue. The restriction to accessing only the front and back elements in this way is the reason for using the queue class.

The methods of the queue class are outlined in the following table:

Name	Description
back	Returns a reference to the last and most recently added element at the back of the queue.
empty	Tests if the queue is empty.
front	Returns a reference to the first element at the front of the queue.
pop	Removes an element from the front of the queue.
push	Adds an element to the back of the queue.
size	Returns the number of elements in the queue.

Refer to the following example for populating the queue class object and accessing the elements:

```
#include <iostream>
#include <queue>

int main()
{
    using namespace std;
    queue<int> q1;
    // Add three integers to the back of the queue
    q1.push(10);
    q1.push(11);
    q1.push(12);
    // Get the integers from the back and front of the queue
    int back = q1.back();
    const int front = q1.front();

    printf("The integer at the back of queue q1 is: %d\n", back);
    printf("The integer at the front of queue q1 is: : %d ", front);
    system("pause>null");
}
```

Because the queue class is defined in the **queue** header, we have to include the header at beginning of the example. In the main program, after creating the queue object and adding three elements to the back of the queue using the **push()** method, we call the **back()** and **front()** methods to get the integers from the **back** and **front** of the queue, respectively. The result of the above example is shown below:

3.5.4 The `stack` Class

The `stack` class supports a **last-in**, **first-out** (**LIFO**) data structure. A good analogy to keep in mind would be a stack of plates. Elements (plates) may be inserted, inspected, or removed only from the **top** of the stack, which is the **last** element at the **end** of the base container. The restriction to accessing only the top element is the reason for using the stack class.

The methods of the stack class are outlined in the following table:

Name	Description
`empty`	Tests if the stack is empty.
`pop`	Removes an element from the top of the stack.
`push`	Adds an element to the top of the stack.
`size`	Returns the number of elements in the stack.
`top`	Returns a reference to an element at the top of the stack.

Refer to the following example for populating the stack class object and accessing the elements:

```cpp
#include <iostream>
#include <stack>

int main()
{
    using namespace std;
    stack<int> s1;
    // Add three integers to the stack, the last one is on the top
    s1.push(10);
    s1.push(20);
    s1.push(30);
    // Get the number of the elements in the stack
    int i = s1.size();
    printf("The stack length is: %d\n", i);

    // Get the top element in the stack
    i = s1.top();
    printf("The element at the top of the stack is: %d\n", i);
    // Remove the element on the top, which is 30
    s1.pop();
```

```
    i = s1.size();
    printf("After a pop, the stack length is: %d\n", i);
    // Get the top element again, now it's 20
    i = s1.top();
    printf("After a pop, the element at the top of the stack is: %d\n",
                                                                    i);
    system("pause>null");
}
```

Because the **stack** class is defined in the **stack** header, we have to include the header at beginning of the example. In the main program, after creating the **stack** object and adding three integers, the number of elements in the stack is printed out. Next, we call the **top()** method to get the **top** element in the stack, and then remove the element on the top, which is **30**, using the **pop()** method. Finally, the **size** and **top** element of the stack are printed out to verify the change of the stack after the **pop()**. The result of the above example is shown below:

3.5.5 The map Class

The **map** class is used for the storage and retrieval of data from a collection in which each element is a **pair** that has **both a data value and a sort key**. The value of the **key** is **unique** and is used to **automatically** sort the data. The data types used for elements and keys are specified as parameters in the class template together with the comparison function and allocator.

The element values are retrieved based on **associated key** values and the value of an element in a map can be changed directly. The key value is a **constant** and **cannot** be changed. Instead, key values associated with old elements must be deleted, and new key values must be inserted for new elements.

The commonly used member functions of the map class are outlined in the following table:

Name	Description
at	Finds an element with the specified key value.

count	Returns the number of elements in a map whose key matches the key specified in a parameter.
emplace	Inserts an element constructed in place into the map.
empty	Returns true if a map is empty.
erase	Removes an element or a range of elements in a map from specified positions.
find	Returns an iterator that points to the location of an element in a map that has a key equal to a specified key.
insert	Inserts an element or a range of elements into the map at a specified position.
size	Returns the number of elements in the map.

Refer to the following example for populating the map class object and accessing the elements:

```cpp
#include <iostream>
#include <map>

int main()
{
    using namespace std;
    map<char, int> m1;
    typedef pair<char, int> Key_Value_Pair;
    // Insert two key and value pairs into the map
    m1.insert(Key_Value_Pair('a', 1));
    m1.insert(Key_Value_Pair('b', 2));
    m1['c'] = 3;
    // Find and show elements
    printf("m1['a'] == %d\n", m1['a']);
    printf("m1.at('b') == %d\n", m1.at('b'));
    // Insert an element constructed in place into the map
    m1.emplace('d', 4);
    printf("The number of elements in the map is: %d\n",
                                        (int)m1.size());
    // Search the map for elements with a key equivalent to the 'e'
    // and returns the number of matches
    if (m1.count('e') > 0)
        printf("'%c' is a key of the map\n", 'e');
    else    // If the count is zero which means no such key
        printf("'%c' is not a key of the map\n", 'e');

    system("pause>null");
}
```

Because the map class is defined in the **map** header, we have to include the header at beginning of the example. In the main program, after creating the **map** object and declaring a new type called **Key_Value_Pair** using the **typedef** keyword and **pair** template, two key and value pairs are inserted into the map using the `insert()` method. Next, we use the `[]` operator and a new key to create a key and value pair in the map and assign the value **directly**.

Then the `[]` operator and `at()` method are used to retrieve the values of two elements respectively and they are printed out to the console. Next, we call the `emplace()` method to **insert** an element, which is **constructed in place**, into the map. After emplacing the element, the size of the map is printed out to verify that the insertion is successful. Finally, we call the count() method and pass in the key to search the map for elements with a key equivalent to the character 'e' and return the number of matches. Because all elements in a map container are unique, the count() method can only return **1** (if the element is found) or **zero** (otherwise). The result of the above example is shown below:

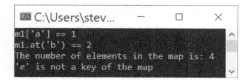

3.6 Summary

C++ is an object-oriented programming language, and in this chapter, we provided useful examples that cover important OOP topics in modern C++ to not only help the readers understand the essential concepts but starting OOP in modern C++.

With the popularity of the multi-core CPU, multithreaded programming has become an important topic in game development. This chapter introduced the essentials of multithreaded programming through practical examples. Multithreading is useful in some special applications, including Artificial Intelligence (AI) and network communication.

Exercises

3.1 Rewrite the `Animal` abstract class given in this chapter to an **interface**. What changes do you have to make to the code?

3.2 Write an **interface** class called **IInteract**, and in the interface, add a member function (method) called **Interact**. Within this method, use the `printf()` function to print out a message string "**E – Interact**" to simulate starting interaction with an NPC. Then write another class called **NPC** that inherits from the **Player** class in this chapter, and also **implements** the **IInteract** interface. Lastly, in the main() function, after creating an **NPC** object called **questGiver** using the new keyword, obtain the **IInteract** interface from the object and call the **Interact()** method to print out the interaction message to the console.

3.3 Rewrite the **AsynTask** class example in this chapter to use the **thread** class instead of the **async** template. What's the difference between the two methods?

Introduction to UE5
Game Programming

UE5 provides two toolsets for programmers which can also be used to accelerate development workflows. New gameplay classes, Slate, and Canvas user interface element printed editor functionality can be written with C++, and all changes will be reflected in Unreal Editor after compiling with either Visual Studio or Xcode. The Blueprint visual scripting system is a robust tool that enables classes to be created in-editor through wiring together function blocks and property references.

C++ classes can be used as a base for Blueprint classes, and in this way, programmers can set up fundamental gameplay classes that are then sub-classed and iterated by level designers.

4.1 UE5 Game Programming Quick Start

In this Quick Start Guide, you will learn how to set up a C++ project in the UE5 and program your first C++ gameplay class in Visual Studio. By the time you have completed this section, you will know how to do the following:

- ❖ Create a new C++ Project.
- ❖ Create a new Actor class in C++.
- ❖ Edit that C++ class in your development environment, adding visual representation and functionality.
- ❖ Compile your project.
- ❖ Test your new Actor in the Unreal Editor.

This guide assumes that you have already set up Visual Studio as your programming environment. If not, please refer to the previous chapter for installing and setting up Visual Studio for the UE5. We also assume that you have some familiarity with using the Unreal Editor before starting this guide, but for your convenience, we will walk through all the steps necessary to create and manage C++ classes from the editor.

The end result of this guide will be a cube that floats softly in mid-air and continually rotates, giving you a simple object to test as you learn to use the development environment for programming.

4.1.1 Required Setup

Launch the UE5, and the **Unreal Project Browser** window will come up, click the **Games** category and select a **Blank** template. Make sure that you have **C++** and **Starter Content** enabled as shown below, choose your preferred **Save Location** and **Name** for this project, and then click the **Create** button. Here, we're naming our project **QuickStart**.

This will automatically create a simple, blank project with only essential C++ code in the solution, and it will automatically open inside both the Unreal Editor and Visual Studio.

Note: Any Blueprint project can be converted to a C++ project. If you have a Blueprint project that you want to add C++ too, create a new C++ class per the next section, and the editor will set up your code environment for you. Also, note that using a C++ project **does not** prevent you from using Blueprint. C++ projects simply set up the base classes for your project in C++ instead of Blueprint.

4.1.2 Creating a New C++ Class

In the **Unreal Editor**, select **Tools** > **New C++ Class...** from the main menu as shown below:

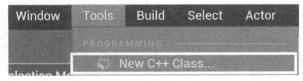

The **CHOOSE PARENT CLASS** menu will display as shown below:

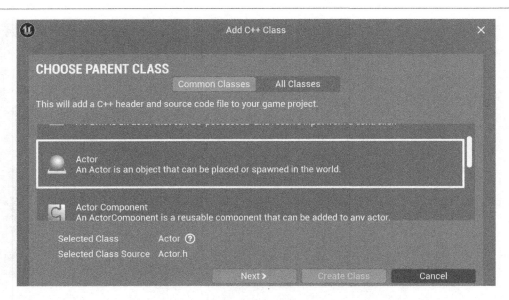

You can choose an existing class to extend, adding its functionality to your own. Here choose **Actor**, as it is the most basic type of object that can be placed in the world, then click **Next**.

In the **NAME YOUR NEW ACTOR** menu, after pressing the **Public** button to set the **Class Type**, a folder called **Public** will be added to the **Path**, then rename your Actor **FloatingActor** as shown below:

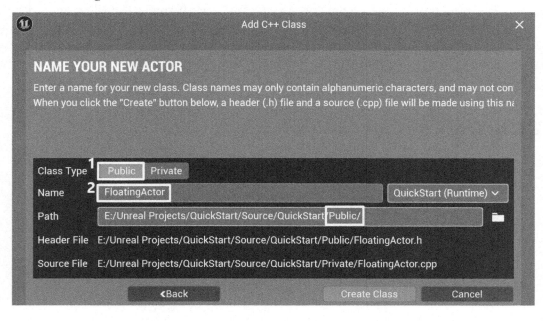

Lastly, click the **Create Class** button to generate the C++ class in Visual Studio. The Unreal Engine will **automatically** compile with the **Live Coding** and **reload** with our new class selected in the Content Browser, and your programming environment will automatically open with the FloatingActor.cpp.

4.1.3 Editing Your C++ Class

Now that the C++ Class has been generated, we're going to switch over to Visual Studio and edit our code as follows:

1. In **Visual Studio**, locate the **Solution Explorer**, and then use it to locate **FloatingActor.h**. In our project, it will be located under Games > **QuickStart** > Source > **QuickStart** > **Public** as shown below:

Note: Because we set the **Class Type** to **Public** in the previous step, UE5 will automatically create the **Public** filter for us in Visual Studio and the **folder** under the project path as well. Besides, the **header** is placed in the **Public** folder and the **.cpp** file is placed under the **Private** filter and folder as shown in the above figure.

2. **Double**-click FloatingActor.h to open it and bring it into focus in the code editor.

    This is a **header** file, and you can also think of it as being sort of like a table of contents for a C++ class. Before building any new functionality, we have to declare any new **Variables** or **Functions** that we're using in this file.

3. Add the following code **underneath** the declaration for the `AFloatingActor()` constructor:

```
UPROPERTY(VisibleAnywhere)
UStaticMeshComponent* VisualMesh;
```

Here we are declaring a **StaticMeshComponent**, which will act as our visual representation for our object. Note that it uses a **UProperty** macro, which makes it **visible** inside **Unreal Editor**.

4. Now open **FloatingActor.cpp** and add the following code inside of `AFloatingActor::AFloatingActor()`, just **before** the **closing** bracket:

```
VisualMesh =
            reateDefaultSubobject<UStaticMeshComponent>(TEXT("Mesh"));
VisualMesh->SetupAttachment(RootComponent);

static ConstructorHelpers::FObjectFinder<UStaticMesh>
        CubeVisualAsset(TEXT("/Game/StarterContent/Shapes/
                                    Shape_Cube.Shape_Cube"));

if (CubeVisualAsset.Succeeded())
{
   VisualMesh->SetStaticMesh(CubeVisualAsset.Object);
   VisualMesh->SetRelativeLocation(FVector(0.0f, 0.0f, 0.0f));
}
```

This function is the **constructor**, and it tells the class how to **initialize** itself when it is **first created**. The code we have added will fill our **VisualMesh** reference in with a new **StaticMeshComponent**, attach it to our Actor, and set it to the **cube** mesh from the **Starter Content** assets.

5. Add the following code inside of `AFloatingActor::Tick(float DeltaTime)`, just **before** the **closing** bracket:

```
FVector NewLocation = GetActorLocation();
FRotator NewRotation = GetActorRotation();
float RunningTime = GetGameTimeSinceCreation();
float DeltaHeight = (FMath::Sin(RunningTime + DeltaTime) -
                                    FMath::Sin(RunningTime));
//Scale our height by a factor of 20
NewLocation.Z += DeltaHeight * 20.0f;
//Rotate by 20 degrees per second
float DeltaRotation = DeltaTime * 20.0f;
NewRotation.Yaw += DeltaRotation;
SetActorLocationAndRotation(NewLocation, NewRotation);
```

The `Tick()` function is where we add code that we want to execute in real time. In this case, it will make our cube simultaneously **rotate** while also **floating up and down**.

4.1.4 Compiling and Testing Your C++ Code

So far the C++ code is ready, it's time to compile and test the code as follows:

1. **Save** your work in **both** FloatingActor.h and FloatingActor.cpp. Then go back to the **Unreal Editor** and press **Ctrl**, **Alt**, and **F11** keys at the same time to **compile** the project. The following **Live Coding** window, which contains the compiling progress, will show up and later you should see a message that says "**Live Coding succeeded**" at the bottom of the screen.

Note: You should always **save** your work **before** attempting to compile, otherwise the changes you make in your code will **not** take effect. Alternatively, you can **turn off** Live Coding from the **Compile options menu** on the bottom of the Unreal Editor or from the **Project Settings** window, and back to Visual Studio, **right**-click the project in the **Solution Explorer**, click the **Build** command in the context menu, and wait for the project to finish compiling.

2. In **Unreal Editor**, go back to the **Content Drawer**, unfold **C++ Classes > QuickStart**, and then locate **FloatingActor** under the **Public** folder as shown below:

3. Click and drag **FloatingActor** onto the Landscape in the **Perspective Viewport** to create an instance of FloatingActor as shown below. It will be selected in the **World Outliner** as "**FloatingActor**" and its properties will be visible in the **Details Panel**.

4. In the **Details Panel** for **FloatingActor**, reset your Actor's **Z Location** to **60** as shown below. This will place it directly **over** the Landscape in the default scene.

Alternatively, you can use the **Move** gizmo to move it there manually as shown below:

5.   Press the **Play In Editor** button, as shown below, at the **top** of the screen.

The result is shown below:

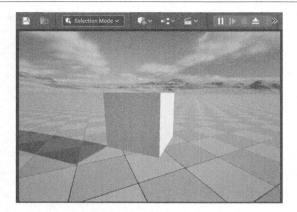

You should now see your cube gently **floating up** and **down** while it slowly **rotates**.

Congratulations! You've created the first Actor class entirely with C++! While this represents quite a simple object and only scratches the surface of what you can do with C++ source code, at this point you have touched on all the essentials of creating, editing, and compiling C++ code for your game. You are now ready for more complex gameplay programming challenges. In the next section, we'll discuss how to extend the above C++ class and create the Blueprint.

4.1.5 Creating Blueprints from the C++ Class

Right-click the above **FloatingActor** class in the **Content Browser**, and you will find the option to extend it, either in C++ or in Blueprint as shown below, enabling you to create new variations of it.

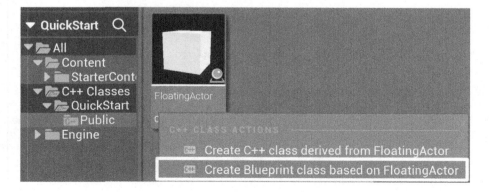

Select **Create Blueprint class based on FloatingActor** from the context menu and the following **Add Blueprint Class** window will appear.

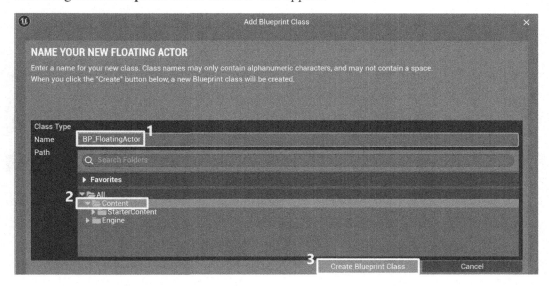

After renaming the **Blueprint** Class to **BP_FloatingActor**, select the **Content** folder as shown above, then press the **Create Blueprint Class** button. The generated Blueprint will be opened in the **Unreal Editor** as shown below:

On the **upper-right** corner of the editor, you'll see the **Parent class** of the Blueprint, here is the C++ **FloatingActor** class. On the **left** side of the editor, the **Components** tab will contain all the Component objects hierarchy created in the **constructor** of the C++ parent class. With the **Visual Mesh** selected as shown above and its properties will show up in the **Details** tab. Find and expand the **Static Mesh** settings, and you'll see that the

Static Mesh field is assigned the static mesh, namely the **Shape_Cube** in the Starter Content folder.

Next, press the drop-down menu to the right of the **Static Mesh** field and select the **Shape_Cone**, as shown below, the **Cone** shape will show up in the Viewport.

After pressing the **Compile** and **Save** button on the Toolbar to save the modification, move the **Cube** shape in the Viewport to the right using the **Move** gizmo, and then drag and drop the **MyFloatingActor** Blueprint to the Viewport as shown below:

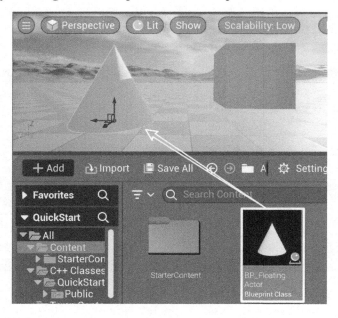

Now press the **Play** button again to run the game and you'll see the **Cone** shape floating up and down just like the Cube shape.

As you can see from the above example, the Blueprints in UE5 provide the **UI** for us to **visually modify** the properties of a gameplay class and **preview** the result. This is the reason why we chose a game engine like UE5 for developing large game projects. Besides, Blueprints also provide **visual scripting** for us to **prototype** a game rapidly, which we'll discuss in the next section.

Recommended Asset Naming Conventions

As you develop projects in UE5, the list of Assets in your Content Browser will expand. This runs the risk of creating redundant variations of assets you're experimenting with or introducing ambiguity with overly similar names. For example, it is possible for you to have a folder named "Soldier" with a Blueprint, a texture, and a model that all have the name "Soldier" in them, but no clear way to tell which is which in a simple list.

For large projects, we recommend you establish a common naming convention for individual Assets early in development. This will make it easier for you and your team to locate files and prevent potential conflicts or ambiguity.

The naming convention described below reflects how Epic Games names Assets in sample projects:

[AssetTypePrefix]_[AssetName]_[Descriptor]_[OptionalVariantLetterOrNumber]

- ❖ **AssetTypePrefix** identifies the type of Asset, refer to the table below for details.

- ❖ **AssetName** is the Asset's name.

- ❖ **Descriptor** provides additional context for the Asset, to help identify how it is used. For example, whether a texture is a normal map or an opacity map.

- ❖ **OptionalVariantLetterOrNumber** is optionally used to differentiate between multiple versions or variations of an asset.

Consider using this naming convention for your own project's Assets, as it will provide multiple ways for your team to locate an Asset when searching the Content Browser.

Note: This naming convention is only a recommendation to simplify setting up your project. Your requirements will always take precedence, and it is likely that you won't use all of these Asset types in your Project.

Recommended Asset Prefixes

This list is not exhaustive, as new features can require new Asset types. If you are using an Asset type not listed, use the existing list as a guideline for your naming convention for that Asset.

Asset	Prefix
General	
HDRI	HDR_
Material	M_
Material Instance	MI_
Physics Asset	PHYS_
Physics Material	PM_
Post Process Material	PPM_
Skeletal Mesh	SK_
Static Mesh	SM_
Texture	T_
Blueprints	
Actor Component	AC_
Animation Blueprint	ABP_
Blueprint Interface	BI_
Blueprint	BP_
Curve Table	CT_
Data Table	DT_
Enum	E_
Structure	F_
Widget Blueprint	WBP_
Particle Effects	

Niagara Emitter	FXE_
Niagara System	FXS_
Niagara Function	FXF_
Skeletal Mesh Animations	
Montages	AM_
Animation Sequence	AS_
Blend Space	BS_

4.2 Introduction to Programming in UE5

After finishing the Quick Start, this section will introduce how to write C++ code in UE5. Do not worry, C++ programming in Unreal Engine is fun, and not hard to get started with! We like to think of Unreal C++ as **"assisted C++"** because UE5 has so many features to help make C++ easier for every game developer.

Before we go on, you must be already familiar with C++ or another programming language. If it is not, please go to the Modern C++ Primer chapter, review the materials and make sure that you understand the essentials of the C++ language. This section is written with the assumption that you have some C++ experience, but if you know C#, Java, or JavaScript, you should find many aspects familiar.

It is possible to write standard C++ code in UE5, but you will be most successful after going through this section and learning the basics of the Unreal programming model. We will talk more about that as we go along.

4.2.1 C++ and Blueprint

UE5 provides two methods, C++ and Blueprint Visual Scripting, to create new gameplay elements. Using C++, programmers add the base gameplay systems that designers can then build upon or with to create the custom gameplay for a level or the game. In these cases, the C++ programmer works in a text editor (like Notepad++) or an IDE (usually Microsoft Visual Studio, or Apple's Xcode) and the designer works in the Blueprint Editor within UE5.

The gameplay API and framework classes are available to both systems, which can be used separately, but show their true power when used in conjunction to complement each other. What does that mean, though? It means that the engine works best when programmers are creating gameplay building blocks in C++ and designers take those blocks and make interesting gameplay.

With that said, let us look at a typical workflow for the C++ programmer that is creating building blocks for the designer. In this case, we are going to create a class that is later extended via Blueprints by a designer or programmer. In this class, we are going to create some properties that the designer can set, and we are going to derive new values from those properties. The entire process is quite easy to do using the tools and C++ macros we provide for you.

Class Wizard

The first thing we're going to do is use the **Class Wizard** within the Unreal Editor to generate the basic C++ class that will be extended by Blueprint later. To open the Class Wizard, please select **Tools > New C++ Class…** from the main menu, and the image below shows the wizard's first step where we are creating a new Actor.

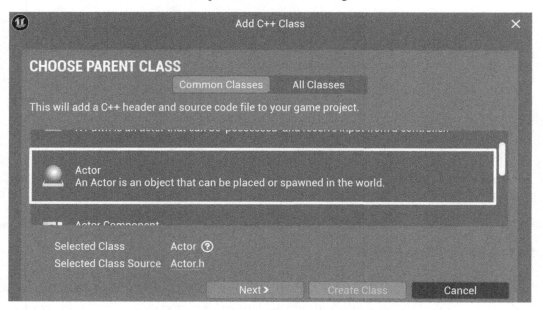

After pressing the **Next** button, the second step in the process tells the wizard the **Type**, **Name**, and **Path** of the class you want to be generated. Here's the second step with the default name used, but this time we want the actor to be placed in a new **Actors** folder under the **Public** folder generated before. So, **add** the path "**/Public/Actors**" to the end of the original path as shown below:

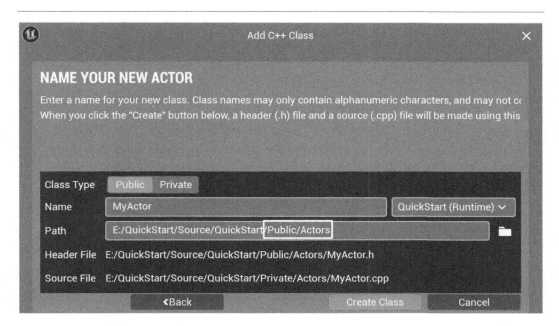

Once you choose to create the class, the wizard will generate the **Actors** folder and the source files in this new folder. After a while, your development environment will open so that you can start editing it. Here is the **class definition** that is generated for you in the **MyActor.h** header file.

```cpp
#pragma once

#include "CoreMinimal.h"
#include "GameFramework/Actor.h"
#include "MyActor.generated.h"

UCLASS()
class QUICKSTART_API AMyActor : public AActor
{
  GENERATED_BODY()

public:
  // Sets default values for this actor's properties
  AMyActor();

protected:
  // Called when the game starts or when spawned
  virtual void BeginPlay() override;

public:
  // Called every frame
  virtual void Tick(float DeltaTime) override;

};
```

The Class Wizard generates your class with **BeginPlay()**, and **Tick()** specified as **overrides**. BeginPlay() is an event that lets you know the Actor has entered the game in a playable state. This is a good place to initiate gameplay logic for your class. Tick() is called once per frame with the amount of elapsed time since the last call passed in. You can do any recurring logic there. However, if you do not need that functionality, it is best to remove it to save yourself a small amount of performance. **If you remove it, make sure to remove the constructor line that indicates ticking should occur.** The constructor below, which is in the generated **MyActor.cpp** file, contains the line in question.

```cpp
// Sets default values
AMyActor::AMyActor()
{
  // Set this actor to call Tick() every frame.
  // You can turn this off to improve performance if you don't need it.
  PrimaryActorTick.bCanEverTick = true;

}
```

Making a Property Show up in the Editor

We have our class, so now we can create some **properties** that designers can set in the Editor. Exposing a property to the Editor is easy with the **UPROPERTY()** Specifier. All you have to do is put **UPROPERTY(EditAnywhere)** on the line **above** your **property declaration**, as seen in the class below:

```cpp
UCLASS()
class QUICKSTART_API AMyActor : public AActor
{
  GENERATED_BODY()

public:
  // Sets default values for this actor's properties
  AMyActor();

  UPROPERTY(EditAnywhere)
  int32 TotalDamage;    // property declaration
    ...

};
```

That is all you need to do to be able to **edit** that value in the **Editor**. There are more ways to control how and where it is edited. This is done by passing more information into the UPROPERTY() Specifier. For instance, if you want the TotalDamage property to appear in a **section** with related properties, you can use the **categorization** feature. The property declaration below shows this.

```
UPROPERTY(EditAnywhere, Category = "Damage")
int32 TotalDamage;
```

When the user looks to edit this property, it now appears under the **Damage** heading and any other properties you have marked with this category name. This is a great way to place commonly used settings together for editing by designers. Next, let us expose that same property to Blueprint as follows:

```
UPROPERTY(EditAnywhere, BlueprintReadWrite, Category = "Damage")
int32 TotalDamage;
```

As you can see, there is a **Specifier** called **BlueprintReadWrite** to make a property available for **reading** and **writing** in Blueprint graphs. There's a separate Specifier, **BlueprintReadOnly**, that you can use if you want the property to be treated as const in Blueprints. There are quite a few options available for controlling how a property is exposed to the Editor and we'll discuss those specifiers in the following chapters.

Before continuing to the section below, let's add a couple of properties to this sample class. There is already a property to control the total amount of damage this actor will deal out but let us take that further and make that damage happen over time. The code below adds one **designer settable** property and one that is **visible** to the designer but **not changeable** by them.

```
UCLASS()
class QUICKSTART_API AMyActor : public AActor
{
  GENERATED_BODY()

public:
  // Sets default values for this actor's properties
  AMyActor();

  UPROPERTY(EditAnywhere, BlueprintReadWrite, Category = "Damage")
  int32 TotalDamage;
  UPROPERTY(EditAnywhere, BlueprintReadWrite, Category = "Damage")
  float DamageTimeInSeconds;
  UPROPERTY(BlueprintReadOnly, VisibleAnywhere, Transient,
                                          Category = "Damage")
  float DamagePerSecond;
    …
};
```

The DamageTimeInSeconds is a property that the designer can modify and the DamagePerSecond property is a **calculated** value using the designer's settings (see the next section). The **VisibleAnywhere** Specifier marks that property as **viewable** but **not**

editable. The **Transient** Specifier means that it **won't** be **saved** or **loaded** from the disk; it is meant to be a **derived, non-persistent** value, so there is no need to store it. The figure below shows the properties in the **Details** tab as part of the class defaults.

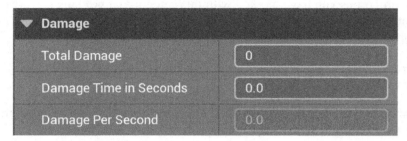

Setting Defaults in the Constructor

Setting default values for properties in a constructor works the same as your typical C++ class. Below are two examples of setting default values in a constructor that are **equivalent** in functionality.

```
AMyActor::AMyActor()
{
  TotalDamage = 200;
  DamageTimeInSeconds = 1.0f;
}


AMyActor::AMyActor() : TotalDamage(200), DamageTimeInSeconds(1.0f)
{
}
```

Here is the same view of the properties after adding default values in the constructor.

Note: If you do not provide a default value for a property, the engine will automatically set that property to **zero**, or **null** in the case of **pointer** types.

Extending a C++ Class via Blueprints

So far, we have created a simple gameplay class with the C++ Class Wizard and added some properties for the designer to set. Now, let's take a look at how a designer can start creating unique classes from our C++ class here.

The first thing we are going to do is create a new Blueprint class from our **AMyActor** class. Back to Unreal Editor and open the Content Drawer. **Right**-click inside the **Content Browser** of the **Content** folder and select **Blueprint Class** from the context menu as shown below:

Then the following **Pick Parent Class** window will appear, and after entering "**My**" in the **search** bar, select the **MyActor** class that appears under the **Actor**, as shown below, then the **Select** button will show up as well.

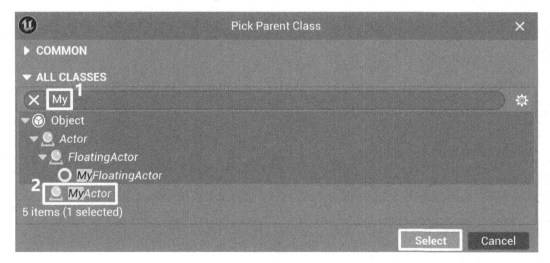

Continue to press the **Select** button, then rename the generated Blueprint to **BP_CustomActor** as shown below:

Calling Functions across the C++ and Blueprint Boundary

So far, we have shown how to expose properties to Blueprints, but there is one last introductory topic that we should cover before you dive deeper into the engine. While creating gameplay systems, designers will need to be able to call functions created by a C++ programmer. So, after the Blueprint is generated, let's create a Blueprint callable function in C++ as follows.

Back to Visual Studio and open the **MyActor.h** header file, add the following **bold** lines in the **public** section:

```
UCLASS()
class QUICKSTART_API AMyActor : public AActor
{
  GENERATED_BODY()

public:
  // Sets default values for this actor's properties
  AMyActor();

  UPROPERTY(EditAnywhere, BlueprintReadWrite, Category = "Damage")
  int32 TotalDamage;
  UPROPERTY(EditAnywhere, BlueprintReadWrite, Category = "Damage")
  float DamageTimeInSeconds;
  UPROPERTY(BlueprintReadOnly, VisibleAnywhere, Transient,
                                          Category = "Damage")
  float DamagePerSecond;

  UFUNCTION(BlueprintCallable, Category = "Damage")
  void CalculateValues();

    ...

};
```

Here we declare a **CalculateValues()** function which is **callable** from Blueprints. Exposing a function to Blueprints is just as simple as exposing a property. It takes only one macro placed **before** the function declaration! The added code snippet above shows what is needed for this.

The **UFUNCTION()** macro handles exposing the C++ function to the reflection system. The **BlueprintCallable** option exposes it to the Blueprint virtual machine. Every Blueprint exposed function **requires a category** associated with it so that the right-click context menu works properly.

Continue to open the **MyActor.cpp** file and **add** the following lines to implement the new function as follows:

```
void AMyActor::CalculateValues()
{
  DamagePerSecond = TotalDamage / DamageTimeInSeconds;
}
```

After saving all the C++ code in Visual Studio, back to **Unreal Editor** and press **Ctrl + Alt + F11** to compile the project. Then open the **BP_CustomActor** Blueprint as shown below:

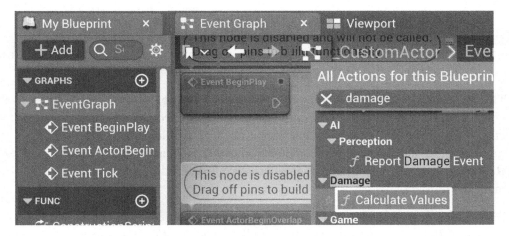

Double-click the **Event Graph** in the **My Blueprint** panel to open the graph editor, then **right**-click in the editor, the context menu will appear as shown above.

Enter "**damage**" in the search bar and you'll see the Blueprint callable function CalculateValues() shows up under the **Damage** category. After clicking the **Calculate Values** function, a new node will be generated in the Event Graph as shown below:

Now drag off from the **Exec** pin of the **Event BeginPlay** Node and plug into the **Exec** pin of the **Calculate Values** Node as shown above. The Blueprint code shows a call to calculate the dependent data after the `BeginPlay` event.

4.2.2 Hot Reloading and Live Coding

Live Coding is a system that can rebuild your application's C++ code and patch its binaries while the engine is running. This functionality is available during the following scenarios:

- ❖ Editing your application in Unreal Editor.
- ❖ Running your application with Play In Editor (PIE).
- ❖ Running a packaged Desktop build of your application attached to the editor for debugging.

This means that without interrupting playtesting sessions or working in the editor itself, you can make changes to C++ classes, compile, and immediately see those changes take effect. This provides significant benefits for iterative development when using C++ runtime logic, such as gameplay code or frontend user interactions. Although the **Hot Reload** system is still available as an alternative, Live Coding is significantly faster and more flexible.

Live Coding is enabled by default for all new Unreal Engine installations. When you open your IDE the Live Coding Console will start automatically but remain hidden. If the console is hidden, it will open when you initiate a Live Coding build. The Live Coding console provides an output log for compilation status. This is separate from the standard **Output Log** and only shows Live Coding build information.

To start a build, press **CTRL+ALT+F11** on your keyboard while using either your IDE or Unreal Engine. A notification will appear in the lower-right corner of the screen to show the status of your build. You can continue working in the editor or testing your project uninterrupted while the build runs.

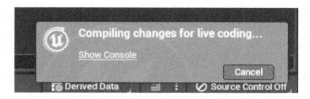

If your build succeeds, you will immediately see changes according to your code.

Live Coding is available when Unreal Editor is open, when using PIE, and when attached to a packaged build in your native desktop environment. It is not available when launching on consoles and mobile devices.

You can find the settings for Live Coding in **Editor Preferences** > **General** > **Live Coding** as shown below:

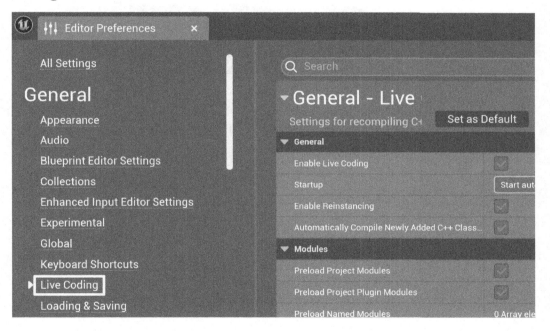

When enabled, Live Coding is Unreal Editor's compilation method. If disabled, Unreal Editor falls back to using **Hot Reload** instead. For example, if you **untick** the **Enable Live Coding** checkbox and go back to Visual Studio. Right-click on the game project and select **Build** from the context menu. The following messages will appear in the **Output** window:

```
Output                                                      ▾  ₊  ×
Show output from:  Build                         ▾  ⌐  ⎺  ⎺  ⌐  ╪  ╥
1>Building 6 actions with 4 processes...                       ▲
1>[1/6] Compile MyActor.gen.cpp                                ▬
1>[2/6] Compile QuickStart.init.gen.cpp
1>[3/6] Compile MyActor.cpp
1>[4/6] Link UnrealEditor-QuickStart-0001.lib
1>   Creating library E:\Unreal Projects\QuickStart\Intermediate\Build\Win64\Unre
1>[5/6] Link UnrealEditor-QuickStart-0001.dll
1>   Creating library E:\Unreal Projects\QuickStart\Intermediate\Build\Win64\Unre
1>[6/6] WriteMetadata QuickStartEditor.target
1>Total time in Parallel executor: 1.86 seconds
1>Total execution time: 6.57 seconds
========== Build: 1 succeeded, 0 failed, 0 up-to-date, 0 skipped ==========  ▾
◄                                                           ►
```

After the Build is successful, you'll see a message shows up on the **lower-right** of the
screen as shown below:

This means the DLL file is reloaded and the editor has applied the changes made in the
C++ code. On the other hand, if the Live Coding is not disabled and the project is rebuilt
in Visual Studio, the following **error** message will appear instead:

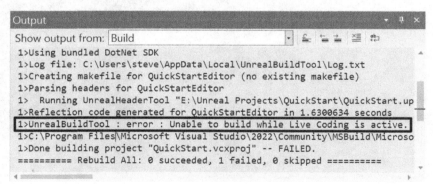

This also means if we need to debug the C++ code in Visual Studio, you have to **close**
the Unreal Editor first and after a while, launch the debugger and the editor.

Note: Although Live Coding is significantly faster and more flexible, the RPG project in this
book is primarily implemented in C++ code, and you may need to trace the code
frequently in Visual Studio. So please keep the Live Coding **disabled** by **unticking** the
Enable Live Coding checkbox in the **Editor Preferences** settings.

4.3 UE5 Class Libraries

This section will introduce the important UE5 built-in classes supporting Gameplay and Math calculations that can help us prototype our games fast. Besides, we are going to dissect the **Third Person Character** Blueprint and explore the essential C++ features that are unique to the UE5.

4.3.1 Gameplay Classes: Objects, Actors, and Components

There are four main class types that you derive from for the majority of gameplay classes. They are **UObject**, **AActor**, **UActorComponent**, and **UStruct**. Each of these building blocks is described in the following sections. Of course, you can create types that do not derive from any of these classes, but they will not participate in the features that are built into the engine. Typical use of classes that are created outside of the **UObject** hierarchy is: integrating third-party libraries, wrapping OS-specific features, and so on.

Unreal Objects (UObject)

The base building block in the Engine is called **UObject**. This class, coupled with **UClass**, provides a number of the Engine's most important services:

- ❖ Reflection of properties and methods.
- ❖ Serialization of properties.
- ❖ Garbage collection.
- ❖ Finding an UObject by name.
- ❖ Configurable values for properties.
- ❖ Networking support for properties and methods.

Each class that derives from **UObject** has a **singleton** **UClass** created for it containing all of the class instance metadata. **UObject** and **UClass** together are at the root of everything that a gameplay object does during its lifetime. The best way to think of the difference between a **UClass** and a **UObject** is that the **UClass** describes what an instance of a **UObject** will look like, what properties are available for serialization, networking, and so on. Most gameplay development does not involve directly deriving from **UObject**, but instead from **AActor** and **UActorComponent**. You do not need to know the details of how **UClass** or **UObject** works to write gameplay code, but it is good to know that these systems exist.

AActor

An **AActor** is a **UObject** that is meant to be part of the gameplay experience. Actors are either placed on a level by a designer or created at runtime via gameplay systems. All objects that can be placed into a level extend from this class. Examples include **AStaticMeshActor**, **ACameraActor**, and **APointLight**. Since **AActor** derives from **UObject**, it enjoys all of the standard features listed in the previous section. Actors can be explicitly destroyed through gameplay code (C++ or Blueprints) or by the standard garbage collection mechanism when the owning level is unloaded from memory. Actors are responsible for the high-level behaviors of your game's objects. **AActor** is also the base type that can be replicated during networking. During network replication, Actors can also distribute information for any **UActorComponents** that they own and that require network support or synchronization.

Actors have their behaviors (specialization through inheritance), but they also act as containers for a hierarchy of Actor Components (specialization through **composition**). This is done through the **RootComponent** member of the Actor, which contains a single **USceneComponent** that, in turn, can contain many others. Before an Actor can be placed in a level, it must contain at least one **Scene** Component, from which the Actor will draw its translation, rotation, and scale.

Actors have a series of **events** that are called during their lifecycles. The list below is a simplified set of the events that illustrate the lifecycle:

- ❖ **BeginPlay**: Called when the Actor first comes into existence during gameplay.
- ❖ **Tick**: Called once per frame to do work overtime.
- ❖ **EndPlay**: Called when the object is leaving the gameplay space.

Runtime Lifecycle

Just above, we discussed a subset of an Actor's lifecycle. For Actors that are placed in a level, understanding the lifecycle is pretty easy to imagine: Actors are loaded and come into existence, and eventually, the level is unloaded, and the Actors are destroyed. Spawning an actor is a bit more complicated than creating a normal object in the game because Actors need to be registered with a variety of runtime systems to serve all of their needs. The initial location and rotation for an Actor need to be set. Physics may need to know about it. The manager responsible for telling an Actor to tick needs to know. And so on. Because of this, we have a method devoted to the spawning of an Actor, **SpawnActor()** (a member of **UWorld**). When the Actor spawns successfully, the Engine will call its **BeginPlay()** method, followed by **Tick()** on the next frame.

Once an Actor has lived out his lifetime, you can get rid of it by calling `Destroy()`. During that process, `EndPlay()` will run, enabling you to perform custom logic before the Actor goes to garbage collection. Another option for controlling how long an Actor exists is to use the `Lifespan` member. You can set the amount of time in the Actor's constructor or with other code at runtime. Once that amount of time has expired, the `Destroy()` method of the Actor will automatically be called to destroy it.

UActorComponent

Actor Components (class **UActorComponent**) have their behaviors and are usually responsible for the functionality that is shared across many types of Actors, such as providing visual meshes, particle effects, camera perspectives, and physics interactions. While Actors are often given high-level goals related to their overall roles in your game, Actor Components usually perform the individual tasks that support those higher-level objectives. Components can also be **attached** to other components or can be the **root** Component of an Actor. A Component can only attach to **one** parent Component or Actor, but it may have many child Components attached to itself. Picture a tree of Components. Child Components have location, rotation, and scaling relative to their parent Component or Actor.

While there are many ways to use Actors and Components, one way to think of the Actor-Component relationship is that Actors might answer the question, "What is this thing?" while Components might answer, "What is this thing **made of**?"

- ❖ **RootComponent**: This is the member of **AActor** that holds the **top**-level Component in the Actor's tree of Components.
- ❖ **Ticking**: Components are ticked as part of the owning Actor's `Tick()` function (**Be sure** to call **Super::Tick()** when writing your `Tick()` function).

Dissecting the Third Person Character

To illustrate the relationship between an **AActor** and its **UActorComponents**, let us dig into the Blueprint that is created when you generate a new project based on the **Third Person Template**.

The figure below is the Component tree for the **BP_ThirdPersonCharacter** Actor. The **RootComponent** is the **CapsuleComponent**. Attached to the **CapsuleComponent** are the **ArrowComponent**, **Mesh**, and **CameraBoom**. The leaf Component is "**FollowCamera**", which is parented to the CameraBoom, meaning that the FollowCamera is **relative** to the Camera Boom.

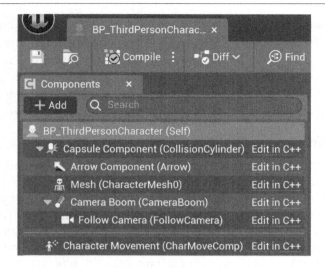

Visually, this tree of Components looks like the figure below, where you see all of the Components in 3D space.

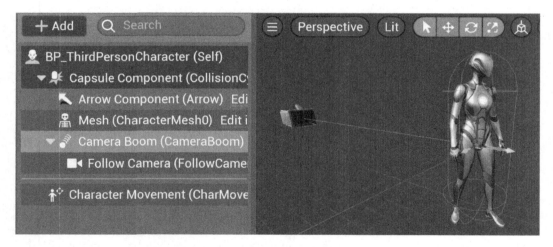

This tree of Components is attached to the one Actor class. As you can see from this example, you can build complex gameplay objects using **both inheritance** and **composition**.

Use **inheritance** when you want to **customize** an existing `AActor` or `UActorComponent`. Use **composition** when you want **many** different `AActor` types to **share** the functionality. In the next chapter, we are going to explore the functionality of the above components in C++ code.

UStruct

To use a UStruct, you do not have to extend from any particular class, you just have to mark the struct with the **USTRUCT()** macro and the build tools will do the base work for you. Unlike a UObject, UStruct instances are **not garbage collected**. If you create dynamic instances of them, you **must** manage their lifecycle yourself. A UStruct should be a plain data type with UObject reflection support for editing within the Unreal Editor, Blueprint manipulation, serialization, networking, etc.

Class Naming Prefixes

Unreal Engine provides tools that generate code for you during the build process. These tools have some class-naming expectations and will trigger warnings or errors if the names do not match the expectations. The list of class prefixes below delineates what the tools are expecting.

- ❖ Classes derived from **Actor** prefixed with **A**, such as AController.
- ❖ Classes derived from **Object** are prefixed with **U**, such as UComponent.
- ❖ **Enums** are prefixed with **E**, such as EFortificationType.
- ❖ **Interface** classes are usually prefixed with **I**, such as IAbilitySystemInterface.
- ❖ **Template** classes are prefixed by **T**, such as TArray.
- ❖ Classes that derive from **SWidget** (Slate UI) are prefixed by **S**, such as SButton.
- ❖ Everything else is prefixed by the letter **F**, such as FVector.

Now that we have talked about the basic hierarchy used in our gameplay class construction, in the next section, we will continue to discuss the two important **Math**-related classes.

4.3.2 Math Class Libraries in UE5

Every game engine has Math-related classes and UE5 is no exception. In this section, we will discuss the three most useful math classes in UE5, namely the **FVector**, **FVector2D**, and **FRotator** classes.

Before we start, let's review some math about the **Vector**. A vector is a set of numbers and can be represented in terms of an arrow as illustrated in the following figure:

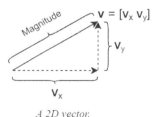

A 2D vector.

The arrow is used to represent the direction of the vector. The **magnitude** (length) of a vector, **v**, denoted as |**v**|, is determined by the **Pythagorean** theorem as follows:

$$|\mathbf{v}| = \sqrt{v_x^2 + v_y^2}$$

Here the V_x is the **horizontal** displacement and V_y is the **vertical** displacement of the vector, respectively.

A **unit** vector is a vector whose **magnitude** is **one**, for example, [1 0] and [0 1] are two 2D unit vectors. and [1 0 0] is a 3D unit vector representing the **X**-axis in the 3D coordinate system.

The **dot product** of two 2D vectors **v** and **u** can be calculated using the following formula, and its result is a **scalar**:

$$\mathbf{v} \cdot \mathbf{u} = \mathbf{v}_x \times \mathbf{u}_x + \mathbf{v}_y \times \mathbf{u}_y$$

For example, given two vectors, **v** = [1 -2] and **u** = [-1 2], the dot product will be 1 × -1 + -2 × 2 = -5, which is a scalar.

The dot product is useful for determining the angle between two vectors as shown below:

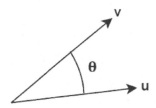

Because the dot product of two vectors **v** and **u** is also equal to the product of their magnitudes and the cosine of the angle between them as shown in the following formula:

$$\mathbf{v} \cdot \mathbf{u} = |\mathbf{v}||\mathbf{u}| \cos \theta$$

To find the angle in between any two vectors, we rewrite the formula and isolate the angle to the left side as follows:

$$\theta = \cos^{-1} \frac{\mathbf{v} \cdot \mathbf{u}}{|\mathbf{v}||\mathbf{u}|}$$

For example, the angle formed by two vectors [1 0] and [0 1] can be calculated as follows:

$$\theta = \cos^{-1}\frac{[1\ 0]\cdot[0\ 1]}{|[1\ 0]||[0\ 1]|}$$
$$= \cos^{-1}\frac{0}{1\times 1}$$
$$= \cos^{-1}0$$
$$= 90^{\circ}$$

In UE5, the three most used **unit direction** vectors, namely the **forward (X)**, **right (Y)**, and **up (Z)** vectors, are used to describe the orientation of a scene object as shown below in terms of **red**, **green**, and **blue** axes, respectively.

The FVector Template

The FVector represents a 3D vector or points with floating-point precision. This template is used throughout UE5 to pass 3D positions and directions around. It also contains functions for doing common vector operations. The most commonly used constructors, variables, and functions are outlined as follows.

FVector Constructors

- ❖ FVector(float InX, float InY, float InZ)
- ❖ FVector()

The above common constructors create a new vector with given X, Y, and Z components, or no initialization (default constructor).

FVector Variables

- ❖ X
- ❖ Y
- ❖ Z

The X, Y, and Z variables represent the X, Y, and Z components of the vector, respectively.

FVector Functions

- ❖ `CrossProduct()`
- ❖ `Dist()`
- ❖ `DistSquared()`
- ❖ `DotProduct()`
- ❖ `IsNormalized()`
- ❖ `Normalize()`
- ❖ `PointsAreNear()`
- ❖ `Rotation()`
- ❖ `Size()`
- ❖ `VectorPlaneProject()`

The `CrossProduct()` function returns the **cross product** of two vectors. The `Dist()` returns the **Euclidean** distance between two **points**. The `DistSquared()` returns the **squared** distance between two points. The `DotProduct()` returns the **dot product** of two vectors. The `IsNormalized()` function checks whether the vector is normalized and the `Normalize()` function normalizes this vector in place if it is larger than a given tolerance or leaves it unchanged if not.

The `PointsAreNear()` function compares **two points** and sees if they're within a specified distance. The `Rotation()` returns the **FRotator** orientation corresponding to the direction in which the vector points. The `Size()` gets the length (magnitude) of this vector and the `VectorPlaneProject()` function calculates the projection of a vector on the plane defined by the plane's **Normal** vector.

The FVector2D Template

The `FVector2D` represents a vector in 2D space composed of components (X, Y) with floating-point precision. It has constructors, variables, and functions which are similar to the `FVector` template, but only involve two components.

The FRotator Template

The `FRotator` implements a container for **rotation** information. All rotation values are stored in **degrees**. The variables, most commonly used constructors, and functions of the `FRotator` are outlined as follows.

FRotator Variables

- ❖ `Pitch`
- ❖ `Roll`
- ❖ `Yaw`

The `Pitch` variable stores the rotation around the **right** axis (around the **Y**-axis), looking **up** and **down** (**0** = **Straight Ahead**, +Up, -Down). The `Roll` variable stores the rotation around the **forward** axis (around the **X-axis**), **tilting** your head (0 = Straight, +**Clockwise**, -**CCW**). The Yaw variable stores the rotation around the **up** axis (around the **Z-axis**), **running in circles** (0 = East, +North, -South).

FRotator Constructors

❖ `FVector(float InPitch, float InYaw, float InRoll)`
❖ `FVector()`

The above common constructors create a new FRotator with given **Pitch**, **Yaw**, and **Roll** components, or no initialization (default constructor).

FVector Functions

❖ `Add()`
❖ `Clamp()`
❖ `MakeFromEuler()`
❖ `Quaternion()`
❖ `RotateVector()`

The Add() function adds to each component of the rotator. The Clamp() gets the rotation values, so they fall within the range [**0,360**]. The MakeFromEuler() function converts a **vector** of floating-point **Euler** angles (in **degrees**) into a FRotator. The Quaternion() gets rotation as a **quaternion**. The RotateVector() function rotates a vector rotated by this rotator.

4.3.3 UE5 Numeric Types, Strings, and Containers

This subsection will discuss the common **Numeric Types**, **Strings**, and **Containers** in UE5.

Numeric Types

Since different platforms have different sizes for basic types such as **short**, **int**, and **long**, UE5 provides the following types which you should use as an alternative:

❖ **int8/uint8**: **8**-bit signed/unsigned integer.
❖ **int16/uint16**: **16**-bit signed/unsigned integer.
❖ **int32/uint32**: **32**-bit signed/unsigned integer.
❖ **int64/uint64**: **64**-bit signed/unsigned integer.

Floating-point numbers are also supported with the standard **float** (**32**-bit) and **double** (**64**-bit) types.

Strings

UE5 provides several different classes for working with strings, depending on your needs.

FString

FString is a **mutable** string, analogous to std::string. FString has a large suite of methods for making it easy to work with strings. To create a new FString, use the TEXT() macro:

```
FString MyStr = TEXT("Hello, Unreal 5!").
```

FText

FText is similar to FString, but it is meant for **localized** text. To create a new FText, use the NSLOCTEXT() macro. This macro takes a **namespace**, **key**, and a **value** for the default language:

```
FText MyText = NSLOCTEXT("Game UI", "Health Warning Message",
                                                "Low Health!")
```

You could also use the LOCTEXT() macro, so you only have to define a namespace once per file. Make sure to **undefine** it at the bottom of your file.

```
// In GameUI.cpp
#define LOCTEXT_NAMESPACE "Game UI"
//...
FText MyText = LOCTEXT("Health Warning Message", "Low Health!")
//...
#undef LOCTEXT_NAMESPACE
// End of file
```

FName

An FName stores a commonly recurring string as an identifier to save memory and CPU time when comparing them. Rather than storing the complete string many times across every object that references it, FName uses a smaller storage footprint index that maps to a given string. This stores the contents of the string once, saving memory when that string is used across many objects. FName comparison is fast because UE5 can simply check their index values to see if they match, without having to do a character-by-character comparison.

TCHAR

The TCHAR type is used as a way of storing characters independent of the character set being used, which may differ between platforms. Under the hood, UE5 strings use TCHAR **arrays** to store data in the **UTF-16** encoding. You can access the raw data by using the overloaded dereference operator, which returns TCHAR.

This is needed for some functions, such as FString::Printf(), where the "**%s**" string format specifier expects a TCHAR instead of an FString.

```
FString Str1 = TEXT("World");
int32 Val1 = 123;
FString Str2 = FString::Printf(TEXT("Hello, %s! You have %i points."),
                                                      *Str1, Val1);
```

The FChar type provides a set of **static** utility functions for working with individual **TCHAR** characters and the following is an example:

```
TCHAR Upper('A');
TCHAR Lower = FChar::ToLower(Upper); // 'a'
```

The FChar type is defined as TChar<TCHAR> as it is listed in the API.

Containers

Containers are classes whose primary function is to store collections of data. The most common of these classes are TArray, TMap, and TSet. Each of these is **dynamically sized**, and so will grow to whatever size you need.

The TArray Class

Of these three containers, the primary container you'll use in Unreal Engine 5 is TArray, it functions much like std::vector does, but offers a lot more functionality. Here are some common operations:

```
TArray<AActor*> ActorArray = GetActorArrayFromSomewhere();
// Tell how many elements (AActors) are currently stored in ActorArray.
int32 ArraySize = ActorArray.Num();
// TArrays are 0-based (the first element will be at index 0)
int32 Index = 0;
// Attempt to retrieve an element at the given index
AActor* FirstActor = ActorArray[Index];
// Add a new element to the end of the array
AActor* NewActor = GetNewActor();
ActorArray.Add(NewActor);
// Add an element to the end of the array only if it is not already in
// the array
ActorArray.AddUnique(NewActor); // Won't change the array because
                                // NewActor was already added
// Remove all instances of 'NewActor' from the array
ActorArray.Remove(NewActor);
// Remove the element at the specified index
// Elements above the index will be shifted down by one to fill the
// empty space
```

```
ActorArray.RemoveAt(Index);
// More efficient version of 'RemoveAt', but does not maintain the order
// of the elements
ActorArray.RemoveAtSwap(Index);
// Remove all elements in the array
ActorArray.Empty();
```

TArray has the added benefit of having its elements **garbage collected**. This assumes that the TArray stores UObject-derived pointers. We'll cover the garbage collection in-depth in a later section.

The TMap Class

After TArray, the most commonly used container in UE5 is TMap. This container stores data as **key-value** pairs (TPair<KeyType, ValueType>), using keys only for storage and retrieval, which is similar to std::map. TMap has quick methods for finding, adding, and removing elements based on their keys. You can use any type for the key, as long as it has a GetTypeHash() function defined for it.

There are two types of maps: TMap and TMultiMap. The difference between these two is that TMap keys are **unique**, while TMultiMap supports storing **multiple**, **identical keys**. When adding a new key-value pair to a TMap with a key that matches an existing pair, the new pair will **replace** the old one. In a TMultiMap, the container will store **both** the new pair and the old.

Please refer to the following code for some common operations:

```
// Create an empty TMap of strings that are identified by integer keys
TMap<int32, FString> FruitMap;
// The standard way to populate a map is to call the Add() function with
// a key and a value
FruitMap.Add(5, TEXT("Banana"));
FruitMap.Add(2, TEXT("Grapefruit"));
// FruitMap == [
//   { Key: 5, Value: "Banana"     },
//   { Key: 2, Value: "Grapefruit" },
// ]
// The Add() function can accept a key without a value. When this
// overloaded Add() is called, the value will be default-constructed
FruitMap.Add(4);
// Like TArray, we can also use Emplace() instead of Add() to avoid the
// creation of temporaries when inserting into the map
FruitMap.Emplace(3, TEXT("Orange"));
// Call the Num() function to find out how many elements are currently
// in the map
int32 Count = FruitMap.Num();
// To determine whether or not a map contains a specific key,
// call the Contains() function
bool bHas2 = FruitMap.Contains(2); // bHas2 == true
```

```
// Using the operator []
FString Val2 = FruitMap[2];  // Val2 == "Grapefruit"
// The Find() function returns a pointer to the value of the element if
// the map contains the key, or a null pointer if it does not
FString* Ptr2 = FruitMap.Find(2); // *Ptr2 == "Grapefruit"
FString* Ptr8 = FruitMap.Find(8); //  Ptr8 == nullptr
// Elements can be removed from maps by using the Remove() function and
// providing the key of the element to remove
FruitMap.Remove(2);
```

If you mark the TMap with the UPROPERTY() macro and one of the "editable" keywords (EditAnywhere, EditDefaultsOnly, or EditInstanceOnly), you can add and edit elements in the Editor.

```
UPROPERTY(Category = Maps, EditAnywhere)
TMap<int32, FString> FruitMap;
```

4.4 Memory Management and Garbage Collection

In the last section, we will go over basic memory management and the **garbage collection** system in UE5.

4.4.1 UObjects and Garbage Collection

UE5 uses the reflection system to implement a garbage collection system. With garbage collection, you will not have to manually manage to delete UObject instances, you just need to maintain valid references to them. Your classes need to derive from UObject to be enabled for garbage collection. Here is the simple example class we will be using:

```
UCLASS()
class MyGCType : public UObject
{
    GENERATED_BODY()
};
```

In the garbage collector, there is a concept called the **root set**. The root set is a list of objects that the collector knows will **never** be garbage collected. An object will not be garbage collected as long as there is a path of references from an object in the root set to the object in question. If no such path to the root set exists for an object, it is called **unreachable** and will be **collected** (**deleted**) the next time the garbage collector runs. The engine runs the garbage collector at certain intervals.

Any `UObject` pointer stored in a `UPROPERTY` or a UE5 **container** class (such as `TArray`) is considered a "**reference**" for garbage collection. Let us start with a simple example.

```
void CreateDoomedObject()
{
  MyGCType* DoomedObject = NewObject<MyGCType>();
}
```

The above function creates a new `UObject` but does not store a pointer to it in any `UPROPERTY` or UE5 container, and it **isn't** a part of the root set. Eventually, the garbage collector will detect that this object is unreachable and destroy it.

4.4.2 Actors and Garbage Collection

Actors are not usually garbage collected, aside from during a Level's shutdown. Once spawned, you must **manually** call `Destroy()` on them to remove them from the Level without ending the Level. They will be removed from the game immediately, and then fully deleted during the **next** garbage collection phase.

This is a more common case, where you have Actors with `UObject` properties.

```
UCLASS()
class AMyActor : public AActor
{
    GENERATED_BODY()

public:
    UPROPERTY()
    MyGCType* SafeObject;

    MyGCType* DoomedObject;

    AMyActor()
    {
      SafeObject = NewObject<MyGCType>();
      DoomedObject = NewObject<MyGCType>();
    }
};

void SpawnMyActor(UWorld* World, FVector Location, FRotator Rotation)
{
    World->SpawnActor<AMyActor>(Location, Rotation);
}
```

When calling the above function, we spawn an Actor into the world. The Actor's constructor creates two objects. One get assigned to a `UPROPERTY`, the other to a bare pointer. Since Actors are automatically a part of the root set, `SafeObject` will not be garbage collected because it can be reached from a root set object. `DoomedObject`, however, will not fare so well. We didn't mark it with `UPROPERTY`, so the collector **does not** know it is being referenced, and will eventually **destroy** it, leaving a **dangling pointer**!

When an `UObject` is garbage collected, all `UPROPERTY` references to it will be set to **null** for you. This makes it safe for you to check if an object has been garbage collected or not as follows:

```
if (MyActor->SafeObject != nullptr)
{
    // Use SafeObject
}
```

This is important since, as mentioned before, actors that have had `Destroy()` called on them are not removed until the garbage collector runs again. You can check the `IsPendingKill()` method to see if a `UObject` is awaiting its deletion. If that method returns `true`, you should consider the object dead and not use it.

4.4.3 UStructs and Non-UObject References

`UStructs`, as mentioned earlier, are meant to be a **lightweight** version of a `UObject`. As such, `UStructs` **cannot** be garbage collected. If you must use **dynamic** instances of `UStructs`, you may want to use **smart pointers** instead.

Normal C++ objects (**not** derived from `UObject`) can also have the ability to add a reference to an object and prevent garbage collection. To do that, your object must derive from **FGCObject** and **override** its **AddReferencedObjects()** method. Here is an example:

```
class FMyNormalClass : public FGCObject
{
public:
    UObject* SafeObject;

    FMyNormalClass(UObject* Object) : SafeObject(Object)
    {
    }

    void AddReferencedObjects(FReferenceCollector& Collector) override
    {
        Collector.AddReferencedObject(SafeObject);
    }
};
```

We use the `FReferenceCollector` to **manually** add a **hard reference** to the `UObject` we need and do not want garbage collected. When the object is deleted and its **destructor** is run, the object will automatically clear all references that it added.

4.5 Summary

In this chapter, we started the introduction to the UE5 game programming by creating a Quick Start tutorial at the beginning. After the Quick Start, we had dived into the engine further by exposing the C++ variables and functions of the Unreal Class to the Unreal Editor for viewing and editing. We also demonstrated how to call functions across the C++ and Blueprint boundary followed by exploring the UE5 Class Libraries which include Gameplay and Math-related classes. Lastly, basic memory management and the garbage collection system in UE5 were introduced. In the next chapter, we'll start the first topic in RPG design which is the **Combat** system.

Exercises

4.1 Create a new C++ Actor class named **SphereActor** in the **Actors** folder generated in this chapter. Then add a **static mesh component** property called `SphereMesh` to the class in the generated **header** and **expose** the property to the Blueprint using the **UPROPERTY** macro. Continue to open the generated **SphereActor.cpp** file, and in the **constructor**, enter the C++ code to **create** the static mesh component and **attach** it to the **RootComponent** as we have done for the **FloatingActor** class in the Quick Start section. Finally, build the project in Visual Studio and make sure no errors occur.

4.2 Continued from the previous exercise, back to Unreal Editor and locate the **SphereActor** class under the **C++ Classes** folder hierarchy in the **Content Browser**. Then create a Blueprint called **BP_SphereActor** from the C++ class in the **Content > Actors** folder. Next, after opening the Blueprint, with the **Sphere Mesh** selected in the **Components** panel, and then find the **Static Mesh** field in the **Details** panel. Lastly, from the drop-down menu, select the **Shape_Sphere** for the static mesh component.

4.3 Consult the online Unreal Engine Document and explore the UE5 built-in functions, templates, or classes used in the **FloatingActor** C++ class presented in this chapter.

Combat for Action RPGs

The **role-playing video game** (RPG) is a popular game genre that every beginner in game development has to be familiar with. In this chapter, we'll start with the first subject for developing an action RPG, which is the **Combat** system.

Besides, other essential topics, including creating player characters, animations, camera controls, and melee weapon collision detection, will be discussed as well. The rest of the other topics, such as dialogues, quests, and character customization, will be covered in detail in the next volume of this book.

5.1 Creating Art Assets for RPGs

Before starting our RPG project, in this section, we are going to create the UE5 project, and the art assets required for the following chapters.

5.1.1 Creating the C++ RPG Project

Start UE5 and in the **Unreal Project Browser**, after selecting the **GAMES** and pressing the **C++** button, rename the **Project Name** to **RPG** as shown below:

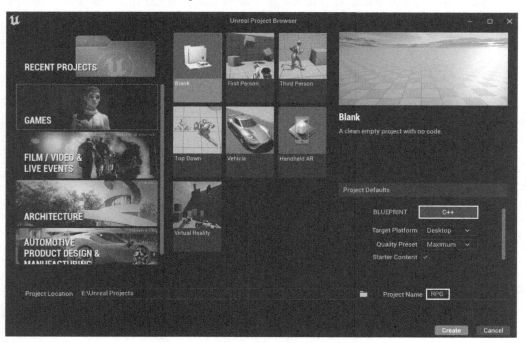

Next, press the **Create** button to create the project in the specified path.

5.1.2 Creating an Open World Level

One of the new features in UE5 is called **World Partition**, which is a new data management and **distance**-based **level streaming** system that provides a complete solution for large world management.

This section will discuss how to use this new feature to build an **open world** level for our action RPG. First, create a new folder called **Levels** in the project's **Content** folder and, from the main menu, choose **File** > **New Level...** to open the **New Level** window as shown below:

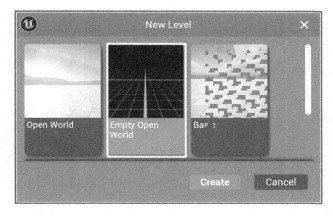

After selecting the **Empty Open World** in the list, press **Create** to create an **empty** level.

Creating Light and Sky

Then choose **Window** > **Place Actors** from the main menu to open the **Place Actors** tab as shown below:

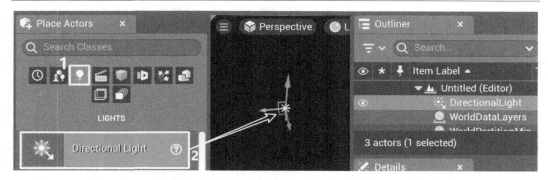

Next, after pressing the **Lights** icon on the tab, drag and drop the **Direction Light** onto the Viewport as shown above to represent the sun.

Continue to click on the **Visual Effects** icon on the tab, then drag and drop the **Sky Atmosphere** onto the Viewport as shown below:

Now you'll see the sky is becoming **blue** instead of black. Next, drag and drop the **Volumetric Cloud** onto the Viewport as shown below:

Then you'll see the clouds appearing in the sky as shown above. Now that the Light and Sky are created, we'll build the **landscape** in the next step.

Creating Heightmaps from Real-World Data

Although UE5 provides tools to create landscapes, for Indie developers to create photo-realistic landscapes still is a challenge. Fortunately, there is an alternative easy way to generate professional terrains from real-world data.

In this subsection, we are going to use the free **TerreSculptor**[3] terrain creation software to import real-world terrain data from the **USGS Earth Explorer**[4] website and then export the **Heightmaps** into UE5 to generate landscapes.

First, go to the USGS Earth Explorer website as shown below:

Press the **Login** on the upper-right, and after creating an account, sign in with the username and password. Then scroll down and use the mouse wheel to zoom in on the map, move the map to the location you are interested as shown below:

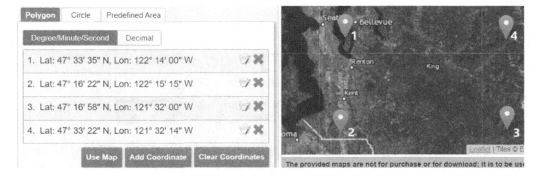

---

[3] **TERRESCULPTOR**, http://www.demenzunmedia.com/home/terresculptor/.
[4] **USGS Earth Explorer**, https://earthexplorer.usgs.gov.

Click on the map **four** times to mark a **rectangular** area as shown above, and their coordinates will be shown in the **Polygon** tab. Continue to press the **Data Sets** tab as shown below:

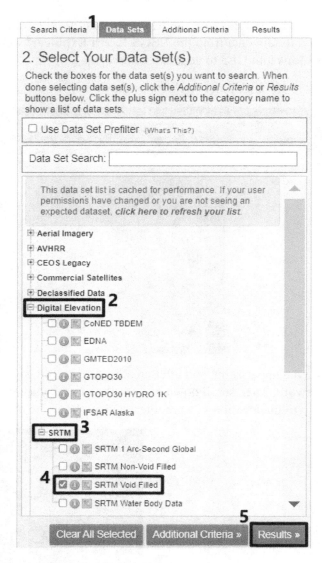

After expanding the **Digital Elevation** and **SRTM** hierarchy, **tick** the **SRTM Void Filled** checkbox as shown above and then click the **Result >>** button to see the search results as shown below:

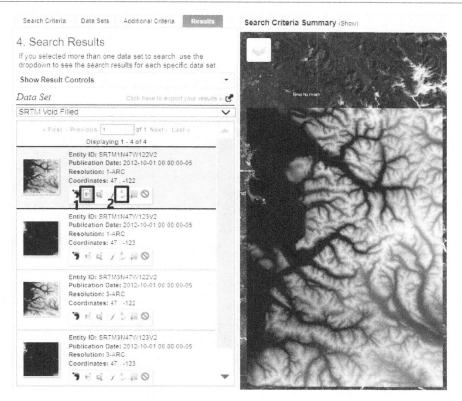

The results will consist of many **blocks** on the map as shown in the **Results** tab, and you can press the **Show Browse Overlay** to preview the block before downloading. Here we choose the **1-ARC** version of the block which means **30 meters** per pixel resolution. Then press the **Download Options** button and the following window will show up.

Lastly, press the **Download** button to the **left** of the **BIL 1 Arc-second** to download the terrain data.

Making Height Map using TerreSculptor

Next, we are going to use **TerreSculptor** to create the height map for the terrain. After starting TerreSculptor, the following window will appear.

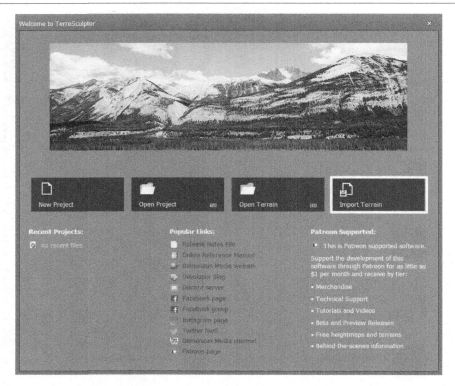

Press the **Import Terrain** button and in the following **Import Terrain** window, choose the **BIL Binary DEM USGS NED** file format from the drop-down menu as shown below:

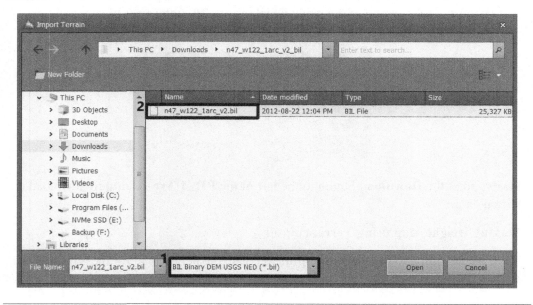

After selecting the downloaded **BIL** file, as shown above, press the **Open** button, and then in the **Import USGS BIL DEM** window, press the **OK** button to import the terrain. You'll see the terrain appears in the viewport as shown below:

Because UE5 can only import specific dimensions of terrains, we have to resample the terrain as follows. Select **Tools** > **Settings…** from the main menu to open the **Settings** window as shown below:

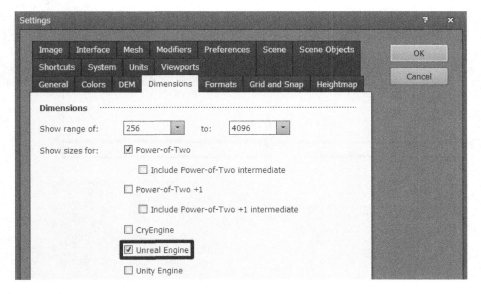

After selecting the **Dimensions** tab, **tick** the **Unreal Engine** checkbox as shown above and then press the **OK** button. Next, select **Modify** > **Resample…** from the main menu to open the **Resample** window as shown below:

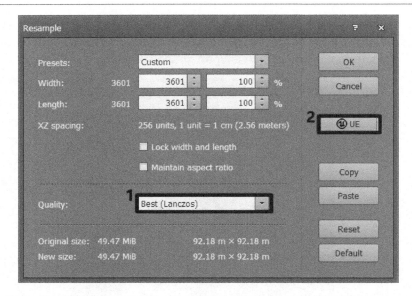

Select the **Best (Lanczos)** for the **Quality** field and then press the **UE** button to open the following **Unreal Engine Landscape Sizes** window:

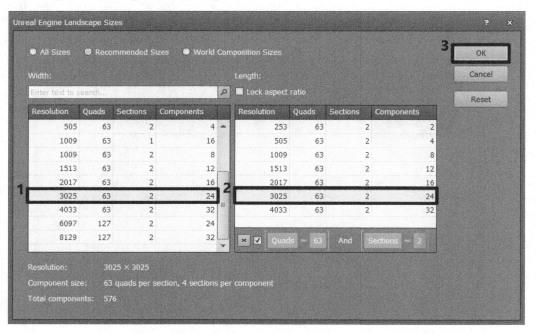

After selecting both the **3025** in the lists for the **Width** and **Length**, as shown above, the **OK** button will be enabled. Then press the OK button to back to the Resample window as shown below:

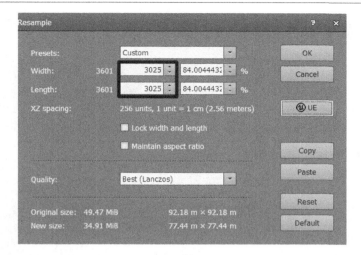

You'll see the number **3025** appears in the **Width** and **Length** fields as shown above and then press the **OK** button to resample the terrain. Please note that depending on the computer speed, you can select a higher resolution of the terrain here.

After resampling the terrain to meet the requirement for the UE5, it's time to export the terrain. Select **File** > **Export Terrain…** from the main menu to open the following **Export Terrain** window:

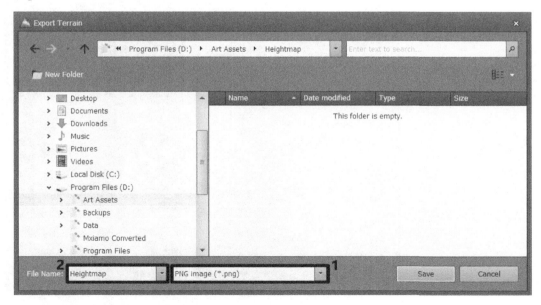

Because the heightmap will be saved in an image file, select the **PNG Image** file format from the drop-down menu as shown above, then change the **File Name** to **Heightmap**

and after pressing the **Save** button, continue to press the **OK** in the following **Export PNG** window to save the file.

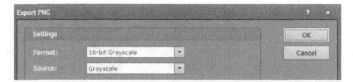

Importing the Height Map File

Now back to Unreal Editor, press the drop-down menu on the toolbar, and switch to **Landscape Mode** as shown on the right:

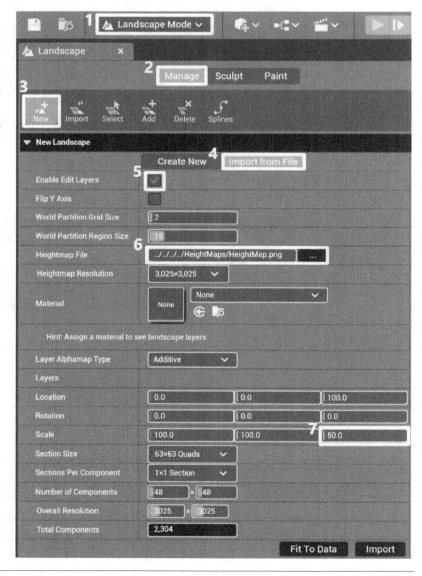

Under the **Manage** tab, select the **New** tab and the **Import from File** tab respectively, then **tick** the **Enable Edit Layers** checkbox, select the **Heightmap.png** file created before for the **Heightmap File** field, and change the **Z** Scale value to **50**, as shown above, to make the terrain **flatter** in the **Z** direction. Lastly, press the **Import** button to import the landscape.

After the landscape is imported, you'll see a message says **No Regions Loaded** as shown below:

Loading and Unloading Landscape Cells

As mentioned before, **World Partition** is the new world streaming system in UE5, regions of the world called **cells** are streamed in and out of view visibility based on their distance from the streaming source usually the player.

In Unreal Editor, UE5 provides a minimap in the **World Partition Editor** for us to load or unload world cells. From the main menu, select **Window** > **World Partition** > **World Partition Editor** to open the panel as shown below:

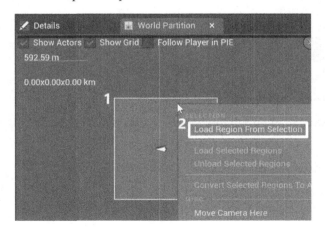

After selecting the regions (cells) using the mouse, as shown above, right-click on the selected cells and choose **Load Region From Selection** from the context menu. The result is shown in the minimap as shown on the right:

So, if for some reason the landscape does not show up correctly in the viewport, you have to check if landscape cells are loaded in the minimap. To unload a certain region, with the region selected, right-click on the region and select **Unload Selected Regions** as shown below:

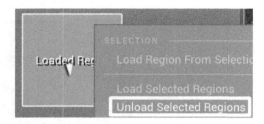

Then after pressing the **Paint** tab as shown below, move the mouse cursor into the Viewport, and we're ready to sculpt and paint the terrain.

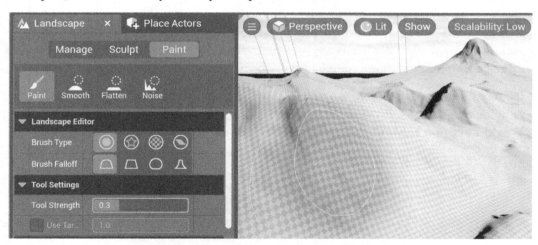

Now press the **Save** icon on the toolbar to save the level in the **Levels** folder and rename it to **MainMap**.

Importing Megascans Textures using Quixel Bridge

Megascans now is integrated into UE5 and through the built-in **Quixel Bridge**, we can access a library of real-world physical objects that have been scanned into Unreal Engine and they're all free.

To open the **Quixel Bridge**, choose **Windows** > **Quixel Bridge** from the main menu to open the window as shown below:

After clicking the **User Account** icon on the **Upper-Right** corner, press **Sign In** from the drop-down menu, and then in the **Login** panel, choose **one** of the accounts to sign into your Epic Account.

After signing in, enter "**uncut grass**" in the **search** bar and press **Enter**, you'll see a list of uncut grass textures under the **Surface** category in the left panel as shown below:

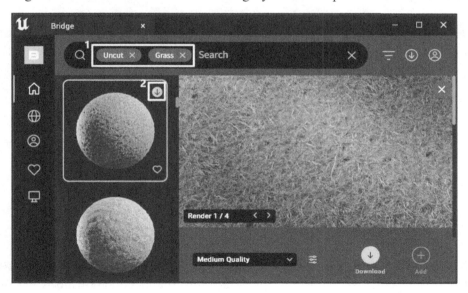

Scroll down the list and find an **UNCUT GRASS** texture like above, then press the **Download** icon to download the textures to the UE5 project.

After the uncut grass asset has been downloaded, click the **Add** icon, as shown below, on the lower right corner to add the asset to your project.

Then the **Content Browser** will show up and you'll see a new folder called **Megascans** appears under the **Content**, as shown below, the UNCUT GRASS textures will be stored in the folder under the **Surfaces** folder.

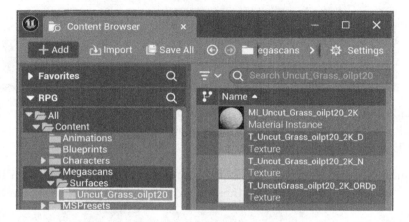

Next, enter "**dried grass**" in the **search** bar and press **Enter**, find the **DRIED GRASS ON SOIL** texture as shown below, press the **Download** icon to download the texture, and then **Add** it to your project.

Continue to enter "**rock cliff surface**" in the **search** bar and press **Enter**, find a **ROCK CLIFF** texture as shown below, then press the **Download** icon to download and **Add** the texture.

Landscape Materials

Now that the terrain textures are ready, let's create the landscape material as follows. First, right-click in the **Content Browser** of the **Levels** folder and select **Material** from the context menu to create a new material. After renaming the Material to **M_LandscapeMaterial**, double-click on it to open the **Material Graph** editor as shown below:

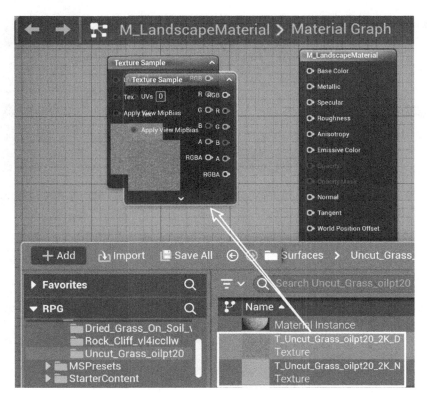

Then drag and drop the **Uncut** Grass **Diffuse** and **Normal** textures into the Graph as shown above. Similarly, drag and drop the **Dried** Grass **Diffuse** and **Normal** textures into the Graph and re-arrange the Nodes as shown below:

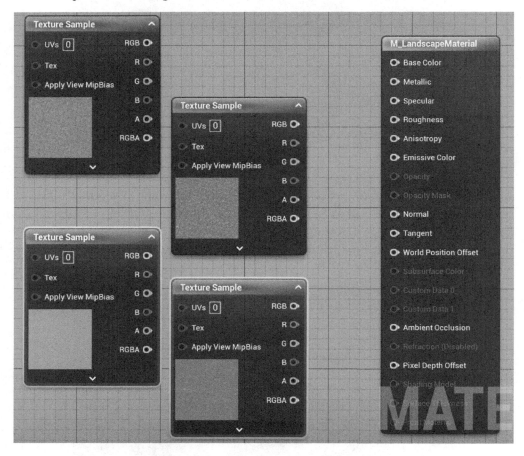

Next, right-click in the Graph and enter "**make**" in the search bar as shown below:

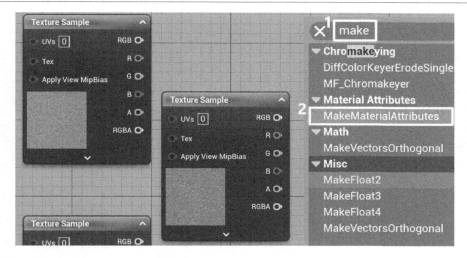

Select the **MakeMaterialAttributes** from the list to create a **MakeMaterialAttributes** Node as follows:

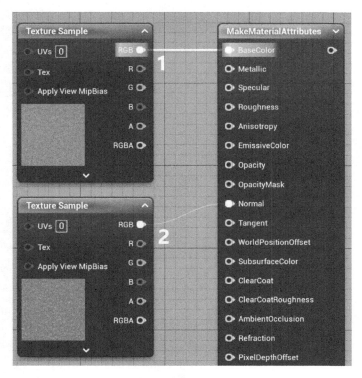

Drag off from the **RGB** pin of the Uncut Grass Texture Sample Node and plug into the **BaseColor** pin of the **MakeMaterialAttributes** Node as shown above. Similarly, plug the **RGB** pin of the **Normal** Texture Sample Node into the **Normal** input.

Next, after creating another **MakeMaterialAttributes** Node in the Graph, repeat the above steps for the **Dried Grass** Texture Sample Nodes as shown on the right:

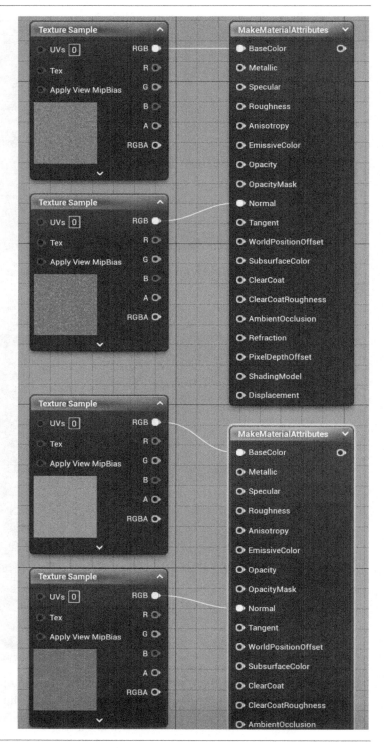

Next, right-click on the Graph and enter "**landscape**" in the search bar as shown below:

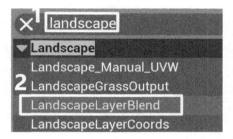

Select the **LandscapeLayoutBlend** from the list to create a **Layer Blend** Node. With the Node selected and in the Details tab, press the + icon, to the right of the **Layers**, **twice** to create **two** Layers as shown below:

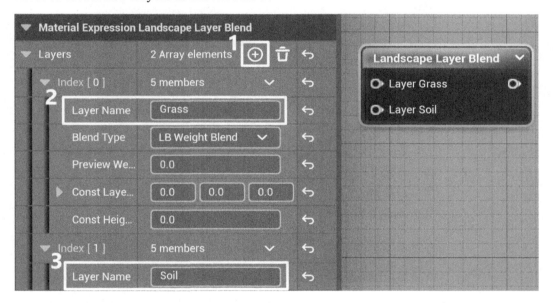

After expanding the two layers, change the **first** layer's name to **Grass** and the **second** layer's name to **Soil** as shown above.

Then plug the **output** pin of the **first MakeMaterialAttributes** Node into the **Layer Grass** pin of the **Layer Blend** Node as shown below. Similarly, plug the output pin of the **second** MakeMaterialAttributes Node into the **Layer Soil** pin of the Layer Blend Node.

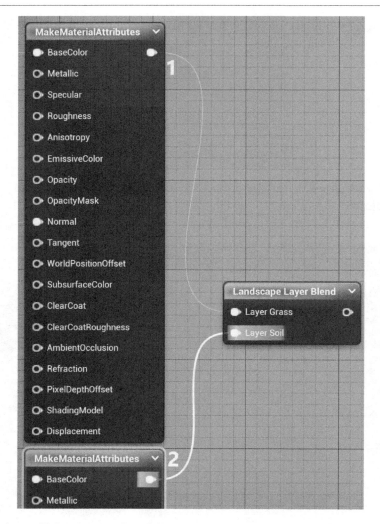

Continue to drag off the output pin of the **Layer Blend** Node, as shown below, and enter "**break**" in the search bar, then select **BreakMaterialAttributes** from the list to create a **BreakMaterialAttributes** Node.

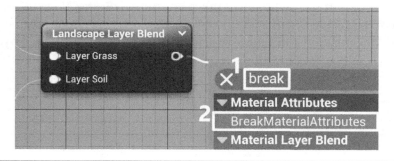

Lastly, plug the **BaseColor** and **Normal** pins of the BreakMaterialAttributes Node into the **Base Color** and **Normal** pins of the LandscapeMaterial Node respectively as shown below:

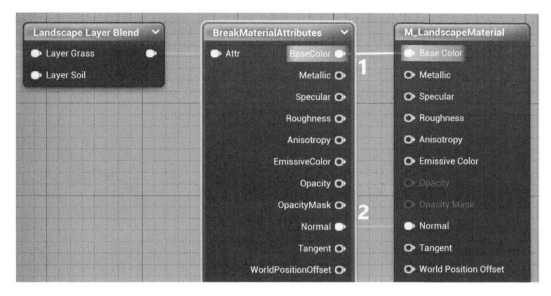

Now press **Apply** and **Save** to confirm all modifications, next we'll assign the material to the landscape. Switch back to the **Select Mode**, with the **Landscape** selected in the **Outliner** panel and after pressing the **All** tab, find the **Landscape Material** field and select the above **M_LandscapeMaterial** for it as shown below:

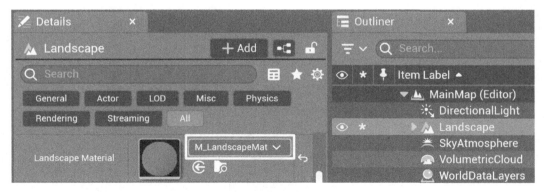

Note: Depending on the landscape size and the speed of your computer, it may take a while to apply the material to your landscape.

Then switch to the **Landscape Mode** again and press the **Paint** tab, as shown below, after expanding the **Layers** settings, you'll see the **Grass** layer and the **Soil** layer, which are created in the landscape material.

Currently, the terrain is all **Black** because no base texture has been assigned so far, and we have to create the **LayerInfo** assets for the two layers. Continue to press the + icon to the **right** of the **Grass** Layer, as shown above, and select the **Weight-Blended Layer (Normal)** to create the **Layer Info** Object. In the next step, Unreal will create a **default** folder for us to store the asset as shown below:

After pressing the **Save** button to save the asset, you'll see a Layer Info Object named **Grass_Layerinfo** appears on the **Grass** Layer as shown below:

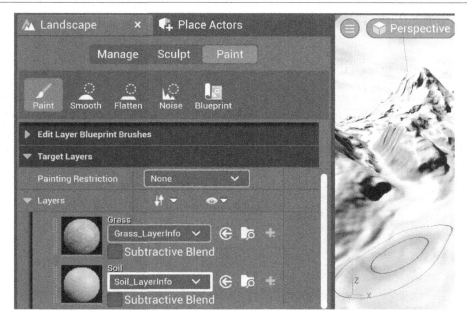

Now the terrain will be painted using the **Uncut Grass** texture as shown in the Viewport. Repeat the same step to create the **Soil_Layerinfo** Object for the **Soil** Layer as shown above. With the **Soil Layer** selected, and after expanding the **Brush Settings**, as shown below, reset the **Brush Size** to a **smaller** value such as **700** here.

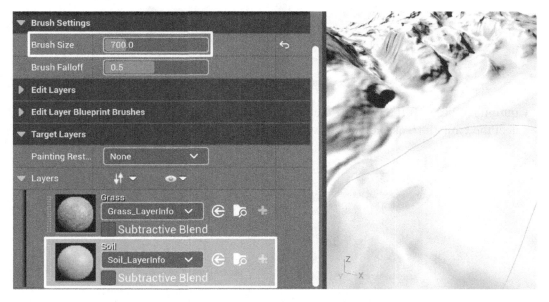

Then move the cursor into the Viewport, and you'll see the new Brush Size as shown above. Now press the **left** mouse button to **paint** the **Soil** Texture on the landscape. With the **Shift** key and **left** mouse button pressed, you can **erase** the Soil Texture from the terrain.

Landscape Textures Tiling

Next, we'll continue to improve our landscape material, and the first task to do is to control the texture tiling using parameters. Open the **M_LandscapeMaterial** Material again and right-click in the Graph, after typing "**landscape**" in the search bar, select the **LandscapeLayerCoords**, as shown below, to create the **LandscapeCoords** Node.

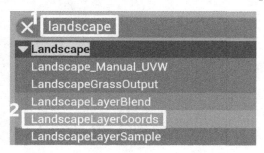

Drag off the output pin of the **LandscapeCoords** Node and type "**div**" in the search bar, select the **Divide**, as shown below, to create a **Divide** Node.

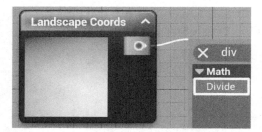

Continue to drag off the **B** pin of the **Divide** Node and type "**const**" in the search bar, select the **Constant**, as shown below, to create a **Constant** Node.

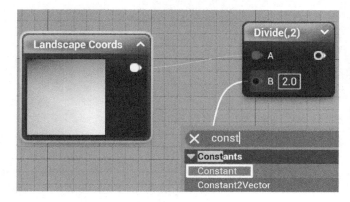

Then right-click on the **Constant** Node and select **Convert to Parameter** from the pop-up menu to convert it to a **Parameter** Node.

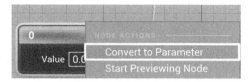

With the **Parameter** Node selected, as shown below, set the **Parameter Name** to **Tiling** and the **Default Value** to **4**.

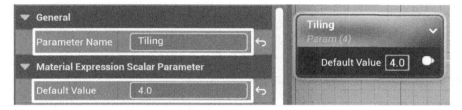

Lastly, plug the output pin of the **Divide** Node into the **UVs** pins of the **four** Texture Sample Nodes respectively as shown on the right:

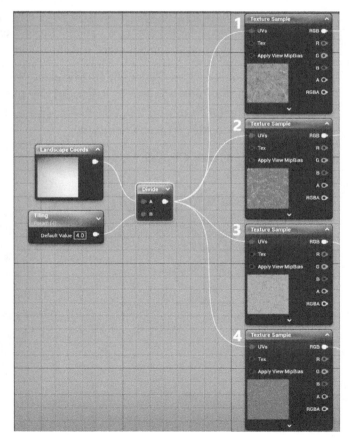

Now press **Apply** and **Save** to apply the modification and after the compile is finished, fly the camera **near** the landscape and you'll see the grass show up as shown below:

Fixing Landscape Texture Repetition

Now that the tiling of the landscape textures can be controlled by parameters, in the next step, we need to hide the texture repetition on the landscape as follows. The first technique we can use to fix this issue is called **Macro Texture Variation**, which is built into the materials existing in the **StarterContent** folder.

Before we start, create a new folder called **Material_Functions** in the **Levels** folder, then double-click the folder to open it. Right-click in the Content Browser, select **Materials** > **Material Function** from the context menu to create a Material Function and then rename it to **MF_MacroVariation**.

Next, find the **M_Metal_Copper** Material in the **StarterContent** > **Materials** folder as shown below:

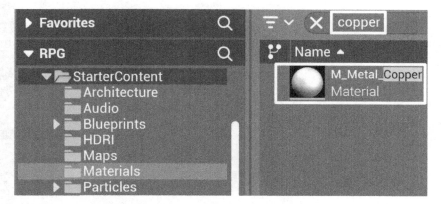

Double-click on the material to open the Material Graph as shown below:

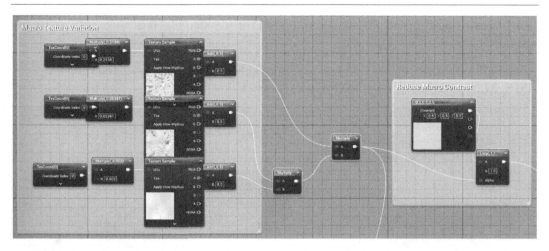

Find the above **Macro Texture Variation** related nodes, with them selected, press the **Ctrl + C** key to copy the nodes, and then open the **MF_MacroVariation** Material Function as shown below:

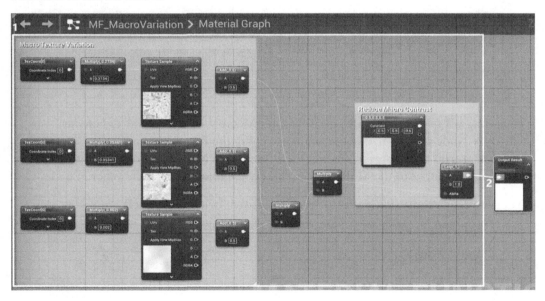

Press **Ctrl + V** key to paste the copied Nodes, as shown above, then plug the **output** pin of the **Lerp** Node into the **input** pin of the **Output Result** Node. Now press **Apply** and **Save** to confirm the modification.

As you can see from the nodes, the **Macro Texture Variation** technique uses a tileable texture with some light to dark variations. Here it uses the texture **three** times with

different tiling for each. Then all textures will be blended together with your landscape texture.

Then after opening the **M_LandscapeMaterial** Material, firstly drag and drop the **MF_MacroVariation** into the Graph as shown below:

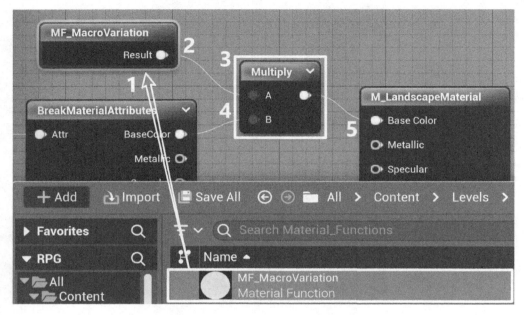

Then drag off from the **Result** pin of the MF_MacroVariation Node and create a **Multiply** Node as shown above. Continue to plug the **BaseColor** pin of the **BreakMaterialAttributes** Node into the **B** pin of the **Multiply** Node, followed by plugging the output of the Multiply into the **Base Color** of the main material node.

After pressing **Apply** and **Save**, the result is shown below on the **left**:

Compared with the previous terrain shown above on the **right**, the repetition issue is greatly reduced.

Noise-based Texture Blending

To make the landscape more photorealistic, we'll blend the Grass and Soil textures with **Noise** in this sub-section, and before doing so, let's create another **Material Function** called **MF_GrassSoil** in the **Material_Functions** folder. Then, after selecting the following Nodes in the **M_LandscapeMaterial** Material, press **Ctrl + C** to copy the Nodes.

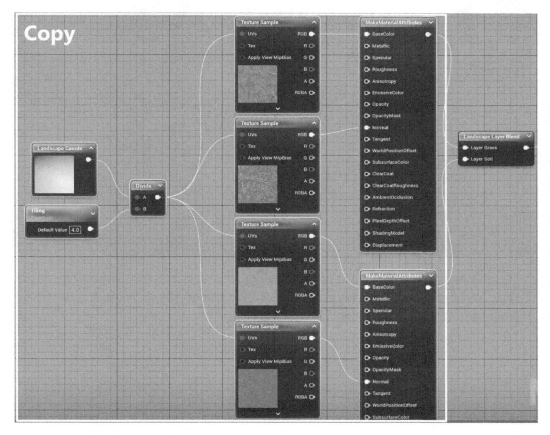

Next, open the **MF_GrassSoil** Material Graph, as shown below, and press **Ctrl + V** to paste the copied Nodes in the Graph.

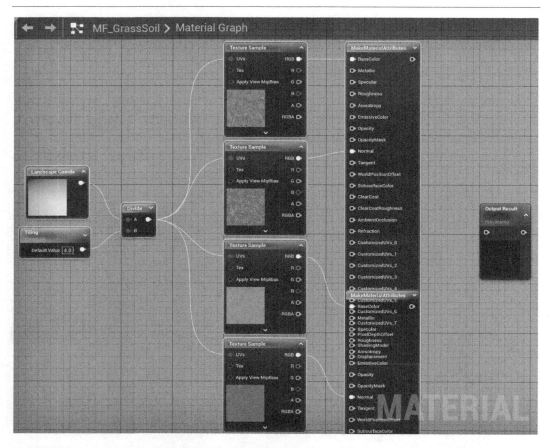

With the **LandscapeCoords**, **Divide**, and **Tiling** Node selected, duplicate a copy of the Nodes, as shown below, then plug the output of the **second** Divide Node into the **UVs** input pins of the two **Soil** Texture Sample Nodes.

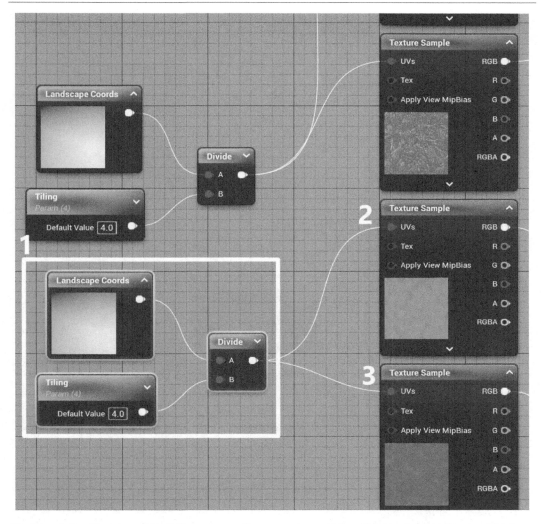

To blend the Grass and Soil Textures, after creating a **BlendMaterialAttributes** Node, as shown below, plug the output pins of the two **MakeMaterialAttributes** Nodes into the **A** and **B** pins of the **BlendMaterialAttributes** Node respectively, then plug the output of the BlendMaterialAttributes Node into the input pin of the **Output Result** Node.

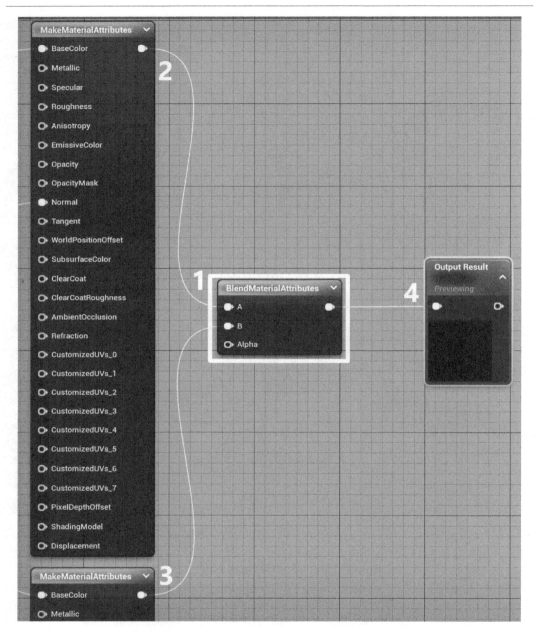

Re-arrange the Nodes and **add** the following new Nodes with the **Comment** as shown below:

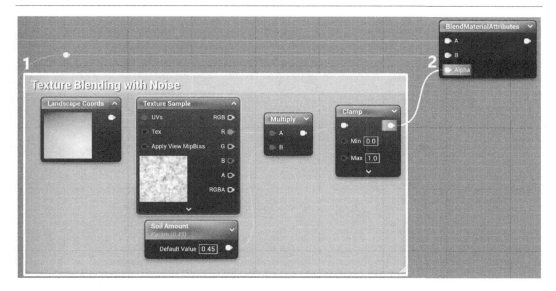

To create a Comment for a group of Nodes, with the Nodes selected and press the **C** key. Here we use the **Perlin Noise** Texture existing in the **StarterContent** folder and the node's setting is as shown below:

The **R** (Red) channel of the Texture Sample node is multiplied with a Parameter called **Soil Amount** as shown above. The parameter is to control the amount of the Soil Texture, and it's set to **0.45** in this case. The **Clamp** Node is to **clamp** the output value of the **Multiply** Node to the range of **0** to **1**, and lastly plug the output of the **Clamp** Node into the **Alpha** pin of the **BlendMaterialAttributes** Node.

Distance-based Texture Blending

Next, we'll use a technique called **Distance Blend** to blend the textures using the **Distance_Blend** Node as follows. First, with the following Nodes selected press **Ctrl + C** to copy the Nodes.

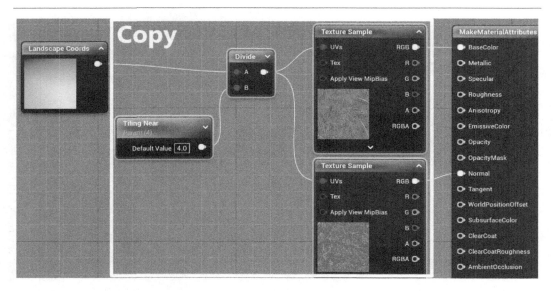

Next, press **Ctrl + V** to **duplicate** a copy of the Nodes as shown below:

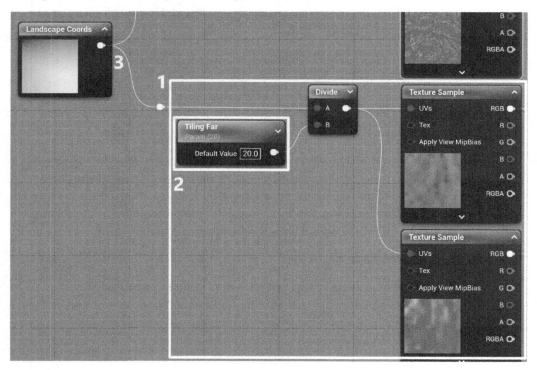

After changing the **name** of the duplicated **Parameter** Nodes to **Tiling Far** as shown above, reset the **Default Value** of the **Tiling Far** parameter to **20**, and re-plug the output of the **LandscapeCoords** Node into the **A** pin of the duplicated **Divide** Node.

Continue to change the **name** of the **Tiling** Parameter Node to **Tiling Near** as shown below:

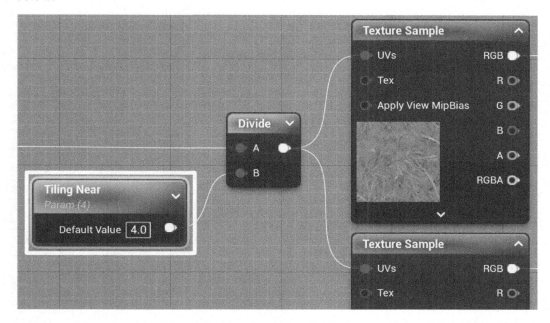

Next, after creating two **Linear Interpolate (Lerp)** Nodes, as shown below, plug the **RGB** pins of the two **Uncut Grass** Texture Sample Nodes into the **A** and **B** pins of the **first** Lerp Node, respectively.

Similarly, plug the **RGB** pins of the two **Normal** Texture Sample Nodes into the **A** and **B** pins of the **second** Lerp Node. Continue to plug the output pins of the first and second Lerp Nodes into the **BaseColor** and **Normal** pins of the **MakeMaterialAttributes** Node, respectively.

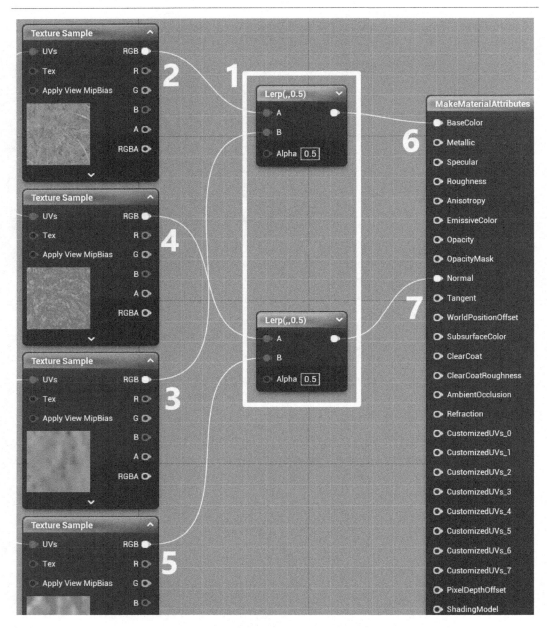

Finally, after creating a **Distance_Blend** Node and two **Parameter** Nodes called **Blend Range** and **Start Offset**, change the **Default** Values of the Parameter Nodes to **1000** and **-200** as shown below:

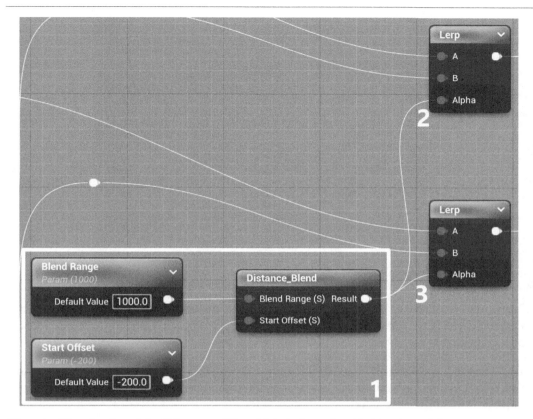

Plug the **Result** pin of the **Distance_Blend** Node into the **Alpha** pins of the two Lerp Nodes respectively as shown above.

Now press **Apply** to confirm the modification and go back to the **M_LandscapeMaterial** Graph. With the **Layer Blend** Node selected, modify the **first** Layer Name to **GrassSoil** as shown below:

After pressing **Apply** and switching to **Landscape Mode**, you'll see the old **Grass** Layer becomes a big question mark and a new Layer is created as shown below:

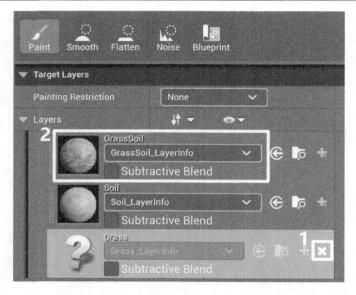

Now press the **Delete (X)** icon to **delete** the old **Grass** Layer, and after confirming the deletion, **create** the **GrassSoil_LayerInfo** asset for the new **GrassSoil** Layer as shown above.

Because we have duplicated all the Texture and Normal Nodes into the **MF_GrassSoil** function, back to the Material Graph. After **deleting** all the nodes which **have been copied**, drag and drop the **MF_GrassSoil** Material Function into the Graph, as shown below, and re-plug the **Result** of the MF_GrassSoil into the **Layer GrassSoil** pin of the Layer Blend Node.

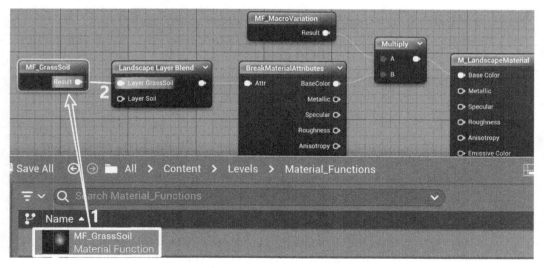

Next, with the **Layer Blend** Node selected, reset the name of the **Soil** Layer to **RockCliff** as shown below:

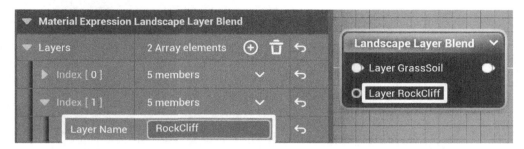

Then, after creating a **Material Function** called **MF_RockCliff** in the **Levels** > **Material_Functions** folder, double-click on it to open the Material Graph as shown below:

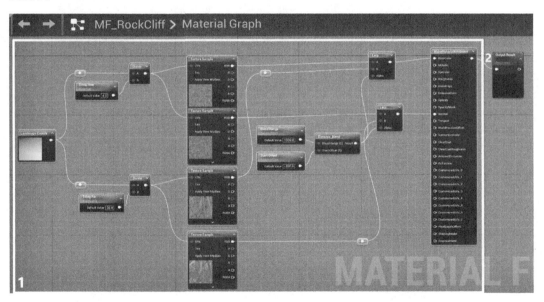

Duplicate the above Nodes from the **MF_GrassSoil** Material Function and plug the output of the **MaterialAttributes** Node into the input pin of the **Output Result** Node.

Then reset the **Texture** fields of the **Texture** and **Normal** Sample Nodes to the imported **Rock Cliff** textures and normals respectively as shown below:

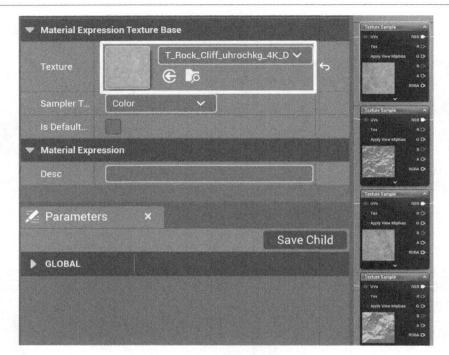

After pressing **Apply** and **Save** to confirm the modification, back to the **LandscapeMaterial** Graph, drag and drop the **MF_RockCliff** into the Graph, and lastly plug the **Result** of the MF_RockCliff Node into the **Layer RockCliff** of the Layer Blend Node as shown below:

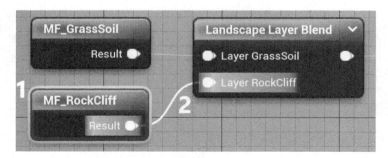

Now press **Apply** and **Save**, switch to **Landscape Mode**, and create the **RockCliff_LayerInfo** asset for the RockCliff Layer as shown below:

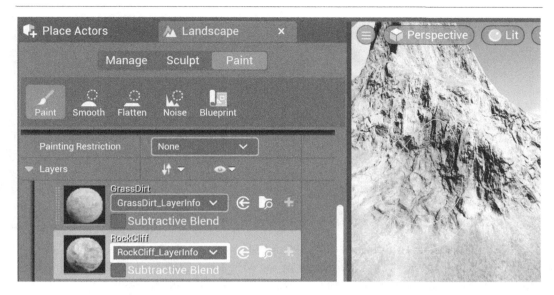

With the **RockCliff** Layer selected, we can paint the Cliff texture in the Viewport as shown above, but this is probably not correct in real terrain, because the Cliff textures mostly appear in steep slope areas on the terrain.

Auto Landscape Material

UE5 provides the **WorldAlignedBlend** Node for us to automatically place the Cliff texture on the terrain according to the specified **slope** of the landscape. With the **Layer Blend** Node selected, add a new Layer called **Auto** as shown below:

Then, after **adding** the following Nodes to the Graph, plug the **Result** of the **MF_GrassSoil** Node into the **B** pin of the **BlendMaterialAttributes** Node as shown below:

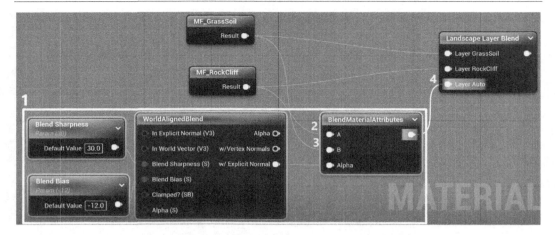

After setting the **Default Values** of the **Blend Sharpness** and **Blend Bias** parameters to **30** and **-12** respectively, plug the **Result** of the **MF_RockCliff** Node into the **A** pin of the **BlendMaterialAttributes** Node as shown above, and plug the output of the **BlendMaterialAttributes** Node into the **Layer Auto** pin of the Layer Blend Node.

Now press **Apply** and you'll see the **Auto** Layer appears under the **Layers** settings as shown below:

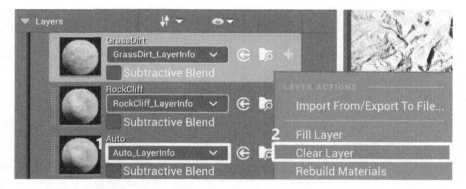

After creating the **Auto_LayerInfo** asset for it, **right**-click on the **GrassSoil** Layer as shown above and select **Clear Layer** from the context menu to **clear** the Grass and Soil texture painted on the landscape.

Then right-click on the **RockCliff** Layer as shown below and select **Fill Layer** to paint the landscape automatically by blending the Grass, Soil, and Cliff textures.

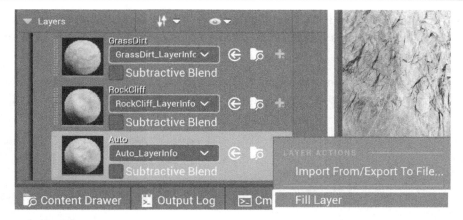

Finally, to control the **Specular** of the LandscapeMaterial, after creating a **Parameter** called **Specular** in the Graph, as shown below, plug the output of the Parameter Node into the **Specular** pin of the LandscapeMaterial Node.

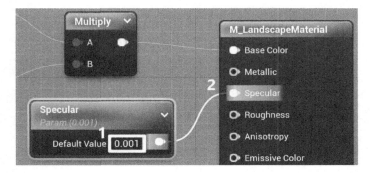

Now reset the **Default Value** of the **Specular** parameter to a **low** value, for example, **0.001**, the result is as shown below on the **left**. After adjusting its value, the Specular of the landscape will be changed in **real-time** as shown below on the **right**.

Painting Foliage

After the landscape is ready, it's time to put some foliage and trees on the terrain. We will use the free 3D plants and trees provided for Unreal Engine by **Quixel Megascans** in this subsection.

From the main menu, choose **Window** > **Quixel Bridge** to open the **Bridge** window, and after signing in, select the **Vegetation** from the **COLLECTIONS** menu as shown below:

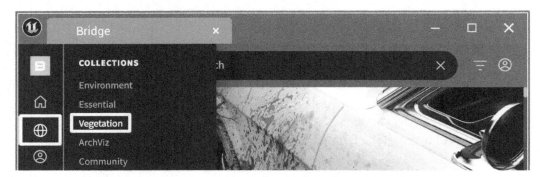

Then scroll down the panel and look for the plants you like as shown below:

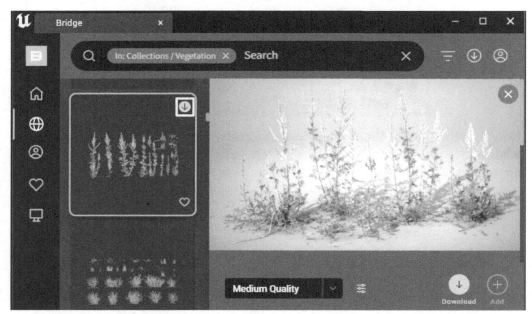

Click on the plants to preview them on the right panel, then press the **Download** icon to download the plants. After the download is ready, press the **Add** icon to add the plants to the project as shown below:

Now open the **Content Drawer** and you'll find a folder called **3D_Plants** appears in the project as shown below:

Under the **3D_Plants** folder, you can find the plants just added as shown above. Next, please follow the same steps to download more plants into the project.

After the plants are ready, switch to **Foliage Mode** from the toolbar, and in the **Foliage** tab, choose **Select** on the menu as shown below. Then drag and drop all the foliage you like to put on the terrain from the **Content Browser** into space under the **+ Drop Foliage Here**.

You'll see the following **Choose Location for Foliage Type Asset** window shows up:

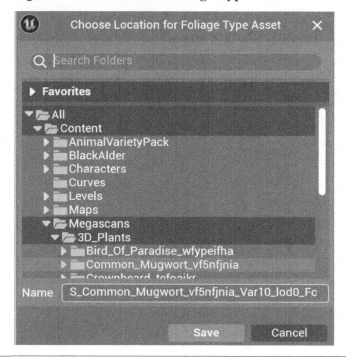

After pressing the **Save** for all the foliage you selected, the result is shown below:

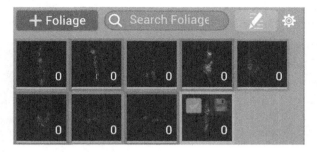

Please note that **all** of the plants will be selected by default. Now choose the **Paint** on the menu as shown below:

After changing the **Brush Size**, **Paint Density**, and **Erase Density** to appropriate values, as shown above, move the mouse into the **Viewport** and press the mouse button to paint the foliage on the terrain. The **number** of planted foliage will be shown on the foliage list.

The World Partition Cell Size

The cell size determines the size of the grid that is used to generate the streaming levels and the default cell size is 12800 world units in centimeters which is 128 **square meters**. The cell size property can be adjusted in the **World Settings** panel as shown below:

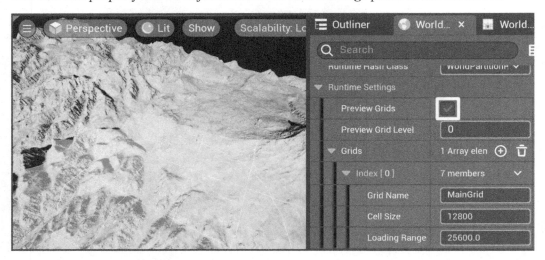

You can **tick** the **Preview Grids** checkbox to preview the grids as shown above in the viewport.

After increasing the **Cell Size** and **Loading Range** to **20000** and **78000** respectively, the result is shown below:

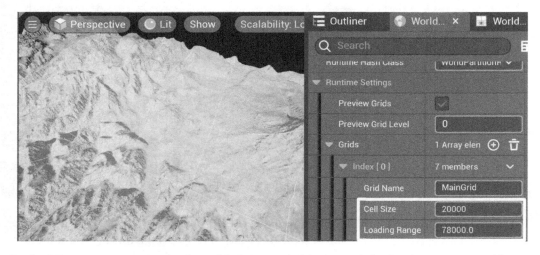

In the Viewport, you can see the grid size now is bigger and the landscape covered by the grids is also getting bigger.

5.1.3 Player Characters

After the landscape is ready, we are going to create the art assets for the player characters in this section.

Creating Warrior Characters from Mixamo

Please use the web browser to connect to **www.mixamo.com**, after entering the account and password, the screen is as follows:

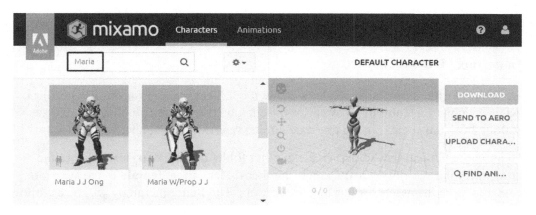

Enter the string "Maria" in the search input field under the **Characters** tab, the female characters will appear in the **left** panel, as shown above, then click on the Maria J J Ong character icon, and you'll see the character appears in the preview panel on the right.

As shown above, press the **DOWNLOAD** button to open the **DOWNLOAD SETTINGS** window as shown below:

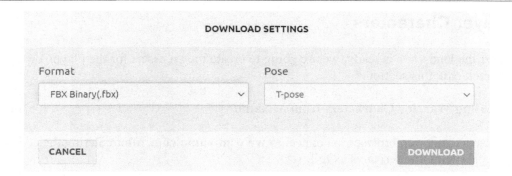

Next, press the DOWNLOAD button and wait for the FBX file to be downloaded.

Importing Mixamo Characters

Before importing our characters, let's create the folder structure for our RPG project. After opening the **Content Browser**, right-click on the **Content** folder, and choose **New Folder** from the context menu to create a folder named **Characters**.

Next, in the **Characters** folder, create another folder named **Warriors** to store the content for our warriors. Lastly, create another folder called **Female** in the Warriors folder to store the assets for our female warriors. The folder hierarchy will be as follows:

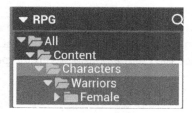

After opening the **Female** folder, **drag and drop** the downloaded **Maria J J** female character into the **Content Browser**, then the **FBX Import Options** window will show up as shown below:

Next, click the **Import** button to import the character, and a warning message saying, **"No smoothing group information was found in this FBX scene."** will show up, please **ignore** this message and press the **CLEAR** button to continue. After the importing is complete, you'll see the character, its textures, and the materials that Unreal created for us as shown below:

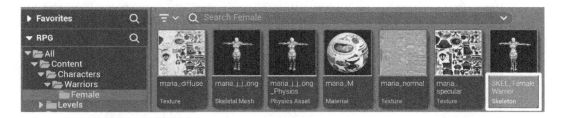

Rename the Skeleton as **SKEL_FemaleWarrior** as shown above just in case you share the skeleton with other characters or animations.

5.1.4 Enemy Characters and Trees

This section will introduce how to download the art assets from the **Unreal Marketplace** for our enemy characters and trees including the **Animal Variety Pack**, **Quadruped Creatures**, and **Megascans Trees**.

Animal Variety Pack

Open the **Epic Games Launcher** and press the **Marketplace** tab as shown below:

Type "**Animal Variety**" in the Search bar and after a while, the drop-down menu will appear as shown above. Click the **ANIMAL VARIETY PACK** and the following page will show up:

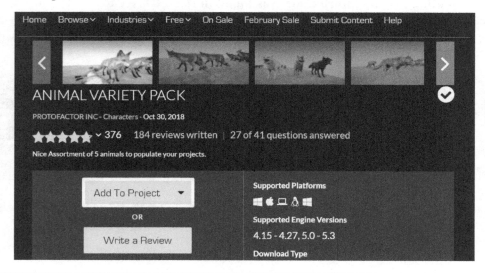

After clicking the **Add To Project** button, in the next step select the current **RPG** project and then press the **Add to Project** button as shown below:

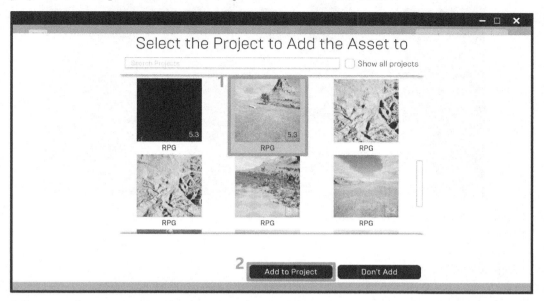

Note: After opening the Epic Games Launcher, if the **Marketplace** tab does **not** show up, back to Unreal Editor, and choose **Window** > **Open Marketplace** from the main menu. Then you'll see the tab appears in the Launcher's window.

When the download is complete, back to Unreal Editor and you'll see the **AnimalVarietyPack** folder appears in the Content Browser as shown below:

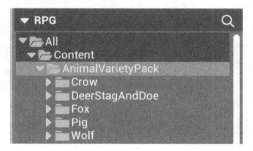

Quadruped Fantasy Creatures

Similarly, find the **Quadruped Fantasy Creatures** in the Marketplace as shown below:

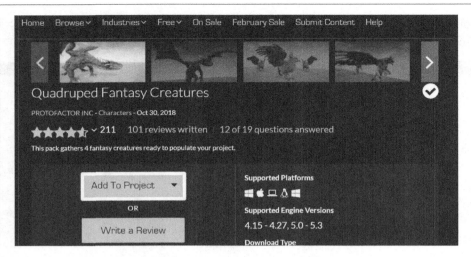

Press the **Add To Project** button and select the **RPG** project in the next step to install the Asset Pack.

Megascans Trees - European Black Alder

This collection is an early access tree pack with 22 unique models of various maturity to build a photorealistic black alder forest. The pack includes a powerful foliage master material to control seasons and wind.

Type "**megascans trees**" in the search bar and press **Enter**, the **Megascans Trees** will appear in the panel as shown below:

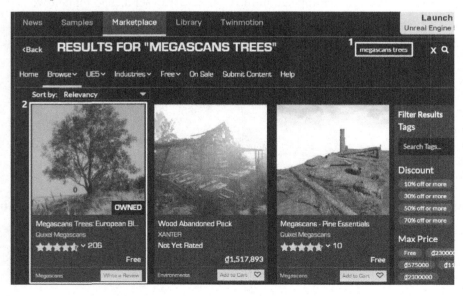

Click on it and the following page will show up:

Press the button to install the asset and after a while, you'll see the **BlackAlder** folder appears in the project as shown below:

Now you can drag and drop the tree under the **Geometry** > **PivotPainter** folder into the scene as shown above, or you can paint the trees on the landscape in the **Foliage** mode.

5.1.5 The Great Sword Weapon

The **Great Sword** weapon shown below is what we are going to use in the project.
Please go to the book's website and download the **GreatSword.fbx** file and its textures.

Or you can use any sword weapon found in the Unreal Marketplace, for example, the
Free Fantasy Weapon Sample Pack.

Importing the Great Sword

Now create a new folder called
Weapons under the **Content**, then
drag and drop the GreatSword.fbx
file into this folder.

Then you'll see the **FBX Import
Options** window as shown on the
right:

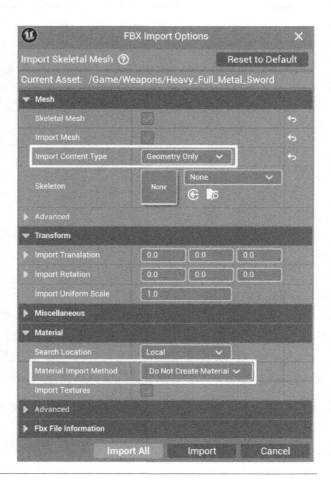

After selecting the **Geometry Only** for the **Import Content Type**, click to open the **Material** settings and select **Do Not Create Material** for the **Material Import Method** as shown above. Next, press the **Import** button to import the great sword as shown below:

Then **rename** the imported **Skeletal Mesh** and the generated **Skeleton** to **SK_GreatSword** and **SKEL_GreatSword,** respectively.

Continue to drag and drop the **T_GreatSword_BaseColor**.png and **T_GreatSword_Normal**.png files into the **Weapons** folder as shown below:

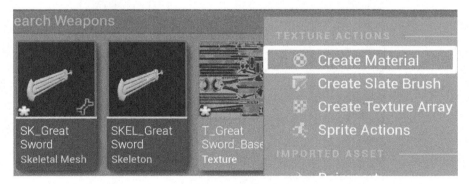

Then **right**-click on the imported **T_GreatSword_BaseColor** texture, select **Create Material** from the context menu, as shown above, to create a Material. After renaming it to **M_GreatSword**, double-click on the material to open the **Material Graph** as shown below:

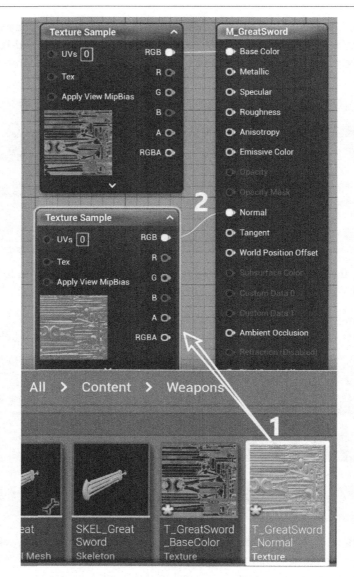

Drag and drop the **T_GreatSword_Normal** texture onto the graph editor, then drag off from the **RGB** pin of the created **Texture Sample** node and plug into the **Normal** pin of the **M_GreatSword** node as shown above.

Finally, double-click the **SK_GreatSword** Skeletal Mesh to open the asset editor as shown below:

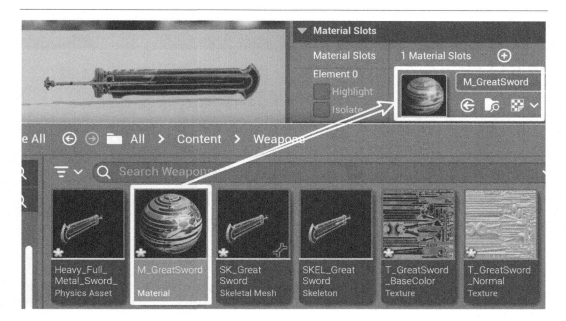

Drag and drop the **M_GreatSword** material onto the **first** Material Slot (**Element 0**) on the **Asset Details** panel to assign the material for the great sword as you can see in the Viewport.

5.1.6 Animation Sequences

In this section, we are going to download the animations that are required for our action RPG, including the **locomotion** and **sword-playing** animations, from the **Mixamo** website.

Locomotion Animations

Go to the **Mixamo** website, click on the Animations tab, and enter "idle" in the search bar as shown below:

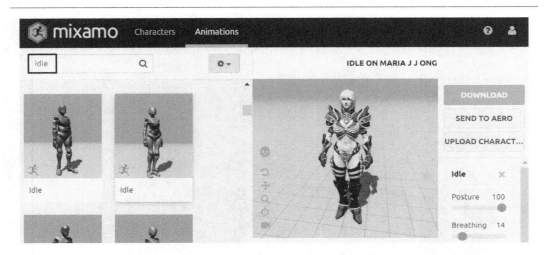

Select one of the **Idle** animations to preview it on the right panel, you can adjust the parameters, such as **Breathing** or **Character Arm-Space**, under the animation's name tab to modify it. Then press the DOWNLOAD button again to open the **DOWNLOAD SETTINGS** window as shown below:

Because we only need the animation keyframes data inside the FBX file, click on the **Skin** drop-down and select **Without Skin**. Then press DOWNLOAD to download the FBX file of the Idle animation.

Next, enter "walking" and press Enter in the search bar, you'll see the **Walking** animation shows up in the left panel, click on it to preview in the right panel as shown below:

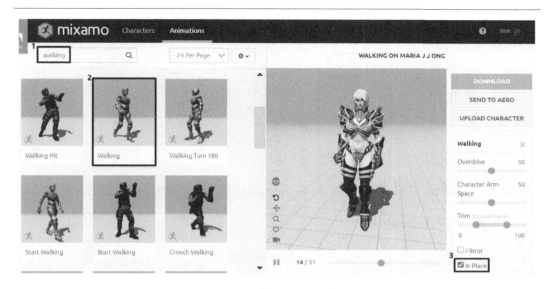

Tick the **In Place** checkbox, as shown above, to let the character stay in place. Then press the DOWNLOAD button again to download the **Walking** animation **without** skin. Similarly, search for the **Running** animation you prefer and download the FBX file without skin and in place.

Continue to type "**falling**" in the search bar and press Enter, find, and click the **Falling Idle** animation as shown below:

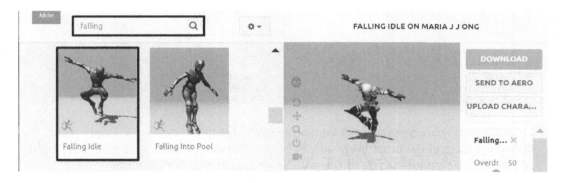

Press the DOWNLOAD button to download the animation **without** skin. Then type "**jump**" in the Search bar and press Enter, find, and click the **Jumping Down** animation as shown below:

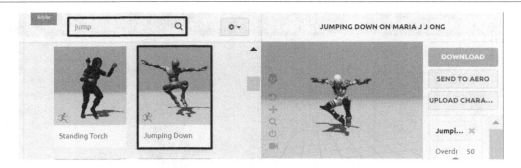

Press the DOWNLOAD button again to download the animation without skin.

Sword-Playing Animations

Next, type "**sword**" in the search bar and press Enter to look for **Light Attack** sword-playing melee animations as shown below:

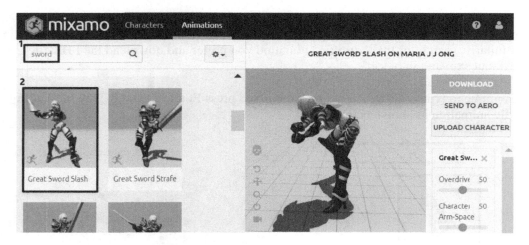

Click on the **Great Sword Slash** animation in the list to preview on the right panel, then download the animation **without** skin as before. Similarly, look for another **two** Light Attack melee animations you like and download them after previewing.

Then, type "**sword jump attack**" in the search bar and press Enter to look for **Heavy Attack** melee animations for the Great Sword. Find and click the **Great Sword Jump Attack** in the left panel, and you'll notice that the character is moving while attacking as shown below on the viewport:

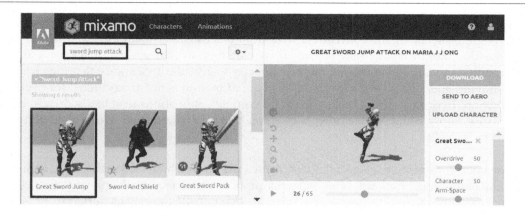

After downloading the animation, continue to search and download another **two** Heavy Attack melee animations including the Great Sword **Slide Attack** animation.

Finally, type "**draw**" and press Enter in the Search bar to look for **sword-drawing** animations as shown below:

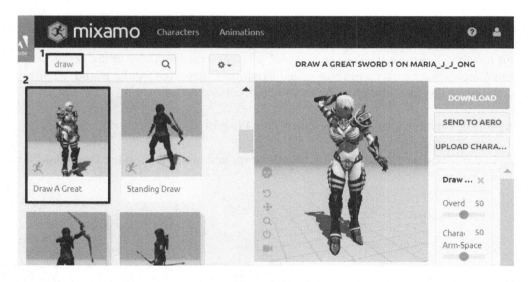

Click the **Draw A Great Sword 1** animation, and then download the animation without skin.

Note: You can find and download all animations used in this book from the Author's website.

5.1.7 ARPG Root Motions

Typically, in-game animation, a character's collision capsule (or another shape) is driven through the scene by the **controller**. Data from this capsule is then used to drive animation. For instance, if the capsule is moving forward, the system then knows to play a running or walking animation on the character to give the appearance that the character is moving under its power. However, this type of motion is not always ideal for every situation. In some cases, it makes sense for complex animations to actually drive the collision capsule and not the other way around. This is where **Root Motion** handling becomes critical for your games.

Consider, for example, a special attack from a player in which the mesh had been pre-animated to lunge forward. If all character motion were based on the player capsule, such animations would cause the character to step outside the capsule, effectively **losing collision**.

Put simply, Root Motion is the motion of a character that is based on animation from the **root bone** of the skeleton. Most in-game animations are handled via cycles in which the character's root remains stationary. To handle this, we need to take the motion of the root away from the character and apply it to the character's capsule instead.

To enable the Root Motion in Unreal, all the character skeletons must have a bone named **root**, but unfortunately, the Mixamo character and the animations currently **do not** have the bone, so we have to add such a bone to the hierarchy of the skeleton. Fortunately, there exists a **plug-in** called **Mixamo Converter** for the **Blender** software to complete this task, the procedures will be discussed as follows.

Installing Blender and Mixamo Converter Plug-in

Go to the **Blender** website at **www.blender.org**, and after clicking the **Download** tab as shown below:

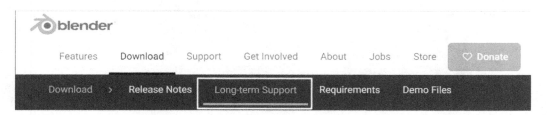

Press the **Long-tern Support** button on the page, and in the next step, press the **Blender 3.3 LTS** tab as shown below:

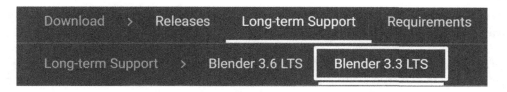

Scroll down the page until you see the **3.3.18 LTS** version as shown below:

Please download and install the software for your computer platform.

On Windows platform, you can also download **Blender** in the **Microsoft Store** as follows. Open the Microsoft Store application, and enter "blender 3.3 lts" on the **Search Bar** as shown below:

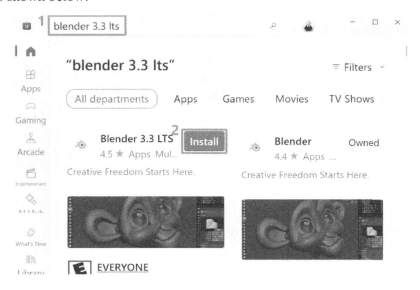

After pressing the **Get** button, and then you will see the **Install** appears, click on it, and wait for the installation to be complete.

After the Blender is installed, let's go to the **Mixamo Converter** [5] GitHub page and download the Mixamo Converter repository as **ZIP (no need to unpack it)**. Next, open up Blender and select **Edit** > **Preferences...** from the main menu to open the **Preferences** window as shown below:

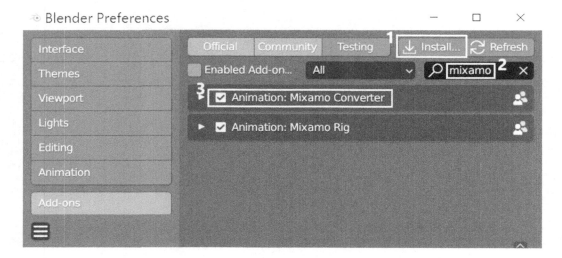

Make sure that the **Add-ons** tab is pressed, click the **Install...** button on the top, then select the **ZIP** you downloaded and click the **Install Add-on** button. After it's installed, it should be in the list (search for **mixamo**), and you can **enable** it as shown above.

Adding A Root Bone to Mixamo Animations

Before converting, please move the T-pos female **character** and **all** the downloaded **animations** to an **empty** folder such as **Mixamo** in our case. Then press on the **Mixamo** tab in **Blender** to open the **Mixamo Rootbaker** panel as shown below:

---

[5] **Mixamo Converter**, https://github.com/enziop/mixamo_converter.

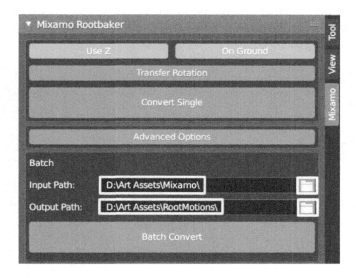

After clicking on the **folder** icon to the **right** of the **Input Path** field, select the folder, for example, the **Mixamo** folder in our case, which contains all the animations to be converted as shown above. Then click on the folder icon to the right of the **Output Path** field, and select the folder, such as the **RootMotions** here, which will store the **converted files**.

Next, press the **Batch Convert** button to add a **root** bone to all the skeletons in the files, and after a while, a message will appear above the status bar and show how many files have been converted.

Regenerating the Skeleton from Mesh

Now drag the **converted** T-pos **female character** into the **Female** folder to **replace** the imported character, a message will appear as follows:

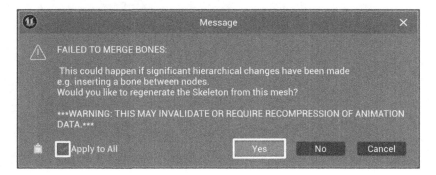

After **ticking** the **Apply to All** checkbox, press the **Yes** button to regenerate the skeleton, then the following message window will show up, press the **Yes** button to ensure all bones are merged.

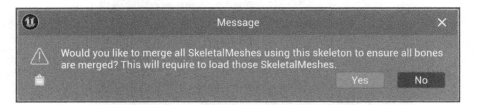

Double-click on the **SKEL_FemaleWarrior** to open it in the editor, and you'll see a new bone named **root** has been added to the top hierarchy as shown on the right:

Importing Animations

Make a new folder named **Animations** in the **Characters** > **Female** folder, then drag all **converted** animations into this new folder, the **FBX Import Options** window will appear as shown below:

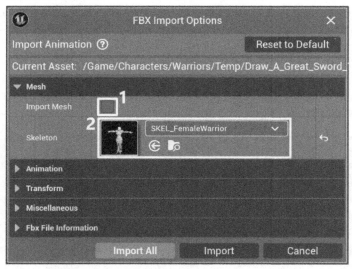

Because our animations are **without** skins, **untick** the **Import Mesh** option first as shown above, then click on the drop-down menu and select the **SKEL_FemaleWarrior** for our animations, finally press **Import All** to import all animations.

Enabling Root Motions

The Root Motion of an animation can be visualized during **playback** in the editor. Simply open up an animation in which the **root** bone is **moving**, for example, the imported Great Sword **Jump Attack** animation sequence, and in the **Viewport**, press the **Character** button on the top and choose **Bones > All Hierarchy** from the drop-down.

If you have **not** enabled the **Root Motion** for the animation, you will notice a **red** line that appears as the character's root moves. This illustrates the Root Motion of the animation as shown below:

Now select **Window > Asset Details** from the main menu to open the panel, find and **tick** the **EnableRootMotion** option to **enable** the Root Motion, this red line will **disappear** as shown below:

Now, the character will move **in place** in the Viewport. This is because the character's root will no longer move from its original position which means that it can still have the same motion that the animator intended, but it can also respond properly to in-game collisions and other physics and gameplay events.

Finally, please open **each** of the rest imported **melee** animations that the **root bone moves, enable** the **Root Motion** by **ticking** its **EnableRootMotion** option, and press **Save** to confirm the modification.

5.2 Blend Spaces

Blend Spaces are special assets that can be sampled in **AnimGraphs** that allow for the blending of animations based on the values of two inputs. Simple blending between two animations based on a single input can be performed using one of the standard Blend nodes available in Animation Blueprints. Blend Spaces provide a means of doing more complex blending between multiple animations based on multiple values (currently limited to two).

The goal of Blend Spaces is to reduce the need for creating individual, hard-coded nodes to perform blending based on specific properties or conditions. By allowing the animator or programmer to specify the inputs, the animations, and how the inputs are used to blend between animations, virtually any type of blending can be performed using the generic Blend Space.

5.2.1 Creating Blend Spaces for Warriors

Right-click in **Content Browser** of the **Female** > **Animations** folder, select **Animation** > **Blend Space** from the context menu to open the **Pick Skeleton** dialog as shown below:

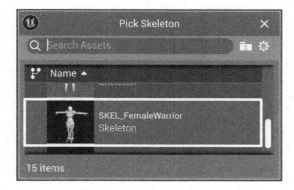

After selecting the **SKEL_FemaleWarrior** as shown above, a new Blueprint will be created for us. After renaming to **BS_FemaleWarrior**, double-click on it to open the Blend Space editor as shown below:

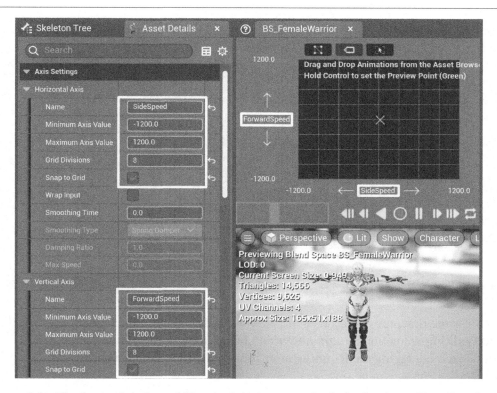

Expand the **Horizontal Axis** and **Vertical Axis** respectively in the **Asset Details** tab, and modify the **Name, Minimum**, and **Maximum Axis Value** fields of the **Horizontal Axis** to **SideSpeed, -1200**, and **1200,** respectively. Similarly, modify the **Name, Minimum**, and **Maximum Axis Value** fields of the **Vertical Axis** to **ForwardSpeed**, -1200, and 1200 respectively as shown above. Lastly, reset both **Grid Divisions** to **8** and **tick** the **Snip to Grid** checkboxes for the Horizontal and Vertical Axes.

After the modification, you'll see the **names** of the **Horizontal** Axis and **Vertical** Axis under the **viewport** will be changed as well. Besides, all the imported animations in this folder will show up in the **Asset Browser** tab on the **bottom right** of the editor.

Sample Poses

With your Axis Settings defined, the next thing you'll need to do is add some animations to sample from the **Blend Space Editor** grid. First, drag the **Idle** animation from the Asset Browser onto the **middle** of the grid as shown below:

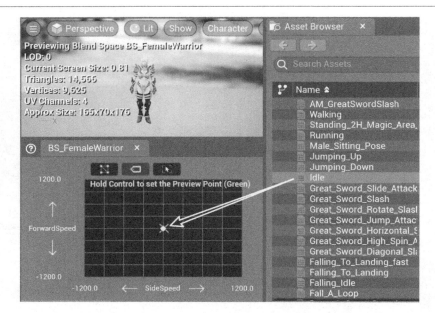

At the same time, the character in the viewport will play the **Idle** animation. Next, drag the **Walking** animation to right **above** and **below** the Idle animation on the grid, followed by dragging the **Running** animation to the **top** and **bottom** locations respectively as shown below:

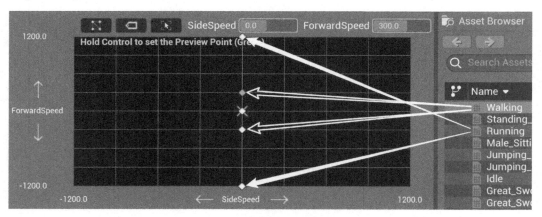

Similarly, drag the **Walking** animation onto the **left** and **right** of the Idle animation on the grid, respectively. Finally, drag the **Running** animation onto the **furthest left** and **furthest right** locations respectively as shown below:

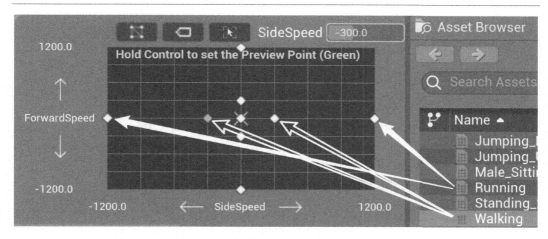

Previewing Blend Spaces

Once you have a few sample poses placed on the grid, you can hold the **Ctrl** (Control) key and drag the **Preview Point (green)** around to view the blend between poses as shown on the right:

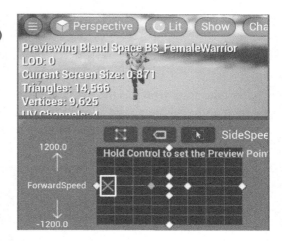

Besides, when you move the cursor **near** the preview point, the actual sample values will show up as well as shown below:

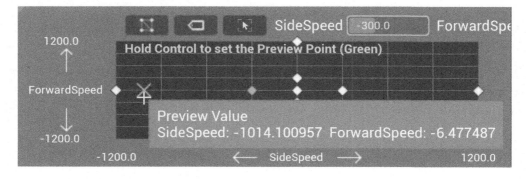

5.2.2 Creating Blend Spaces for Wolves

Now you know what a Blend Space is and how to create it. Let's continue to create the Blend Space for the **Wolf** in the **Animal Variety Pack**.

Right-click in the **Wolf** folder under the **Animal Variety Pack**, then under the **CREATE ADVANCED ASSET** section, select **Animation > Blend Space** to open the **Pick Skeleton** dialog as shown below:

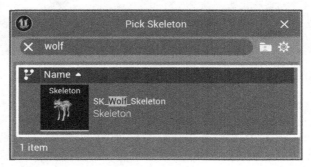

After entering "**wolf**" in the **Search Assets** field, choose the **SK_Wolf_Skeleton** as shown above to create the Blend Space, and rename it to **BS_Wolf**. Double-click to open it in the Editor, and expand the **Horizontal Axis** settings in the **Assets Details** tab as shown below:

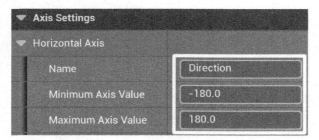

Change the **Name** field to **Direction**, **Minimum Axis Value** to **-180**, and **Maximum Axis Value** to **180** respectively as shown above.

Next, after expanding the **Vertical Axis** settings, change the **Name** field to **ForwardSpeed**, **Minimum Axis Value** to **0**, **Maximum Axis Value** to **300**, and also reset the **Grid Divisions** to **2** respectively as shown below:

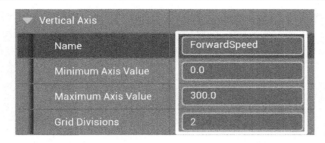

Then drag and drop the **ANIM_Wolf_IdleBreathe** sequence onto the **five** positions on the grid at the bottom as shown below:

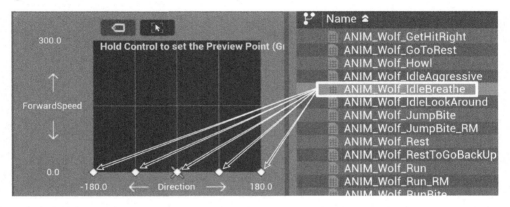

Then drag and drop the **ANIM_Wolf_Walk** sequence onto the **middle** position on the grid as shown below:

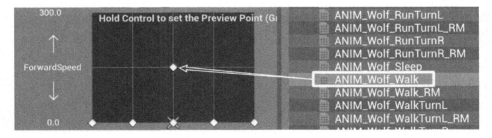

Then drag and drop the **ANIM_Wolf_WalkTurnR** and **ANIM_Wolf_WalkTurnL** sequences onto the **middle right** and **middle left** positions on the grid as shown below:

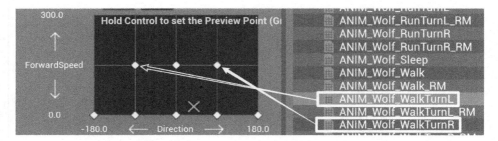

Then drag and drop the **ANIM_Wolf_Run** sequence onto the **top** position on the grid as shown below:

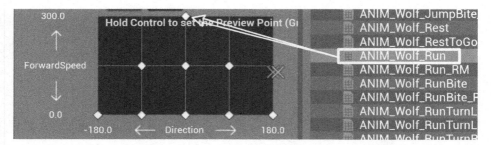

After previewing the blend between poses, press **Save** to confirm the modification.

5.3 The Character and Camera Controls

This section will discuss the design of third person ARPG character and camera controls which are inspired by the latest Chinese action RPG called **Sword and Fairy 7**.[6]

5.3.1 The Character Controller

In this subsection, we'll design and implement an action RPG-style character controller and before doing so, let's build an RPG player character first.

Creating the RPG Character Class

Select **Tools** > **New C++ Class** on the main menu to open the **Add C++ Class** window as shown below:

---

[6] **Sword and Fairy 7**, https://pal7.cubejoy.com/index.html.

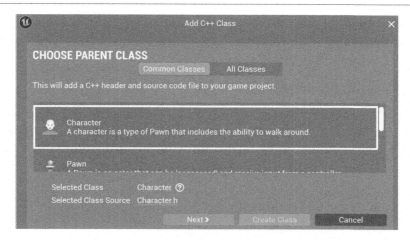

After clicking on the **CHARACTER** class, press **NEXT** to continue. In the next step, after setting the Class Type to **Public**, rename the class to **RPGCharacter** as shown below:

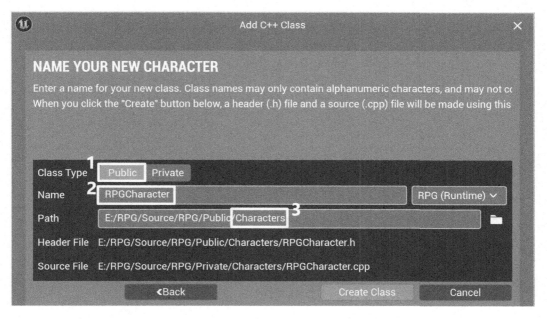

Next, to put the class in the **Characters** folder, add "Characters" to the Path as shown above. Then press **Create Class** button to generate the C++ class in Visual Studio. After the class is compiled, a message will show up and say "Live coding succeeded" on the bottom of the screen.

As we mentioned in the previous chapter, please **turn off** the **Live Coding** from the **Compile options menu** at the **bottom** of the Unreal Editor or from the **Project Settings** window.

Adding Camera Components in C++

In this subsection, we'll continue to extend the **RPGCharacter** class, and add a third-person camera for it in C++. Open the **RPGCharacter.h** header file in the code editor, add the following two lines, as shown in **bold**, right **above** the #include `"RPGCharacter.generated.h"` line:

```
#include "CoreMinimal.h"
#include "GameFramework/Character.h"
#include "Camera/CameraComponent.h"
#include "GameFramework/SpringArmComponent.h"
#include "RPGCharacter.generated.h"
```

Because the camera-related classes are defined in the **CameraComponent.h** and the **SpringArmComponent.h** header files, we have to include both headers.

Note: **All user added** includes **must** be placed **above** the **.generated.h** include line; for example, the #include `"RPGCharacter.generated.h"` line here, otherwise a compile error will occur! In other words, the **.generated.h** file should always be the **last** #include in a header.

Next, add the following lines shown in **bold** in the **public** section **below** the constructor:

```
    ...
public:
    // Sets default values for this character's properties
    ARPGCharacter();

    // Player follow camera
    UPROPERTY(VisibleAnywhere, BlueprintReadWrite)
    UCameraComponent* FollowCamera;
    // Spring Arm Component to follow the camera behind the player
    UPROPERTY(VisibleAnywhere, BlueprintReadWrite)
    USpringArmComponent* CameraBoom;
protected:
    ...
```

In the above code, we declare a **camera component**, representing the third-person camera that follows the player character, using the **UCameraComponent** class. Then a camera boom component is declared using the **USpringArmComponent** class, and it's used to control the camera to **zoom** in/out or **orbit** around the player character.

Next, open the **RPGCharacter.cpp** file in the code editor, and add the following lines shown in bold in the **constructor**:

```
ARPGCharacter::ARPGCharacter()
{
  PrimaryActorTick.bCanEverTick = true;

  // Instantiate your class Components
  CameraBoom =
          CreateDefaultSubobject<USpringArmComponent>(TEXT("CameraBoom"));
  FollowCamera =
          CreateDefaultSubobject<UCameraComponent>(TEXT("FollowCamera"));
  // Attach your class Components to the default RootComponent
  CameraBoom->SetupAttachment(RootComponent);
  FollowCamera->SetupAttachment(CameraBoom,
                                        USpringArmComponent::SocketName);
  CameraBoom->TargetArmLength = 300.0f;
}
```

In the above code, we create the camera and camera boom objects using the engine's built-in function **CreateDefaultSubobject()** and with the required types, respectively. The **TEXT()** macro is used to generate the name for each object.

Then the camera boom is attached to the root component of the character using its **SetupAttachment()** method, followed by attaching the follow camera to the camera boom also by calling its **SetupAttachment()** method, but passing in the **CameraBoom** object as the first parameter. Finally, the **length** of the camera boom is set to **300 cm** by setting its **TargetArmLength** property.

Now right-click on the project, choose **Build** from the context menu to build the project, and make sure that no errors show up in the **Output** window.

Creating the Warrior Class in C++

Next, let's create the **Warrior** class in C++. From the main menu, choose **Tools** > **New C++ Class...** to open the **Add C++ Class** panel as shown below:

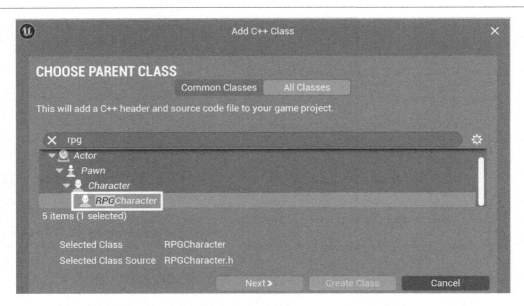

After clicking the **All Classes** tab, type "rpg" in the Search bar and then select the **RPGCharacter** class under the **Character** as shown above. Press the **NEXT** button to continue.

In the next step, rename the class to **WarriorCharacter** and then change its **Path** to under the **Public/Characters** folder as shown below:

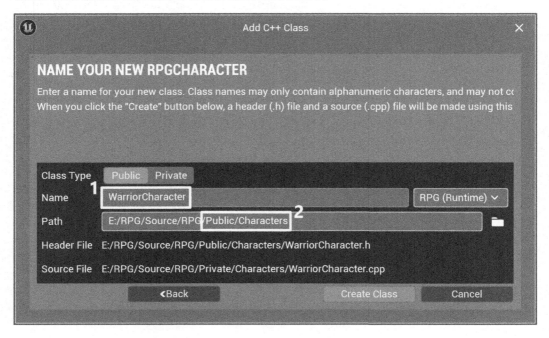

Press the **Create Class** button to generate the class in Visual Studio. Then open the **WarriorCharacter.h** header file, and add the following **bold** lines to add a **public** section in which we declare a **constructor** and three **overridden** methods:

```
UCLASS()
class RPG_API AWarriorCharacter : public ARPGCharacter
{
  GENERATED_BODY()
public:
  AWarriorCharacter();

  // Called to bind functionality to input
  virtual void SetupPlayerInputComponent(class UInputComponent*
                                   PlayerInputComponent) override;
  virtual void BeginPlay() override;
  virtual void Tick(float DeltaTime) override;
};
```

Next, open the **WarriorCharacter.cpp** file, and add the following lines to implement the constructor and methods:

```
AWarriorCharacter::AWarriorCharacter() : Super()
{
}

void AWarriorCharacter::SetupPlayerInputComponent(class UInputComponent*
                                   PlayerInputComponent)
{
  Super::SetupPlayerInputComponent(PlayerInputComponent);
}

void AWarriorCharacter::BeginPlay()
{
  // Note: Call parent's BeginPlay() is required!
  Super::BeginPlay();
}

// Called every frame
void AWarriorCharacter::Tick(float DeltaTime)
{
  Super::Tick(DeltaTime);
}
```

In the above code, the constructor of the parent class, which is the **RPGCharacter**, is called first using the **Super()** method. Then within the three **overridden** methods, their parent's methods are called using the **Super** keyword.

Note: In the overridden **BeginPlay()** method, you have to call the **parent's** BeginPlay() **at the first line**; otherwise, the Unreal Editor may **crash**!

Now, build the project and ensure that no errors occurred during the Compile.

The Female Warrior Blueprint

Back to Unreal Editor, open the **Content Browser**, and in the **Warriors** folder, create a new folder named **Blueprints** to store the blueprints for our warriors.

Next, right-click **in** the **Blueprints** folder, and choose **Blueprint Class** from the context menu to open the **Pick Parent Class** window as shown below:

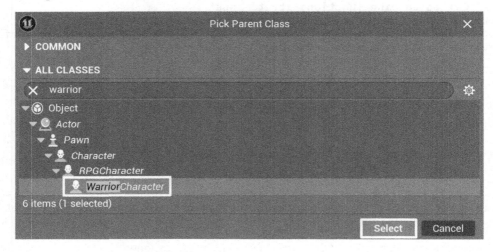

Enter "**warrior**" in the search bar under **ALL CLASSES**, you'll find the **WarriorCharacter** class, created in our C++ project, shows up under the **RPGCharacter** class. Now press the **SELECT** button to create the blueprint in the folder, then rename it as **BP_FemaleWarrior**.

Double-click the **BP_FemaleWarrior** to open it in the editor, in the **Components** panel on the left side of the editor, you'll see the hierarchy of the components, created by the C++ code, as shown below:

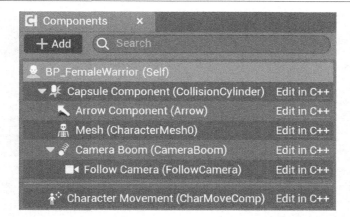

Besides, on the upper-right corner of the blueprint editor window, you'll see its parent class that is the **WarriorCharacter** created in the C++ code as shown below:

Parent class: **Warrior Character**

Now click on the **Mesh** component, its properties will appear in the **Details** panel as shown below:

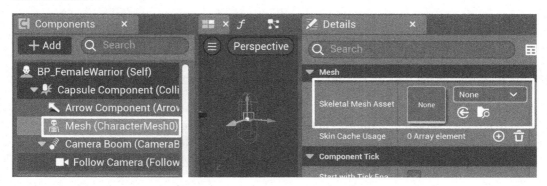

Please scroll down and find the **Mesh** section, click on it to see the further properties of the mesh. Currently, the **Skeletal Mesh** field is **empty** such that **no** character mesh appears in the Viewport.

Then drag the imported **female** character skeletal mesh from the folder onto the **Skeletal Mesh** field as shown below:

Now you can see the skeletal mesh appears in the viewport window, but it's **not** facing the direction of the **Arrow** Component and **not** totally within the **Capsule** Component as well.

To make the character facing the same direction as the arrow is and inside the range of the capsule, in the **Details** panel, click on the **TRANSFORM** tab and enter both **-90** in the **third (Z)** field of the **Location** and **Rotation** respectively as shown below:

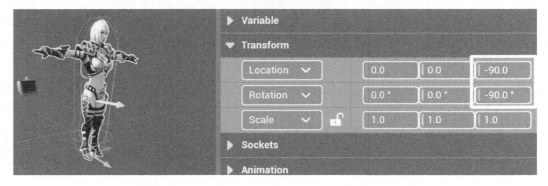

Lastly, press **Save** to confirm all modifications.

5.3.2 Animation Classes and Blueprints

This section will create the C++ **Animation Instance** class and the Blueprint to control the animation playing for our player characters.

Creating the AnimInstance Class in C++

From the main menu, click the Tools > New C++ Class... to open the **Add C++ Class** window. After clicking the **All Classes** tab, enter "**animin**" in the Search bar. You'll see the **AnimInstance** class appears under the **Object** class, select it, and press the **NEXT** button to continue as shown below:

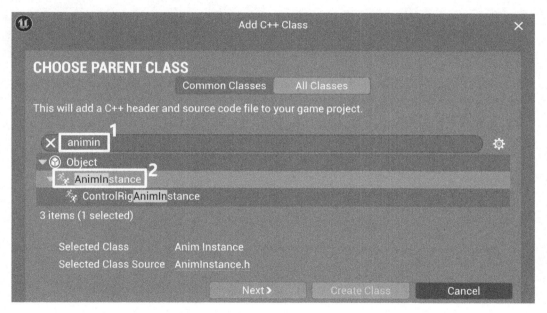

Next, after modifying the class name as **RPGAnimInstance**, add "**Public/Animation**" to the **Path** as shown below. Finally, press **Create Class** button to generate the class in Visual Studio.

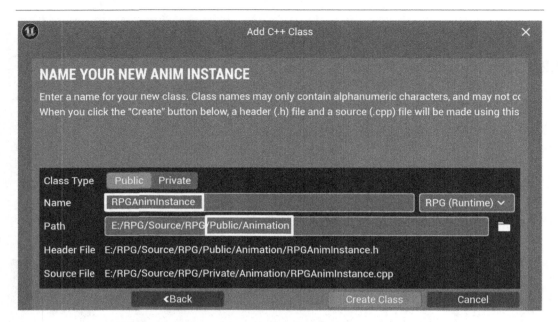

Back to Visual Studio, expand the **Animation** filter and open the **RPGAnimInstance.h** header, add the following **bold** lines in the class:

```
class RPG_API URPGAnimInstance : public UAnimInstance
{
  GENERATED_BODY()

public:
  UPROPERTY(EditAnywhere, BlueprintReadWrite, Category = "Speed")
  float ForwardSpeed;
  UPROPERTY(EditAnywhere, BlueprintReadWrite, Category = "Speed")
  float SideSpeed;
  UPROPERTY(EditAnywhere, BlueprintReadWrite, Category = "Locomotion")
  bool IsFalling;

  virtual void NativeUpdateAnimation(float DeltaSeconds) override;
};
```

Here, we declare two floats to store the **forward** and **side** speeds of the player character and the flag IsFalling represents whether the character is **falling**. We also override the inherited **NativeUpdateAnimation()** method which is called when the animation is **playing**.

Next, open the **RPGAnimInstance.cpp** file and add the following lines:

```
#include "Characters/RPGCharacter.h"
// The following include is required for the GetMovementComponent() method
#include "GameFramework/PawnMovementComponent.h"
```

```
void URPGAnimInstance::NativeUpdateAnimation(float DeltaSeconds)
{
  Super::NativeUpdateAnimation(DeltaSeconds);

  ARPGCharacter* owningActor = Cast<ARPGCharacter>(GetOwningActor());

  if (IsValid(owningActor))
  {
    float Speed = owningActor->GetVelocity().Size();

    ForwardSpeed = owningActor->Direction.Y * Speed;
    SideSpeed = owningActor-> Direction.X * Speed;
    IsFalling = owningActor->GetMovementComponent()->IsFalling();
  }
}
```

In the code above, because we'll use the **RPG character** class, its header has to be included first. Then, in the overridden **NativeUpdateAnimation()** method, after calling the parent's constructor, we get the owning character and **cast** it to the RPG character. After checking its validation, the **speed** of the player character is obtained. Then, we multiply the axis values stored in the **Axis** vector by the speed respectively to get the **forward** and **side** speeds. Finally, the **IsFalling()** method of the player movement component is called to return the status of the character.

Continue to open the **RPGCharacter.h** header, and add the following **bold** lines in the **public** section:

```
class RPG_API ARPGCharacter : public ACharacter
{
  GENERATED_BODY()
public:
  // Sets default values for this character's properties
  ARPGCharacter();

    ...
  UPROPERTY(VisibleAnywhere, BlueprintReadOnly, Category = "Direction")
  FVector2D Direction;

protected:
    ...
};
```

In the above code, we declare a **2D** vector variable, **Direction**, to represent the player's moving direction. Here [**1** 0] means moving to the **right**, [**-1** 0] means moving to the **left**, [0 **1**] means moving **forward**, and [0 **-1**] means moving **backward** respectively, which are all relative to the facing of the camera. Now build the project and ensure that no errors occur.

Animation Blueprints for Player Characters

After the C++ classes are ready, it's time to create the blueprint for our animation instance class. Back to Unreal Editor, in the **Warriors** > **Blueprints** folder, right-click and select **Animation** > **Animation Blueprint** from the context menu to open the **Create Animation Blueprint** window as shown on the right:

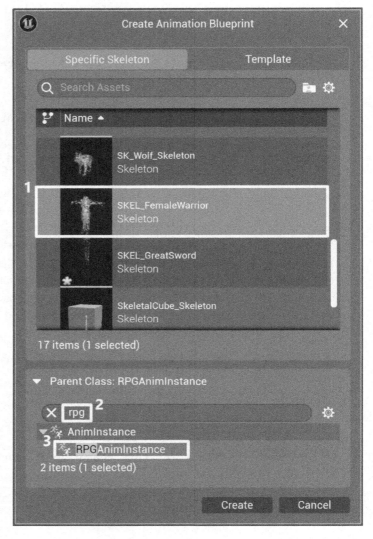

In the **Specific Skeleton** list on the top, find and click the **SKEL_FemaleWarrior** to select it as the target skeleton for our animation instance. Then, after typing "rpg" in the search bar, select the **RPGAnimInstance** class created in C++ in the **Parent Class** panel. Finally, press the **Create** button to generate the blueprint and rename it as **ABP_FemaleWarrior**.

Double-click the **ABP_FemaleWarrior** to open it in the editor, **right-click** within the **AnimGraph** of your Animation Blueprint, find and choose **State Machines** > **State Machine** from the context menu as shown below:

Click the **New State Machine** in the **My Blueprint** panel and type "**Locomotion**" as shown below:

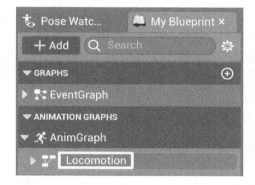

Now, you can **double-click** the **Locomotion** State Machine in the **AnimGraph** to open and create States and Transitions. This will open a new graph tab with nothing but an **Entry** point, which essentially kicks off the animation.

Creating States and Conduits

Next, drag off from the **Entry** node into an **empty** portion of the graph and release the mouse, and the context menu will show up as shown below:

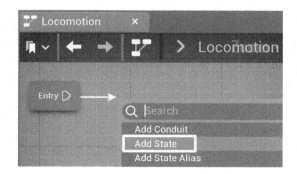

Choose **Add State…** to add a new state and then rename it as **Idle/Run** as shown below:

Next, double-click on the **Idle/Run** state to open it in the editor and find the **BS_FemaleWarrior** under the **Animations** folder. Drag it into the **Idle/Run (state)** panel as shown below:

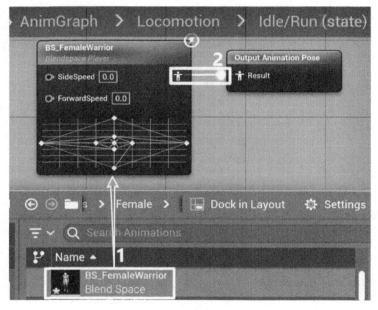

Now, drag off from the **output pin** of the blend space and plug it into the **input** (**Result**) pin of the **Output Animation Pose** node as shown above.

Next, right-click within the Idle/Run panel to open the **All Actions for this Blueprint** window as shown below:

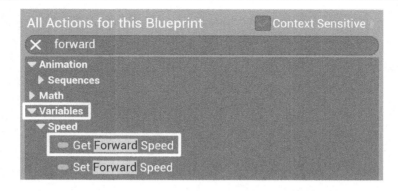

In the search bar, after entering "**forward**", you can find **Get Forward Speed** under the **Speed** category as shown above. Click on it to create a **Forward Speed** node in the panel as shown below:

Then drag off from the **output** pin of the **Forward Speed** node and plug into the **ForwardSpeed** input pin of the blend space to make a transition as shown above.

Right-click in the **Idle/Run** tab again and select the **Get Side Speed** under the **Speed** in the list to create a **Side Speed** node in the panel. Then drag off from the **Side Speed** node and plug into the **SideSpeed** input pin of the blend space as shown below:

Next, after switching to the **Locomotion** tab, drag off from the **Idle/Run** state and add a new state called **FallingIdle** as shown below:

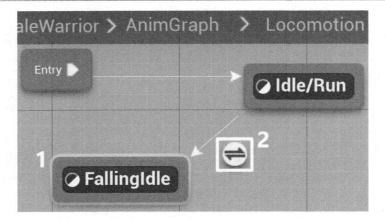

Continue to double-click on the **Transition Rule** icon to open the tab as shown below:

After getting the **IsFalling** variable declared in the C++ code, drag off from the output of the node and plug it into the **Can Enter Transition** pin of the **Result** node, as shown above, which means if the **IsFalling** flag is **true**, the locomotion will be switched to the **FallingIdle** state.

Back to the **Locomotion** tab, drag off from the **FallingIdle** state, and add a new state called **FallingToLanding** as shown below:

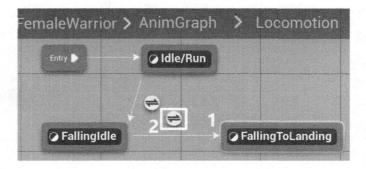

Double-click on the new **Transition Rule** icon to open the tab as shown below:

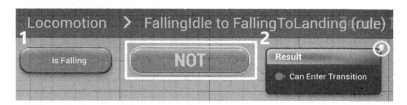

After getting the **IsFalling** variable, drag off from the output of the node and select the **NOT Boolean** under the **Math** > **Boolean** to create a **NOT** node as shown above. Then make a transition from the **NOT** node to the **Result** node, which means if the **IsFalling** flag is **not** true (**false**), the locomotion will be switched to the **FallingToLanding** state.

Back to the Locomotion tab, double-click to open the **FallingToLanding** state as shown below:

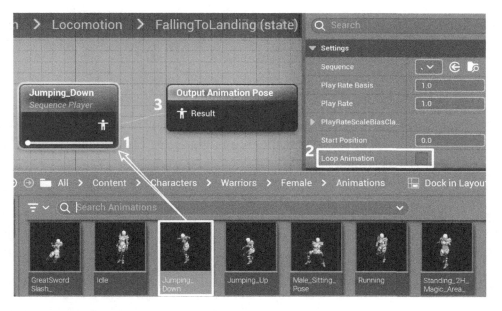

Find the imported **Jumping_Down** animation in the Content Browser, drag and drop it into the panel as shown above, and in the **Details** tab, **untick** the **Loop Animation** checkbox. Then drag off from the **output** pin of the **Jumping_Down** node and plug it into the **Result** pin of the **Output Animation Pose** node.

Back to the **Locomotion** tab, and drag off from the **FallingToLanding** node to make a transition to the **Idle/Run** state as shown below:

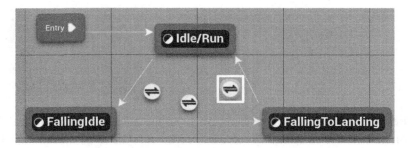

Double-click on the **Transition Rule** icon to open the tab as shown below:

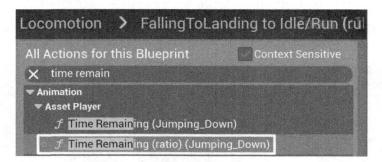

After right-clicking on the panel and entering "**time remain**" in the Search bar, as shown above, select the **Time Remaining (ratio) (Jumping_Down)** function from the context menu to generate the node as shown below:

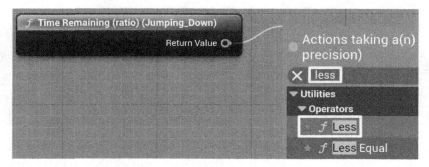

Continue to drag off from the **Return Value** pin of the node, and after typing "less" in the Search bar, as shown above, select the **Less** function from the context menu to generate the node as shown below:

Modify the value of the **Less** node to **0.1** as shown above, which means that when the time remaining **ratio** of the **Jumping Down** animation is less than 0.1, the state will be switched to the **Idle/Run**.

Back to the **Locomotion** tab, double-click the **FallingIdle** state to open the tab as shown below:

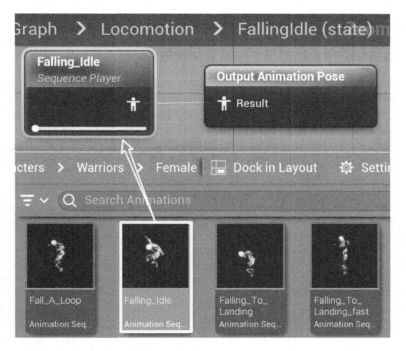

Then drag and drop the **Falling_Idle** animation into the state, as shown above, and make a transition from the **Falling_Idle** node to the **Output Animation Pose** node.

Finally, double-click the **AnimGraph** in the **ANIMATION GRAPHS** panel on the left to open it, then within the tab, drag off from the output of the **Locomotion** node and plug into the **Result** pin of the **Output Pose** as shown below:

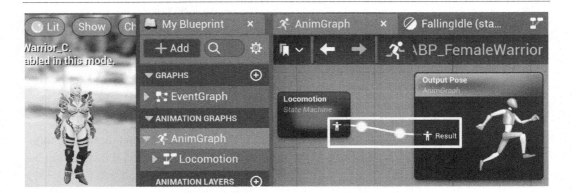

After the transition is established, press **Compile** on the toolbar to compile the blueprint, and you'll find that the **Idle** animation is playing in the **Viewport** on the left. Lastly, press **Save** to save the blueprint.

Associating Animation and Character Blueprints

After the animation blueprint is ready, we have to associate the created animation Blueprint with the Blueprint of our **player character**. Navigate to the **Warriors** > **Blueprints** folder in the **Content Browser** and open the **BP_FemaleWarrior** Blueprint.

After selecting **Mesh** in the **Components** tab, set the **Anim Class** for the **Mesh** to the **ABP_FemaleWarrior** Animation Blueprint just created, then you will see the **Idle** animation is played in the Viewport as shown below:

Finally, do not forget to **Compile** and **Save** the Blueprint before closing it.

Next, we will add input settings for the character using the new **Enhanced Input System** that has been introduced in UE5.

Using the Enhanced Input System for Interaction

For UE5 projects that require more advanced input features, like complex input handling or runtime control remapping, the **Enhanced Input Plugin** provides developers with an upgrade path and backward compatibility from the default input system from UE4. This plugin implements features like radial dead zones, chorded actions, contextual input, and prioritization, as well as the ability to extend your own filtering and processing of raw input data in an **Asset**-based environment. As the Axis and Action mappings are now deprecated, so in this new edition, we will start using the new input system.

The Enhanced Input system has four main concepts:

- ❖ **Input Actions** are the communication link between the Enhanced Input system and your project's code. An Input Action can be anything that an interactive character might do, like jumping or opening a door. It can also be used to indicate user input states, like holding a button that changes a character's walking movement to running. Input Actions are separate from raw input; an Input Action is not concerned with the specific input that triggered it but does know its current state and can report an input value on up to three independent floating-point axes.

As an example, a "pick up item" Action might only need an on/off state, indicating whether or not the user wants the character to pick something up, while a "walk" Action might require two axes to describe the direction and speed at which the user wants the character to walk.

- ❖ **Input Mapping Contexts** map user inputs to Input Actions and can be dynamically added, removed, or prioritized for each user. You can apply one or more of these Contexts to a local player through its Enhanced Input Local Player Subsystem and prioritize them to resolve collisions between multiple Actions trying to consume the same input.

For example, consider a single button that can either open doors while the character is walking around in the world, or select an item while the character is looking through a backpack.

Whenever the character is near a door, you add the "open door" Context. If the character opens the backpack, you add a "select item" Input Mapping Context that out-prioritizes the "open door" Context, so that characters looking through a backpack while standing near a door can still select backpack items. When the character closes the backpack, you remove the "select item" Context, enabling the "open door" Context to take effect.

This ensures that the user's inputs will be interpreted correctly based on the character's situation and prevents the need to program code at the input-handling level with awareness of the door and backpack systems.

❖ **Modifiers** adjust the value of raw input coming from the user's devices. An Input Mapping Context can have any number of modifiers associated with each raw input for an Input Action. Common Modifiers include dead zones, input smoothing over multiple frames, conversion of input vectors from local to world space, along with several others that are included in the plugin. Developers can also create their own Modifiers.

❖ **Triggers** use post-Modifier input values, or the output magnitudes of other Input Actions, to determine whether or not an Input Action should activate. Any Input Action within an Input Mapping Context can have one or more Triggers for each input. For example, taking a photograph might require that the user hold down the Left Mouse Button for a quarter of a second while a separate Input Action for aiming the camera is active.

By combining these concepts, developers can quickly set up input systems ranging from simple to complex and adjust these systems without having to change project code.

Setting up Input Actions

Open your Content Browser and add a folder called **Input** under the **Content**. Inside the folder, create another folder named **Actions**. Right-click and select **Input** > **Input Action** to create an Input Action asset. After renaming it **IA_Move**, create **five** other Input Actions and name them **IA_Look**, **IA_Jump**, **IA_Zoom**, **IA_Sprint**, and **IA_Interact,** respectively.

Firstly, to set up the **IA_Move** action, open it and simply change **Value Type** to **Axis2D (Vector2D)** as shown below:

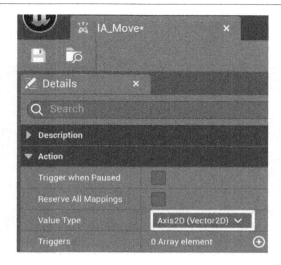

Similar to the setting of the IA_Move, continue to open the **IA_Look** asset, and change **Value Type** to **Axis2D (Vector2D)**.

Next, let's edit the **IA_Jump** action, here we have to activate the **Jump** action by pressing a key (or button). To do so, double-click on the asset to open it and check that **Value Type** has been set to the **default** value of **Digital (bool)** as shown below:

Similar to the setting of the IA_Jump, open the **IA_Sprint** and **IA_Interact** assets respectively, and check that the **Value Type** has been set to **Digit (bool)**.

Continue to open the **IA_Zoom** asset, and set its **Value Type** to **Axis1D(float)** as shown below:

This action will be activated when you scroll the mouse **wheel** and its value, which is a **float**, will be returned and passed to the C++ code.

Now that the basic actions have been defined, it's time to create the Mapping Context and set its properties.

Creating the Input Mapping Context

As described before, **Input Mapping Contexts** map user inputs to Input Actions and can be dynamically added, removed, or prioritized for each user. Through the Mapping Context we will create here, you can define the mappings between the base actions that a character can do and the inputs from various devices.

Right-click on the **Input** folder and select **Input** > **Input Mapping Context**. After naming the newly generated asset **IMC_Warrior**, double-click to open it for editing as shown below:

Click the + button to the right of the **Mappings** as shown above. After selecting the **IA_Move** in the drop-down menu, repeat this step **five** more times to add **IA_Look**, **IA_Jump**, **IA_Zoom**, **IA_Sprint**, and **IA_interact**.

Now that the context has been created, let's set up the player input mappings as follows. First, to set up the **IA_Move** mapping, click the drop down icon to see the setting for the IA_Move as shown below:

As you can see, a **keyboard** mapping named **None** has been created for us and this means that there is no keyboard input for this action. Because we will let the player use the **W/A/S/D** keys on the keyboard to move the character, let's add the mappings one by one as follows:

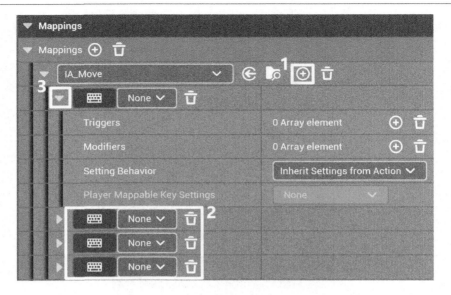

Click the + icon **three** times to create three more mappings, and after expanding the first mapping, click the drop down and select **Keyboard** > **W** key from the menu for the mapping as shown below:

Then after clicking on the + icon to the right of **Modifiers** field to add one modifier, select **Swizzle Input Axis Values** for it. Here the **Swizzle Input Axis Values** means to make the **W** key register as **Y**-Axis instead of the default X-Axis.

In the next step, after selecting **Keyboard** > **S** key for the **second** mapping, press the + icon **twice** to add two modifiers as shown below:

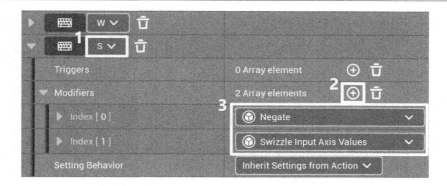

Then select **Negate** and **Swizzle Input Axis Values** for the two modifiers, respectively. Since each key reports a **positive** value of either **0.0** or **1.0** on any given tick. Besides **switching** the axis order, here we also use the **Negate** to make S key (**down** input) register as **negative**.

Continue to select **D** and **A** keys for the **third** and **fourth** mappings respectively as shown below:

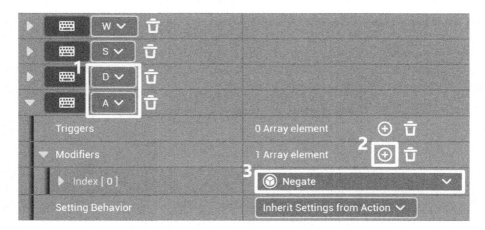

Here the **Negate** is used to make the **A** key (**left** input) register as **negative**.

The **IA_Look** action will be controlled by the mouse movement. So, after selecting **Mouse XY 2D-Axis** for the mapping as shown below, click the + icon on the **Modifiers** field to add a modifier, and then select **Negate** for it.

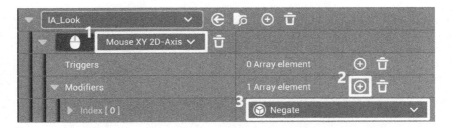

Next, for the player to jump by pressing the space bar, after selecting **Keyboard** > **Space Bar** for the **IA_Jump** as shown below:

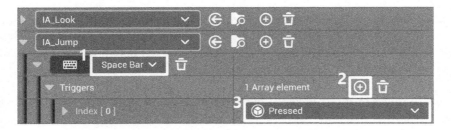

Press the + icon on the **Triggers** field to add a trigger, and then select **Pressed**.

The **IA_Zoom** will let the player use the mouse wheel to control the length of the camera boom to achieve the effect of camera zooming. So, select **Mouse** > **Mouse Wheel Axis** for the mapping as shown below:

The **IA_Sprint** action is similar to the IA_Jump. But the action is **activated** when the **Shift** key is pressed while moving and is **deactivated** after the player **releases** the Shift key. So here we have to use **Triggers** to achieve this purpose as shown below:

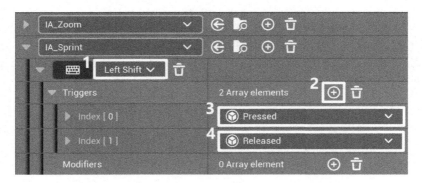

After selecting **Left Shift** for the mapping, click the + icon **twice** to add **two** Triggers. Then select **Pressed** and **Released** for them, respectively.

Lastly, the settings of the **IA_Interact** are as follows:

Here the **E** key is selected for the **interact** button, and after adding a Trigger, select **Pressed** for it.

Adding the Enhanced Input Module

Before using the Enhanced Input System, we have to **import** the module first by adding the module declaration in the **Build.cs** file as follows. Open **RPG.Build.cs** in the **Source > RPG** folder of the C++ project, add the following code in **bold** to add the Enhanced Input module:

```
PublicDependencyModuleNames.AddRange(new string[] { "Core",
          "CoreUObject", "Engine", "InputCore", "EnhancedInput" });
```

Declaring Input Properties and Functions

To use the Enhanced Input System in C++, we need to declare a **pointer** to the **UInputMappingContext** type of the Input Mapping Context, and also declare pointers to the **UInputAction** type of all Input Actions.

Now back to Visual studio, open the **RPGCharacter.h** header, add the following **includes**, which are required for the Enhanced Input System, as shown in **bold**:

```
    ...
#include "EnhancedInputSubsystems.h"
#include "EnhancedInputComponent.h"
#include "InputActionValue.h"
#include "RPGCharacter.generated.h"
```

Next, add the following lines of code in the **Public** section:

```
// A pointer to the Input Mapping Context
UPROPERTY(EditAnywhere, BlueprintReadOnly, Category = "Input")
```

```
class UInputMappingContext* InputMappingContext;
// A pointer for each Input Action
UPROPERTY(EditAnywhere, BlueprintReadOnly, Category = "Input")
class UInputAction* MoveAction;
UPROPERTY(EditAnywhere, BlueprintReadOnly, Category = "Input")
class UInputAction* JumpAction;
UPROPERTY(EditAnywhere, BlueprintReadOnly, Category = "Input")
class UInputAction* ZoomAction;
UPROPERTY(EditAnywhere, BlueprintReadOnly, Category = "Input")
class UInputAction* LookAction;
UPROPERTY(EditAnywhere, BlueprintReadOnly, Category = "Input")
class UInputAction* SprintAction;
UPROPERTY(EditAnywhere, BlueprintReadOnly, Category = "Input")
class UInputAction* InteractAction;
UPROPERTY(EditAnywhere, BlueprintReadOnly, Category = "Input")
class UInputAction* LightAttackAction;
UPROPERTY(EditAnywhere, BlueprintReadOnly, Category = "Input")
class UInputAction* HeavyAttackAction;
UPROPERTY(EditAnywhere, BlueprintReadOnly, Category = "Input")
class UInputAction* DismountAction;
UPROPERTY(EditAnywhere, BlueprintReadOnly, Category = "Input")
class UInputAction* CastFireballAction;
UPROPERTY(EditAnywhere, BlueprintReadOnly, Category = "Zoom")
int ZoomSpeed = 20;
// To be bound to the input actions
void Move(const FInputActionValue& value);
void DoubleJump(const FInputActionValue& value);
void Look(const FInputActionValue& value);
void Zoom(const FInputActionValue& value);
void ShiftKey(const FInputActionValue& value);
void Interact(const FInputActionValue& value);
virtual void LightAttack(const FInputActionValue& value);
virtual void HeavyAttack(const FInputActionValue& value);
virtual void Dismount(const FInputActionValue& value);
virtual void PlayCastFireballMontage(const FInputActionValue& value);
```

In the above code, the **InputMappingContext** is a pointer to the Input Mapping Context. Next, we declare a pointer for each Input Action followed by declaring an integer variable storing the camera zoom speed.

Lastly, the above methods are declared to be bound to their corresponding input actions, and please note that the last **four** methods are also **virtual** functions that will be **overridden** by child classes.

Implementing the Mapping Context

Continue to open **RPGCharacter.cpp** file and add the following block of code:

```
void ARPGCharacter::Move(const FInputActionValue& value)
{
```

```
}

void ARPGCharacter::DoubleJump(const FInputActionValue& value)
{
}

void ARPGCharacter::Look(const FInputActionValue& value)
{
}

void ARPGCharacter::Zoom(const FInputActionValue& value)
{
}

void ARPGCharacter::ShiftKey(const FInputActionValue& value)
{
}

void ARPGCharacter::Interact(const FInputActionValue& value)
{
}

void ARPGCharacter::LightAttack(const FInputActionValue& value)
{
}

void ARPGCharacter::HeavyAttack(const FInputActionValue& value)
{
}

void ARPGCharacter::Dismount(const FInputActionValue& value)
{
}

void ARPGCharacter::PlayCastFireballMontage(const FInputActionValue&
                                                             value)
{
}
```

The above binding functions will be implemented after we finish the following camera and character controller code.

Then, in the BeginPlay() method, add the following **bold** lines:

```
void ARPGCharacter::BeginPlay()
{
  Super::BeginPlay();

    // Get the player controller
    if (APlayerController* controller =
                        Cast<APlayerController>(GetController()))
    {
```

```
    // Get the local player subsystem
    if (UEnhancedInputLocalPlayerSubsystem* subSystem =
      ULocalPlayer::GetSubsystem<UEnhancedInputLocalPlayerSubsystem>(
                                        controller->GetLocalPlayer()))
    {
      // Clear out existing mapping and add the control mapping context
      subSystem->ClearAllMappings();
      subSystem->AddMappingContext(InputMappingContext, 0);
    }
  }
}
```

In the above code block, firstly we try getting the **PlayerController** and then use it to get the local player subsystem. Finally, we call the `ClearAllMappings()` method, followed by the `AddMappingContext()` to clear out existing mapping and add the input mapping context.

In the final step, we will bind the input actions to their corresponding binding functions declared before in the `SetupPlayerInputComponent()` method. So please look for the method and add the **bold** lines:

```
// Called to bind functionality to input
void ARPGCharacter::SetupPlayerInputComponent(UInputComponent*
PlayerInputComponent)
{
  Super::SetupPlayerInputComponent(PlayerInputComponent);

  // Get the Enhanced Input Component
  if (UEnhancedInputComponent* enhancedInputComponent =
            CastChecked<UEnhancedInputComponent>(PlayerInputComponent))
  {
    // Bind the actions
    enhancedInputComponent->BindAction(MoveAction,
          ETriggerEvent::Triggered, this, &ARPGCharacter::Move);
    enhancedInputComponent->BindAction(LookAction,
          ETriggerEvent::Triggered, this, &ARPGCharacter::Look);
    enhancedInputComponent->BindAction(JumpAction,
          ETriggerEvent::Triggered, this, &ARPGCharacter::DoubleJump);
    enhancedInputComponent->BindAction(ZoomAction,
          ETriggerEvent::Triggered, this, &ARPGCharacter::Zoom);
    enhancedInputComponent->BindAction(SprintAction,
          ETriggerEvent::Triggered, this, &ARPGCharacter::ShiftKey);
    enhancedInputComponent->BindAction(InteractAction,
          ETriggerEvent::Triggered, this, &ARPGCharacter::Interact);
    enhancedInputComponent->BindAction(LightAttackAction,
          ETriggerEvent::Triggered, this, &ARPGCharacter::LightAttack);
    enhancedInputComponent->BindAction(HeavyAttackAction,
          ETriggerEvent::Triggered, this, &ARPGCharacter::HeavyAttack);
    enhancedInputComponent->BindAction(DismountAction,
          ETriggerEvent::Triggered, this, &ARPGCharacter::Dismount);
    enhancedInputComponent->BindAction(CastFireballAction,
```

```
            ETriggerEvent::Triggered, this,
                    &ARPGCharacter::PlayCastFireballMontage);
    }
}
```

Here, after getting the enhanced input component, the **BindAction()** method of the input component is called to bind each input action to its corresponding method. Now build the project and ensure there are no unexpected errors that pop up.

Updating the Character Blueprint

So far, the C++ code is ready, and it is time to assign the input actions and mapping context to our properties. Back to Unread Editor, and open the **BP_FemaleWarrior** as shown below:

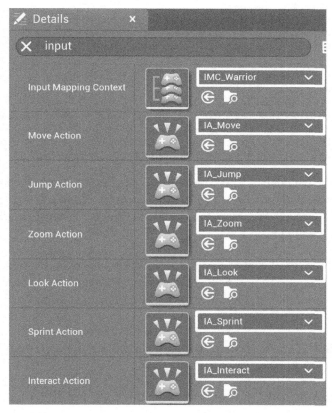

After entering "**input**" in the search bar, you will see the Input Mapping Context property along with the **five** input actions declared in the C++ code. Then press the drop-down button for the **Input Mapping Context** and select the **IMC_Warrior** asset.

Finally, select the corresponding input action asset, as shown above, for each input action property.

5.3.3 The ARPG Third-Person Camera Controller

This subsection discusses how to make a third person ARPG **camera controller**, by which the player can control the camera to **orbit** and look around to see the player character in 360 degrees.

Back to Visual Studio, open the **RPGCharacter.h** header, and in the **public** section of the class, add the following lines:

```
UPROPERTY(EditDefaultsOnly, BlueprintReadWrite, Category = "MouseLook")
float MaxMousePitch = 80.0f;
UPROPERTY(EditDefaultsOnly, BlueprintReadWrite, Category = "MouseZoom")
float MinTargetArmLength = 100.0f;
UPROPERTY(EditDefaultsOnly, BlueprintReadWrite, Category = "MouseZoom")
float MaxTargetArmLength = 800.0f;

// Control the zooming of the camera
void MouseZoom(float val);
// Add input (affecting Yaw) to the Controller's ControlRotation
virtual void AddControllerYawInput(float Val) override;
// Add input (affecting Pitch) to the Controller's ControlRotation
virtual void AddControllerPitchInput(float Val) override;
```

In the above code, we declare three properties where `MaxMousePitch` represents the **maximum degrees** that the player can **pitch** around his character. `MinTargetArmLength` and `MaxTargetArmLength` represent the **minimum** and **maximum** lengths of the camera boom arm to the character.

The `MouseZoom()` method is used to control the **zooming** of the camera. The `AddControllerYawInput()` and `AddControllerPitchInput()`, both are **overridden** methods, are to add inputs (affecting **Yaw** and **Pitch**) to the controller's **ControlRotation**, respectively.

Next, open the **RPGCharacter.cpp** file, and add the following lines to implement the three new methods:

```
void ARPGCharacter::AddControllerYawInput(float Val)
{
  if (Val != 0) {
    // Update the camera boom's current Yaw rotation by adding the input
    // Yaw value
    CameraBoom->AddRelativeRotation(FRotator(0, Val, 0));
  }
```

```
}

void ARPGCharacter::AddControllerPitchInput(float Val)
{
  Super::AddControllerPitchInput(Val);
  // Get the new Pitch rotation by adding the input Pitch value
  float pitch = CameraBoom->GetRelativeRotation().Pitch + Val;
  // Clamp the Pitch to an appropriate value
  pitch = FMath::Clamp(pitch, -MaxMousePitch, MaxMousePitch);
  // Update the camera boom's rotation by the new Pitch and its current
  // Yaw value
  FRotator rotation = FRotator(pitch, CameraBoom->
                                    GetRelativeRotation().Yaw, 0);
  CameraBoom->SetRelativeRotation(rotation);
}

void ARPGCharacter::MouseZoom(float val)
{
  // Get the new arm length by adding the input value
  float armLength = CameraBoom->TargetArmLength + val;
  // Update the camera boom's arm length by the clamped arm length
  CameraBoom->TargetArmLength = FMath::Clamp(armLength,
                            MinTargetArmLength, MaxTargetArmLength);
}
```

In the `AddControllerYawInput()` method, we update the camera boom's current **Yaw** rotation by adding the input `Yaw` value when the player moves the mouse. Within the `AddControllerPitchInput()` method, the new **Pitch** rotation is obtained by adding the input `Pitch` value, then after the value is **clamped** to an appropriate value, we update the camera boom's **rotation** by a **Rotator** using the new Pitch and its **current Yaw** value.

In the `MouseZoom()` method, after obtaining the new arm length by adding the input value, we update the camera boom's arm length by the **clamped** arm length.

Finally, add the following **bold** lines in the **Zoom()** and **Look()** binding methods as follows:

```
void ARPGCharacter::Look(const FInputActionValue& value)
{
  // Get the input action value
  const FVector2D lookAxisValue = value.Get<FVector2D>();
  // Call the methods and pass in the mouse axis values
  AddControllerYawInput(lookAxisValue.X);
  AddControllerPitchInput(lookAxisValue.Y);
}

void ARPGCharacter::Zoom(const FInputActionValue& value)
{
  // Get the input action value
  const float zoomValue = value.Get<float>();
```

```
  // Call the MouseZoom() and pass in the scaled value
  MouseZoom(zoomValue * ZoomSpeed);
}
```

In the `Look()` method, after getting the input action value which is a 2D Vector from the passed in **value** parameter, the mouse **X** and **Y** axis values are passed into the `AddControllerYawInput()` and `AddControllerPitchInput()` methods respectively to control the **Yaw** and **Pitch** of the camera.

In the `Zoom()` method, we call the `MouseZoom()` method, and pass in the scaled **float** value, to control the length of the camera boom.

Moving the Player Character

To move the player character in C++, open the **RPGCharacter.h** header again, and add the following lines in the **public** section:

```
UPROPERTY(EditDefaultsOnly, Category = "Speed")
float WalkSpeed = 300.0f;
UPROPERTY(EditDefaultsOnly, Category = "Speed")
float RunSpeed = 1200.0f;
// Functions to bind to movement axes
void MoveForward(float axis);
void MoveBackward(float axis);
void MoveRight(float axis);
void MoveLeft(float axis);
// Set movement speed
void Walk();
void Sprint();
```

First, the `WalkSpeed` and `RunSpeed` represent the **walk** and **run** speeds respectively. Then the `MoveForward()` and `MoveBackward()` functions are bound to the **forwards/backward** input; the `MoveRight()` and `MoveLeft()` functions are bound to the **right/left** side input, respectively. Lastly, the `Walk()` and `Sprint()` functions are to set the **maximum** walking speed.

Next, open the **RPGCharacter.cpp** file, and add the following lines to implement the new methods:

```
void ARPGCharacter::MoveForward(float axis)
{
  if (axis > 0) {
    // Obtain the current Yaw rotation of the camera boom
    float controllerYaw = CameraBoom->GetRelativeRotation().Yaw;
    // Rotate the player character toward the camera's facing direction
    GetWorld()->GetFirstPlayerController()->SetControlRotation(
                                      FRotator(0, controllerYaw, 0));
    // Move the character in the Forward direction
```

```cpp
    AddMovementInput(GetActorForwardVector(), axis);
    // Here [0 1] means moving forward
    Direction.X = 0;
    Direction.Y = axis;   // axis = 1
  }
}

void ARPGCharacter::MoveBackward(float axis)
{
  if (axis < 0) {
    // Obtain the Yaw rotation to the backward of the camera by adding
    // 180 degrees to the current Yaw rotation of the camera boom
    float controllerYaw = CameraBoom->GetRelativeRotation().Yaw + 180.0f;
    GetWorld()->GetFirstPlayerController()->SetControlRotation(
                                        FRotator(0, controllerYaw, 0));
    AddMovementInput(GetActorForwardVector(), -axis);
    // Here [0 -1] means moving backward
    Direction.X = 0;
    Direction.Y = axis; // axis = -1
  }
}

void ARPGCharacter::MoveRight(float axis)
{
  if (axis > 0) {
    // Obtain the Yaw rotation to the right of the camera by adding 90
    // degrees to the current Yaw rotation of the camera boom
    float controllerYaw = CameraBoom->GetRelativeRotation().Yaw + 90.0f;
    // Rotate the player character to face the Right side of the camera
    GetWorld()->GetFirstPlayerController()->SetControlRotation(
                                        FRotator(0, controllerYaw, 0));
    AddMovementInput(GetActorForwardVector(), axis);
    // Here [1 0] means moving to the right
    Direction.X = axis;
    Direction.Y = 0;
  }
}

void ARPGCharacter::MoveLeft(float axis)
{
  if (axis < 0) {
    // Obtain the Yaw rotation to the left of the camera by subtracting
    // 90 degrees to the current Yaw rotation of the camera boom
    float controllerYaw = CameraBoom->GetRelativeRotation().Yaw - 90.0f;
    // Rotate the player character to face the Left side of the camera
    GetWorld()->GetFirstPlayerController()->SetControlRotation(
                                        FRotator(0, controllerYaw, 0));
    // Move forward in the facing direction
    AddMovementInput(GetActorForwardVector(), -axis);
    // Here [-1 0] means moving to the left
    Direction.X = axis;
    Direction.Y = 0;
```

```
  }
}
void ARPGCharacter::Walk()
{
  // Set the maximum ground speed when walking
  GetCharacterMovement()->MaxWalkSpeed = WalkSpeed;
}

void ARPGCharacter::Sprint()
{
  GetCharacterMovement()->MaxWalkSpeed = RunSpeed;
}
```

In the `MoveForward()` method, if the `axis` value is **greater** than **0**, meaning that moving **forward**. Then, after obtaining the current **Yaw** rotation of the **camera boom**, we call the **SetControlRotation()** of the **PlayerController** and pass in the new rotation to rotate the player character toward the **camera's facing** direction. Lastly, move the character **forward** by calling the inherited `AddMovementInput()` method to add movement in that direction and store the incoming `axis` value to the `Direction` 2D vector.

Similarly, within the `MoveBackward()` method, if the `axis` value is **less** than **0**, meaning that moving **backward**. Then, after obtaining the **Yaw** rotation to the **backward** of the camera by **adding 180 degrees** to the current **Yaw** rotation of the camera boom, we rotate the player character to face the **backward** of the **camera**, then move the character in its new **Forward** direction and store the incoming `axis` value. The following figure illustrates the situation:

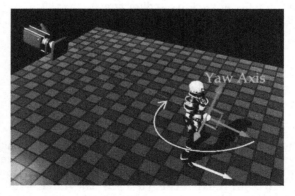

In the `MoveRight()` method, if the `axis` value is **greater** than **0**, after obtaining the Yaw rotation to the **right** of the camera by **adding 90** degrees to the current Yaw rotation of the camera boom, we rotate the player character to face the **right** side of the camera, then move the character forward at its new facing direction and store the incoming `axis` value. The following figure illustrates the situation:

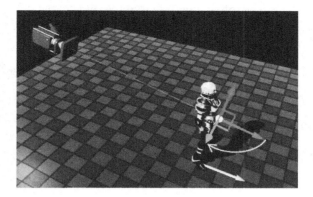

Similarly, within the `MoveLeft()` method, if the `axis` value is **less** than **0**, after obtaining the Yaw rotation to the **left** of the camera by **subtracting 90** degrees to the current Yaw rotation of the camera boom, we rotate the player character to face the **left** side of the camera, then move the character forward at its new facing direction and store the incoming `axis` value.

Finally, in the `Walk()` and `Sprint()` methods, we assign the `WalkSpeed` and `RunSpeed` to the **MaxWalkSpeed** of the `CharacterMovementComponent`, respectively.

Next, add the following **bold** lines in the **Move()** binding function:

```
void ARPGCharacter::Move(const FInputActionValue& value)
{
  // Get the Vector2D value
  const FVector2D moveValue = value.Get<FVector2D>();
  // Forward/Backward direction
  if (moveValue.Y > 0)
    MoveForward(moveValue.Y);
  else if (moveValue.Y < 0)
    MoveBackward(moveValue.Y);
  // Right/Left direction
  if (moveValue.X > 0)
    MoveRight(moveValue.X);
  else if (moveValue.X < 0)
    MoveLeft(moveValue.X);
}
```

In the above code, after getting the Vector2D value, because the **X** and **Y** values of the vector represent the movement direction respectively, here if the Y value is **greater than** 0 that means moving in the **Forward** direction, we call the **MoveForward()** method to move the character forward. Otherwise, we call the **MoveBackward()** method to move the character backward.

Similarly, we call the **MoveRight()** method to move the character to the right if the **X** value is greater than 0. Otherwise, the **MoveLeft()** method is called to move the character to the left.

Continue to add the following **bold** lines in the **ShiftKey()** binding function:

```
void ARPGCharacter::ShiftKey(const FInputActionValue& value)
{
  const bool shiftKeyPressed = value.Get<bool>();

  if (shiftKeyPressed)
    Sprint();
  else
    Walk();
}
```

After getting the passed in **bool** value, which represents whether the player **pressed** the **Shift** key, if the key was pressed, we call the Sprint() method to change the maximum ground speed; otherwise, the Walk() method is called.

Finally, after adding the following **bold** line in the **BeginPlay()** method to set the initial walking speed:

```
void ARPGCharacter::BeginPlay()
{
  Super::BeginPlay();

  GetCharacterMovement()->MaxWalkSpeed = WalkSpeed;
  ...
}
```

Add the following **include** at the **beginning** of the file:

```
#include "GameFramework/CharacterMovementComponent.h"
```

Now build the project and back to Unreal Editor.

Finishing up Character Blueprint Settings

Before testing the game, some properties have to be set. Open the **BP_FemaleWarrior** Blueprint in the editor, with the **Camera Boom** component selected, **untick** the **Inherit Yaw** field under the **Camera Settings** as shown below:

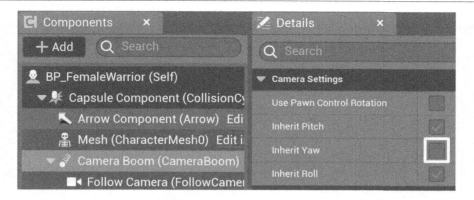

That's because we'll control the Camera Boom by C++ code instead of using the inherited Yaw values. Next, with the **BP_FemaleWarrior** selected, **untick** the **Use Controller Rotation Pitch** as shown below, because the **Rotation Pitch** will not be used.

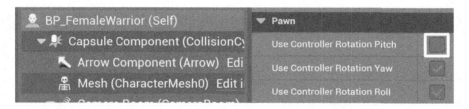

Finally, press **Compile** and **Save** to confirm the modification.

5.3.4 Maps and GameMode

Before testing our character controller, we have to spawn the Warrior character in the level, and this can be done by setting the **GameMode** in the **Project Settings**. The Game Mode defines the game's set of rules, which include what default pawn the player will spawn when the game is launched.

Creating the RPGGameMode class

Select **Tools** > **New C++ Class...** from the main menu, find and choose the **Game Mode Base** class in the window as shown below:

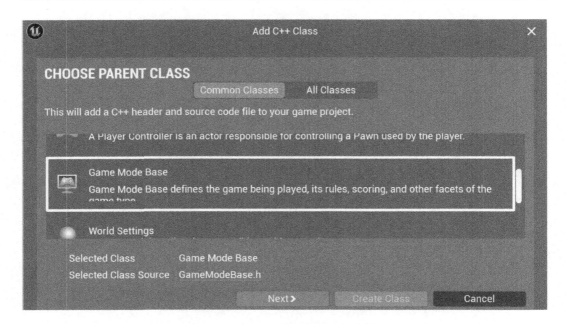

After pressing **Next**, rename the class as **RPGGameModeBase**, and add "**Public**" to the **Path** as shown below:

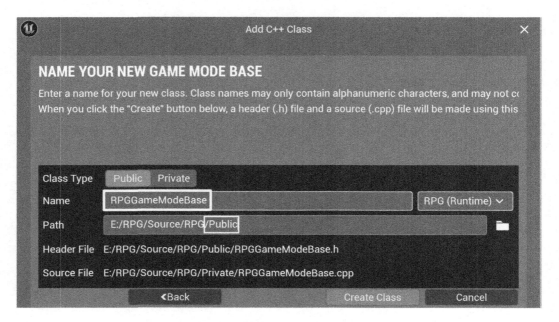

Lastly, after pressing **Create Class** to create the class in the C++ project, build the solution.

Note: On older UE5 versions, after the C++ project is created, the **RPGGameModeBase** class will be generated for us automatically. So, if you are using older versions than UE**5.3**, please check if the class was already created for you!

Creating the GameMode Blueprint

To set up the GameMode, we have to create a **GameMode Blueprint** first from the **RPGGameModeBase** class.

Create a folder called **RPG** under the **Content** folder in the **Content Browser**, then right-click in the folder and choose **Blueprint Class** from the context menu. In the next step, select the **RPGGameModeBase** class as shown below to create a new Blueprint named **BP_RPGGameMode** in the folder.

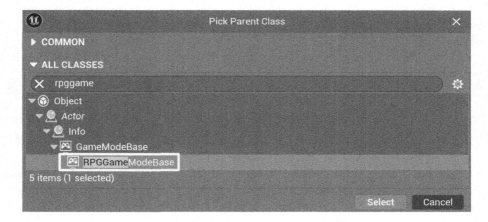

Maps and GameMode Setup

Next, we have to assign the above **GameMode Blueprint** in the project settings. From the main menu, choose **Edit** > **Project Settings...** to open the **Project Settings** window as shown below:

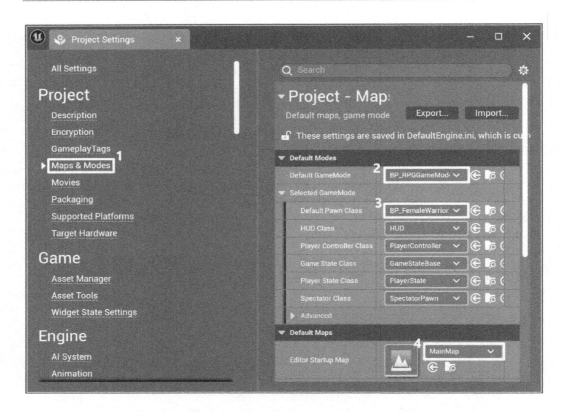

In the **left** panel, click **Maps & Modes**, and its settings will show up in the **right** panel as shown above. Click the drop-down menu and choose the **BP_RPGGameMode** as the **Default GameMode**, then you'll see the settings, under the **Selected GameMode** section, which are allowed to be modified now.

Finally, click the drop-down menu on the right, and choose **BP_FemaleWarrior** Blueprint as the **Default Pawn Class** as shown above. Also, select the **MainMap** as the **Editor Startup Map**. Now close the window and the settings will automatically apply for our project.

Creating Player Starts

To spawn the player character in a specific location on the terrain, Unreal Editor provides the **Player Start** class for us to spawn a player when the game begins. Open the **Place Actors** window and drag and drop a **Player Start** from the **BASIC** panel onto the terrain as shown below:

The Player Start will be automatically put right **above** the landscape as shown above. Now press the **Play** button to run the game in the editor, you'll see the female warrior character is created and placed on the **Player Start** location.

After moving the mouse, you can **look around** the character and when scrolling the mouse wheel, you can **zoom** in/out the camera by increasing or decreasing the arm length of the camera boom. Click the movement keys (W/A/S/D) with the **Left Shift** key pressed, you can make the character **sprint** according to the direction the **camera** is facing. The results are shown in the following figures:

5.3.5 Double and Multiple Jump

A **Double Jump**[7] is a jumping move performed in mid-air, which was introduced in **Unreal Tournament 2003** (UT2003). It can be performed at the apex of the movement parabola to increase the total jump height.

We'll implement the double and multiple jumps in this section. Open the **RPGCharacter.h** header and add the following **bold** lines in the class:

```
UCLASS()
class RPG_API ARPGCharacter : public ACharacter
{
  GENERATED_BODY()

public:
  // Sets default values for this character's properties
  ARPGCharacter();

  UPROPERTY(EditDefaultsOnly, Category = "Jump")
  int MaxJumpCount = 2;
  int jumpCount = 0;
  // Override the built-in Landed() method
  void Landed(const FHitResult& Hit) override;
    ...
}
```

The `MaxJumpCount` property represents the maximum number of the allowed jumps, and the `jumpCount` variable stores the current number of the jumps.

The `Landed()` function is an **overridden** method that will be called after the player character is landing on the ground.

---

[7] **Double Jump,** https://unreal.fandom.com/wiki/Jumping.

Then open the **RPGCharacter.cpp** file and look for the **DoubleJump()** binding function. Add the following **bold** lines:

```
void ARPGCharacter::DoubleJump(const FInputActionValue& value)
{
  // Increase the jump count
  jumpCount++;

  if (jumpCount <= MaxJumpCount) {
    // Get the JumpZVelocity from the CharacterMovement component and make
    // a velocity vector
    FVector velocity = FVector(0, 0,
                                GetCharacterMovement()->JumpZVelocity);
    // Set a velocity in the Z axis whenever the Jump key is pressed
    LaunchCharacter(velocity, false, true);
  }
}
```

In the `DoubleJump()` method, after increasing the jump count, if it's less than or equal to the maximum allowed jumps, then the **JumpZVelocity** of the **CharacterMovementComponent** is obtained first and it's used to make a `velocity` vector. Next, we call the built-in **LaunchCharacter()** method to set a pending launch velocity on the Character on the **Z** axis. This velocity will be processed on the next CharacterMovementComponent tick and will set it to the "**falling**" state. Also note that here the **third** parameter is set to `true`, which means to replace the **Z** component of the character's velocity instead of adding to it.

Finally, add the following lines to re-implement the **Landed()** method:

```
void ARPGCharacter::Landed(const FHitResult& Hit)
{
  jumpCount = 0; // Reset the jump count
}
```

In the **overridden** `Landed()` method, after the character is landing on the ground, we reset the `jumpCount` to 0.

Now build the project and back to Unreal Editor. Open the **BP_FemaleWarrior** Blueprint and find the **Jump** settings as shown below:

For testing purposes, set the **Max Jump Count** to **3** as shown above, and press **Save** to confirm the modification.

So far the code and settings are complete, press Play to run the game. After pressing the **Space Bar** three times in a row, the result is shown below:

You can see the character now can jump remarkably high and the animation is played according to the state of the player.

5.4 Stats in RPGs

Before we dive into the programming of the combat system, let's discuss an important topic about developing any RPG that is the **Stats**. The content of this section is a summary of the excellent web article archives: **How to Make an RPG: Stats.**[8]

5.4.1 What Is a Stat?

A **statistic**, or **stat**, is a number describing an aspect of a game entity. A game entity might be a monster, character, weapon, or spell. Stats define game entities in the world. In RPGs, the player character's stats can be increased to benefit the player.

If you attack a monster the computer needs a way to decide if you hit it and if you do, how much damage you inflict, and finally, it needs to check if the blow killed the creature. To make these decisions the computer runs simulation code using the stats.

Let's take a look at example stats for an Action RPG character:

---

[8] **How to Make an RPG: Stats,** http://howtomakeanrpg.com/a/how-to-make-an-rpg-stats.html.

❖ **Health Points or HP** - represents the amount of damage a character can take before dying or being knocked out.

❖ **Magic Points or MP** - represents the amount of magical power a character has. The higher the power, the more spells can be cast.

❖ **Strength** - represents the character's physical strength. Determines the number of damage attacks inflict.

❖ **Stamina** - represents the amount of energy a character has. It's used as a way to limit the ability of players to do repeated actions such as the Sprint.

❖ **Speed** - represents how fast the character moves. Determines the frequency of attacks and the chance to dodge incoming attacks.

❖ **Intelligence** - represents how clever the character is. Determines the power of spells and the ability to resist magic attacks.

If you play ARPGs you'll already be familiar with these stats, they're quite common, but the exact effect of each stat varies according to the game. **Stats are a description the computer can understand,** Stats describe aspects of game entities that are important for a combat simulation.

We've listed the stats a character might have but characters aren't the only game entities involved in combat - what about weapons, armor, and spells? These are all important in combat and are described using stats.

❖ **Attack type** - is it a physical attack? magical? elemental? or a combination!

❖ **Attack power** - how much damage can this weapon inflict?

❖ **Defense power** - how much damage can this weapon block?

❖ **Attack rate** - how quickly can the weapon be used to attack? Is it a small knife or a giant two-handed hammer?

These stats describe a sword but it's worth thinking about other entities as well. What stats might a spell have, a piece of armor, a magic ring? Try coming up with a few examples and think about what information that computer is going to need.

Notice how similar the sword stats are to the character stats. Attack power is similar to character strength; they both determine the amount of damage inflicted. The attack rate is similar to speed they both determine how often an attack can take place. Stats that seem to have a similar effect combined in the combat simulation, according to a formula, to get a single, final number, we'll call a **derived stat**.

Derived Stats

All the stats we've looked at so far are called base stats. Base stats represent one pure aspect of an entity, they can't be broken down into smaller parts. Derived stats, on the other hand, are built up from multiple smaller parts. Derived stats are calculated from several base stats to form a new number that represents them both. This calculation might be as simple as adding them, or it may be more complicated.

Base stats are rarely used in combat simulation directly, instead, they're often transformed into derived stats that make the calculations easier. When simulating combat, we might want to know the **total attack power** of a character, this would be a **derived** stat. The calculation might look like this:

total_attack_power = char.strength + weapon.power

The final attack power is derived from the weapon's power and the character's strength. In this case, the calculation is simple and intuitive but in a finished game, it's likely to be more complicated.

5.4.2 Why Have Stats at All?

Reality is made from nothing but atoms and space, there are no stats, a cheetah does not have some intrinsic speed stat to compare with a human, both are just billions of atoms combined in different ways.

Computer games need a higher level of abstraction to make things simpler. Stats are part of that abstraction. How do we decide who wins in a battle between a dragon and a giant squid? We plug the stats into a simulation, and we find out!

Stats without the simulation aren't especially useful. The stats and simulation together help us answer questions important for an RPG, such as:

- ❖ How well does the magic potion heal my character?
- ❖ How much damage does my ax strike do to this troll?
- ❖ Will this Dragon's fireball kill my character?
- ❖ Do I have enough magical energy to teleport my party?

Gameplay has to be the designer's most important consideration when coming up with a simulation. In ARPGs the most important simulation is the combat, stats exist to make combat interesting and enjoyable.

What Stats Should a Game Have?

Games differ wildly depending on how many stats they have. An RPG doesn't need a lot of stats to be good but nearly all RPGs will have some stats. When deciding on the number of stats the most important question to ask is: "**Is each stat important in the** game?" If it is, that's fine, add the stat. But don't have a stat for swimming if your game doesn't have any water!

The greater the number of stats, the greater the number of inputs into the combat simulation. Too few stats and the combat might be **dull** and **predictable**, too many and it may be difficult for a player to understand how the stats influence it.

As a rough guide, for base stats, I wouldn't go higher than 10. For base weapons and armor, I'd try to keep it no more than 5. The combat system presented in this book keeps the number of stats minimal, so the combat simulation is clear and easy to understand.

Secret Stats

Hiding stats from players is a good idea if showing them doesn't add much to the game. In Zelda there's no real choice about weapons and armor, it's a linear progression, you find sword 1 then sword 2, and then sword 3, and each is better than the last. You don't need to know the weapon on stats. In more traditional RPGs there are multiple weapons to choose from and they have different stats, with different trade-offs, making for an interesting choice. Luck stats that affect loot, dodging, and critical hits are a favorite to keep as a hidden stat.

5.4.3 Implementing Stats

Now that we have a definition of what a stat is, in this subsection, we'll start on the implementation. To begin with, let's first make a **CharacterStats** class for our characters.

Creating the CharacterStats Class

From the main menu, choose **Tools** > **New C++ Class...**, and in the **Add C++ Class** window, after pressing the **All Classes** tab, select the **Object** as the **Parent** class as shown below:

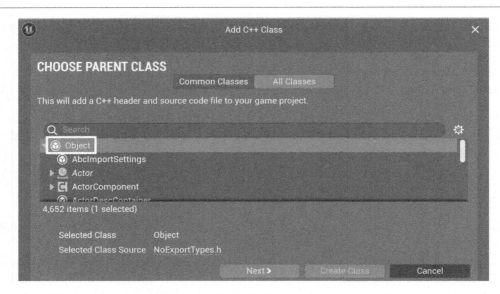

Press the **NEXT** button, and in the next step, rename the class to **CharacterStats** and then add "**Public/Stats**" to the **Path** as shown below:

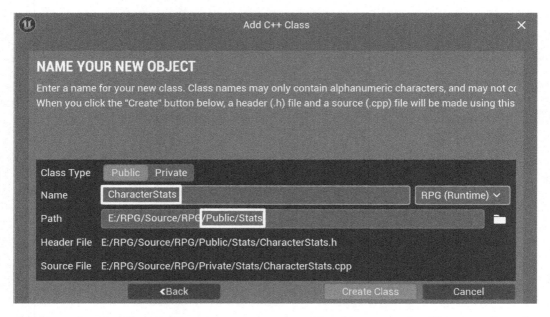

After pressing the **Create Class** button to generate the class, open the **CharacterStats.h** header in Visual Studio, and add the following code in **bold**:

```
UCLASS(Blueprintable, DefaultToInstanced, EditInlineNew)
class RPG_API UCharacterStats : public UObject
{
```

```
  GENERATED_BODY()
public:
  UCharacterStats();

  // Base stats: MaxHP, MaxMp, Strength, Speed, Intelligence
  UPROPERTY(EditDefaultsOnly, BlueprintReadOnly, Category = "BaseStats")
  TMap<FString, int> BaseStats;

  void SetStatValue(FString name, int value);
};
```

In the `UCLASS()` declaration, we add the **Blueprintable specifier** to expose this class as an acceptable base class for creating Blueprints. The **DefaultToInstanced** keyword means all instances of this class are considered "**instanced**". The **EditInlineNew** specifier indicates that Objects of this class can be created from the Unreal Editor **Property** window, as opposed to being referenced from an existing Asset.

Then a `public` section is added, in which we declare a default constructor. At the simplest level, a stat is a **name** associated with a **number** and the **TMap** is a good data structure to describe an entity using several stats. So, the `BaseStats` property of the `TMap` type is used to store the base stats which can be accessed by its **name** string as the **key**. The `SetStatValue()` method is used to set the value of a base stat in the `BaseStats` property.

Next, open the **CharacterStats.cpp** file again and add the following lines to implement the constructor and method:

```
UCharacterStats::UCharacterStats()
{
}

void UCharacterStats::SetStatValue(FString name, int value)
{
  BaseStats.Emplace(name, value);
}
```

Within the `SetStatValue()` method, we call the `Emplace()` method of the `TMap` to replace the **value** of the **Stat** in the property using the Stat's **name** as the key.

Now build the project and make sure that no errors occur.

Modifiers

RPGs are complicated and **base stats** are commonly **modified**. Here are some examples of modifiers:

❖ A magic sword that +5 to the player's strength.
❖ A ring that adds 5% to the maximum hp.

❖ A curse that reduces strength, speed, and intelligence by 5.
❖ The character becomes enraged doubling his strength and halving his intelligence.

Without careful planning, these types of modifications can quickly give rise to a heap of special cases and spaghetti codes. We need a general way to deal with modifying player stats. In general, there are **two** types of modifiers, modifiers of **addition** and modifiers of **multiplication**. So, let's create a C++ class to represent the Stats modifier.

Creating the StatsModifier Class

Back to Unreal Editor, and from the main menu, choose **Tools** > **New C++ Class...** to create another class named **StatsModifier** and choose **Object** as the parent class in the **Public/Stats** folder. Open the **StatsModifier.h** header and add the following code shown in **bold**:

```
UENUM()
enum EModifierTypes
{
  Add          UMETA(DisplayName = "Add"),
  Multi        UMETA(DisplayName = "Multi")
};

UCLASS(Blueprintable, DefaultToInstanced, EditInlineNew)
class RPG_API UStatsModifier : public UObject
{
  GENERATED_BODY()
public:
  UPROPERTY(EditDefaultsOnly, BlueprintReadOnly, Category = "Type")
  TEnumAsByte<EModifierTypes> Type;
  UPROPERTY(EditDefaultsOnly, BlueprintReadOnly, Category = "Map")
  TMap<FString, float> ModifierValues;
};
```

First, we declare an `enum` type **EModifierTypes** which includes two members, namely the `Add` and `Multi`, representing the **Addition** and **Multiplication** modifiers, respectively. The **UENUM()** macro allows us to create an `enum` whose members will show up in a drop-down menu inside the Unreal Editor.

Then, in the `public` section, the above `EModifierTypes` type is used to declare a property `Type`. Please note that here we **have to** use the `TEnumAsByte<>` template with the `enum` type to declare the property; otherwise, a compile error will occur!

Lastly, the `ModifierValues` property is to store the modifier's value and key pairs.

Next, let's extend the **CharacterStats** class code to apply the above modifiers. Open the **CharacterStats.h** header, and add the following **bold** lines:

```
#include "CoreMinimal.h"
#include "UObject/NoExportTypes.h"
#include "StatsModifier.h"
#include "CharacterStats.generated.h"

UCLASS(Blueprintable, DefaultToInstanced, EditInlineNew)
class RPG_API UCharacterStats : public UObject
{
  GENERATED_BODY()
public:

    ...

  UPROPERTY(EditDefaultsOnly, Category = "Modifiers")
  TArray<UStatsModifier*> Modifiers;
  void AddModifier(UStatsModifier* modifier);
  void RemoveModifier(UStatsModifier* modifier);
  int GetStatValue(FString name);
};
```

The **Modifiers** property is an array to store the modifiers. To add and remove modifiers, two new methods AddModifier() and RemoveModifier() are added.

The **GetStatValue()** method gets a **base** stat with **all** modifications applied.

Next, open the **CharacterStats.cpp** file and add the following lines to implement the new methods:

```
void UCharacterStats::AddModifier(UStatsModifier* modifier)
{
  Modifiers.Add(modifier);
}

void UCharacterStats::RemoveModifier(UStatsModifier* modifier)
{
  Modifiers.Remove(modifier);
}

int UCharacterStats::GetStatValue(FString name)
{
  // Note: We have to check if the BaseStats is not empty and contains the
  //       key; otherwise, a run-time error may occur!
  if (!BaseStats.IsEmpty() && BaseStats.Contains(name)) {
    int total = BaseStats[name];
    float multiplier = 0.0f;

    for (UStatsModifier* modifier : Modifiers)
    {
      if (modifier->Type == EModifierTypes::Add)
        total += modifier->ModifierValues[name];
      else
        // Note: We add all the multipliers but not multiply!
```

```
            multiplier += modifier->ModifierValues[name];
        }

        return FMath::RoundHalfFromZero(total + (total * multiplier));
    }
    else
        return 0;
}
```

The AddModifier() method is called when the player **equips a weapon**, is affected by a spell, or uses a special skill. The RemoveModifier() simply looks up the modifier and deletes it from the array. This is used when **unequipping** a weapon or when a spell expires.

The GetStatValue() function gets a **base** stat **with all modifications applied**. In a combat simulation, we'll rarely need the base **Strength** stat, we'll want to use the **fully modified** one. The fully modified Stat is calculated by first getting the **base** number and then applying all **add** modifiers in the array that affect that stat.

Modifiers are **combined** using a for-each loop. The **add** modifiers are added to the base stat **directly**. The multiplier modifiers have their **values summed** and are applied **after** the **add** modifiers. Lastly, the static RoundHalfFromZero() method converts the result floating-point number to the **nearest** integer. Also note that, at beginning of the method, we have to check if the **BaseStats** is **not empty** and **contains** the key; otherwise, **a runtime error may occur!**

Finally, let's modify the **RPGCharacter** class to add a **Stats** property for it. Open the **RPGCharacter.h** header, and add the following **bold** lines:

```
    ...
#include "Stats/CharacterStats.h"
#include "RPGCharacter.generated.h"

UCLASS()
class RPG_API ARPGCharacter : public ACharacter
{
    GENERATED_BODY()

public:
    // Sets default values for this character's properties
    ARPGCharacter();

    UPROPERTY(Instanced, EditAnywhere, Category = "Stats")
    UCharacterStats* Stats;
    ...
};
```

In the UPROPERTY() declaration, the **Instanced** keyword indicates that we **can edit** the Stats property in the Unreal Editor.

Now build the project and ensure that no errors occur. In the next step, we'll initialize the Stats for the **warrior** character in the Blueprint.

Assigning Stats in the Blueprint

Back to Unreal Editor and open the **BP_FemaleWarrior** Blueprint, and in the **Details** panel, find and expand the **Stats** section, after selecting **Character Stats** for the **Stats** field from the drop-down menu as shown below:

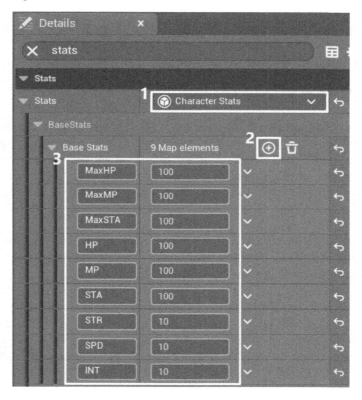

Then after pressing the + icon to add one **Map** element, enter **MaxHP** in the **left** empty field and **100** in the **right** empty field, which means the **MaxHP** Stat's **value** is **100**. Repeat the same procedure **eight** more times, and enter the **MaxMP**, **MaxSTA**, **HP**, **MP**, **STA**, **STR**, **SPD**, and **INT** Stats in the **left** column and their **values** in the **right** column respectively as shown above.

Finally, press **Compile** and **Save** to confirm the modification.

5.4.4 Implementing the Stamina System

Before diving into the combat system, in this section, we'll first implement the stamina system, which is an important feature in an Action RPG. Recall that in the previous section we implemented the mechanism for the player to sprint by holding down the **Shift** key. After defining the **Stamina** stat for our characters, we can apply constraints to the ability to sprint, such as a compulsory waiting period between uses, and make our ARPG more interesting and challenging. In online-based games and MMOs, the stamina system is typically a way to prevent macros, bots, or other devices from completing basic tasks while the user is not controlling the game.[9]

We'll also implement the stamina bar in this section to display the current player's stamina and its ratio. The stamina and bar will decrease with the player's sprinting and when a player's stamina is below a certain level, he or she will not be able to sprint.

Creating the Stamina Bar with UMG

User Interfaces (UIs) and **Heads-up Displays (HUDs)** are the games' way of providing information about the game to the player and in some cases allowing the player to interact with the game. The game's Interface is used to convey information to the player and provide a means of prompting the user for directed input. A game interface generally consists of two main elements: the heads-up display (HUD) and menus or user interfaces (UIs).

The HUD refers to the status and information overlaid on the screen during gameplay. The purpose of the HUD is to inform the player of the current state of the game, i.e., the score, their health and stamina, the amount of time remaining, etc.

Unreal Motion Graphics UI Designer (UMG) is a visual UI authoring tool that can be used to create UI elements such as in-game HUDs, menus, or other interface-related graphics you wish to present to your users. In this subsection, we'll create the game HUD with a stamina bar in the UMG, and before doing so, let's create a `StaminaBarWidget` class in C++ as follows.

The StaminaBarWidget Class

Choose **Tools > New Class...** from the main menu, and in the next step, select the **UserWidget** class under the **Widget** as the PARENT CLASS as shown below:

---

[9] **Stamina Bar Concept**, https://www.giantbomb.com/stamina-bar/3015-3569/.

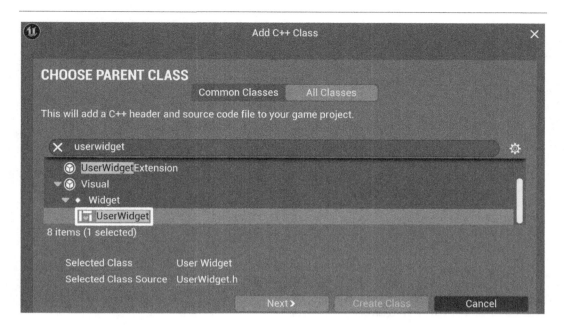

After pressing the **Next** button, change the class name to **StaminaBarWidget** in the next step, and add "**Public/UI**" to the **Path** as shown below:

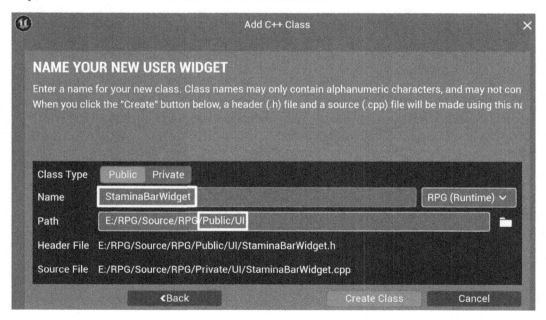

Press the **Create Class** button to generate the class under the **UI** filter in Visual Studio, and then add the following **bold** lines in the **StaminaBarWidget.h** header:

```
#include "CoreMinimal.h"
#include "Blueprint/UserWidget.h"
#include "Components/ProgressBar.h"
#include "Components/TextBlock.h"
#include "StaminaBarWidget.generated.h"

UCLASS()
class RPG_API UStaminaBarWidget : public UUserWidget
{
  GENERATED_BODY()
public:
  UPROPERTY(EditAnywhere, BlueprintReadWrite, meta = (BindWidget))
  UProgressBar* StaminaBar;
  UPROPERTY(EditAnywhere, BlueprintReadWrite, meta = (BindWidget))
  UTextBlock* Stamina;
  UPROPERTY(EditAnywhere, BlueprintReadWrite, meta = (BindWidget))
  UTextBlock* MaxStamina;

  UFUNCTION()
  void ResizeStaminaBar(float percent);
  void SetStamina(int stamina);
  void SetMaxStamina(int maxStamina);
};
```

Because **Progress Bar** and **Text Block** components are used to display the stamina bar and the stamina number, we have to include ProgressBar.h and TextBlock.h headers.

The StaminaBar property refers to the stamina bar which is a progress bar, and the Stamina and MaxStamina properties are text blocks used to display stamina and maximum stamina numbers.

The ResizeStaminaBar() method is to resize the stamina bar. The SetStamina() and SetMaxStamina() methods are to set the stamina and maximum stamina numbers displayed on the text blocks, respectively.

Then open the **StaminaBarWidget.cpp** file, and add the following lines to implement the three methods:

```
void UStaminaBarWidget::ResizeStaminaBar(float percent)
{
  // Resize the stamina bar by setting the Percent value
  StaminaBar->SetPercent(percent);
}

void UStaminaBarWidget::SetStamina(int stamina)
{
  // Set the text of the Stamina text block
  Stamina->SetText(FText::FromString(FString::FromInt(stamina)));
}
```

```
void UStaminaBarWidget::SetMaxStamina(int maxStamina)
{
  // Set the text of the MaxStamina text block
  MaxStamina->SetText(FText::FromString(FString::FromInt(maxStamina)));
}
```

In the ResizeStaminaBar() method, we resize the stamina bar by calling its
SetPercent() method to set the Percent value. In SetStamina() and SetMaxStamina()
methods, after converting stamina and maximum stamina values to the FString
respectively, we call the SetText() method and pass in the string to update the text.

Creating the StaminaBar UI Blueprint

Now that the C++ class is complete, back to Unreal Editor and create a new folder called
UI in the **Content** folder to store the stamina bar widget. Right-click in the **UI** folder,
select **Blueprint Class** from the context menu, and in the next step, pick the
StaminaBarWidget class as the Parent Class as shown below:

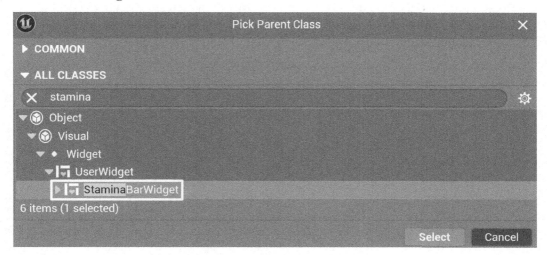

After pressing the **Select** button to generate the Blueprint, rename it to
WBP_StaminaBar and then double-click the Blueprint to open the **UMG Usigner** as
shown below:

In the **Palette** tab, find and expand the **PANEL,** as shown above, drag and drop the **Canvas Panel** widget onto the **WBP_StaminaBar** in the **Hierarchy** tab to become its child widget. Continue to drag and drop the **Overlay** widget onto the **Canvas Panel** to become its child widget as shown below:

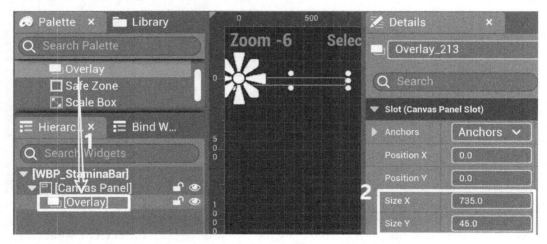

Continue to drag and drop the **Progress Bar** widget under the **COMMON** onto the **Overlay** to become its child widget as shown below:

Click on the generated **ProgressBar** in the **Hierarchy** tab and change its name to **StaminaBar** as shown above. Then after setting the **Horizontal** and **Vertical** Alignment to **Fill Horizontally** and **Fill Vertically** respectively, change the **Percent** value to **1.0** and you'll see the progress bar is filled with the default **Fill Color**.

Continue to expand the **Style** settings, and after expanding the **Background Image** > **Tint** settings, reset the **RGBA** values, as shown below, to make the background **semi-transparent**. Then set the **Draw As** field to **Rounded Box**.

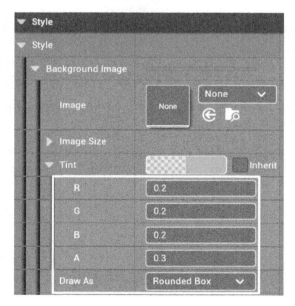

Similarly, after expanding the **Fill Image** settings, set the **Draw As** field to **Rounded Box** as well as shown below:

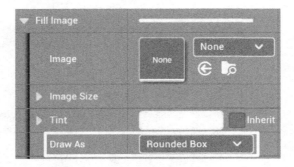

Next, drag and drop the **Horizontal Box** widget onto the **Overlay** in the **Hierarchy** tab to become its child widget as shown below:

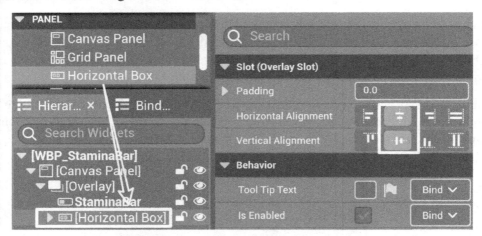

Reset the **Horizontal** and **Vertical** Alignment to **Center Align Horizontally** and **Center Align Vertically** respectively.

Continue to drag and drop the **Size Box** widget onto the **Horizontal Box** to become its child widget, and then add a **Text Block** widget to the **Size Box** as a child as shown below:

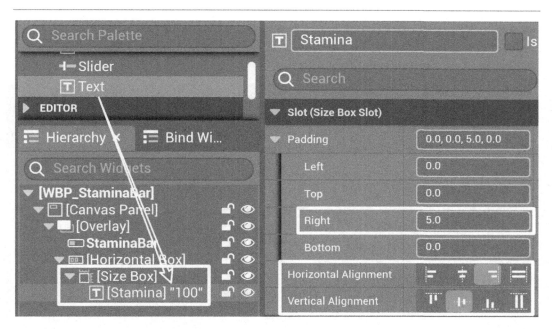

After renaming it to **Stamina**, expand the **Padding** settings, and set the **Right** value to **5** as shown above. Then reset the **Horizontal** and **Vertical** Alignment to **Right Align Horizontally** and **Center Align Vertically** respectively.

Continue to expand the **Content** and **Appearance** settings, and then change the **Text** field to **100**, and the **RGB** values to **0.3**, **0**, and **0** respectively as shown below. Lastly, change the **Font Size** to **26**.

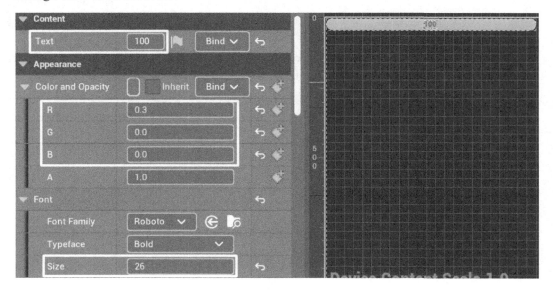

Next, drag and drop a **Text Block** widget onto the **Horizontal Box** to become its child widget, and after changing the **Text** to /, reset the **RGB** values to all **0** as shown below, and change the **Font Size** to **26**.

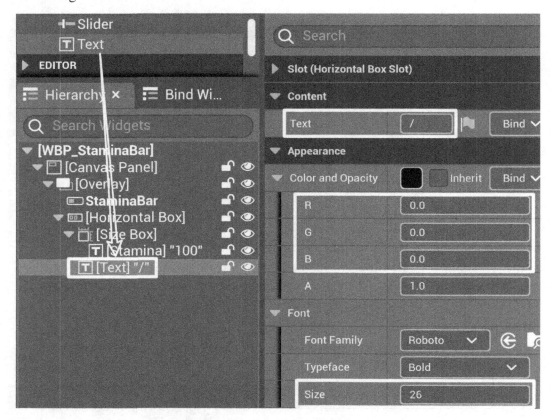

Now with the **Size Box** and **Stamina** Text Block selected, **right**-click on them and select **Copy** from the context menu as shown below:

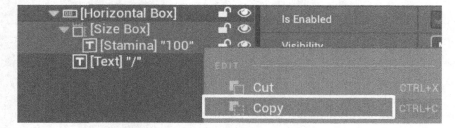

Then right-click on the **Horizontal Box** and select **Paste** to duplicate a copy of them as shown below:

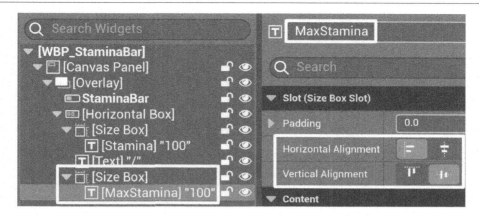

With the **copy** of the **Stamina** selected, rename it to **MaxStamina** as shown above, and reset its **Horizontal** Alignment to **Left Align** Horizontally.

Finally, with the **Overlay** selected, press the **Anchors** drop-down in the **Details** panel as shown below:

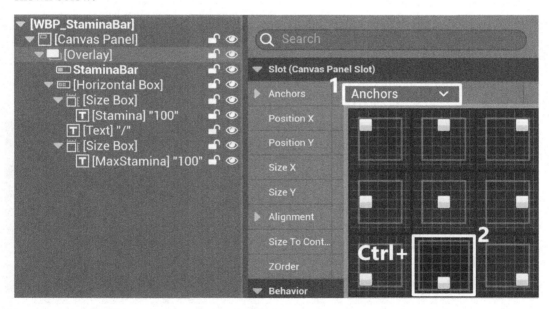

Hold **Ctrl** and press the align to the bottom icon as shown above to update the **position** to match. Next, press the **Anchors** again and this time hold the **Shift** and press the align to bottom icon again to update the **alignment** to match. The result can be previewed in the Viewport as shown below:

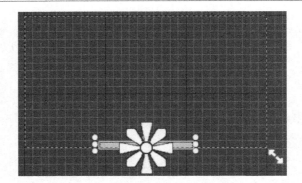

So far the Stamina UI is complete, press **Compile** and **Save** to confirm the modification, and make sure that no errors occurred.

The RPGHUD Class

The **HUD** is the base object for displaying elements overlaid on the screen. Every human-controlled player in the game has their instance of the **AHUD** class which draws to their Viewport. In the case of split-screen multiplayer games, multiple Viewports share the same screen, but each HUD still draws to its Viewport. The type, or class, of HUD to use is specified by the game type being used.

From the main menu, choose **Tools > New C++ Class…**, and in the **Add C++ Class** window, find and select the **HUD** as the **Parent** class as shown below:

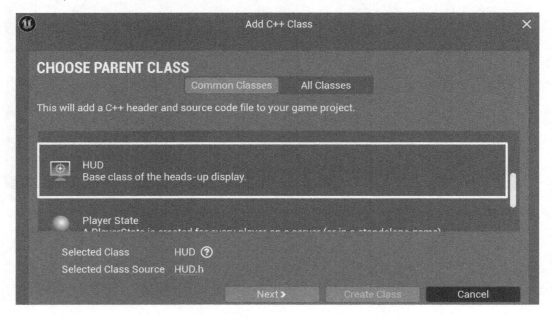

After pressing the **Next** button, change the class name to **RPGHUD** in the next step, and add "**Public/UI**" to the **Path** as shown below:

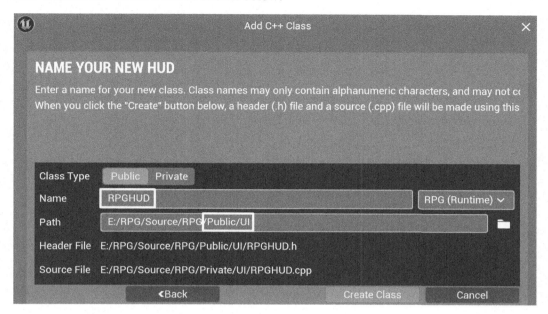

Press the **Create Class** button to generate the class in Visual Studio, and then add the following **bold** lines in the **RPGHUD.h** header:

```
#include "CoreMinimal.h"
#include "GameFramework/HUD.h"
#include "StaminaBarWidget.h"
#include "RPGHUD.generated.h"

UCLASS()
class RPG_API ARPGHUD : public AHUD
{
  GENERATED_BODY()
public:
  UPROPERTY(EditDefaultsOnly, Category = "Widgets")
  TSubclassOf<UUserWidget> StaminaBarWidgetClass;
  UPROPERTY(VisibleAnywhere, Category = "Widgets")
  UStaminaBarWidget* StaminaBarWidget;
protected:
  void AddStaminaBarWidget();
  virtual void BeginPlay() override;
};
```

The StaminaBarWidgetClass property refers to the **Blueprint** class used to create the stamina bar. The StaminaBarWidget property stores the reference of the stamina bar widget. In the protected section, the `AddStaminaBarWidget()` method is to create and add the stamina bar to the Viewport. Besides, we also override the `BeginPlay()` method.

Then open the **RPGHUD.cpp** file and add the following lines to implement the methods:

```
void ARPGHUD::BeginPlay()
{
  Super::BeginPlay();

  AddStaminaBarWidget();
}

void ARPGHUD::AddStaminaBarWidget()
{
  if (IsValid(StaminaBarWidgetClass))
  {
    // Create the stamina bar widget
    StaminaBarWidget = CreateWidget<UStaminaBarWidget>(GetWorld(),
                                            StaminaBarWidgetClass);
    // Add the stamina bar to the viewport
    if (StaminaBarWidget)
    {
      StaminaBarWidget->AddToViewport();
    }
  }
}
```

In the `BeginPlay()` method, we call the `AddStaminaBarWidget()` method to create and add the stamina bar to the Viewport.

In the `AddStaminaBarWidget()` method, we first check if the `StaminaBarWidgetClass` property is assigned and valid, then the built-in `CreateWidget()` method is called, and the class property is passed in to create the stamina bar and it's assigned to the `StaminaBarWidget` property. Lastly, we call the `AddToViewport()` method of the stamina bar to add it to the Viewport.

Now build the project and make sure that no error occurred.

Creating the RPGHUD Blueprint

Next, let's create the Blueprint for the RPGHUD. Right-click in the Content Browser of the **UI** folder, choose **Blueprint Class** from the Context menu, and in the next step, find and select the **RPGHUD** class as the Parent Class as shown below:

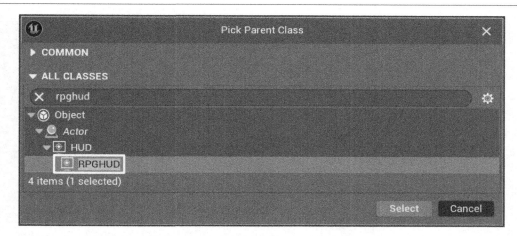

After pressing the **Select** button to generate the Blueprint, rename it to **BP_RPGHUD**. Double-click the Blueprint to open it, and after expanding the **Widgets** category as shown below:

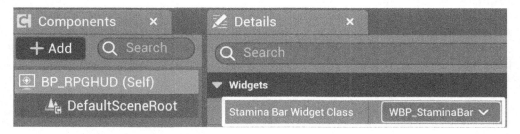

Select the **WBP_StaminaBar** from the drop-down menu for the **Stamina Bar Widget Class**. Now press **Save** to confirm the modification.

Assigning the RPGHUD in the Project Settings

After the Blueprint is complete, we have to assign it to the **HUD** class in the Project Settings. Open the **Project Settings** window, after selecting the **Maps and Modes**, select the **BP_RPGHUD** from the drop-down menu for the **HUD Class** as shown below:

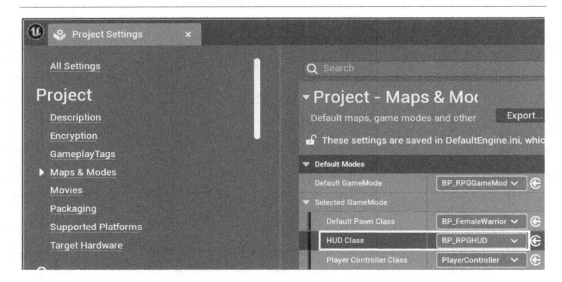

Implementing the Sprint Drain

After the UI classes are complete, we'll implement the sprint drain for the player character in this subsection. Open the **RPGCharacter.h** header, and add the following **bold** lines:

```
    …
#include "Stats/CharacterStats.h"
#include "UI/RPGHUD.h"
#include "RPGCharacter.generated.h"

UCLASS()
class RPG_API ARPGCharacter : public ACharacter
{
    GENERATED_BODY()

public:
    // Sets default values for this character's properties
    ARPGCharacter();

    UPROPERTY(EditDefaultsOnly, Category = "Sprint")
    bool IsSprinting = false;
    UPROPERTY(EditDefaultsOnly, Category = "Constraints")
    float SprintCost = 10;
    UPROPERTY(EditDefaultsOnly, Category = "Stamina")
    float StaminaRecoveryRate = 0.2f;
    ARPGHUD* RPGHUD;
    FTimerHandle SprintDrainTimerHandle;
    FTimerHandle RegenerateStaminaTimerHandle;

    UFUNCTION()
```

```
    void SprintDrain();
    UFUNCTION()
    void RegenerateStamina();
    void ClearTimer();
    void RestartTimer();
    void UpdateStaminaUI(int stamina, int maxStamina = 0);
    UPROPERTY(Instanced, EditAnywhere, Category = "Stats")
    UCharacterStats* Stats;
        ...
};
```

The `IsSprinting` property represents whether the player is sprinting. The `SprintCost` property refers to the value that will be deducted from the stamina after sprinting. The `StaminaRecoveryRate` property represents the stamina recharge rate. The `RPGHUD` refers to the HUD in the game to display the stamina bar. The `SprintDrainTimerHandle` and `RegenerateStaminaTimerHandle` are two **Timer** handles.

`SprintDrain()` and `RegenerateStamina()` methods are two delegates for the **Timer** to call and drain and regenerate the stamina, respectively. The `ClearTimer()` and `RestartTimer()` methods are to clear and restart the timer for regenerating the stamina respectively which will be used for the following horse riding system. The `UpdateStaminaUI()` method is to update the stamina bar and values.

Then open the **RPGCharacter.cpp** file, and add the following lines to implement the new methods:

```
void ARPGCharacter::SprintDrain()
{
  // Get current stamina
  int stamina = Stats->GetStatValue("STA");
  // Decrease the stamina
  stamina -= SprintCost;
  // Reset the stamina
  Stats->SetStatValue("STA", stamina);
  // Update the stamina bar
  UpdateStaminaUI(stamina);

  if (stamina < SprintCost) {
    GetCharacterMovement()->MaxWalkSpeed = WalkSpeed;
    // Clear the timer to stop the sprint drain
    GetWorldTimerManager().ClearTimer(SprintDrainTimerHandle);
    IsSprinting = false;
  }
}
```

In the `SprintDrain()` method, after getting the current stamina of the player, the sprint cost is deducted from the stamina, then we reset the stamina stat, and call the `UpdateStaminaUI()` method to update the stamina bar. Lastly, if the stamina is less than the sprint cost, after setting the `MaxWalkSpeed` of the **CharacterMovement** component to the walking speed, the built-in `ClearTimer()` of the **Timer instance** in the actor's world to clear the timer and stop the sprint drain. Lastly, the `IsSprinting` flag is set to `false`.

```
void ARPGCharacter::RegenerateStamina()
{
    // Note: Must check Stats otherwise crash!
    if (!IsSprinting && Stats) {
        int stamina = Stats->GetStatValue("STA");
        // Only recharge when we don't have the max stamina
        if (stamina != Stats->GetStatValue("MaxSTA")) {
            // Regernate the stamina
            stamina += StaminaRecoveryRate * Stats->GetStatValue("STR");

            int maxStamina = Stats->GetStatValue("MaxSTA");
            if (stamina >= maxStamina)
                stamina = maxStamina;

            UpdateStaminaUI(stamina);
            // Reset the stamina
            Stats->SetStatValue("STA", stamina);
        }
    }
}
```

In the `RegenerateStamina()` method, if the player is **not** sprinting and the **Stats** property is initialized, after getting the current stamina of the player, if it's not equal to the **maximum** stamina, we regenerate the stamina by adding a value from the product of the `StaminaRecoveryRate` and the **STR** stat. Then we check if the new stamina is greater or equal to the maximum stamina, and if it is, its value is reset to the maximum stamina. Next, we call the `UpdateStaminaUI()` method and pass in the new stamina to update the stamina bar. Lastly, the stamina stat is reset to the new value.

```
void ARPGCharacter::UpdateStaminaUI(int stamina, int maxStamina)
{
    if (RPGHUD)
    {
        UStaminaBarWidget* staminaBar = RPGHUD->StaminaBarWidget;

        if (staminaBar) {
            staminaBar->SetStamina(stamina);
            // If the incoming maxStamina parameter is not zero, also update
            // the maximum stamina value
            if (maxStamina != 0)
                staminaBar->SetMaxStamina(maxStamina);
            staminaBar->ResizeStaminaBar((float)stamina /
                                         Stats->GetStatValue("MaxSTA"));
        }
```

```
    }
}
```

In the `UpdateStaminaUI()` method, after obtaining the stamina bar widget, we update the stamina value and if the incoming `maxStamina` parameter is **not zero**, we also update the **maximum** stamina value. Lastly, the stamina bar is resized according to the ratio of the stamina and its maximum value.

```
// Stop the timer for regenerating the stamina
void ARPGCharacter::ClearTimer()
{
  GetWorldTimerManager().ClearTimer(RegenerateStaminaTimerHandle);
}

// Restart the timer for regenerating the stamina
void ARPGCharacter::RestartTimer()
{
  GetWorld()->GetTimerManager().SetTimer(RegenerateStaminaTimerHandle,
                  this, &ARPGCharacter::RegenerateStamina, 0.5f, true);
}
```

In the `ClearTimer()` method, after getting the **World Timer Manager**, we call its built-in `ClearTimer()` function to **stop** the timer for regenerating the stamina.

In the `RestartTimer()` method, after getting the top level timer manager, we call the built-in `SetTimer()` function to **restart** the timer for regenerating the stamina.

Next, add the following **bold** lines in the `Sprint()` method:

```
void ARPGCharacter::Sprint()
{
  if (Stats->GetStatValue("STA") >= SprintCost)
  {
    GetCharacterMovement()->MaxWalkSpeed = RunSpeed;
    IsSprinting = true;
    // Call SprintDrain() once per 0.5 seconds, starting zero seconds from
    // now
    GetWorldTimerManager().SetTimer(SprintDrainTimerHandle, this,
                      &ARPGCharacter::SprintDrain, 0.5f, true, 0.0f);
  }
}
```

In the `Sprint()` method, if the player's current stamina is greater or equal to the sprint cost, then after the `IsSprinting` flag is set to `true`, we call the built-in `SetTimer()` method and call the `SprintDrain` delegate once per **0.5** seconds, starting **zero** seconds from now.

Finally, add the following **bold** lines in the **BeginPlay()** method:

```
void ARPGCharacter::BeginPlay()
```

```
{
  Super::BeginPlay();

  GetCharacterMovement()->MaxWalkSpeed = WalkSpeed;

  GetWorld()->GetTimerManager().SetTimer(RegenerateStaminaTimerHandle,
                       this, &ARPGCharacter::RegenerateStamina, 0.5f, true);
  RPGHUD = Cast<ARPGHUD>(GetWorld()->GetFirstPlayerController()
                                                       ->GetHUD());
}
```

In the `BeginPlay()` method, after setting the `MaxWalkSpeed`, we start the **Timer** and call the `RegenerateStamina()` function **indefinitely**. Finally, we obtain the game **HUD** reference from the first **Player Controller**.

So far all of the C++ code and Blueprints are complete, build the project and make sure no errors occurred. Now press **Play** to run the game, and you'll see the stamina bar appears on the bottom of the screen. When pressing any movement key while holding down the Shift key to sprint, you'll see the stamina bar getting shorter and the stamina value decreasing. After releasing the Shift key, you'll notice that the stamina is regenerated, and the stamina bar is getting longer as shown below:

5.5 Action RPG Combat

In this section, we'll implement the **Combat** in ARPGs, and before we start, let's complete the design of the **Health Bar** interface first for our characters.

5.5.1 Character Health and GUI Design

Before starting the Health Bar UI design in the UMG, let's create a C++ class for it first. Choose **Tools** > **New Class...** from the main menu, and in the next step, select the **UserWidget** class under the **Widget** as the **PARENT** CLASS.

After pressing the **Next** button, change the class name to **HealthBarWidget** in the next step, and add "**Public/UI**" to the **Path** as shown below:

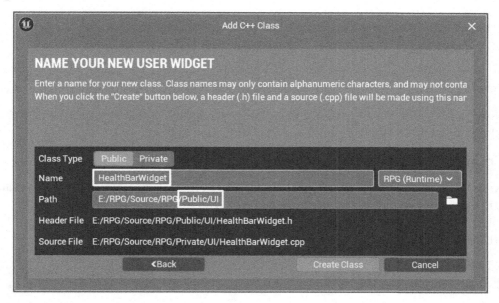

Press the **Create Class** button to generate the class in Visual Studio, and then add the following **bold** lines in the **HealthBarWidget.h** header:

```cpp
#include "CoreMinimal.h"
#include "Blueprint/UserWidget.h"
#include "Components/ProgressBar.h"
#include "HealthBarWidget.generated.h"

UCLASS()
class RPG_API UHealthBarWidget : public UUserWidget
{
  GENERATED_BODY()
public:
  UPROPERTY(EditAnywhere, BlueprintReadWrite, meta = (BindWidget))
  UProgressBar* HealthBar;

  UFUNCTION()
  void ResizeHealthBar(float percent);
};
```

The `HealthBar` property is a **progress bar** to bind a widget in the designer. Here the **BindWidget** metadata keyword allows easy native access to designer-defined controls. The `ResizeHealthBar()` method is to resize the health bar.

Then add the following lines in the **HealthBarWidget.cpp** file to implement the method:

```
void UHealthBarWidget::ResizeHealthBar(float percent)
{
  // Use SetPercent() instead of assign value to the percent
  HealthBar->SetPercent(percent);
}
```

In the method, we call the **SetPercent()** method and pass in the `percent` value to resize the progress bar.

Now build the project and make sure no errors occur. In the next step, we'll create the Blueprint for the health bar and design the UI in Unreal Designer.

Creating the HealthBar UI Blueprint

After the C++ class is complete, back to the Unreal Editor and create a new folder called **UI** in the **Content** folder to store the health bar widget. Right-click in the **UI** folder, select **Blueprint Class** from the context menu, and in the next step, pick the **HealthBarWidget** class as the Parent Class as shown below:

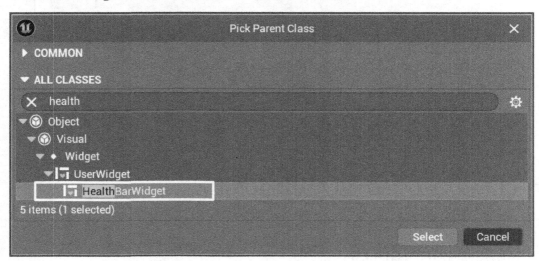

After pressing the **Select** button to create the Blueprint, change its name to **WBP_HealthBarWidget** and then double-click to open it in the Designer as shown below:

In the **Palette** tab, find and expand the **PANEL,** as shown above, drag and drop the **Canvas Panel** widget onto the **WBP_HealthBar** in the **Hierarchy** tab to become its child widget.

Continue to drag and drop the **Progress Bar** widget under the **COMMON** onto the **Canvas Panel** to become its child widget as shown below:

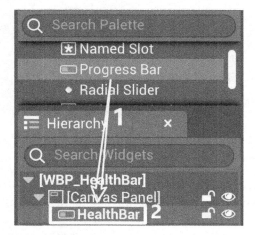

Click on the generated **ProgressBar** in the **Hierarchy** tab and change its name to **HealthBar** as shown above.

Next, with the **HealthBar** selected in the Hierarchy, click on the drop-down to the **right** of the **Anchors** field to open the menu in the **Details** tab as shown below:

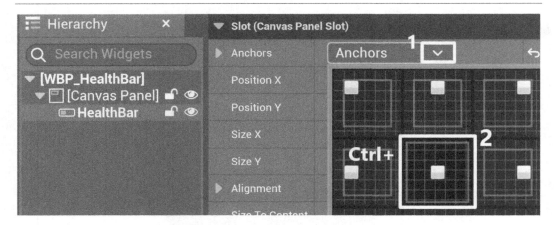

Hold the **Ctrl** key and press the alignment to the **middle** option as shown above. The result is shown below:

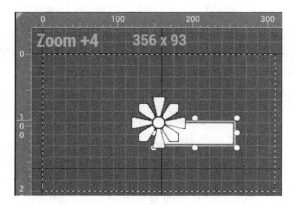

The progress bar will be **moved** to the **middle** in the **Canvas Panel** and the **Anchor** is on its **top-left** corner as shown above.

Next, click on the **Anchors** drop-down again and this time, with the **Shift** key pressed, and select the alignment to the **middle** option again, the result is shown below:

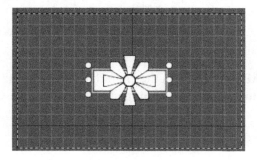

Now the progress bar is moved again and aligned to the middle of the Canvas Panel as shown above.

Then, in the **Details** tab, after expanding the **Style** > **Background Image** > **Tint** field as shown below:

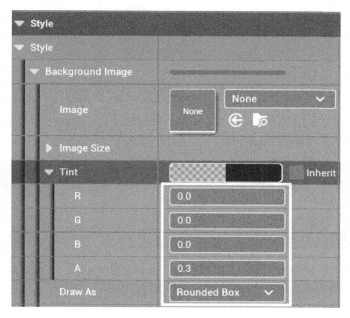

After changing the **R**, **G**, and **B** fields all to **0.0** (Black) and the **A** (Alpha) field to **0.3** as shown above to make the background **semi-transparent**, select **Rounded Box** for the **Draw As** field.

Next, after expanding the **Fill Image** field, select **Rounded Box** for the **Draw As** filed as shown below:

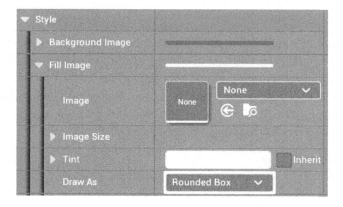

Continue to expand the **Appearance** > **Fill Color and Opacity** field as shown below:

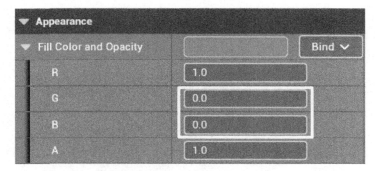

Change both the **G** and **B** fields to **0.0**, which makes the health bar filled with **red** color. Finally, expand the **Progress** field as shown below:

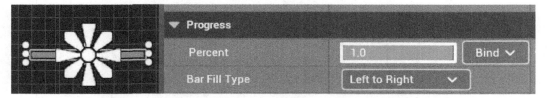

After changing the **Percent** field to **1.0** (100%), you'll see the health bar will be filled in **red** and the corners will be **rounded** as shown above.

5.5.2 Animation Montages

An **Animation montage** (or **montage** for short) provides a way for you to control an animation asset directly through Blueprint or C++ code. They can also be used to create a wide variety of animation effects, including intelligent loops of animation, logic-based animation switching, and much more.

With an Animation Montage, you can combine several different animation sequences into a single asset that you can break up into **sections** for playback either individually or in combination. You can also fire off **events** within a montage that can perform a variety of local or replicated tasks, such as playing sound cues or particle effects, changing player values like ammunition count, or even replicating root motion in networked games (provided root motion is enabled on the animation).

Creating an Attack Montage

To create an Attack Montage, right-click in the **Content Browser** of the **Animations** folder, and choose **Animation** > **Animation Montage** to open the **Pick Skeleton** window as shown below:

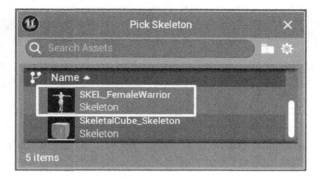

After selecting the **SKEL_FemaleWarrior**, a Montage will be created, then rename the Montage to **AM_GreatSwordSlash**. Next, double-click the montage to open it, and the panel will appear **empty** as shown on the right:

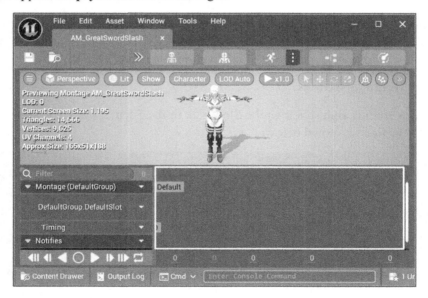

Adding Animation Sequences to a Montage

Now it's time to add the great sword-attacking **Animation Sequences** that will comprise the Montage inside the **Montage** area. Open the **AM_GreatSwordSlash** Montage, inside the **Asset Browser** window drag and drop an attacking animation, here is the imported **Great_Sword_Rotate_Slash** animation sequence, into the Montage **Slot** track as shown below:

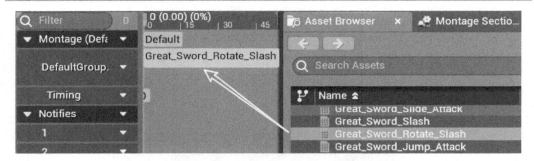

Once you drop the animation on the **Slot** track, the animation will be added. Next, drag and drop the **Great_Sword_Jump_Attack**, **Great_Sword_Slide_Attack**, **Great_Sword_Horizontal_Slash**, and **Great_Sword_Diagonal_Slash** animations respectively onto the Slot track and they will be added sequentially as shown below:

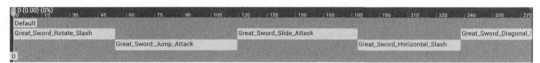

Animations will **automatically alternate** between the first and second Slot tracks to help distinguish where each animation starts and stops. You can also left-click and drag and drop the animations on the Slot track to **re-order** them.

Creating Montage Sections

To create a Section, right-click on the Slot track or the Section track and select **New Montage Section** as shown below:

When prompted, enter the desired Section name, which is "**JumpAttack**" in this case, as shown below:

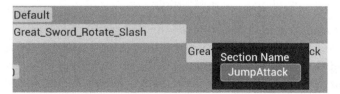

When adding a new Section, it will be added to the **Sections** track as well as inside the **Montage Section** tab as shown below:

Note: By default, all Animation Montages include a **Default** Section that, when used by itself, will play the **entire** Montage.

You can move Sections around by left clicking and dragging the Section to the desired location. Here we move the **JumpAttack** section to the **end** of the **Greate_Sword_Rotate_Slash** as shown above.

Continue to right-click on the Slot track or the Section track and select **New Montage Section** to add the other sections respectively, namely the **SlideAttack**, **HorizontalSlash**, and **DiagonalSlash** as shown below:

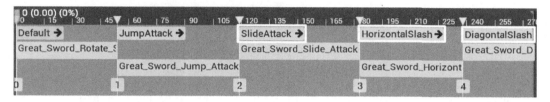

Then, move the markers of the sections respectively to the **start** of each animation as shown above.

Now click the **Default** section and, in the Details panel, change its name to **RotateSlash** as shown below:

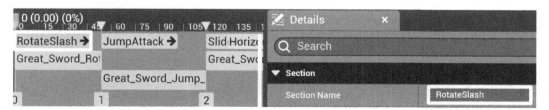

Finally, we have to **remove** all of the links created in the **Montage Sections** tab, as shown below:

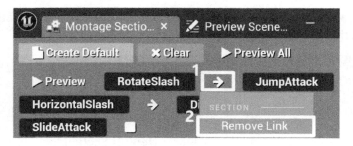

Please click each arrow icon and choose the **Remove Link** from the context menu to **unlink** the animations, the result is shown below:

Now press the **Play** button on the bottom of the left panel to preview the Montage, you'll find that only the first section is played not the entire Montage.

Creating the Montage from an Animation Sequence

Another way to create a Montage is from the imported **Animation Sequence**. Right-click the **Draw_A_Great_Sword** animation and choose **Create > Create AnimMontage** from the context menu to create a new Montage called **AM_Draw_A_Great_Sword**. Then open the Montage, and you'll see the panel will have the animation inside as shown below:

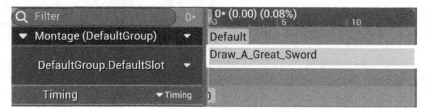

Because we only need the animation to affect the **Upper Body** of the character, in the next step, we'll use **Montage Slots** to achieve this goal.

Montage Slots

With Slots, you can take a group of related animations and assign them to different Slots within the Montage. Through Blueprint or C++, you can then tell one of the Slots to play the Montages it contains.

To create a new Slot, in the **Animation** Editor, choose **Window > Anim Slot Manager** from the menu, as shown below if the tab does not show up in the editor.

Then you'll see the **Anim Slot Manager** tab on the **lower-right** panel as shown below:

Click the **Add Slot** button and assign a new unique name called **UpperBody** to which we can assign our Montage as shown above.

After adding the slot, we can assign the Montage to the newly created **UpperBody** Slot as follows. Click the **Slot** drop-down to the right of the **DefaultGroup.DefaultSlot** on the left panel and choose **Slot name > DefaultGroup.UpperBody** to assign the Montage to the new **UpperBody** Slot as shown below:

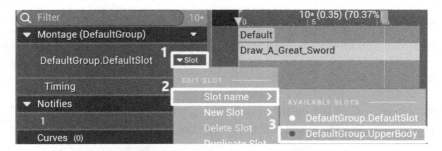

Now, press **Save** to confirm the modification. Please note that currently, you have to **save** the Montage first and **re-open** it to preview the Montage animations and Slot changing.

Next, right-click the **Draw_A_Great_Sword** animation again and choose **Create** > **Create AnimMontage** from the context menu to create another Montage, rename it to **AM_Unload_A_Great_Sword**. Then open the Montage and **re-assign** the Montage to the **UpperBody** Slot as well. Finally, press **Save** to confirm the modification.

Anim Graph Setup for Montages

In this subsection, we'll set up our **AnimGraph** to handle the blending of our **AnimMontage** and the movement pose from our State Machine.

Find and open the **ABP_FemaleWarrior** Animation Blueprint, and in the **MyBlueprint** panel, click to open the **AnimGraph**. Drag off the **Locomotion** State Machine and search for and add a **New Save cached pose** as shown below:

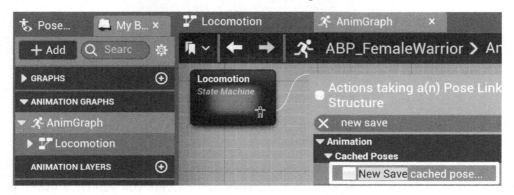

Here we are getting the resulting pose from our **Locomotion** State Machine and storing it in a **cached pose** that we can use elsewhere.

Give the cached pose a name, such as **LocomotionCache**, by pressing **F2** on the node as shown below:

Right-click in the graph and add the **Use cached pose 'LocomotionCache'** (or whatever you named the cached pose) as shown below:

Continue to drag off the **Use cached pose** node, as shown below, search for and add the **Layered blend per bone** node.

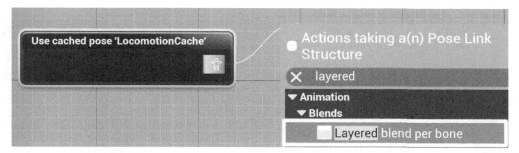

The **Layered Blend Per Bone** node will allow us to **blend** animations from a **specified** bone on the Skeleton.

Copy/Paste the **Use cached pose 'LocomotionCache'** node as shown below, then drag off it and select the **Slot 'DefaultSlot'** under **Montage** to create a **Slot** node.

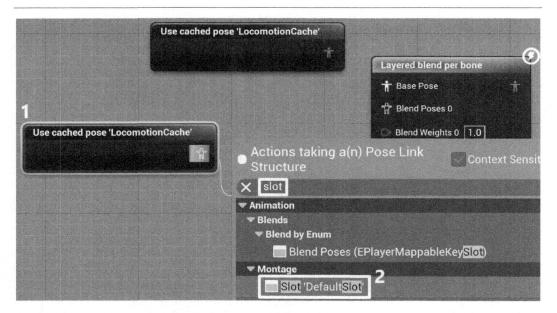

In the **Settings** for the **Slot** node in the **Details** tab, click on the drop-down menu and select DefaultGroup.**UpperBody** as shown below:

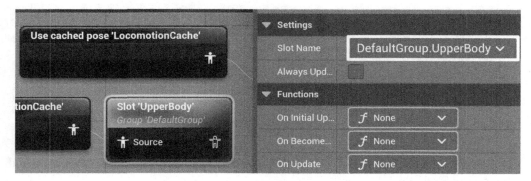

When an Animation Montage that uses this slot is called to play, it will now be called inside our AnimGraph.

Connect the **Slot** to the **Blend Poses 0** pin on the **Layered blend per bone** node, as shown below:

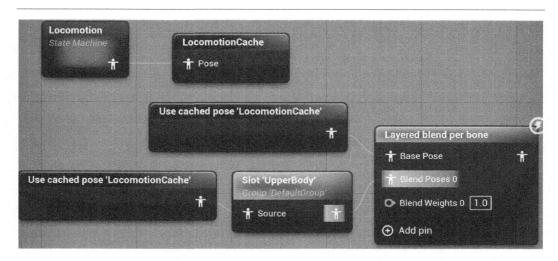

Layered Blend Per Bone Setup

In this step, we define the method in which to layer our blended animation and which **bone** to start the blend from. Inside the **AnimGraph**, click on the **Layered blend per bone** node, then expand the **Layer Setup** section and click the + sign as shown below:

With these settings, we can blend the **upper body** AnimMontage, which is the **AM_Draw_A_Great_Sword** in our case, onto our Skeleton starting from the **Spine** bone.

Finalizing the Blend Settings

Copy/Paste the **Use cached pose 'LocomotionCache'** node, then drag off it and add another **Layered blend per bone** node as shown below:

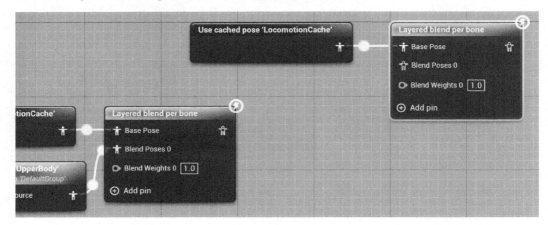

Continue to drag off the **previous** Layer blend per bone node and add another **Slot 'DefaultSlot'** node as shown below:

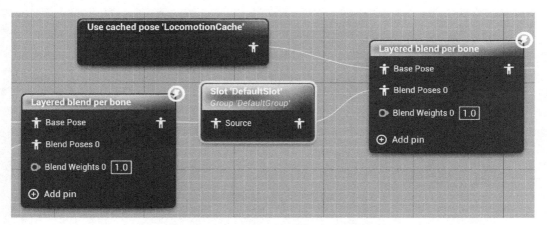

Connect the **Slot** to the **Blend Poses 0** pin on the new **Layered blend per bone** node, as shown above.

Then, with the **second** Layered blend per bone node selected, expand the **Layer Setup** section in the **Details** panel and click the + sign to add a new element as shown below:

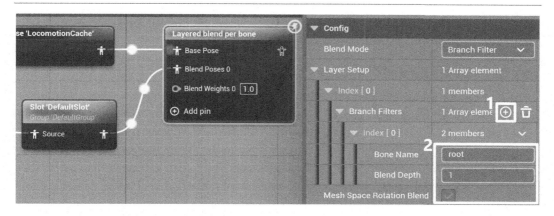

This time set the **Bone Name** field to **root**, which means to blend all the great sword attack montages, onto our Skeleton starting from the **root** bone.

Finally, connect the **Layered blend per bone** node out to the **Result**, and our AnimGraph is complete as shown below:

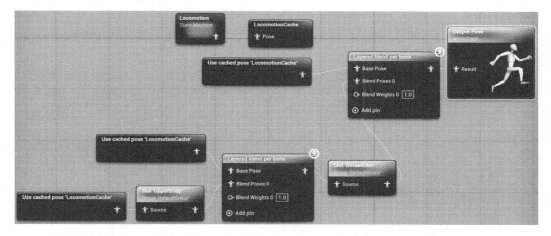

Now press **Compile** and **Save** to confirm the modification.

5.5.3 Combos in ARPGs

In video games, a **combo** (short for **combination**) is a set of actions performed in sequence, usually with strict timing limitations, which yield a significant benefit or advantage. The term originates from fighting games which are based upon the concept of a striking combination. Combos are commonly used as an essential gameplay element in ARPGs.

In this section, we'll use the **Animation Notify State** class to implement Combos in our ARPG.

Using Animation Notifications

Animation Notifications (AnimNotifies or just **Notifies)** provide a way for animation programmers to set up events to occur at specific points during an **Animation Sequence** or **Montage**. Notifies are commonly used to add effects like footstep sounds during a walk or run animation or spawning a particle system during animation. However, they can have any number of different uses, as the system can be extended with custom notification types to cater to the needs of any type of game.

Animation Notifications in Unreal include **two** classes, namely the **AnimNotify** and **AnimNotifyState** classes. The main difference between them is that the **Anim Notify State** has **three** distinct events, namely the **Notify Begin**, **Notify End**, and **Notify Tick** that Anim Notify does not.

In this subsection, we'll use **Anim Notify State** to trigger events at the **end** of each great sword slash animation to implement the Combo mechanism in C++. First, click **Tools > New C++ Class…** and select the **AnimNotifyState** class as our parent class as shown below:

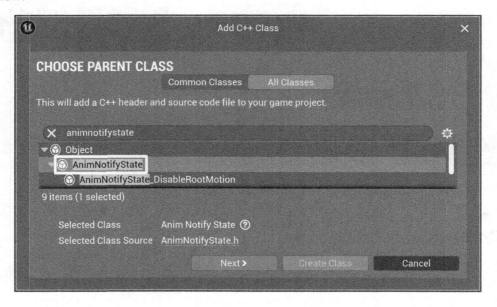

After pressing the **Next** button, rename the class to **SwordAnimNotifyState** in the next step, and change the **Path** to under the **Public/Animation** folder as shown below:

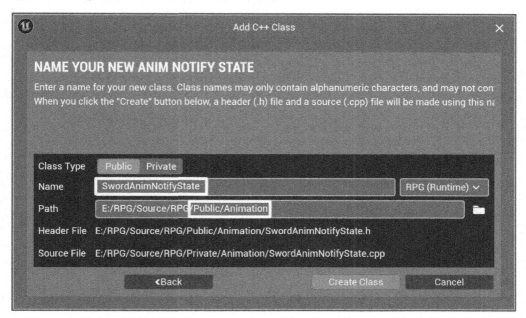

Press the **Create Class** button to generate the class in Visual Studio, then open the **SwordAnimNotifyState.h** header and add the following **bold** lines:

```
UENUM()
enum EComboSections
{
  None                   UMETA(DisplayName = "None"),
  HorizontalSlash        UMETA(DisplayName = "HorizontalSlash"),
  DiagontalSlash         UMETA(DisplayName = "DiagontalSlash"),
  JumpAttack             UMETA(DisplayName = "JumpAttack"),
  SlideAttack            UMETA(DisplayName = "SlideAttack"),
  RotateSlash            UMETA(DisplayName = "RotateSlash")
};

UCLASS()
class RPG_API USwordAnimNotifyState : public UAnimNotifyState
{
  GENERATED_BODY()
public:
  // Note: EditAnywhere is required for editing its value, otherwise it
  //       will not show up in the Montage editor!
  UPROPERTY(EditAnywhere, BlueprintReadWrite, Category = "Combo")
  TEnumAsByte<EComboSections> NextLightComboSection;
  UPROPERTY(EditAnywhere, BlueprintReadWrite, Category = "Combo")
  TEnumAsByte<EComboSections> NextHeavyComboSection;
```

```
    virtual void NotifyEnd(USkeletalMeshComponent* MeshComp,
                                UAnimSequenceBase* Animatioin) override;
};
```

The enum type **EComboSections** defines the **section names** created in our great sword slash Montage. Then in the class, we add a `public` section and declare two properties, **NextLightComboSection** and **NextHeavyComboSection**, to store the next light and heavy attack sections in the Montage. Finally, **NotifyEnd()** is the overridden method used as the event handler.

Next, switch to the **SwordAnimNotifyState.cpp,** and add the following lines to implement the overridden method:

```
#include "Characters/WarriorCharacter.h"

void USwordAnimNotifyState::NotifyEnd(USkeletalMeshComponent* MeshComp,
                                UAnimSequenceBase* Animation)
{
  AWarriorCharacter* warrior = Cast<AWarriorCharacter>(
                                        MeshComp->GetOwner());

  if (warrior)
  {
    // If we have the next Combo to play
    if (warrior->NextComboType != EComboTypes::Empty) {
      FText sectionName;
      // Get the Montage
      UAnimMontage* montage = Cast<UAnimMontage>(Animation);
      // Find the enum type object
      const UEnum* EnumPtr =
                    FindFirstObjectSafe<UEnum>(TEXT("EComboSections"));
      // Play the next Combo
      switch (warrior->NextComboType) {
        case EComboTypes::LightMelee:
          if (EnumPtr)
            sectionName =
              EnumPtr->GetDisplayNameTextByValue(NextLightComboSection);

          if (montage) {
            warrior->PlayComboMontage(FName(sectionName.ToString()),
                                                montage);
          }
          break;
        case EComboTypes::HeavyMelee:
          if (EnumPtr)
            sectionName =
              EnumPtr->GetDisplayNameTextByValue(NextHeavyComboSection);

          if (montage) {
            warrior->PlayComboMontage(FName(sectionName.ToString()),
```

```
                                                        montage);
        }
      break;
    }
    // Reset the next combo
    warrior->NextComboType = EComboTypes::Empty;
  } else {
    // No next combo to play, reset the IsAttacking flag
    warrior->IsAttacking = false;
  }
 }
}
```

First, within the method, after getting the warrior character by calling `GetOwner()` method of the incoming `MeshComp`, and if we have the next combo section to play, after obtaining the Montage to play from the passed in **Animation** parameter and the `EComboSections` type object pointer, we play the **next** Combo according to its type.

If it's a **light** attack and because the `NextLightComboSection` variable stores the index **not** the **name** of the section, we have to get the **section name** by using the `GetDisplayNameTextByValue()` method through the `enum` type pointer. Then the section in the Montage is played by calling the `PlayComboMontage()` method of the warrior object. On the other hand, if the next Combo is a **heavy** attack, the code is similar.

Lastly, we reset the next Combo of the warrior to `EComboTypes::Empty`, which means if the timing of the combo key pressing or mouse clicking is **after** the **end** of the animation notify state, this Combo is ignored and treated as a normal attack.

On the other hand, if we don't have the next combo to play, the `IsAttacking` flag of the warrior is reset to `false`. The code is not complete yet and we have to modify the `WarriorCharacter` class as follows.

Playing Combos in C++

Continue to open the **WarriorCharacter.h** header, and add the following **bold** lines:

```
#include "CoreMinimal.h"
#include "RPGCharacter.h"
#include "Animation/SwordAnimNotifyState.h"
#include "WarriorCharacter.generated.h"

UENUM()
enum EComboTypes
{
  Empty              UMETA(DisplayName = "Empty"),
  LightMelee         UMETA(DisplayName = "LightMelee"),
  HeavyMelee         UMETA(DisplayName = "HeavyMelee")
};
```

```
UCLASS()
class RPG_API AWarriorCharacter : public ARPGCharacter
{
  GENERATED_BODY()
public:
  …

  // Note: EditDefaultsOnly attribute is required, otherwise you are
  //       unable to assign the montage!
  UPROPERTY(EditDefaultsOnly, BlueprintReadOnly, Category = "Montages")
  UAnimMontage* GreatSwordSlashMontage;
  UPROPERTY(EditDefaultsOnly, BlueprintReadOnly, Category = "Combo")
  TEnumAsByte<EComboSections> DefaultLightSlashSection;
  UPROPERTY(EditDefaultsOnly, BlueprintReadOnly, Category = "Combo")
  TEnumAsByte<EComboSections> DefaultHeavySlashSection;
  TEnumAsByte<EComboTypes> NextComboType;
  UPROPERTY(EditDefaultsOnly, BlueprintReadOnly, Category = "Combo")
  bool IsAttacking = false;

  virtual void PlayComboMontage(FName section, UAnimMontage* montage = 0,
                                               float rate = 1.0f);
  virtual void LightAttack(const FInputActionValue& value) override;
  virtual void HeavyAttack(const FInputActionValue& value) override;
};
```

The **EComboTypes** enum type defines the next Combo types in which LightMelee and HeavyMelee represent the **light** and **heavy** attacks respectively, and the **Empty** means no next Combo.

Within the class, the GreatSwordSlashMontage property is to store the sword attack Montage. The DefaultLightSlashSection and DefaultHeavySlashSection enum properties represent the **default light** slash and **heavy** slash sections in the Montage to play when the player presses the key or clicks the mouse to attack. The **NextComboType** enum variable is to store the type of the **next** Combo to be played. The **IsAttacking** property represents whether the player is attacking.

Note: The above three **UENUM** variables have to be declared using the **TenumAsByte<>** template to store enumeration values as bytes in a **type-safe** way; otherwise, compile errors will occur!

Besides, three methods are declared, the PlayComboMontage() method is used to play the Montage. The LightAttack() and HeavyAttack() are overridden binding methods that are used to play the attack Montage when the player presses the key or clicks the mouse button.

Now open the **WarriorCharacter.cpp** source file, and add the following lines to implement the above three methods:

```cpp
void AWarriorCharacter::LightAttack(const FInputActionValue& value)
{
  IsAttacking = true;
  // If the sword attack Montage is not playing
  if (!GetMesh()->GetAnimInstance()
                        ->Montage_IsPlaying(GreatSwordSlashMontage)) {
    if (IsValid(GreatSwordSlashMontage)) {
      FText sectionName;
      const UEnum* EnumPtr =
                  FindFirstObjectSafe<UEnum>(TEXT("EComboSections"));
      // Get the default light attack section name
      if (EnumPtr)
        sectionName =
            EnumPtr->GetDisplayNameTextByValue(DefaultLightSlashSection);
      // Play the default light attack
      PlayComboMontage(FName(sectionName.ToString()));
    }
  }
  else // Otherwise set the next Combo type
    NextComboType = EComboTypes::LightMelee;
}

void AWarriorCharacter::HeavyAttack(const FInputActionValue& value)
{
  IsAttacking = true;
  if (!GetMesh()->GetAnimInstance()
                        ->Montage_IsPlaying(GreatSwordSlashMontage)) {
    if (IsValid(GreatSwordSlashMontage)) {
      FText sectionName;
      const UEnum* EnumPtr =
                  FindFirstObjectSafe<UEnum>(TEXT("EComboSections"));
      // Play the default heavy attack
      if (EnumPtr)
        sectionName =
          EnumPtr->GetDisplayNameTextByValue(DefaultHeavySlashSection);

      PlayComboMontage(FName(sectionName.ToString()));
    }
  }
  else
    NextComboType = EComboTypes::HeavyMelee;
}

void AWarriorCharacter::PlayComboMontage(FName section, UAnimMontage*
                                          montage, float rate)
{
  // Play the specified section in the Montage
  if(IsValid(montage))
    PlayAnimMontage(montage, rate, section);
  else
    PlayAnimMontage(GreatSwordSlashMontage, rate, section);
}
```

When the **LightAttack** mouse button is pressed, the above LightAttack() method will be called. Within the method, after setting the IsAttacking flag to true, if the sword attack Montage is not playing yet, after getting the assigned default light attack **section name**, the default light melee animation is played. Otherwise, if the Montage is playing, we set the **next** Combo type to LightMelee.

When the **HeavyAttack** mouse button is pressed, the above HeavyAttack() method will be called. The code in the method is similar to the LightAttack() method.

In the PlayComboMontage() method, we play the specified section in the Montage by calling the built-in PlayAnimMontage() function.

Now build the project and ensure that no errors occurred during the compilation.

The Animation Notify State Blueprint

After the C++ classes are ready, we have to create the Blueprint to specify the declared properties in the editor.

Back to the Unreal Editor, right-click in the **Content Browser** of the **Female** > **Animations** folder, after choosing **Blueprint Class** from the context menu, select the **SwordAnimNotifyState** class as the Parent Class as shown below:

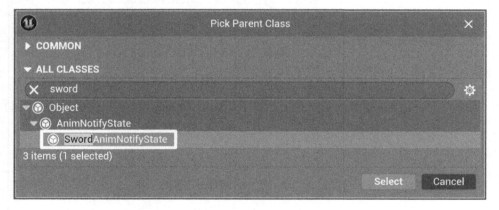

Rename the created Blueprint to **BP_SwordAnimNotifyState** and open the **AM_GreatSwordSlash** in the editor. To add Anim Notify State for our Montage, right-click on the **first** track (**1**) under the **Notifies** section, choose **Add Notify State...** > **BP_SwordAnimNotifyState** from the context menu as shown below:

After the state is created, use the **handles** on both ends of the state to adjust its length as shown below:

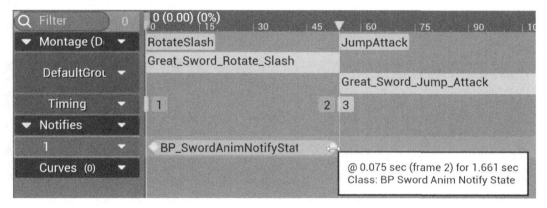

Move the **left** end to the **start** of the **RotateSlash** section, and the **right** end to the **end** of the section as shown above.

With the **BP_SwordAnimNotifyState** state selected, and in the Details panel, click on the drop-down menus to the **right** of the **Next Light Combo Section** and **Next Heavy Combo Section** respectively, **and** choose **HorizontalSlash** and **JumpAttack** as shown below:

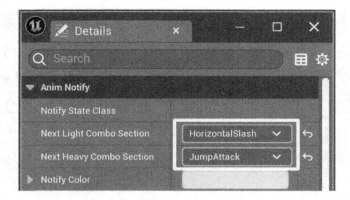

This means that if the **RotateSlash** section is playing and the **light** attack Combo key is pressed, then the **HorizontalSlash** section will be played next in the sequence. Otherwise, if the **heavy** attack Combo key is pressed during the RotateSlash section is playing, the **JumpAttack** section will be played next.

Repeat the above step **four** times to create four more states for the rest sections as shown below:

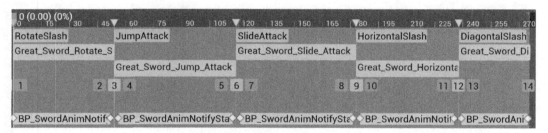

Finally, after adjusting the length of each state to match the **start** and **end** of each section respectively and setting the **Next Light Combo Section** and **Next Heavy Combo Section** properties for each state, press **Save** to confirm the modification.

Now that the montage is ready, let's finish up the Blueprint and Project Settings to play the Combos. First, open the **BP_FemaleWarrior** Blueprint and in the **Details** tab, after expanding the **Montages** and **Combo** settings as shown below:

Select the **AM_GreatSwordSlash** from the drop-down menu for the Great Sword Slash Montage field, **HorizontalSlash** for the Default Light Slash Section, and **JumpAttack** for the Default Heavy Slash Section respectively as shown above.

Adding Input Actions

After compiling and saving the Blueprint, go to the Content > **Input** folder, right-click in the folder, and select **Input** > **Input Action** to create an Input Action asset named **IA_LightAttack**. Continue to create another Input Action named **IA_HeavyAttack** in the folder.

Then open the **IMC_Warrior** mapping context asset, press the + next to the Mappings **twice** to add two more mappings as follows:

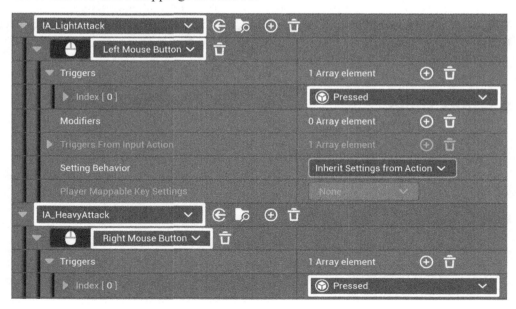

Select **IA_LightAttack** and **IA_HeavyAttack** for them, respectively. To set up the IA_LightAttack mapping, select **Mouse > Left Mouse Button** from the dropdown menu followed by creating a trigger, then click the dropdown and select **Pressed**.

The settings of the **IA_HeavyAttack** are similar to the IA_LightAttack, but we select the **Right Mouse Button** for the mapping instead.

Updating the Warrior Blueprint

Finally, open the **BP_FemaleWarrior** Blueprint again, and in the **Details** panel, look for the **Light Attack Action** and **Heavy Attack Action** fields as shown below:

After selecting the corresponding Input Action assets for them, press Compile and save the blueprint.

So far the code and the setup for playing the Combos are done, now press **Play** to run the game. After pressing the **left** mouse button, the **default light** attack section in the Montage will be played, and if you **right-click** the mouse during the animation, the **Next Heavy Combo Section** specified in the **Sword Anim Notify State** Blueprint will be played in sequence.

5.5.4 Damage Rolls

In this subsection, the weapon's hit detection and its caused damage will be implemented, and before we start, let's discuss some theories about **Damage Rolls**[10] in RPGs.

Damage Rolls

---

[10] **Probability and Games: Damage Rolls**, https://www.redblobgames.com/articles/probability/damage-rolls.html.

Damage rolls are used to calculate attack damage in Paper-and-dice role-playing games like Dungeons & Dragons. This makes sense for a game based on **dice**. Many computer RPGs calculate damage and other attributes (strength, magic points, agility, etc.) with a similar system.

Typically, you'll write some code to call the `Random(N)` method, for example, the random number generator, which returns a random integer from **0** to **N-1**. Then you'll adjust the numbers and tweak the results to get the behavior you want in your game.

Let's start with a single die. This histogram shows the results of rolling a single **12**-sided die: `1+Random(12)`. Since `Random(12)` returns a number from 0 to **11**, and we want a number from **1** to **12**, we add **1** to it. The x-axis is the damage; the y-axis shows how often that damage occurs. With a single die, a damage roll of 2 or 12 is just as likely as a damage roll of 7.

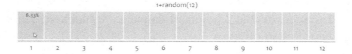

For multiple dice rolls, it'll help to use a bit of notation from dice games: *N*d*S* means roll an *S-sided* die *N* times. Rolling the **single 12**-sided die above would be written **1d12**; 3d4 means to roll a **4**-sided die **three** times; we'd code it as `3 + Random(4) + Random(4) + Random(4)`.

Let's roll **two** 6-sided dice (**2d6**) and add up the results:

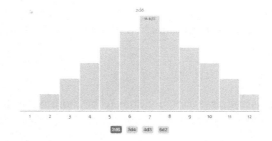

The outcomes could be anywhere from 2 (both dice roll 1) to 12 (both dice roll 6). It's more likely to roll **7** than 2 or 12.

What happens if we increase the number of dice, but decrease their size? Please refer to the following two examples:

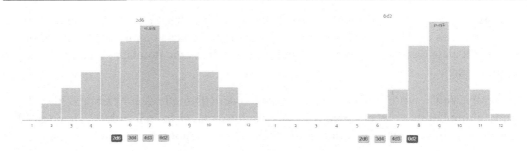

The main effect is that the distribution goes from **wide** to **narrow**. There's also a second effect, where the peak **shifts** to the **right**. Let's first investigate the uses of shifts.

Constant Shifts

Some weapons in Dungeons & Dragons give bonus damage. We could write 2d6+**5** to indicate +**5** bonus damage. In some games, armor or shields **negate** some damage. We could write 2d6-**2** to indicate that **2** points of damage are **blocked**; The two distributions are as shown in the following figures:

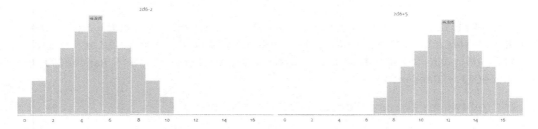

Adding bonus damage or subtracting blocked damage simply **shifts** the **entire** distribution **left** or **right**.

Asymmetry

Suppose you'd like higher-than-average values to be more common than lower-than-average values. This is less common for damage but can be used for attributes like **strength**, **intelligence**, etc. One way to do this is to roll **several** times and pick the **best** roll.

To illustrate this situation, let's define a method RollDice(N,S) for N repeated rolls of Random(S+1), returning a number from 0 to N*S. Let's try RollDice(2,12) **twice** and pick the **higher** roll, the result is shown below, and you'll find the shape now is **asymmetric**.

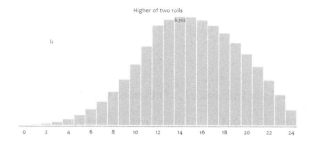

Critical hits

Another way to create occasional **bursts** of high damage is to implement it more directly. In some games, a "critical hit" provides some **bonus**. The simplest bonus is extra damage. In the following code the critical hit damage is added **5%** of the time:

```
int damage = RollDice(3,4);
if(Random(100) < 5)
  damage += RollDice(3,4);
```

The result is shown below:

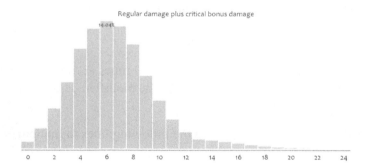

Other approaches to adding asymmetry include affecting **further** attacks: make the critical hits have a chance to trigger further critical hits; make critical hits trigger a second attack that skips defenses, or make critical hits cause the opponent to miss an attack.

Implementing the DiceRoll class

Now you understand how a die can be used for the damage rolls. Then let's create the **DiceRoll** class to model the behavior of rolling dice.

Choose **Tools > New C++ Class…** from the main menu to create a class named **DiceRoll** and choose **Object** as the parent class in the **Public/Stats** folder. Then open the **DiceRoll.h** header and add the following code shown in **bold**:

```
UCLASS(Blueprintable, EditInlineNew)
class RPG_API UDiceRoll : public UObject
{
  GENERATED_BODY()
public:
  UDiceRoll();
  UDiceRoll(int rolls, int faces, int modifier);

  UPROPERTY(EditDefaultsOnly, BlueprintReadOnly, Category = "DiceRoll")
  int Rolls;
  UPROPERTY(EditDefaultsOnly, BlueprintReadOnly, Category = "DiceRoll")
  int Faces;
  UPROPERTY(EditDefaultsOnly, BlueprintReadOnly, Category = "DiceRoll")
  int Modifier;

  static int Die(int rolls, int faces, int modifier = 0);
  int Roll();
};
```

First, add the **Blueprintable** and **EditInlineNew** Class Specifiers to the class declaration because we'll create Blueprints from this class that is derived from UObject. The **EditInlineNew** Specifier indicates that objects of this class can be created from the Unreal Editor **Property** window. Then a public section is added to the class, in which we declare two constructors, one of which has three parameters to initialize the **three** properties namely the Rolls, Faces, and Modifier.

The static Die() method is used to roll a die several times according to the parameters passed in and get the sum of the outcomes with the modifier. The Roll() method calls the Die() and uses the three properties.

Next, open the **DiceRoll.cpp** file and add the following lines to implement the constructors and methods:

```
UDiceRoll::UDiceRoll()
{
  // Default is the normal die with 6 faces, roll once
  Rolls = 1;
  Faces = 6;
  Modifier = 0;
}

UDiceRoll::UDiceRoll(int rolls, int faces, int modifier)
{
  Rolls = rolls;
  Faces = faces;
  Modifier = modifier;
}

int UDiceRoll::Die(int rolls, int faces, int modifier)
{
```

```
  int total = 0;
  // Roll a die several times
  for (int i = 1; i <= rolls; i++)
  {
    // Accumulate the outcomes
    total += FMath::RandRange(1, faces);
  }
  // Apply the modifier
  return total + modifier;
}

int UDiceRoll::Roll()
{
  return Die(Rolls, Faces, Modifier);
}
```

In the `Die()` method, we use a `for` loop to simulate rolling a die several times and accumulate the outcomes. Here the `RandRange()` method will return an **integer** ranging from **1** to the specified **faces**. Lastly, the modifier's value is added to the total and the result is returned. In the `Roll()` method, the `Die()` is called and the values of the three properties are passed in.

Now build the project and the class for damage rolls is complete, next we are going to create other classes for our weapons as follows.

5.5.5 Weapon Classes

In this section, we are going to create weapon-related classes and Blueprints.

The EquipmentStats Class

From the main menu, choose **Tools** > **New C++ Class…** from the main menu to create a class called **EquipmentStats** under the **Public/Stats** folder, and choose the **Object** as the Parent Class. Then open the **EquipmentStats.h** header, and add the following code in **bold**:

```
UCLASS(Blueprintable, DefaultToInstanced, EditInlineNew)
class RPG_API UEquipmentStats : public UObject
{
  GENERATED_BODY()

public:
  UPROPERTY(Instanced, EditAnywhere, Category = "Stats")
  class UDiceRoll* DefensePower;
};
```

Firstly, add the **Blueprintable, DefaultToInstanced** and **EditInlineNew** class specifiers to the class declaration. The **DefaultToInstanced** Specifier means that all instances of this class are considered "**instanced**". Instanced classes (components) are duplicated upon construction, and this Specifier is **inherited by subclasses**.

Then, in the **public** section, we use the above **UDiceRoll** class to declare a new property, namely the **DefensePower**, representing the **defense** power. Please note that the **Instanced** Specifier is required for you to select and reset the Stats inside Unreal Editor.

The WeaponStats Class

Continue to create a C++ class called **WeaponStats** under the **Public/Stats** folder and choose the above **EquipmentStats** as the Parent Class. Then open the **WeaponStats.h** header, and add the following code in **bold**:

```
UCLASS()
class RPG_API UWeaponStats : public UEquipmentStats
{
  GENERATED_BODY()

public:
  UPROPERTY(Instanced, EditAnywhere, Category = "Stats")
  class UDiceRoll* AttackPower;
  UPROPERTY(EditDefaultsOnly, BlueprintReadOnly, Category = "Stats")
  float AttackRate = 1.0f;
};
```

In the **public** section, the **AttackPower** property represents the attack power, and the **AttackRate** property represents the attack speed **modifier** using the weapon.

After building the project, we'll continue to create the **Item** class.

The Item Class

Back to Unreal Editor and choose **Tools** > **New C++ Class...** to create a class called **Item**, choose **Actor** as the parent class, and add "**Public/Inventory**" to the **Path** as shown below:

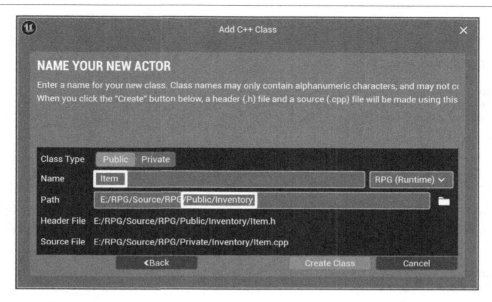

After pressing **Create Class** to generate the class in Visual Studio, open the **Item.h** header and add the following **bold** lines in the **public** section:

```
UCLASS()
class RPG_API AItem : public AActor
{
  GENERATED_BODY()

public:
  // Sets default values for this actor's properties
  AItem();

  UPROPERTY(EditDefaultsOnly, BlueprintReadWrite, Category = "Name")
  FString Name;
  UPROPERTY(EditDefaultsOnly, BlueprintReadOnly, Category = "Mesh")
  class USkeletalMeshComponent* Mesh;
     ...
};
```

Because each item has a name, a property called Name is declared to store the item's name. The Mesh property, which is a **USkeletalMeshComponent**, is to store the weapon skeletal mesh. Now build the project and make sure that no errors occur.

The Equipment Class

Back to Unreal Editor, create another C++ class called **Equipment** in the **Public/Inventory** folder, and choose the above **Item** as the parent class.

Open the **Equipment.h** header, add the following **bold** lines as shown below:

```
UCLASS()
class RPG_API AEquipment : public AItem
{
  GENERATED_BODY()

public:
  UPROPERTY(Instanced, EditAnywhere, Category = "Stats")
  class UEquipmentStats* Stats;
};
```

In the `Public` section, we add an instanced **Stats** property for every equipment.

The Weapon Class

Continue to create another C++ class called **Weapon** in the **Public/Inventory** folder and choose the above **Equipment** as the parent class. Open the **Weapon.h** header and add the following **bold** lines:

```
UENUM()
enum EAttackTypes
{
  Melee         UMETA(DisplayName = "Melee"),
  Magical       UMETA(DisplayName = "Magical")
};

UCLASS()
class RPG_API AWeapon : public AEquipment
{
  GENERATED_BODY()
public:
  UPROPERTY(EditDefaultsOnly, BlueprintReadOnly, Category = "Attack")
  TEnumAsByte<EAttackTypes> AttackType;
};
```

Before the class declaration, we declare an `enum` type **EAttackTypes** to represent the attack types for weapons. In the class, the `AttackType` represents the attack type of the weapon.

Now build the project and back to Unreal Editor. From the main menu, choose **Tools > New C++ Class...** to create another class called **Sword** in the **Public/Inventory** folder as well, and this time choose the **Weapon** as the parent class.

Open the **Sword.h** file and add the following **bold** lines in the header:

```
UCLASS()
class RPG_API ASword : public AWeapon
{
  GENERATED_BODY()
public:
  ASword();
```

```
};
```

Next, open the **Sword.cpp** file and add the following lines to implement the constructor:

```
ASword::ASword()
{
  Mesh =
        CreateDefaultSubobject<USkeletalMeshComponent>(TEXT("SwordMesh"));
  Mesh->SetupAttachment(RootComponent);
}
```

In the constructor, we create the **Skeletal Mesh** Component, and attach it to the **RootComponent**.

The EquipmentComponent Class

Now build the project and back to Unreal Editor. Choose **Tools** > **New C++ Class…** from the main menu, and select the **SkeletalMeshComponent** as the parent class:

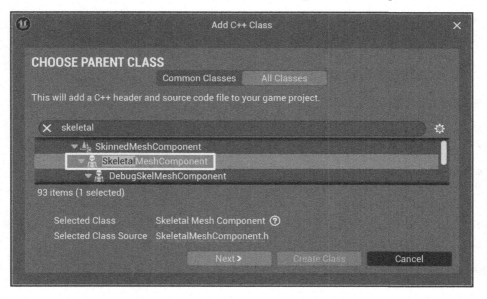

After pressing **Next**, in the next step, name the class **EquipmentComponent** and add "Public/**Inventory**" to the Path as follows:

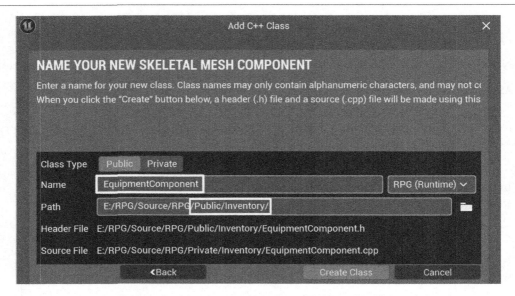

Next, press **Create Class** to generate the class, then in Visual Studio, open the
EquipmentComponent.h header, add the following **bold** lines:

```
UCLASS()
class RPG_API UEquipmentComponent : public USkeletalMeshComponent
{
  GENERATED_BODY()

public:
  // Refer to the equipment object
  UPROPERTY()
  class AEquipment* Equipment;
  bool isEquipped;
};
```

In the public section, the Equipment pointer refers to the equipment object, and the
isEquipped Boolean variable represents if the equipment is equipped.

The SwordEquipmentComponent Class

Back to Unreal Editor, create another C++ class called **SwordEquipmentComponent** in
the **Public/Inventory** folder, and choose the above **EquipmentComponent** as the
parent class.

Then in Visual Studio, open the **SwordEquipmentComponent.h** header, add the
following **bold** lines:

```
UCLASS()
```

```
class RPG_API USwordEquipmentComponent : public UEquipmentComponent
{
  GENERATED_BODY()

public:
  virtual void BeginPlay() override;

};
```

In the public section, we declare the **BeginPlay()** method.

Next, open the **SwordEquipmentComponent.cpp** file, and add the following lines to implement the **BeginPlay()** method:

```
void USwordEquipmentComponent::BeginPlay()
{
  Super::BeginPlay();

}
```

Now build the project and ensure that no errors occur. Next, we will deal damage with hit detection using the UE5 built-in tracing mechanism.

Dealing Damage

In this subsection, we will deal damage to enemies using Anim Notify State and a sphere trace to determine if we have hit the enemies. Firstly, create a new C++ class named **SwordDamageAnimNotifyState** in the **Public/Animation** folder, and choose the **AnimNotifyState** as the parent class.

Then open the **SwordDamageAnimNotifyState.h** header, and add the following **bold** lines:

```
UCLASS()
class RPG_API USwordDamageAnimNotifyState : public UAnimNotifyState
{
  GENERATED_BODY()

public:
  UPROPERTY(EditAnywhere, BlueprintReadWrite, Category = Trace)
  float TraceRadius = 20.0f;
  UPROPERTY(EditAnywhere, BlueprintReadWrite, Category = Trace)
  TArray<TEnumAsByte<EObjectTypeQuery>> DamageObjectTypes;

  virtual void NotifyTick(USkeletalMeshComponent* MeshComp,
              UAnimSequenceBase* Animation,float FrameDeltaTime) override;
};
```

In the `public` section, the `TraceRadius` property represents the damage radius of the **Sphere** trace, and the `DamageObjectTypes` property is an **Array** to store the **Object Types** that the great sword can cause damage to them.

The `NotifyTick()` event method will be called continuously each tick, during the execution of an AnimNotifyState.

Continue to open the **SwordDamageAnimNotifyState.cpp** file, add the following lines to implement the **NotifyTick()** method:

```cpp
#include "Characters/WarriorCharacter.h"
#include "Inventory/Sword.h"
#include "Interfaces/Health.h"
#include "Kismet/KismetSystemLibrary.h"
#include "Stats/DiceRoll.h"
#include "Inventory/SwordEquipmentComponent.h"

void USwordDamageAnimNotifyState::NotifyTick(USkeletalMeshComponent*
            MeshComp, UAnimSequenceBase* Animation, float FrameDeltaTime)
{
  AWarriorCharacter* warrior = Cast<AWarriorCharacter>(MeshComp->
                                                        GetOwner());

  if (warrior && warrior->RightHandWeapon)
  {
    // Get the TraceStart and TraceEnd sockets
    FVector traceStart = warrior->RightHandWeapon->
                                        GetSocketLocation("TraceStart");
    FVector traceEnd = warrior->RightHandWeapon->
                                        GetSocketLocation("TraceEnd");
    // The Hit results
    TArray<FHitResult> HitArray;
    // Ignore the sword owner for the Sphere Trace
    TArray<AActor*> ActorsToIgnore;
    ActorsToIgnore.Add(warrior);
    // Perform the Sphere Trace and show the trace hits in blue color
    // Note: warrior->GetWorld() is required instead of GetWorld();
    //       otherwise the SphereTrace will not work!
    bool isHit = UKismetSystemLibrary::SphereTraceMultiForObjects(
        warrior->GetWorld(), traceStart, traceEnd, TraceRadius,
        DamageObjectTypes, false, ActorsToIgnore,
        DrawDebugTrace::ForDuration, HitArray,
                true, FLinearColor::Red, FLinearColor::Blue, 0.1f);

    // If some target is hit
    if (isHit)
    {
      for (const FHitResult HitResult : HitArray) {
        IHealth* health = Cast<IHealth>(HitResult.GetActor());
        // Get the IHealth interface
        if (health && !health->IsDead()) {
```

```
        // Obtain the hit bone's name from the result
        FName boneName = HitResult.BoneName;

        ASword* greatSword = Cast<ASword>(warrior->RightHandWeapon
                                                        ->Equipment);
        // Only apply damage if has Stats
        if (greatSword && greatSword->Stats) {
          UWeaponStats* weaponStats = Cast<UWeaponStats>(greatSword
                                                          ->Stats);

          if (warrior->Stats) {
            // Calculate the total damage from the sword's attack power
            // plus player's current strength
            int damage = weaponStats->AttackPower->Roll() +
                            warrior->Stats->GetStatValue(TEXT("STR"));
            // Apply the damage through the interface
            health->ApplyDamage(damage, warrior);
          }
          else
            // If the warrior does not have stats, use the sword's
            // attack power as the damage
            health->ApplyDamage(weaponStats->AttackPower->Roll(),
                                                          warrior);
        }
      }
    }
  } // if isHit
  }
}
```

In the NotifyTick() method, we perform the collision detection and apply the damage for the sword attack as follows. First, the positions of the **TraceStart** and **TraceEnd** sockets are obtained. Then we declare an **FHitResult** array to store the Hit results, and after declaring an array variable, the sword owner that is the warrior is added to the ActorsToIgnore array.

Next, we call the built-in SphereTraceMulti() function to perform the collision detection. This function will sweep a **sphere** along the given line, starting from the **TraceStart** socket to the **TraceEnd** socket, and return **all hits** encountered up to and including the first blocking hit that belongs to one of the Damage Object Types.

Then if some target is hit, try getting the IHealth interface from the hit actor, and if the actor implements the IHealth and is **not** dead, after calculating the total damage from the sword's attack power plus the player's current strength, we apply the damage to the hit actor through the interface. On the other hand, if the warrior does not have stats, we use the sword's attack power as the damage.

Now build the project and back to Unreal Editor. Open the **AM_GreatSwordSlash** montage, and add the following **Sword Damage Anim Notify States** as shown below:

To create the **second** Notify Track, click the dropdown button next to the **Notifies**, and select **Add Notify Track**. Then, after adding a **Sword Damage** Anim Notify State under each section, adjust their length to represent the period that the great sword will do the damage.

Lastly, after adding an element to each **Sword Damage Anim Notify State** by pressing the + to the right of the **Damage Object Types** field in the **Details** panel, select **Pawn** from the dropdown menu as shown below:

Our code is **not** complete yet, because we have to create an **IHealth** interface class for our characters.

The IHealth Interface Class

Back to Unreal Editor and choose **Tools** > **New C++ Class...** and then choose the **UNREAL INTERFACE** as the **PARENT CLASS** as shown below:

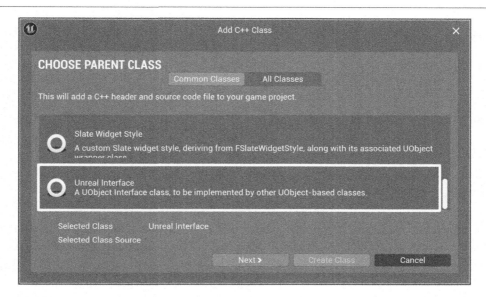

Press the **NEXT** button and in the next step, after renaming the class to **Health**, add "**Public/Interfaces**" to the **Path** as shown below:

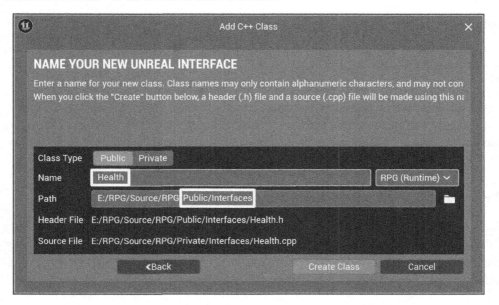

Click the **Create Class** to create the Unreal Interface and open the **Health.h** header in Visual Studio. You'll find **two** classes exist in the header as follows:

```
// This class does not need to be modified.
UINTERFACE(MinimalAPI)
class UHealth : public UInterface
```

```
{
  GENERATED_BODY()
};

/**
 *
 */
class RPG_API IHealth
{
  GENERATED_BODY()

  // … the class that will be inherited to implement this interface.
public:
};
```

The **UHealth** class is **not** supposed to be modified, as shown in the comments, and the IHealth is the **interface** class **that will be inherited to implement this interface**.

Then add the following **bold** lines to the **IHealth** class:

```
class RPG_API IHealth
{
  GENERATED_BODY()
…
public:
  // Note: Pure virtual methods (=0) are required!
  virtual void ApplyDamage(int damageValue, AActor* owner) = 0;
  virtual bool IsDead() = 0;
};
```

In the **public** section, we add two **pure virtual** methods. The ApplyDamage() method is used to apply damage to the character implementing this interface and the IsDead() method returns a Boolean value indicating whether the actor is dead.

Now you can build the project and make sure that no errors occur.

Creating Blueprints for the Great Sword

Back to Unreal Editor, open the **Content Drawer** and in the **Warriors** > **Blueprints** folder, create a new folder called **Weapons**. Then right-click in the Content Browser of the **Weapons** folder, choose **Blueprint Class** from the context menu, and in the next step, pick the **Sword** class as the Parent Class as shown below:

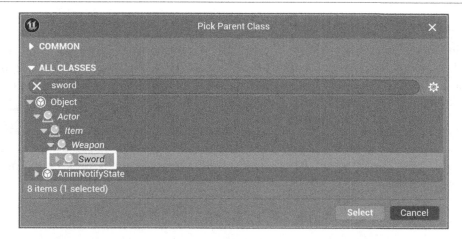

Press the **Select** button to create the Blueprint and rename it to **BP_GreatSword**.

Next, create a new folder called **Stats** in the **Warriors** > **Blueprints** folder, then right-click in the Content Browser of the **Stats** folder, choose **Blueprint Class** on the context menu, and in the next step, pick the **DiceRoll** class as the Parent Class as shown below:

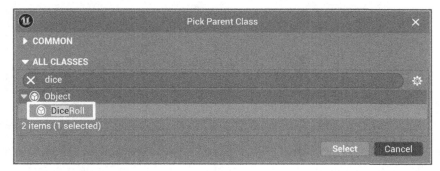

Press **Select** to create the Blueprint and rename it to **BP_GreatSwordDamage**.

Now open the **BP_GreatSwordDamage** in the editor, and within the **Details** panel, enter the desired values for the damage rolls of the great sword weapon as shown on the right:

Then press **Compile** and **Save** to confirm the modification.

Continue to create another Blueprint called **BP_GreatSwordDefense** in the **Stats** folder and also pick the **DiceRoll** class as its Parent Class. Then double-click to open it in the editor, and within the **Details** panel, enter the desired values for the **defense** rolls of the great sword.

Next, open the **BP_GreatSword** Blueprint, and in the Details panel, find the **Stats** section, and after expanding it, select the **Weapon Stats** from the drop-down menu for the **Stats field**, then select the **BP_GreatSwrodDamage** for the **Attack Power** property as shown below:

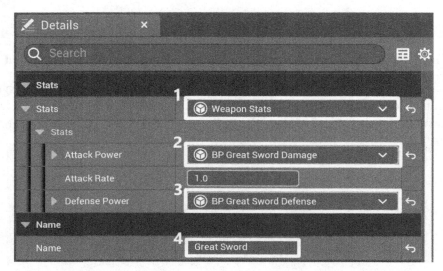

For the **Defense Power** property, choose the **BP_GreatSwordDefense** for it as shown above. Also, in the **Name** field, enter "**Great Sword**" for the **Name** property.

With the **Mesh** component selected under the **Components** tab, drag and drop the imported **SK_GreatSword** skeletal mesh onto the **Skeletal Mesh Asset** field in the **Details** panel as shown below:

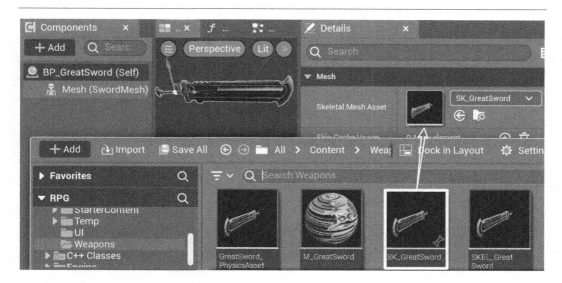

The great sword mesh will show up in the Viewport as shown above.

Now that the great sword Blueprint is complete, press **Compile** and **Save** to confirm the modification. In the next step, we'll create **Sockets** for the great sword to denote its damage range.

Creating Sphere Trace Sockets

To denote the damage range of the weapon, here is the great sword, we'll create **two** sockets on the static mesh. Double-click on the **SK_GreatSword** skeletal mesh to open it in the editor. In the **Skeleton Tree** panel on the right, with the **GreatSword** selected, click the + icon to create a socket as shown below:

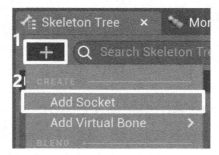

After the socket is created, rename it to **TraceStart** as shown below:

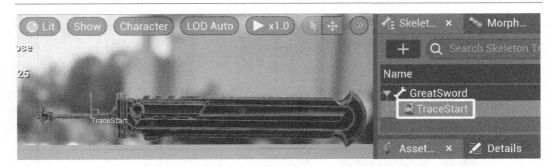

Then move the **TraceStart** socket in the direction of the **Y-axis** in the **Viewport** to the appropriate location on the **blade** as shown below:

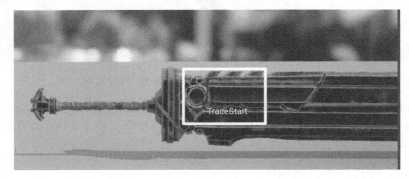

Continue to press the + icon to create another socket called **TraceEnd** and move it to the **top** of the blade as shown below:

Now press **Save** to confirm the modification.

5.5.6 Enemy Classes and Animation Setup

In this section, we'll create the enemy-related classes and set up the animations and Montages.

The NPC Class

Before creating the **Enemy** class to represent the enemies, let's create the **base** class called **NPC** to represent the **non-playable characters**. Choose Tools > **New C++**

Class... from the main menu, and in the next step, choose the **Character** as the parent class. Then after changing the class name to **NPC** in the next step as shown below:

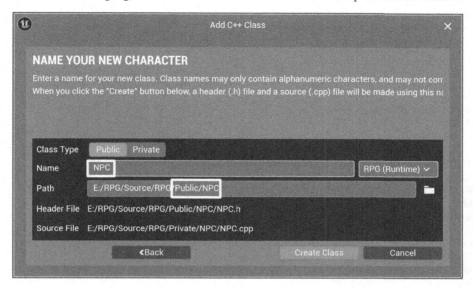

Add "**Public/NPC**" to the **Path**, then press **Create Class** to generate the class. Open the **NPC.h** header and add the following **bold** lines to the header:

```cpp
UCLASS()
class RPG_API ANPC : public ACharacter
{
  GENERATED_BODY()

public:
  // Sets default values for this character's properties
  ANPC();

  UPROPERTY(EditDefaultsOnly, BlueprintReadWrite, Category = "Name")
  FString Name;
    ...
};
```

Because each NPC has its name, we declare a property called `Name` in the `public` section.

The Enemy Class

After building the project, back to Unreal Editor, continue to create a new C++ class called **Enemy**, and choose the newly created **NPC** class as the parent class in the **Public/NPC** folder.

Open the **Enemy.h** header and add the following code shown in **bold**:

```
#include "CoreMinimal.h"
#include "NPC.h"
#include "Components/WidgetComponent.h"
#include "Interfaces/Health.h"
#include "Stats/CharacterStats.h"
#include "Enemy.generated.h"

UCLASS()
class RPG_API AEnemy : public ANPC, public IHealth
{
   GENERATED_BODY()
public:
   AEnemy();

   UPROPERTY(Instanced, EditAnywhere, Category = "Stats")
   UCharacterStats* Stats;
   UPROPERTY(VisibleAnywhere, BlueprintReadOnly, Category = "Widgets")
   UWidgetComponent* HealthBar;
   UPROPERTY(EditDefaultsOnly, BlueprintReadOnly, Category = "Montages")
   TArray<UAnimMontage*> DeathMontages;
   UPROPERTY(EditDefaultsOnly, BlueprintReadOnly, Category = "Montages")
   TArray<UAnimMontage*> GetHitMontages;
   UPROPERTY(EditDefaultsOnly, BlueprintReadOnly, Category = "Montages")
   TArray<UAnimMontage*> AttackMontages;

   virtual void ApplyDamage(int damageValue, AActor* causer) override;
   virtual bool IsDead() override;
   virtual void PlayDeathMontage();
   virtual void PlayGetHitMontage();
   void ResizeHealthBar(int hp);
private:
   bool isDead = false;
};
```

The Enemy class has to implement the **IHealth** interface and override its two methods namely the ApplyDamage() and IsDead() which are declared in the public section.

The **Stats** property represents the enemy Stats. The **HealthBar** widget component property refers to the health bar widget. The DeathMontages, GetHitMontages, and AttackMontages array properties are to store the death, get hit, and attack Montages, respectively. We also declare an isDead Boolean variable in the private section to indicate whether the enemy is dead.

The PlayDeathMontage() and PlayGetHitMontage() are the methods to play the death and get hit Montages, respectively. The ResizeHealthBar() method is to resize the health bar.

Next, open the **Enemy.cpp** file and add the following lines to implement the constructor and methods:

```
#include "UI/HealthBarWidget.h"

AEnemy::AEnemy()
{
  HealthBar =
        CreateDefaultSubobject<UWidgetComponent>(TEXT("HealthBarWidget"));
  HealthBar->SetupAttachment(RootComponent);
}

void AEnemy::ResizeHealthBar(int hp)
{
  // Get the health bar widget
  UHealthBarWidget* healthBar = Cast<UHealthBarWidget>(
                                    HealthBar->GetUserWidgetObject());

  if (healthBar) {
    // Get the enemy's maximum HP
    int maxhp = Stats->GetStatValue("MaxHP");
    // Resize the health bar
    if(maxhp != 0)
      healthBar->ResizeHealthBar(hp / (float)maxhp);
  }
}
```

In the constructor, after creating the health bar widget component, it's attached to the root component.

In the ResizeHealthBar() method, after getting the health bar widget and the enemy's maximum HP, we resize the health bar by calling its ResizeHealthBar() method and passing in the **ratio** of the new HP to the enemy's **MaxHP** Stat value. Here the maxHP is converted to a **float** first and thus the result of the division is a float as well.

```
void AEnemy::ApplyDamage(int damageValue, AActor* causer)
{
  if (Stats) {
    // Get the enemy's current HP
    int hp = Stats->GetStatValue("HP");
    // Apply the damage
    hp -= damageValue;
    // If the HP is less than 0 after the damage, reset it to 0
    // and set the isDead to true
    if (hp <= 0) {
      hp = 0;
      isDead = true;
      // Play the death Montage
      PlayDeathMontage();
    } else
      PlayGetHitMontage(); // Play the Get Hit Montage

    // Resize the health bar
    ResizeHealthBar(hp);
```

```
        // Save the new HP
        Stats->SetStatValue("HP", hp);
    }
}

void AEnemy::PlayDeathMontage()
{
    if (DeathMontages.Num() != 0)
    {
        // Get a random integer from 0 to the array size minus one
        int num = FMath::RandRange(0, DeathMontages.Num() - 1);
        // Play the Montage
        PlayAnimMontage(DeathMontages[num]);
    }
}

void AEnemy::PlayGetHitMontage()
{
    if (GetHitMontages.Num() != 0)
    {
        int num = FMath::RandRange(0, GetHitMontages.Num() - 1);
        PlayAnimMontage(GetHitMontages[num]);
    }
}

bool AEnemy::IsDead()
{
    return isDead;
}
```

Within the ApplyDamage() method, after getting the enemy's current HP value, we apply the damage by **substrating** it from the HP. If the new HP value is **less than** 0 after the damage, reset it to 0. Then after setting the isDead to **true**, the death Montage is played. Otherwise, if the enemy is not dead, we play the **Get Hit** Montage. Finally, after resizing the health bar, the new HP value is saved.

In the PlayDeathMontage() and PlayGetHitMontage() methods, we **randomly** choose one Montage from the array and call the PlayAnimMontage() method to play the Montage. In the IsDead() method, the isDead flag value is returned.

The Wolf Class

After building the project, back to Unreal Editor. Continue to create another C++ class called **Wolf** in the **Public/NPC** folder and choose the newly created **Enemy** class as the parent class.

Open the **Wolf.h** header and add the following **bold** lines to declare a constructor in the header:

```
UCLASS()
class RPG_API AWolf : public AEnemy
{
  GENERATED_BODY()
public:
  AWolf();
};
```

Next, open the **Wolf.cpp** file and add the following lines to implement the constructor:

```
AWolf::AWolf()
{
}
```

The EnemyAnimInstance Class

Next, let's create a C++ **Anim Instance** class for our enemies. From the main menu, choose **Tools > New C++ Class...** and in the next step, select the **RPGAnimInstance** as the parent class as shown below:

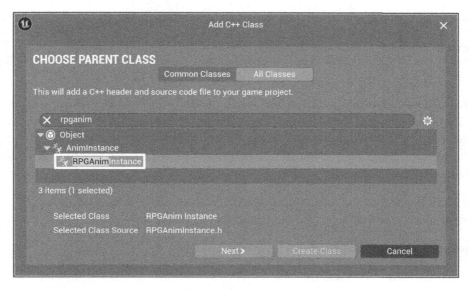

After pressing the **NEXT** button, rename the class to **EnemyAnimInstance** in the next step, and then add "**Public/Animation**" to the **Path**. Finally, press **Create Class** to generate the class in Visual Studio. Open the **EnemyAnimInstance.h** header and add the following **bold** lines:

```
UCLASS()
class RPG_API UEnemyAnimInstance : public URPGAnimInstance
{
  GENERATED_BODY()
public:
```

```
UPROPERTY(EditAnywhere, BlueprintReadWrite, Category = "States")
bool IsResting = false;
UPROPERTY(EditAnywhere, BlueprintReadWrite, Category = "States")
bool IsMoving = false;
UPROPERTY(EditAnywhere, BlueprintReadWrite, Category = "Direction")
float Direction;

virtual void NativeUpdateAnimation(float DeltaSeconds) override;
};
```

In the `public` section, the `IsResting` and `IsMoving` properties represent the movement states of the enemy. The `Direction` property is to store the degree of the angle between velocity and Rotation forward vector.

Next, open the **EnemyAnimInstance.cpp** file and add the following lines to implement the `NativeUpdateAnimation()` method:

```
void UEnemyAnimInstance::NativeUpdateAnimation(float DeltaSeconds)
{
  FVector velocity = GetOwningActor()->GetVelocity();
  FRotator rotation = GetOwningActor()->GetActorRotation();

  ForwardSpeed = velocity.Size();
  Direction = CalculateDirection(velocity, rotation);   // -180 to 180
}
```

In the overridden `NativeUpdateAnimation()` method, after getting the actor's velocity and rotation, we obtain the forward speed from the velocity and call the built-in `CalculateDirection()` method to calculate the **angle** between the velocity and rotation forward vector. The range of return will be from -180 to 180, and this will be used to feed blendspace directional value.

Now build the project and ensure that no errors occur. Since the C++ classes are complete, let's continue to create the Blueprints as follows.

Creating Blueprints for Enemies

Open the **Content Browser**, right-click in the **Wolf** folder under the **Animal Variety Pack** and choose **Animation** > **Animation Blueprint** from the context menu. In the next step, select the **EnemyAnimInstance** class in the list as the Parent Class as shown below:

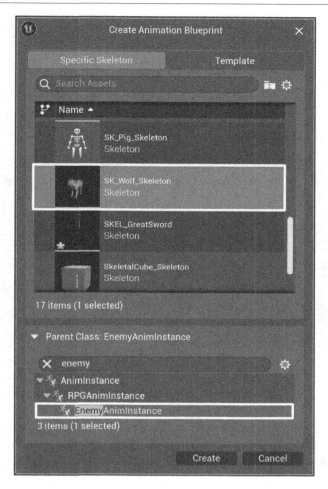

Select the **SK_Wolf_Skeleton** as the **Specific Skeleton**, then press the **Create** button to create a Blueprint named **ABP_Wolf** in the folder.

Double-click on the **ABP_Wolf** to open it in the editor, right-click within the **AnimGraph** of your Animation Blueprint, find and choose **State Machines > State Machine** from the context menu to create a **Node**, and rename it to **Locomotion**.

Now double-click on the **Locomotion** node to open the State Machine for creating states and conduits. Then drag a wire from the **Entry** node into an **empty** portion of the graph and release the mouse, from the context menu choose **Add State** to add a new state and rename it to **Idle/Run** as shown below:

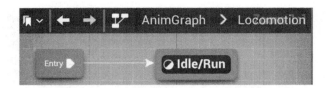

Next, double-click on the **Idle/Run** state to open it in the editor and find the **BS_Wolf** under the **Wolf** folder. Drag it into the **Idle/Run** panel as shown below:

Now, drag a wire from the **output pin** icon of the blend space and make a transition to the input (**Result**) pin of the **Output Animation Pose** node as shown above.

Next, right-click within the **Idle/Run** panel to open the **All Actions for this Blueprint** window. In the input field, after entering the "Forward" string, you can find **Get Forward Speed** under the **Speed** category. Click on it to create a **Forward Speed** node in the panel as shown below:

Then drag a wire from the **output** pin of the **Forward Speed** node to the **ForwardSpeed** input pin of the Blend Space to make a transition as shown above.

Right-click within the **Idle/Run** panel again and in the window, select the **Get Direction** under the **Variables** > **Direction** hierarchy to create a **Direction** node in the panel. Finally, make a transition between the **Direction** node and the **Direction** input pin of the Blend Space as shown below:

In the **MyBlueprint** window, double-click to open the **AnimGraph**. Drag off the **Locomotion** State Machine and search for and add a **New Save cached pose** as shown below:

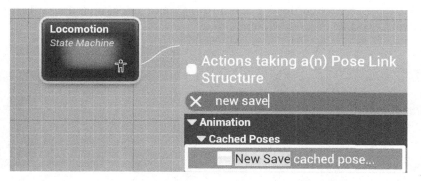

Give the **cached pose** a name called **LocomotionCache** as shown below:

Right-click in the graph and add the **Use cached pose 'LocomotionCache'** (or whatever you named the cached pose) as shown below:

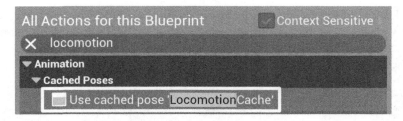

Drag off the **Use cached pose** node and search for and add the **Layered blend per bone** node.

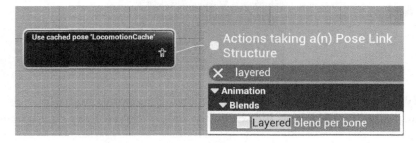

Copy/Paste the **Use cached pose 'LocomotionCache'** node, then drag off it and add the **Slot 'DefaultSlot'** node as shown below:

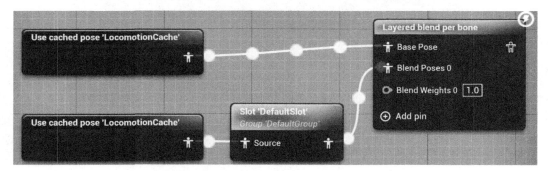

Connect the **Slot** to the **Blend Poses 0** pin on the **Layered blend per bone** node, as shown above.

Now with the **Layer blend per bone** node selected, in the **Details** tab, after adding a **Branch Filter** under the **Config > Layer Setup** section, set the **Bone Name** field to **root** as shown below:

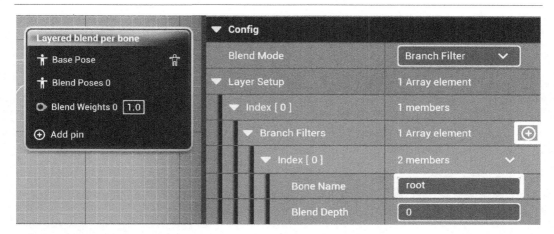

Finally, connect the output pin of the **Layer blend per bone node** to the **Result** pin on the **Output Pose** node, as shown below:

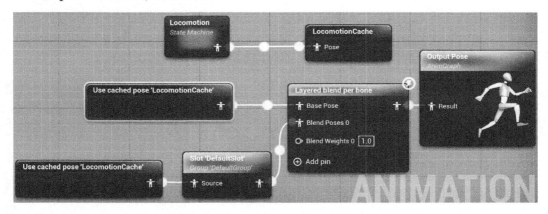

After the transition is established, you'll find that the **Idle** animation is played in the previewing panel on the left. Now click on **Compile** button on the toolbar to compile the blueprint, if no errors appeared, then press the **Save** button to save the blueprint.

Next, let's create the Blueprint for the **Wolf** enemy. Right-click in the **Wolf** folder under the Animal Variety Pack, choose **Blueprint Class** from the context menu, and choose the **Wolf** class under the **Enemy** as the Parent Class as follows:

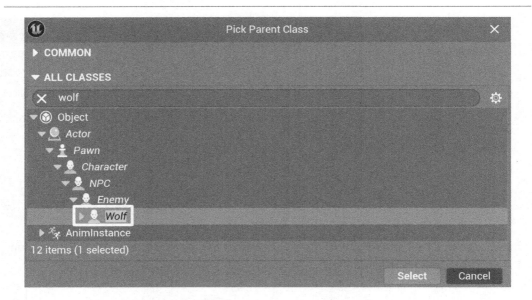

Press **Select** to create the Blueprint, and after renaming it to **BP_Wolf**, double-click to open the Blueprint in the editor as shown below:

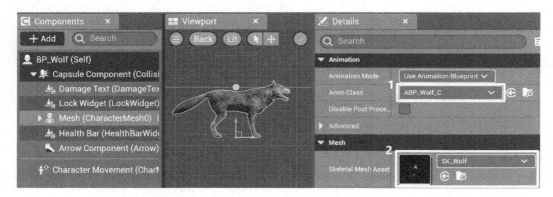

With the **Mesh** selected in the **Components** tab, and in the **Details** tab, select **ABP_Wolf** for the **Anim Class** field and select **SK_Wolf** for the **Skeletal Mesh Asset** field, respectively. Then in the **Viewport**, move the Wolf mesh to **inside** the **Capsule** as shown above.

Next, select the **Capsule Component** in the Components tab, and adjust the **Capsule Half Height** and **Capsule Radius** fields respectively in the **Details** tab as shown below:

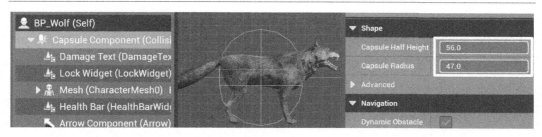

Select the **Mesh** again in the Components tab, and expand the **Transform** settings in the Details tab as shown below:

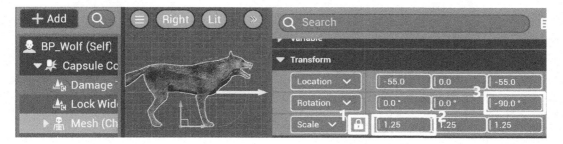

After **resetting** its **Scale** to **1.25** (25% bigger), change the **Z** rotation to **-90** to make the wolf face the direction of the **Arrow** Component as shown above. Finally, move the Wolf mesh in the Viewport until the Capsule covers its head.

Now that the wolf mesh setup is complete, let's add a health bar for it.

Health Bar Setup

With the **Health Bar** selected in the Components tab, and in the Details tab, after expanding the **User Interface** as shown below:

Select the **WBP_HealthBar** Blueprint for the **Widget Class** field as shown above, then move the health bar in the Viewport to **above** the mesh, and if its size is too big or too small, please re-open the Blueprint to adjust the size accordingly.

After the setup is complete, select the **Screen** for the **Space** field as shown below:

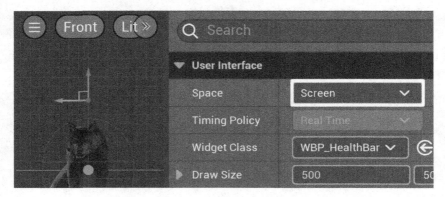

Now the health bar will **disappear** from the Viewport, which means during gameplay the health bar will **always face** the player.

Enemy Stats Setup

With the **BP_Wolf** selected, find the **Stats** section in the Details tab, and after selecting **Character Stats** for the **Stats** field as shown below:

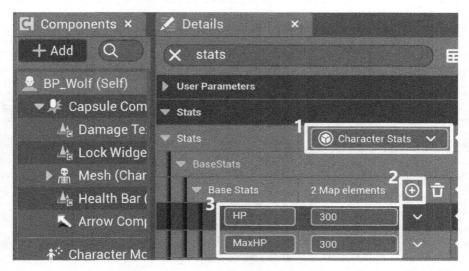

Press the + icon to add a Map element under the **Base Stats** property, enter "**HP**" in the **left** empty field for the Stat's name and **300** in the **right** empty field for the Stat's **value**.

Then press the + again to add another element and enter "**MaxHP**" and **300** in the empty fields respectively as shown above.

Enemy Montage Setup

Find the **ANIM_Wolf_GetHitFront** and **ANIM_Wolf_GetHitLeft** animation sequences in the **Wolf** > **Animations** folder, **right-click** on them respectively and choose **Create** > **Create AnimMontage** from the context menu to create **two** get-hit Montages. Then rename them to **AM_Wolf_GetHitFront** and **AM_Wolf_GetHitLeft** respectively.

Similarly, right-click the **ANIM_Wolf_Death** animation sequence, create a Montage from it, and rename the Montage to **AM_Wolf_Death**. Then open the **BP_Wolf** Blueprint and in the Details tab, find the **Montages** section and press the + icon to the right of the **Death Montages** field to create a new Array element. Then select the **AM_Wolf_Death** for the element as shown below:

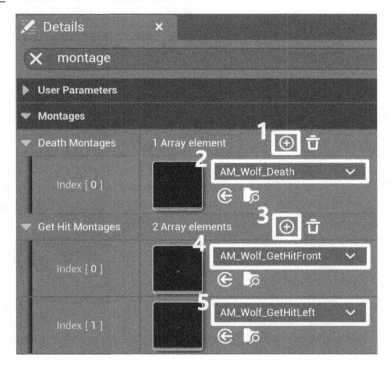

Next, press the + icon to the right of the **Get Hit Montages** field **twice** to create **two** new elements. Then select the **AM_Wolf_GetHitFront** and **AM_Wolf_GetHitLeft** for them respectively as shown above.

After pressing **Compile** and **Save** to confirm the modification, the Wolf enemy Blueprint is complete. Now drag and drop the **BP_Wolf** from the Content Browser onto the map as shown below:

Ensure that the wolf's feet are **right above** the terrain, if it's not, please open the Blueprint and adjust its position accordingly.

5.5.7 Melee Weapon Loading Setup

In this section, we'll finish the setup for loading the great sword on the warrior character. Double-click to open the **SKEL_FemaleWarrior** under the **Warriors** > **Female** folder, and in the **left** panel of the editor, expand the hierarchy until you find the **RightHand** bone as shown below:

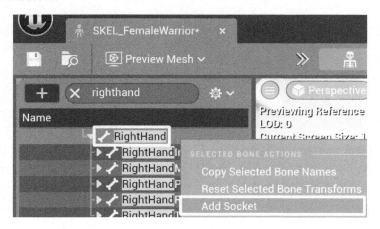

Right-click on it and select **Add Socket** on the context menu to create a socket under the bone, and as shown below, with the **RightHandSocket** socket selected, rename it to **RightHandSwordSocket**.

Then, in the **Viewport**, **move** the socket to **under** the **right palm** as shown below:

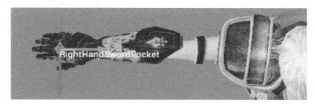

Next, continue to right-click on the **Neck** bone and add another socket called **WeaponRestSocket** as shown below:

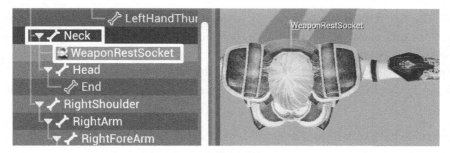

Move it to the **back** of the character in the **Viewport** as shown above. Finally, press **Save** to confirm the modification.

Attaching the Great Sword

Before attaching the great sword to the character, we have to add some code in the warrior class. Open the **WarriorCharacter.h** header in Visual Studio, and add the following **bold** lines in the **public** section:

```
UCLASS()
class RPG_API AWarriorCharacter : public ARPGCharacter
{
  GENERATED_BODY()
public:
```

```
    ...
    UPROPERTY(EditDefaultsOnly, Category = "Weapon")
    TSubclassOf<class AItem> GreatSwordClass;
    UPROPERTY(VisibleAnywhere, BlueprintReadOnly, Category = "Weapon")
    bool IsRightHandWeaponLoaded;
    UPROPERTY(EditDefaultsOnly, BlueprintReadWrite, Category = "Weapon")
    class USwordEquipmentComponent* RightHandWeapon;
    UPROPERTY(EditDefaultsOnly, BlueprintReadWrite, Category = "Weapon")
    FRotator WeaponRestRotation;
    UPROPERTY(EditDefaultsOnly, BlueprintReadWrite,Category = "Weapon")
    FRotator RightHandWeaponMountRotation;
    UPROPERTY(EditDefaultsOnly, BlueprintReadOnly, Category = "Montages")
    UAnimMontage* DrawASwordMontage;
    UPROPERTY(EditDefaultsOnly, BlueprintReadOnly, Category = "Montages")
    UAnimMontage* UnloadASwordMontage;
    TEnumAsByte<EComboTypes> CurrentComboType;

    void EquipAGreatSword();
    void UnloadAGreatSword();
    void DrawAGreatSwordNotify();
    void UnloadAGreatSwordNotify(bool playMontage);
}
```

The **GreatSwordClass** property refers to the great sword blueprint. The IsRightHandWeaponLoaded property represents whether the right-handed weapon is loaded. The RightHandWeapon property is to store the sword equipment component. The WeaponRestRotation and RightHandWeaponMountRotation properties are to store the **rotations** of the weapon when it's **unloaded** or **loaded**. The DrawASwordMontage and UnloadASwordMontage properties are to store the sword drawing and unloading Montages, respectively. The CurrentComboType enum variable stores the current Combo attack type.

The EquipAGreatSword() and UnloadAGreatSword() methods are to **equip** and **unload** a great sword, respectively. The DrawAGreatSwordNotify() or UnloadAGreatSwordNotify() method is called when the Anim Notify is triggered.

Then open the **WarriorCharacter.cpp** file, and after adding the following header:

```
#include "Inventory/SwordEquipmentComponent.h"
```

Add the following **bold** lines in the **constructor**:

```
AWarriorCharacter::AWarriorCharacter() : Super()
{
  RightHandWeapon =
    CreateDefaultSubobject<USwordEquipmentComponent>
                                    (TEXT("RightHandWeapon"));
  // Attach the melee weapon to the socket of the Mesh component
```

```
  RightHandWeapon->SetupAttachment(GetMesh(), "WeaponRestSocket");
  IsRightHandWeaponLoaded = false;
  CurrentComboType = EComboTypes::Empty;
}
```

In the constructor, after creating the **Sword Equipment Component** to store the great sword, we call the `SetupAttachment()` method, passing in the warrior's **Mesh** component and the **socket** name, to attach the weapon to the **socket** of the Mesh component. Finally, the `IsRightHandWeaponLoaded` flag is set and the `CurrentComboType` is initialized to **Empty**.

Then, add the following **bold** lines in the **BeginPlay()**:

```
void AWarriorCharacter::BeginPlay()
{
  Super::BeginPlay();

  // Create the great sword object
  if (IsValid(GreatSwordClass)) {
    ASword* greatSword = NewObject<ASword>(GetWorld(), GreatSwordClass);

    if (greatSword) {
      // Assign the great sword
      RightHandWeapon->Equipment = greatSword;
      // Set the skeletal mesh of the component
      RightHandWeapon->SetSkeletalMesh(greatSword->Mesh-
                                        >GetSkeletalMeshAsset());
    }
  }

  const FTransform swordRestTransform(WeaponRestRotation);
  // Mount the great sword on the back of the character
  RightHandWeapon->SetRelativeTransform(swordRestTransform);
}
```

In the method, after the game is running, we create the great sword object using the **NewObject()** method. Then the object is assigned to the **Equipment** property of the `RightHandWeapon`, followed by setting the skeletal mesh of the component.

Lastly, an **FTransform** object is first created and initialized with the `WeaponRestRotation` rotation, and then we set the **relative transform** of the great sword to mount it on the back of the character.

Next, add the following lines to implement the **four** methods:

```
void AWarriorCharacter::EquipAGreatSword()
{
  // Load the great sword
  RightHandWeapon->AttachToComponent(GetMesh(),
                  FAttachmentTransformRules::KeepRelativeTransform,
```

```
                                          "RightHandSwordSocket");
    const FTransform swordMountTransform(RightHandWeaponMountRotation);
    RightHandWeapon->SetRelativeTransform(swordMountTransform);

    IsRightHandWeaponLoaded = true;
}
```

In the `EquipAGreatSword()` method, we first call the **AttachToComponent()** method of
the child actor component, here we specify the **RightHandSwordSocket** socket of the
Mesh component to attach the sword on the **right** hand of the character and choose to
keep the **relative** transform.

Then, after creating an `FTransform` object and initializing it with the
`RightHandWeaponMountRotation` rotation, we set the relative transform of the great
sword to load it on the right hand of the character. Lastly, the
`IsRightHandWeaponLoaded` flag is set to `true`.

```
void AWarriorCharacter::UnloadAGreatSword()
{
    if (IsRightHandWeaponLoaded) {

        // Load the great sword
        RightHandWeapon->AttachToComponent(GetMesh(),
                        FAttachmentTransformRules::KeepRelativeTransform,
                                               "WeaponRestSocket");
        const FTransform swordRestTransform(WeaponRestRotation);
        RightHandWeapon->SetRelativeTransform(swordRestTransform);

        IsRightHandWeaponLoaded = false;
    }
}
```

In the `UnloadAGreatSword()` method, the code is similar to the above method, we
specify the **WeaponRestSocket** socket of the Mesh component to **unload** the sword and
the `IsRightHandWeaponLoaded` flag is set to `false`.

```
void AWarriorCharacter::DrawAGreatSwordNotify()
{
    // If the great sword is not loaded and we're playing the attack Montage
    if (!IsRightHandWeaponLoaded && CurrentComboType != EComboTypes::Empty)
    {
        // Equip the great sword first
        EquipAGreatSword();

        // Determine which Combo to play, light or heavy
        if (CurrentComboType == EComboTypes::LightMelee)
            LightAttack();
        else if (CurrentComboType == EComboTypes::HeavyMelee)
            HeavyAttack();
        // Reset the current attack to Empty
```

```
      CurrentComboType == EComboTypes::Empty;
  }
}
```

In the `DrawAGreatSwordNotify()` method, if the great sword is not loaded and the attack Montage is playing, after equipping it, we determine which Combo to play; if it's a **light** attack, the `LightAttack()` method is called; otherwise, the `HeavyAttack()` method is called. Lastly, the current Combo type is reset to `Empty`.

```
void AWarriorCharacter::UnloadAGreatSwordNotify(bool playMontage)
{
  if (IsRightHandWeaponLoaded) {
    if (playMontage && IsValid(UnloadASwordMontage))
      PlayAnimMontage(UnloadASwordMontage);
    else // The montage is playing, unload the sword directly
      UnloadAGreatSword();
  }
}
```

In the `UnloadAGreatSwordNotify()` method, if the great sword is loaded and the incoming `playMontage` flag is **true**, which means the character currently is **idle** or **moving**, the `UnloadASwordMontage` Montage is played first to unload the sword.

Otherwise, if the flag is **false**, meaning the unloading Montage is playing, then we call the `UnloadAGreatSword()` method directly to unload the great sword.

Finally, **modify** the `LightAttack()` and `HeavyAttack()` methods respectively, and add the following code in **bold**:

```
void AWarriorCharacter::LightAttack()
{
  IsAttacking = true;

  // If the sword is not loaded yet
  if (!IsRightHandWeaponLoaded) {
    // Set the current Combo type
    CurrentComboType = EComboTypes::LightMelee;
    // Play the DrawASwordMontage Montage
    if(IsValid(DrawASwordMontage))
      PlayAnimMontage(DrawASwordMontage);
  } else if (!GetMesh()->GetAnimInstance()
                        ->Montage_IsPlaying(GreatSwordSlashMontage)) {
    ...
  }
  else
    NextComboType = EComboTypes::LightMelee;
}
```

In the added code, we determine if the sword is **not** loaded yet, and if it's true, after setting the current Combo type, the **DrawASwordMontage** Montage is played and then the sword will be loaded.

```
void AWarriorCharacter::HeavyAttack()
{
  IsAttacking = true;

  if (!IsRightHandWeaponLoaded) {
    CurrentComboType = EComboTypes::HeavyMelee;

    if (IsValid(DrawASwordMontage))
      PlayAnimMontage(DrawASwordMontage);
  } else if (!GetMesh()->GetAnimInstance()
                        ->Montage_IsPlaying(GreatSwordSlashMontage)) {
    …
  }
  else
    NextComboType = EComboTypes::HeavyMelee;
}
```

Similarly, in the `HeavyAttack()` method, after setting the current Combo type to `HeavyMelee`, we play the DawASwordMontage Montage. Now build the project and ensure that no errors occur.

Next, we'll attach the great sword to the player character in the Blueprint. Open the **BP_FemaleWarrior** Blueprint in the editor, with the **Mesh** component **selected**, and click the **+ADD** icon on the **toolbar** as shown below:

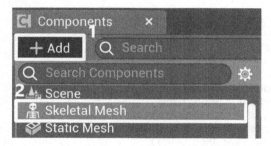

Then select **Skeletal Mesh** in the drop-down menu to create a **SkeletalMesh** under the **Mesh** component as shown below:

In the Details tab, after expanding **Sockets** and **Mesh** sections, select the **RightHandSwordSocket** socket for the **Parent Socket** field by pressing the **Search** tool as shown above. Then select the **SK_GreatSword** from the drop-down menu for the **Skeletal Mesh Asset** field.

Then in the **Viewport**, you'll see the great sword appears on the **right** hand of the character as shown below:

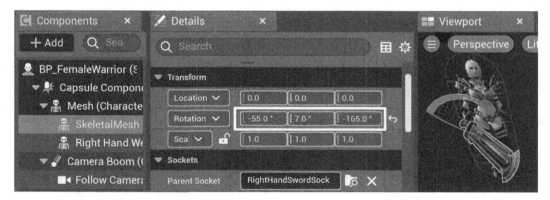

With the **SkeletalMesh** selected in the Viewport, after using the **rotation** gizmo to adjust its **rotation**, as shown above, **record** the **three Rotation values** in the Details tab. We'll use the values later for the **mount rotation** of the right-handed weapon in the C++ code.

Now **delete** the **SkeletalMesh** from the hierarchy in the Components tab, and select the **Right Hand Weapon** component as shown below:

In the Details tab, find the **Mesh** section, click the drop-down menu to the right of the **Skeletal Mesh Asset** field, and select the **SK_GreatSword** as shown above. After using the **rotation** gizmo to adjust its **rotation**, **record** the **three Rotation values** in the Details tab and we'll use the values later for the sword's **rest rotation** in the C++ code.

After the Rotation values have been recorded, click on the dropdown button, and select **Clear** to reset the field to **None** as shown below. That's because we will load the great sword using C++ code in the **BeginPlay()** method when the game starts.

Note: Sometimes, you'll find it's **empty** in the **Details** panel in the Unreal Editor after adding a new UPROPERTY to a C++ class. To solve this issue, choose **File** > **Reparent Blueprint** from the main menu of the **Blueprint Editor** to reparent **temporarily** to its **parent** class, for example, the **RPGCharacter** class. Then **re-do** the reparenting back to the **original desired** class, for example, the **WarriorCharacter** class in our case.

Now with the **BP_FemaleWarrior** selected, and in the Details tab, expand the **Weapon** section, enter the above-recorded rotation values in the **Weapon Rest Rotation** and **Right Hand Weapon Mount Rotation** fields respectively as shown below:

Next, in the **Montages** section, select **AM_Draw_A_Great_Sword** and **AM_Unload_A_Great_Sword** for the Draw ASword Montage and Draw ASword Montage fields respectively as shown below:

Finally, select the **BP_GreatSword** blueprint for the **Great Sword Class** field as follows:

Now press **Compile** and **Save** to confirm the above modification. In the next step, we'll set up the Montages using **Anim Notify** to load and unload the great sword in C++.

Weapon Mounting and Unloading Montage Setup

From the main menu, select **Tools** > **New C++ Class…** and choose the **AnimNotify** class as the PARENT CLASS as shown below:

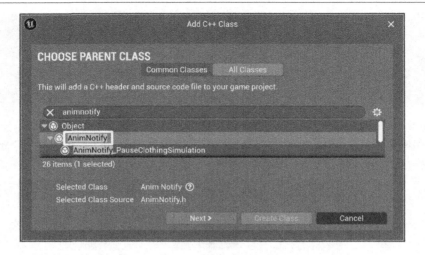

Press the **NEXT** button and in the next step, after renaming the class to **DrawASwordAnimNotify**, add "**Public/Animation**" to the **Path** and press **Create Class** to generate the class.

Open the **DrawASwordAnimNotify.h** header and add the following **bold** lines:

```
UCLASS()
class RPG_API UDrawASwordAnimNotify : public UAnimNotify
{
  GENERATED_BODY()
public:
  virtual void Notify(USkeletalMeshComponent* MeshComp,
                              UAnimSequenceBase* Animation) override;
};
```

In the public section, we override the Notify() method of the **UAnimNotify** class.

Now open the **DrawASwordAnimNotify.cpp** file, and add the following lines to implement the overridden method:

```
#include "Characters/WarriorCharacter.h"

void UDrawASwordAnimNotify::Notify(USkeletalMeshComponent* MeshComp,
                                UAnimSequenceBase* Animation)
{
  // Get the warrior character from the Mesh component's owner actor
  AWarriorCharacter* warrior = Cast<AWarriorCharacter>(
                                        MeshComp->GetOwner());

  if (warrior) {
    warrior->DrawAGreatSwordNotify();
  }
}
```

In the `Notify()` method, after getting the warrior character from the incoming Mesh component's **owner** actor, the `DrawAGreatSwordNotify()` method is called to draw the great sword.

Next, back to Unreal Editor and select **Tools > New C++ Class...** from the main menu to generate another class called **UnloadASwordAnimNotify** in the **Public/Animation** folder, and also choose the **AnimNotify** class as its parent class. Open the **UnloadASwordAnimNotify.h** header and add the following **bold** lines:

```
UCLASS()
class RPG_API UUnloadASwordAnimNotify : public UAnimNotify
{
  GENERATED_BODY()
public:
  virtual void Notify(USkeletalMeshComponent* MeshComp,
                            UAnimSequenceBase* Animation) override;
};
```

In the `public` section, we also override the `Notify()` method of the `UAnimNotify` class.

Then open the **UnloadASwordAnimNotify.cpp** file, and add the following lines to implement the overridden method:

```
#include "Characters/WarriorCharacter.h"

void UUnloadASwordAnimNotify::Notify(USkeletalMeshComponent* MeshComp,
                            UAnimSequenceBase* Animation)
{
  AWarriorCharacter* warrior = Cast<AWarriorCharacter>(
                                  MeshComp->GetOwner());
  // Get the Montage if it's a Montage; otherwise, we have a nullptr
  UAnimMontage* unloadASwordMontage = Cast<UAnimMontage>(Animation);
  // Unload the sword when is not attacking
  if (warrior && !warrior->IsAttacking) {
    if(unloadASwordMontage)
      // Pass in false to unload the great sword directly
      warrior->UnloadAGreatSwordNotify(false);
    else  // Not a montage, pass in true to play the Montage first
      warrior->UnloadAGreatSwordNotify(true);
  }
}
```

In the `Notify()` method, after getting the warrior character and the Montage from the incoming **Animation** parameter, if the warrior is not attacking, we determine whether the animation is a **Montage** by checking the `unloadASwordMontage` **pointer**, and if it's **not** `nullptr`, which means the Montage is playing, then we call the warrior's `UnloadAGreatSwordNotify()` method and pass in **false** to **unload** the great sword directly; otherwise, pass in **true** to the method, and later in the method, the sword unloading Montage will be played first before unloading the sword.

Now build the project and so far the AnimNotify classes are complete, let's add them to the Montages. Back to Unreal Editor and open the **AM_Draw_A_Great_Sword** in the **Animations** folder, then press the **Pause** button on the **bottom** of the viewport to **stop** playing the animation. **Drag** the **red bar** above the timeline to the position where the character's right hand is **behind** the head as shown below:

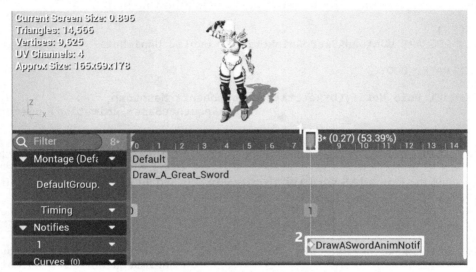

Right-click on the first (**1**) track of the Notifies at the position on the **vertical** line, choose **Add Notify... > Draw ASword Anim Notify** from the drop-down menu to add a **DrawASwordAnimNotify** as shown above. This means that when the Montage is at this position, the Notify() method in the C++ code will be called.

Next, open the **AM_Unload_A_Great_Sword** in the **Animations** folder and press the **Pause** button to **stop** playing the animation. **Drag** the **red bar** above the timeline to the position where the character's right hand is **behind** the head, right-click on the first (**1**) track of the Notifies at the position on the **vertical** line, and add an **UnloadASwordAnimNotify** as shown below:

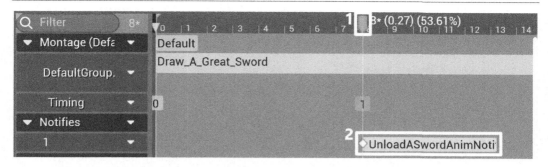

Now press **Save** for the above **two** Montages to confirm the modification.

Continue to open the **Idle** animation sequence in the **Animation** folder, after stopping playing the animation, **drag** the **red bar** above the timeline to the position as shown below:

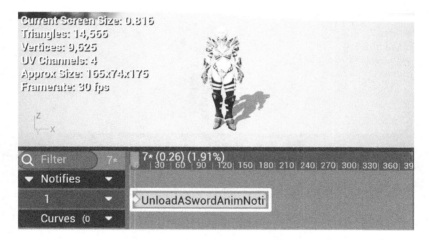

Right-click on the first (**1**) track of the Notifies at the position on the **vertical** line and add an **UnloadASwordAnimNotify** as shown above. This means when the **Idle** animation is played and at this position, the Notify will be fired to **unload** the great sword.

Similarly, open the **Walking** and **Running** animation sequences, in the **Animation** folder, respectively. Again add an **UnloadASwordAnimNotify** notify at the appropriate position for each of them as shown in the following two figures:

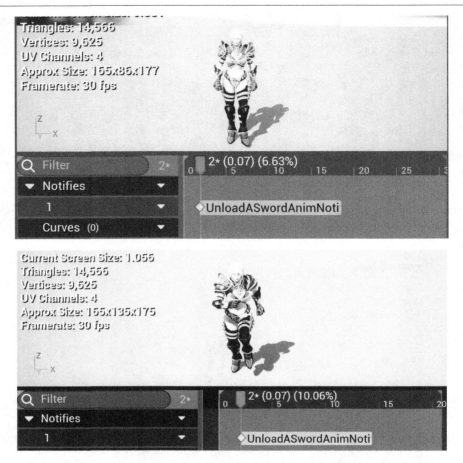

After pressing **Save** to confirm above modifications, the setup for loading and unloading the great sword is complete, now press **Play** to test the game.

The result is as follows, when you click the mouse button, the **AM_Draw_A_Great_Sword** will be played to load the sword first, followed by the **light** attack or **heavy** attack Montage. Finally, when the **Idle**, **Walking** or **Running** animation is playing and the great sword is loaded, after a while, it'll be unloaded to the **back** of the character.

Now move the player character toward the Wolf enemy and right-click the mouse serval times to attack it. When the great sword collides with the wolf, you'll see a **blue** capsule and a **point** inside to indicate the **impact** point as shown below:

Meanwhile, the wolf will play the **get hit** Montage and the health bar will become **shorter** after applying the damage. After it's dead, the **death** Montage will be played as shown below:

5.5.8 Automatic Enemy Locking

Enemy locking is a helpful feature in most ARPGs, and in this section, we'll discuss how to implement this feature in UE5. First, let's create a Blueprint for the lock widget. Open the Content Browser, right-click in the **UI** folder and choose **Blueprint Class** from the context menu. Then select the **UserWidget** as the Parent Class as follows:

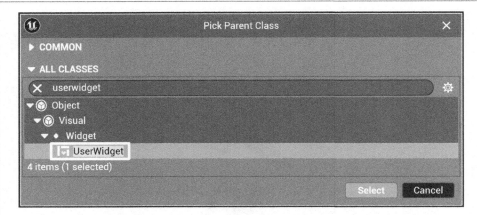

After renaming the Blueprint to **WBP_EnemyLockWidget**, right-click in the **UI** folder and create a new folder called **Icons**, then drag and drop the **EnemyLock.png** image into this folder.

Now double-click the **WBP_EnemyLockWidget** Blueprint to open it in the editor as shown below:

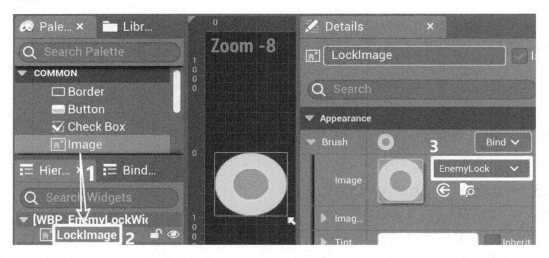

First, drag and drop an **Image** widget into the **Hierarchy** panel and rename it to **LockImage** as shown above. Then, in the Details tab, expand the **Appearance** > **Brush** settings, select the imported **EnemyLock** Texture from the drop-down menu for the **Image** field and you'll see the image appears in the Viewport. Finally, press **Compile** and **Save** to confirm the modification.

Creating the Lock Interface

From the main menu, choose **Tools** > **New C++ Class...** and after choosing **Unreal Interface** as the Parent Class, rename the class to **Lock** and add "**Public/Interfaces**" to the **Path**. After the class is generated in Visual Studio, open the **Lock.h** header and add the following **bold** lines in the **ILock** class:

```
class RPG_API ILock
{
  GENERATED_BODY()

  // Add interface functions to this class. This is the class that will be
     inherited to implement this interface.
public:
  virtual void ShowLocked(bool visible) = 0;
};
```

The ShowLocked() method in the public section is a **pure virtual** function to show the above enemy lock widget.

Implementing the Lock Interface

Next, open the **Enemy.h** header and add the following code in **bold**:

```
  ...
#include "Interfaces/Lock.h"
#include "Enemy.generated.h"

UCLASS()
class RPG_API AEnemy : public ANPC, public IHealth, public ILock
{
  GENERATED_BODY()
public:
  AEnemy();

  UPROPERTY(EditAnywhere, BlueprintReadOnly, Category = "Widgets")
  UWidgetComponent* LockWidget;

  void ShowLocked(bool visible) override;
    ...
};
```

The LockWidget widget component refers to the enemy lock widget and the ShowLocked() method is to show or hide the lock widget according to the incoming visible flag.

Continue to open the **Enemy.cpp** file, and in the constructor, add the following **bold** lines:

```
AEnemy::AEnemy()
{
    ...
```

```
LockWidget =
        CreateDefaultSubobject<UWidgetComponent>(TEXT("LockWidget"));
LockWidget->SetupAttachment(RootComponent);
}
```

In the constructor, after creating the widget component, it's attached to the root component.

Then add the following lines to implement the new method:

```
void AEnemy::ShowLocked(bool visible)
{
  if (LockWidget)
    LockWidget->SetVisibility(visible);
}
```

In the `ShowLocked()` method, we call the `SetVisibility()` method of the lock widget to show or hide the widget.

Continue to open the **RPGCharacter.h** header, and add the following code in **bold**:

```
...
#include "UI/RPGHUD.h"
#include "Components/BoxComponent.h"
#include "RPGCharacter.generated.h"

UCLASS()
class RPG_API ARPGCharacter : public ACharacter
{
  GENERATED_BODY()

public:
  // Sets default values for this character's properties
  ARPGCharacter();

  UPROPERTY(VisibleAnywhere, BlueprintReadOnly, Category = "EnemyLock")
  UBoxComponent* EnemyLockBox;
  UFUNCTION()
  void OnLockBoxBeginOverlap(UPrimitiveComponent* OverlappedComp, AActor*
    OtherActor, UPrimitiveComponent* OtherComp, int32 OtherBodyIndex, bool
                          bFromSweep, const FHitResult& SweepResult);
  UFUNCTION()
  void OnLockBoxEndOverlap(UPrimitiveComponent* OverlappedComp, AActor*
        OtherActor, UPrimitiveComponent* OtherComp, int32 OtherBodyIndex);

  AActor* currentTarget;
    ...
}
```

The `EnemyLockBox` property is a **Box Component** that is used as a **collider**. The `OnLockBoxBeginOverlap()` and `OnLockBoxEndOverlap()` methods are the delegates for the box component's overlay events. Lastly, the `currentTarget` refers to the currently locked actor.

Next, open the **RPGCharacter.cpp** file, and add the following code in **bold**:

```cpp
#include "RPGCharacter.h"
#include "GameFramework/CharacterMovementComponent.h"
#include "Interfaces/Lock.h"
#include "Interfaces/Health.h"

// Sets default values
ARPGCharacter::ARPGCharacter()
{
    …
    EnemyLockBox =
              CreateDefaultSubobject<UBoxComponent>(TEXT("EnemyLockBox"));
    // Attach to the Camera Boom, not the RootComponent
    EnemyLockBox->SetupAttachment(CameraBoom);
    // Register the delegates
    EnemyLockBox->OnComponentBeginOverlap.AddDynamic(this,
                              &ARPGCharacter::OnLockBoxBeginOverlap);
    EnemyLockBox->OnComponentEndOverlap.AddDynamic(this,
                              &ARPGCharacter::OnLockBoxEndOverlap);
}
```

In the constructor, after creating the BoxComponent, it's attached to the **Camera Boom** instead of the root component. That's because here we want to lock enemies that are **in front of** the camera. Then we register `OnLockBoxBeginOverlap()` and `OnLockBoxEndOverlap()` methods as delegates of the **OnComponentBeginOverlap** and **OnComponentEndOverlap** events, respectively.

Finally, add the following lines to implement the **two** new methods:

```cpp
void ARPGCharacter::OnLockBoxBeginOverlap(UPrimitiveComponent*
        OverlappedComp, AActor* OtherActor, UPrimitiveComponent* OtherComp,
    int32 OtherBodyIndex, bool bFromSweep, const FHitResult& SweepResult)
{
  IHealth* health = Cast<IHealth>(OtherActor);

  if (health && !health->IsDead()) {
    // Try getting the ILock interface
    ILock* target = Cast<ILock>(OtherActor);
    // If the target implements the ILock
    if (target)
    {
      // Show the lock widget
      target->ShowLocked(true);
      // Set the current target
      currentTarget = OtherActor;
    }
  }
```

```
}

void ARPGCharacter::OnLockBoxEndOverlap(UPrimitiveComponent*
        OverlappedComp, AActor* OtherActor, UPrimitiveComponent* OtherComp,
                                              int32 OtherBodyIndex)
{
  ILock* target = Cast<ILock>(OtherActor);

  if (target)
  {
    // Hide the lock widget
    target->ShowLocked(false);
    // Reset the current target
    currentTarget = NULL;
  }
}
```

The above `OnLockBoxBeginOverlap()` method will be called when an actor is colliding with the box component. In the method, if the actor implements `IHealth` and `ILock` interfaces, and is not dead, the lock widget on the actor is shown and the actor is set as the current target.

Similarly, in the `OnLockBoxEndOverlap()` method, if the actor, which **left** the box collider, implements the **ILock** interface, we **hide** the lock widget and reset the current target to `NULL`.

Now build the project and make sure no errors occur. Back to Unreal Editor, open the **BP_Wolf** Blueprint and with the **Lock Widget** selected as shown below:

In the Details tab, find and expand the **User Interface** settings, after selecting the **WBP_EnemyLoackWidget** for the **Widget Class** field, as shown above, change the **Draw Size** fields to **32** to make it smaller. Next, set the **Space** field to **Screen** to make it always face the player during gameplay.

Finally, find and expand the **Rendering** settings, and **tick** the **Visible** checkbox, as shown on the right, to temporarily hide the widget.

Enemy Lock Collision Box Setup

Open the **BP_FemaleWarrior** Blueprint and with the **Enemy Lock Box** selected as shown below:

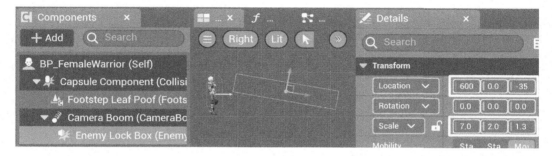

In the **Viewport**, after moving the **Box Collider** to the **front** of the character, as shown above, then change the **X** and **Z** Scale fields respectively in the **Transform** settings to make it **larger** in the X and Z directions. Lastly, press **Compile** and **Save** to confirm the modification.

Now press the **Play** to run the game, the result is shown below:

Move the player character toward the Wolf enemy and rotate the camera to face it. If the distance is near enough, the Box Collider will collide with it, and you'll see the **lock widget** appears as shown above.

Rotating the Player toward the Enemy

Currently, the enemy can be locked but we still need to rotate the player character toward it while attacking. Open the **WarriorCharacter.cpp** file, first add the following include:

```
#include "Kismet/KismetMathLibrary.h"
```

Next, add the following **bold** lines in the LightAttack() and HeavyAttack() methods respectively:

```
void AWarriorCharacter::LightAttack()
{
  FRotator targetRot;
  // If any target is locked
  if (currentTarget) {
    // Find the rotation for the player at the Start location to the point
    // at the Target location
    targetRot = UKismetMathLibrary::FindLookAtRotation(GetActorLocation(),
                                    currentTarget->GetActorLocation());
    GetWorld()->GetFirstPlayerController()->SetControlRotation(targetRot);
  }

  IsAttacking = true;
    ...
}

void AWarriorCharacter::HeavyAttack()
{
  FRotator targetRot;

  if (currentTarget) {
    targetRot = UKismetMathLibrary::FindLookAtRotation(GetActorLocation(),
                                    currentTarget->GetActorLocation());
    GetWorld()->GetFirstPlayerController()->SetControlRotation(targetRot);
  }

  IsAttacking = true;
    ...
}
```

In the above two methods, **before** performing the attack, we check if any target is locked, and if it's true, the **FindLookAtRotation()** built-in function is called to find the **rotation** for the player's location (Start) to the point of the target's location (End). After obtaining the rotation, we call the **SetControlRotation()** method of the PlayerController and pass in the new rotation to rotate the player toward the target before attacking.

Now build the project and back to Unreal Editor, press the **Play** again to run the game, move toward the Wolf, and after it's **locked**, press the mouse button to attack. You'll see the player **rotates toward** the enemy first and the attack Montage is played.

5.5.9 Damage Texts

Damage texts mean texts represent the damage values after an attack and it usually goes with a **floating** animation. This section will implement this mechanism.

The DamageTextWidget Class

From the main menu, choose Tools > **New C++ Class...** to create a C++ class named **DamageTextWidget** in the **Public/UI** folder and select **UserWidget** as its Parent Class. Open the **DamageTextWidget.h** header in Visual Studio and add the following **bold** lines:

```
#include "CoreMinimal.h"
#include "Blueprint/UserWidget.h"
#include "Animation/WidgetAnimation.h"
#include "Components/TextBlock.h"
#include "DamageTextWidget.generated.h"

UCLASS()
class RPG_API UDamageTextWidget : public UUserWidget
{
  GENERATED_BODY()
public:
  UPROPERTY(EditAnywhere, BlueprintReadWrite, meta = (BindWidget))
  UTextBlock* DamageText;
  UPROPERTY(EditAnywhere, BlueprintReadOnly, Transient, meta =
                                        (BindWidgetAnim))
  UWidgetAnimation* FloatingDamageText;

  void SetDamageText(FText damage);
  void PlayFloatingTextAnimation();
};
```

The `DamageText` property is a TextBlock widget that is bound to the damage text. The `FloatingDamageText` property is a **widget animation** that will be bound to the animation created in the editor. The `SetDamageText()` method is to set the damage text and the `PlayFloatingTextAnimation()` method is to play the damage text floating animation.

Next, open the **DamageTextWidget.cpp** file, and add the following lines to implement the two methods:

```
void UDamageTextWidget::SetDamageText(FText damage)
```

```
{
    DamageText->SetText(damage);
}

void UDamageTextWidget::PlayFloatingTextAnimation()
{
    PlayAnimation(FloatingDamageText);
}
```

In the `SetDamageText()` method, we call the `SetText()` method of the TextBlock and pass in the incoming text to set the damage text. In the `PlayFloatingTextAnimation()` method, the built-in `PlayAnimation()` method is called to play the text floating animation.

The Damage Text Blueprint and Animation

After building the project, back to Unreal Editor and open the Content Browser, right-click in the **UI** folder, select the **Blueprint Class** from the context menu, and in the next step, select the above **DamageTextWidget** as the Parent Class to create a Blueprint called **WBP_DamageTextWidget** in the UI folder. Then double-click to open it in the editor as shown below:

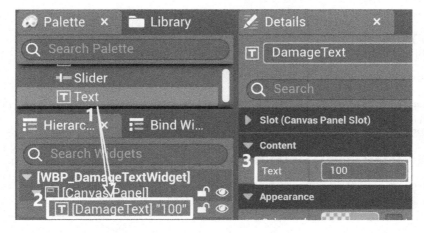

After dragging and dropping a **Canvas Panel** into the Hierarchy tab, drag and drop a **Text** under the **COMMON** onto the Canvas Panel to become its child, as shown above, and rename it to **DamageText** to **match** the property declared in the C++ class. Then in the Details tab, find and expand the **Content**, and change the **Text** field to **100**.

Next, set the **Anchors** field to move and align the **DamageText** to the **middle** of the Canvas Panel as shown below:

Then **tick** the **Size To Content** checkbox as shown above.

Next, expand the **Appearance** settings, and change the **Color and Opacity** field to the color you prefer for the damage text as shown below:

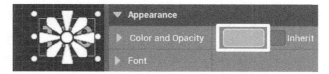

Continue to open the **Animations** window by clicking the **Animations** tab as shown below:

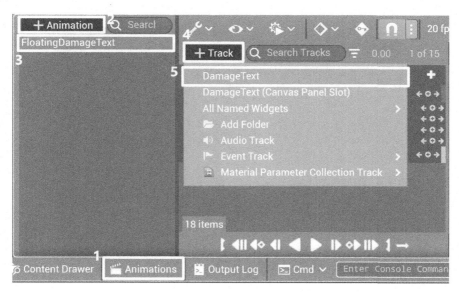

Press the + **Animation** button to add an Animation in the tab and rename it to **FloatingDamageText** to match the **property** declared in the C++ header, as shown above. Then press the + **Track** button and choose **Damage Text** to add an animation track for the **DamageText** as shown below:

Press the + button to the **right** of the **DamageText**, as shown above, and select **Transform** from the pop-up menu to create a **Transform** track under the **DamageText** as shown below:

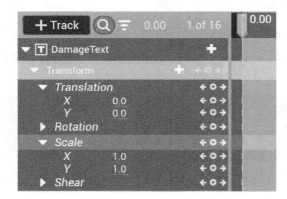

Now move the **red bar** on the Timeline to the position of **0.15** seconds as shown below:

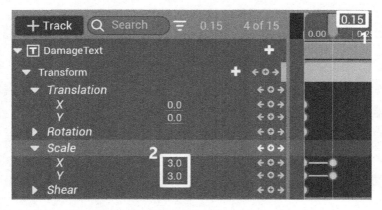

Then after expanding the **Translation** and **Scale** sections, change the **X** and **Y** values both to **3.0** as shown above. After the values are modified, you'll see the **keyframes** generated for us in the **Timeline** window.

Continue to move the red bar to the position of **0.75** seconds as shown below:

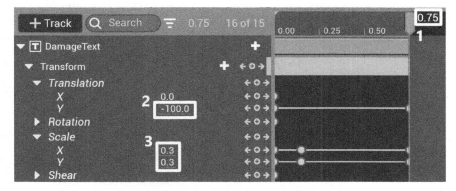

Change the **Y Translation** to **-100** and the **X** and **Y Scale** values both to **0.3** as shown above.

Now press the **Play** button on the **bottom** of the window to preview the animation, **three** frames of the animation are shown below:

The **left** figure above is the first frame, the **middle** figure is the frame at 0.15 seconds which is **three times** bigger, and the right figure above is the frame at **0.6** seconds which is getting **smaller** while being translated **upward**.

After the animation keyframes of the Translation and Scaling are complete, it's time to set up the **Color and Opacity** animation, and before we start, please set the **Alpha (A)** field of the **DamageText** to **0.0**, as shown below, in the Details tab to make it **transparent**.

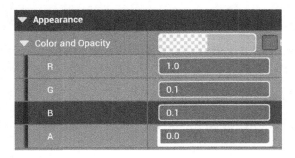

Back to the **Animation** window, press the **+Track** button on the **DamageText** track, and choose **Color and Opacity** from the pop-up menu as shown below:

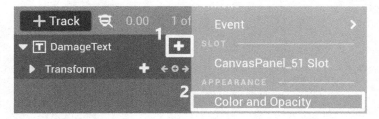

Then after expanding the **Color and Opacity** section as shown below:

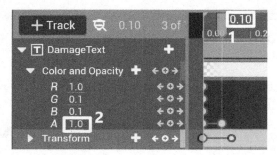

Move the red bar to the position of **0.1** seconds, as shown above, and change the **A** field to **1.0** to make it appear on the screen. Next, move the red bar to the position of **0.75** seconds, as shown below, and change the **A** field to **0.0** to make it **disappear** on the screen at the **end** of the animation.

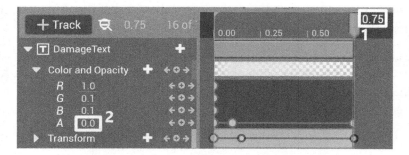

Now that the Blueprint and damage text animation is complete, press **Compile** and **Save** to confirm the modification and make sure that no errors occurred.

Playing Damage Text Animation in C++

Back to Visual Studio, after opening the **Enemy.h** header, add the following **bold** lines in the **public** section:

```
UCLASS()
```

```
class RPG_API AEnemy : public ANPC, public IHealth, public ILock
{
  GENERATED_BODY()
public:
  AEnemy();

  UPROPERTY(EditAnywhere, BlueprintReadWrite, Category = "Widgets")
  UWidgetComponent* DamageText;
    ...
}
```

In the public section, we add a widget component DamageText which refers to the damage text.

Next, open the **Enemy.cpp** file and add the following **bold** lines:

```
#include "UI/DamageTextWidget.h"

AEnemy::AEnemy()
{
    ...
  DamageText =
      CreateDefaultSubobject<UWidgetComponent>(TEXT("DamageTextWidget"));
  DamageText->SetupAttachment(RootComponent);
}
```

In the constructor, we create the DamageText object and attach it to the root component.

```
void AEnemy::ApplyDamage(int damageValue, AActor* causer)
{
  // Get the damage text widget
  UDamageTextWidget* damageText = Cast<UDamageTextWidget>(
                                      DamageText->GetUserWidgetObject());

  if (damageText) {
    // Pass in the string of the damage value and set the damage text
    damageText->SetDamageText(
                    FText::FromString(FString::FromInt(damageValue)));
    // Play the floating text animation
    damageText->PlayFloatingTextAnimation();
  }

  if (Stats) {
    ...
}
```

In the ApplyDamage() method, after getting the damage text widget and converting the incoming damage **value** to an **FText**, we set the damage text and start playing the floating text animation. Here the **FromInt()** method of the FString is called to convert the integer to a string.

Setting up the Damage Text Widget

After building the project, back to Unreal Editor and open the **BP_Wolf** Blueprint. With the **Damage Text** selected in the **Components** tab as shown below:

After expanding the **User Interface** settings, set the **Space** field to **Screen** and select the **WBP_DamageTextWidget** for the **Widget Class** field as shown above. Then, in the **Viewport**, move it to **above** the wolf using the translate gizmo as shown below:

Now press **Compile** and **Save** to confirm the modification, then press **Play** to run the game. The result is shown below:

When the damage is applied, the damage value will appear in the **middle** of the screen and be **translated upward**.

5.6 Integrating Animation and Sound Effects

This section will discuss how to use animation notify for our movement animations to synchronize the footstep sound playing with the animation. First, let's import sound clips to our project.

5.6.1 Importing Sound Clips

Go to the **freesound.org** website and after logging in, search for the **Step/Tap** sound as shown below:

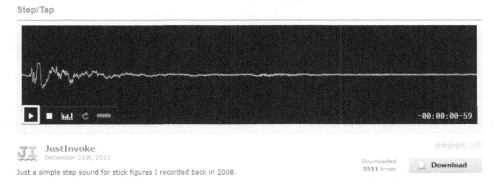

After clicking the **Play** button to preview the sound, press the **Download** button to download the sound clip.

Back to Unreal Editor, after creating a new folder called **Sounds** in the **Content** folder, drag and drop the downloaded step sound into the **Sounds** folder as shown below:

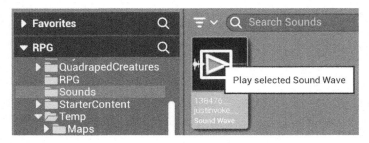

Move the mouse cursor over the sound and you'll see the **Play** button appears, press it to preview the sound. Then **right**-click the sound and choose **Create Cue**, as shown below, to create a sound cue from the sound wave.

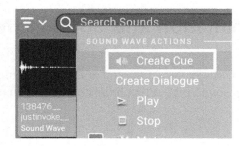

Then rename the sound cue to **Step-tap_Cue** as shown below:

Finally, find another sound you prefer for the footstep on **rock** and create a sound cue for it in the **Sounds** folder.

5.6.2 Physical Materials

After the sounds are ready, we have to set **Physical Surfaces** and create **Physical Materials**, which are used to define the response of a physical object when interacting dynamically with the world, for the landscape layers.

Physical Surfaces

To set Physical Surfaces, from the main menu, open the **Project Settings** window as shown below:

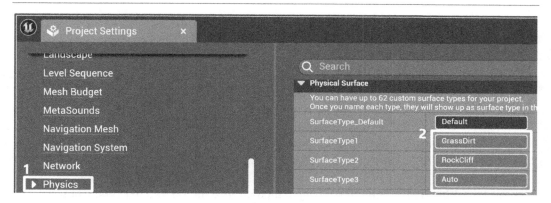

Find the **Engine** > **Physics** settings, as shown above, and set the **SurfaceType1** field to **GrassDirt**, **SurfaceType2** field to **RockCliff**, and **SurfaceType3** field to **Auto**, which is the same as the names of the three landscape layers.

Creating Physical Materials

After the surface types are set, let's create the Physical Materials. First, create a new folder called **PhysicalMaterials** in the **Content** folder, then right-click in the Content Browser of the folder and choose **Physics** > **Physical Material** as shown below:

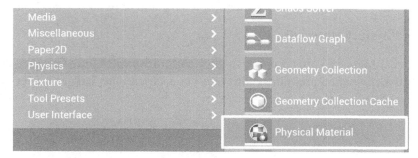

And in the next step, after selecting the **PhysicalMaterial** class as shown below:

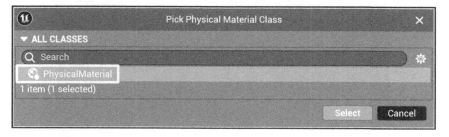

Press the **Select** button to create a Physical Material, and after renaming it to **PM_GrassDirt**, double-click to open it as shown below:

Expand the **Physical Properties** settings, then choose the **GrassDirt** type from the drop-down menu for the **Surface Type** field as shown above.

Next, create another Physical Material called **PM_RockCliff** in the same folder. After opening it, set the **Surface Type** field to **RockCliff** as shown below:

Now press **Save** to confirm the modification for the above two Physical Materials.

Assigning Physical Materials

After Physical Materials are complete, switch to **Landscape Mode** from the toolbar, and in the **Landscape** panel, press the **Paint** tab. Then expand the **Target Layers** > **Layers** settings as shown below:

Press the **Browse** icon to the **right** of the **GrassDirt** layer to open the Content Browser and you'll see the **GrassDirt_LayerInfo** created before as shown below:

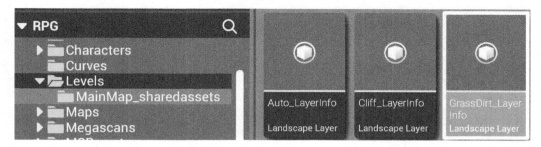

Now double-click to open it, and in the Details tab, select the **PM_GrassDirt** for the **Phys Material** field as shown below:

After pressing **Save** to confirm the modification, open the **RockCliff_LayerInfo** in the same folder as shown below:

Select the **PM_RockCliff** for the **Phys Material** field as shown above, then press **Save** to save the asset.

Next, with the **GrassDirt** layer selected as shown below:

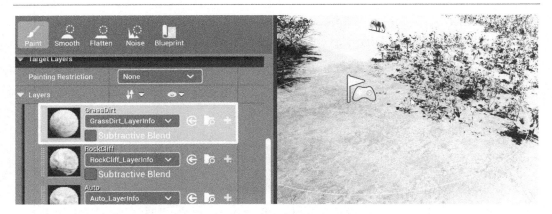

Move the mouse cursor into the Viewport and paint the terrain around the **Player Start** as shown above. Then, with the **RockCliff** layer selected, paint some part of the terrain as shown below:

Finally, switch back to the **Select Mode** and press **Save** to confirm the modification.

5.6.3 Playing Footstep Sound Effects

Now that the sound and Physical Material are complete, in this section, we'll use animation notify to play the footstep sound in C++. First, from the main menu, choose Tools > New C++ Class… and select **AnimNotify** as the Parent Class. Next, after renaming the class to **FootstepAnimNotify**, add "**Public/Animation**" to the **Path**. Finally, press the **Create Class** button to generate the class.

Open the **FootstepAnimNotify.h** header and add the following **bold** lines:

```cpp
#include "CoreMinimal.h"
#include "Animation/AnimNotifies/AnimNotify.h"
#include "Sound/SoundCue.h"
#include "FootstepAnimNotify.generated.h"

UENUM()
enum ESurfaceTypes
{
  Default       UMETA(DisplayName = "Default"),
  GrassDirt     UMETA(DisplayName = "GrassDirt"),
  RockCliff     UMETA(DisplayName = "RockCliff"),
  Auto          UMETA(DisplayName = "Auto")
};

UCLASS()
class RPG_API UFootstepAnimNotify : public UAnimNotify
{
  GENERATED_BODY()
public:
  UPROPERTY(EditDefaultsOnly, BlueprintReadWrite, Category = "SoundCues")
  TArray<USoundCue*> FootstepCues;

  virtual void Notify(USkeletalMeshComponent* MeshComp,
                              UAnimSequenceBase* Animation) override;
};
```

The ESurfaceTypes enum type defines the surface types created in the Project Settings, please note that the **order** must be the same that is the **GrassDirt** number is **1** (**SurfaceType1**), the **RockCliff** number is **2** (**SurfaceType2**), and so on. Because we'll use the number as the **index** to access the **sound cue** in the following array.

In the public section, the FootstepCues array property stores the footstep sound cues on different surface types, the **first** one is for **GrassDirt** and the **second** is for **RockCliff**, etc. The Notify() method is the overridden method to play the footstep sound.

Next, open the **FootstepAnimNotify.cpp** file and add the following lines to implement the method:

```cpp
#include "PhysicalMaterials/PhysicalMaterial.h"
#include "Kismet/GameplayStatics.h"

void UFootstepAnimNotify::Notify(USkeletalMeshComponent* MeshComp,
                              UAnimSequenceBase* Animation)
{
  // Get the owner actor of the Mesh
  AActor* owner = MeshComp->GetOwner();
  // Trace starts from the player's position
```

```
FVector traceStart = owner->GetActorLocation();
// Trace end position is at 150 cm below the player
FVector traceEnd = owner->GetActorLocation() - FVector(0, 0, 150);
// The hit result
FHitResult Hit(ForceInit);
// Collision parameters
FCollisionQueryParams CollisionParams;
// The bReturnPhysicalMaterial parameter has to be turned on (true)
CollisionParams.bReturnPhysicalMaterial = true;
// Ignore the owner actor which is the player
CollisionParams.AddIgnoredActor(owner);
// Perform the line trace
GetWorld()->LineTraceSingleByChannel(Hit, traceStart, traceEnd,
                    ECollisionChannel::ECC_WorldStatic, CollisionParams);
//DrawDebugLine(GetWorld(), traceStart, traceEnd, FColor::Blue, true);
// If we hit some physical material
if (Hit.PhysMaterial != NULL) {
  // Play the sound cue according to the surface type value
  switch (Hit.PhysMaterial->SurfaceType.GetValue()) {
    case ESurfaceTypes::GrassDirt:
      // Play the stepping on the GrassDirt surface sound cue
      if(FootstepCues.Num())
        // Use the GrassDirt surface enum value minus one as the index
        // to get the sound cue
        UGameplayStatics::PlaySoundAtLocation(GetWorld(),
                        FootstepCues[ESurfaceTypes::GrassDirt - 1],
                                    owner->GetActorLocation());
    break;
    case ESurfaceTypes::RockCliff:
      if (FootstepCues.Num())
        UGameplayStatics::PlaySoundAtLocation(GetWorld(),
                        FootstepCues[ESurfaceTypes::RockCliff - 1],
                                    owner->GetActorLocation());
    break;
  }
 }
}
```

Because we'll use **Physical Material** which is defined in the `PhysicalMaterial.h` header and the `PlaySoundAtLocation()` method, which is declared in the `GameplayStatics.h` header, both the headers have to be included.

In the `Notify()` method, firstly the owner actor of the Mesh component is obtained, then we get the trace start position from the player's current position, and the trace end position is **150** cm below the player. Next, an `FHitResult` object is declared to store the hit result, followed by declaring an `FCollisionQueryParams` object for setting collision parameters. Then we set the **bReturnPhysicalMaterial** parameter to **true** for the **Line Trace** below to return the physical material. Also, the **owner** actor, who is the player, is set to be **ignored** for collision detection.

Finally, we call the built-in **LineTraceSingleByChannel()** function to perform the line trace, and if we hit some physical material underneath, the sound cue is played according to the returned surface type **value**. For example, if the type is **GrassDirt**, the stepping on the **GrassDirt** surface sound cue is played by calling the built-in **PlaySoundAtLocation()** method.

Now build the project and make sure that no errors occurred.

Creating the Footstep AnimNotify Blueprint

Back to Unreal Editor, open the Content Browser and right-click in the **Warriors** > **Blueprints** folder, select **Blueprint Class** from the context menu, and in the next step, choose the above **FootstepAnimNotify** class as the Parent Class to create a Blueprint called **BP_FootstepAnimNotify**.

Next, double-click to open it and in the Details tab, expand the **Sound Cues** settings as shown below:

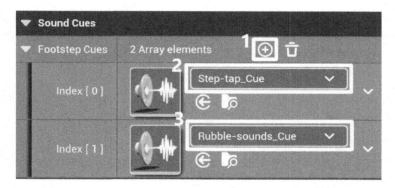

After pressing the + icon **twice** to add two Array elements, as shown above, select the sound cue for stepping on the **GrassDirt** layer in the first element, then choose the sound cue for stepping on the **RockCliff** layer in the second element.

Now press **Compile** and **Save** to save the Blueprint, then open the **Running** animation sequence in the **Female** > **Animations** folder, as shown below:

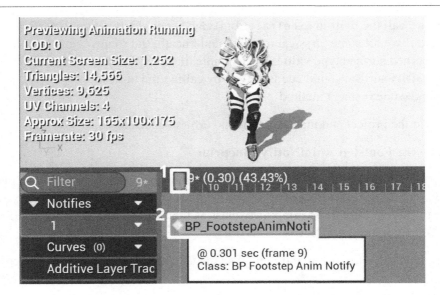

First, stop previewing the animation, and then move the **red bar** on the Timeline to the position when the character's **left** foot is **on** the **ground** as shown above. Next, right-click at the **vertical line** on the track and choose **Add Notify…** > **BP_FootstepAnimNotify** to create an AnimNotify at that time.

Continue to move the **red bar** to the position when the character's **right** foot is on the ground as shown below:

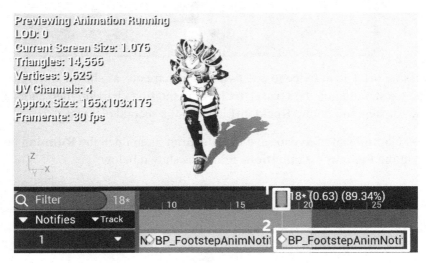

Right-click at the **vertical line** on the track and choose **Add Notify…** > **BP_FootstepAnimNotify** to create another AnimNotify at that time as shown above. Lastly, press **Save** to confirm the modification.

So far all the settings are ready, press **Play** to run the game. When the player character is running and her **left** or **right** foot is stepping on different layers with different physical materials, you'll hear different footstep sounds.

5.7 Horse Riding System

The horse-riding system is helpful for open-world RPGs and almost every commercial game has implemented this feature. So, in this section, we'll discuss how to implement such a system.

5.7.1 Horse Skeletal Mesh and Animations

Currently, it's difficult to find a free and good-looking 3D rigged horse mesh (skeletal mesh). So, in this section, we'll use the **free** Blender Addon called **Rigify Animbox** to create the **Horse** skeletal mesh and animations as follows.

Blender Rigify Animbox Addon Installation

First, go to the **blenderartists.org** website[11], as shown below, to download the Addon.

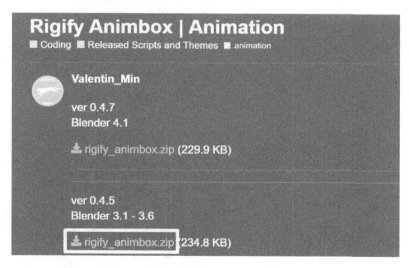

After the download is complete, open **Blender** and after creating a new file, delete **all** the objects in the scene. Continue to open the Blender **Preferences** window by selecting

---

[11] **Rigify Animbox Addon**, https://blenderartists.org/t/rigify- animbox-animation/1248691.

Edit > **Preferences…** from the main menu. Then, after pressing the **Install…** button on the top, find and select the downloaded **rigify_animbox.zip** file as shown below:

Press the **Install Add-on** button to install it and **tick** the checkbox to the **left** of the Add-on, as shown below, to **enable** it.

Automatic Horse Rigging

Next, after downloading the **Horse_Mesh.fbx** file from the Author's website, import the FBX file into the Blender, as shown below, by selecting File > Import > **FBX (.fbx)** from the main menu.

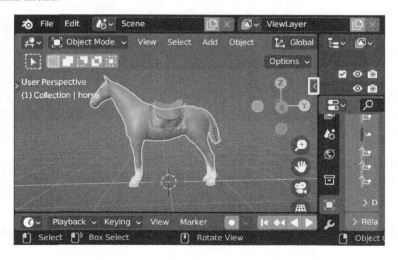

Continue to drag the < handle, on the **right** of the Viewport, to open the Add-on menu as shown below:

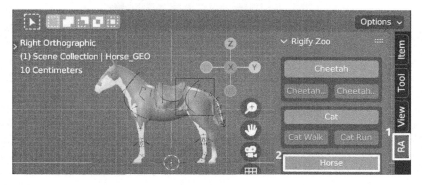

After selecting the **RA** tab and expanding the **Rigify Zoo**, press the **Horse** button to create the **horse_rig** in the scene. Then expand the **horse_rig**, with the **Horse_GEO** selected, as shown below, and **delete** the mesh.

Next, with the **Cloth**, **Horse**, and **Saddle** meshes selected first, as shown below, then with the **Ctrl** key pressed and left click the **horse_rig** to select it.

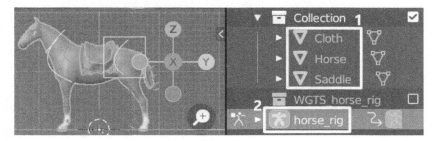

Now move the cursor into the Viewport, press the **Ctrl + P** key, and select **With Automatic Weights** from the context menu, as shown below, to automatically rig the Horse.

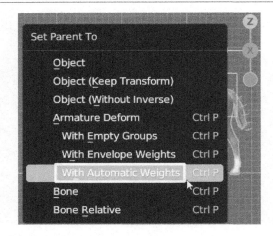

Exporting the Horse Skeletal Mesh

After the Horse is rigged, let's export the skeletal mesh as follows. Select File > **Export** > **FBX (.fbx)** from the main menu, and in the **Blend File View** window, click the **Armature** button first, as shown below, then with the **Shift** key pressed, left click the **Mesh** button to select it as well.

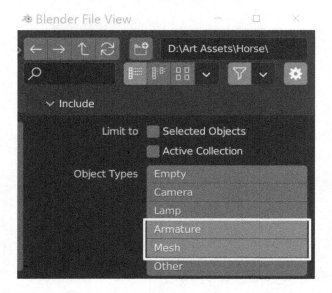

Continue to scroll down and expand the **Armature** settings, as shown below, **tick** the **Only Deform Bones** checkbox, and **untick** the **Add Leaf Bones** and **Bake Animation**, because we don't need the animation for the skeletal mesh.

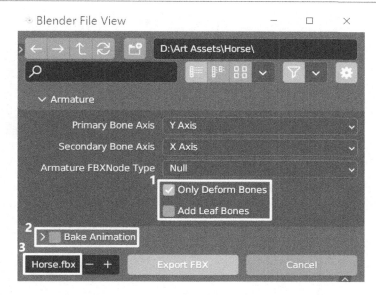

Lastly, after changing the name of the skeletal mesh to **Horse.fbx**, press the **Export FBX** button to export the FBX file in the specified folder.

Animating the Horse

After rigging the Horse, we'll create the **Walk** and **Run** animations for it as follows. First, set the object interaction mode to **Pose Mode** as shown below:

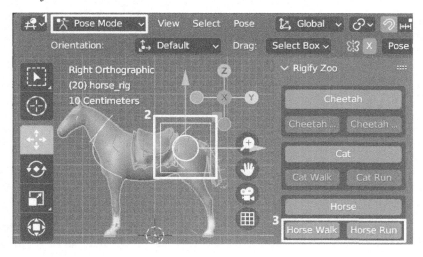

Then select the **Box** shape, as shown above, and the **Horse Walk** and **Run** buttons under the Horse button will be **enabled**. Now press the **Horse Walk** button, and you'll see the animation is playing in the Viewport as shown below:

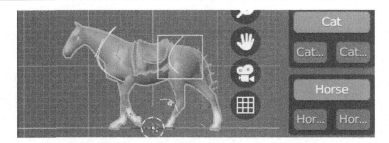

Exporting the Horse Walk Animation

Next, select **File** > **Export** > **FBX (.fbx)** again from the main menu, and this time select only the **Armature** Object Type as shown below:

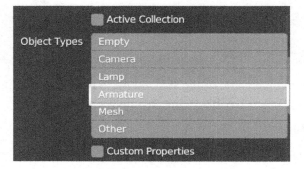

Continue to scroll down and, after **unticking** the Add Leaf Bones, **tick** both the **Only Deform Bones** and **Back Animation** as shown below. Then change the file name to **Horse_Walk.fbx** and press the **Export FBX** button to export the animation.

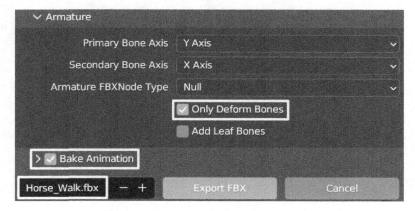

Similarly, create the **Horse Run** animation for the horse and export the animation with the name **Horse_Run.fbx** in the same folder. Lastly, for the Horse **Idle** animation, please go to the **Author's website** and **download** the **Horse_Idle.fbx** file.

5.7.2 Horse Characters

Now that the Hose skeletal mesh and animations are ready, in this section, we are going to create the C++ code for our horse character and the UI with animation indicating the player to interact with it.

Importing the Horse Skeletal Mesh and Animations

Before importing the Horse skeletal mesh, create a new folder called **Horses** inside the **Characters** folder. Then drag and drop the **Horse.fbx** file into this new folder and import the skeletal mesh using the **default** settings.

After **renaming** the **Horse** and **Horse_Skeleton** to **SK_Horse** and **SKEL_Horse** respectively, continue to add another folder called **Animations** in the **Horses** folder, then drag and drop the **Horse_Idle.fbx**, **Horse_Walk.fbx**, and **Horse_Run.fbx** files into this new folder, and choose the **SKEL_Horse** in the **Horses** folder, as shown below, in the **FBX Import Options** window.

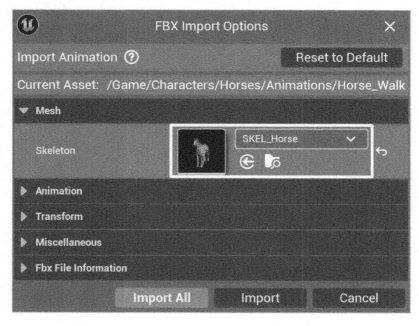

Lastly, press the **Import All** button to import all the animations to the **Animations** folder. So far the art assets for our Horse character are ready, next let's create the UI for suggesting the player interact with it as follows.

Interactable Icon and Text Widgets

From the main menu, choose Tools > **New C++ Class...** and select **UserWidget** as the Parent Class. Next, after renaming the class to **InteractTextWidget**, add "**Public/UI/Interaction**" in the **Path** as shown below:

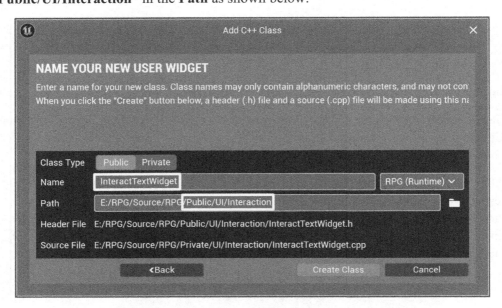

Press the **Create Class** button to generate the class in Visual Studio. Then open the **InteractTextWidget.h** header and add the following **bold** lines:

```
#include "CoreMinimal.h"
#include "Blueprint/UserWidget.h"
#include "Components/TextBlock.h"
#include "InteractTextWidget.generated.h"

UCLASS()
class RPG_API UInteractTextWidget : public UUserWidget
{
  GENERATED_BODY()
public:
  UPROPERTY(EditAnywhere, meta = (BindWidget))
  UTextBlock* InteractText;
};
```

In the public section, we declare the **TextBlock** property InteractText representing the **Interact** text to bind to the widget created in the editor.

Back to Unreal Editor, choose Tools > **New C++ Class...** again, and select **UserWidget** as the Parent Class. Next, after renaming the class to **InteractableIconWidget**, select the **Public/UI/Interaction** folder for its Path. Then press the **Create Class** button to generate the class in Visual Studio.

Open the **InteractableIconWidget.h** header and add the following **bold** lines:

```
UCLASS()
class RPG_API UInteractableIconWidget : public UUserWidget
{
  GENERATED_BODY()
public:
  UPROPERTY(EditAnywhere, meta = (BindWidget))
  class UImage* InteractableIcon;
  UPROPERTY(EditAnywhere, Transient, meta = (BindWidgetAnim))
  UWidgetAnimation* MovingAnimation;
  UFUNCTION()
  void PlayMovingAnimation();
};
```

The `InteractableIcon` **Image** property refers to the **icon** moving above the interactable actor, and the `MovingAnimation` widget animation property refers to the moving animation of the icon. The `PlayMovingAnimation()` method is used to play the animation.

Then add the following lines in the **InteractableIconWidget.cpp** file:

```
#include "Animation/WidgetAnimation.h"

void UInteractableIconWidget::PlayMovingAnimation()
{
  if (MovingAnimation) {
    // Play the animation from the start position and loop indefinitely
    PlayAnimation(MovingAnimation, 0.0f, 0);
  }
}
```

In the `PlayMovingAnimation()` method, we call the built-in `PlayAnimation()` function to play the icon moving animation. Here the **third** parameter is **0** which means to **loop indefinitely**.

After building the project, back to Unreal Editor and create a new folder called **Interaction** in the **UI** folder, right-click in Content Browser of this folder, and choose **Blueprint** from the context menu. In the next step, pick the **InteractTextWidget** under the **UserWidget** as the Parent Class to create the Blueprint.

Next, after renaming the Blueprint to **WBP_InteractTextWidget**, double-click to open it in the editor as shown below:

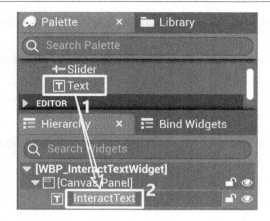

Drag and drop a **CanvasPanel** into the **Hierarchy**, then continue to drag and drop a **Text** onto the **CanvasPanel** to become its child, as shown above, and lastly, after clicking on the **Text**, rename it to **InteractText**.

With the **InteractText** selected, and in the **Details** tab, after resetting the **Text** field to **E – Interact**, as shown below, set the **Color and Opacity** to the **Green** color and **Font Size** to **32** points.

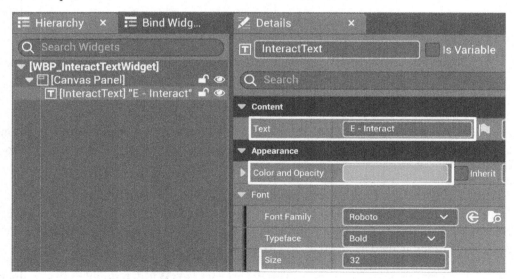

Continue to set the **Justification** to align to the Middle as shown below:

Lastly, change the **Anchors** of the **InteractText** to align it to the **center** of the Canvas Panel as shown below:

Now press **Compile** and **Save** to confirm all modifications. Next, we'll create the **Interactable Icon** widget and before doing so, please prepare the following texture called **InteractableIcon.png** with transparent background for the icon:

After importing the texture to the **UI > Interaction** folder, create another Blueprint called **WBP_InteractableIconWidget** in the same folder and pick the **InteractableIconWidget** under the **UserWidget** as the Parent Class. Double-click to open it in the editor as shown below:

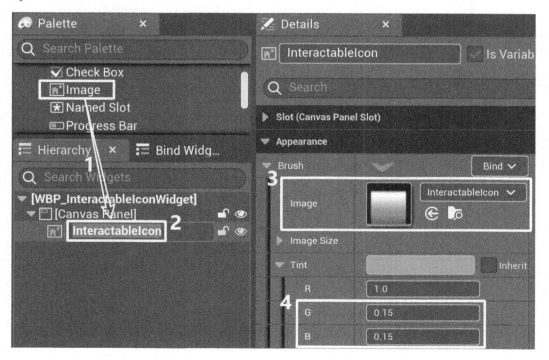

Drag and drop a **CanvasPanel** into the **Hierarchy**, then continue to drag and drop an **Image** onto the **CanvasPanel** to become its child, as shown above, and after clicking on the Image, rename it to **InteractableIcon**.

With the **InteractableIcon** selected, and in the **Details** tab, expand the **Appearance** and **Tint**. Then, after setting the **Image** field to the imported icon, set the **Tint** color values, as shown above, to make it **redder**.

Next, expand the **Anchors**, and after setting the **Size X** and **Y** to **60** and **30** as shown below:

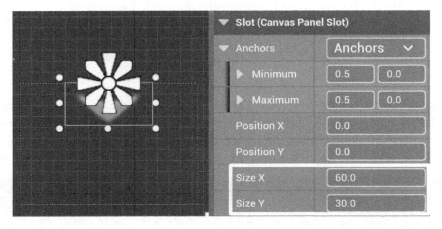

Set the **Anchors** to make the icon aligns to the **Top** and **Middle** as shown above. Lastly, we need to create the **MovingAnimation** declared in C++ code as follows.

Click the **Animations** on the **Status Bar** to open the **Animations** tab as shown below:

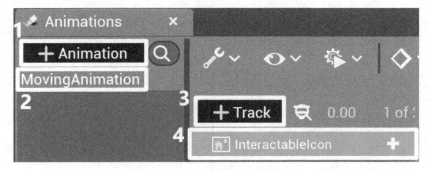

Then, after pressing the **+Animation** to add a new animation, rename it to **MovingAnimation** as shown above. Continue to press the **+Track** on the Track panel and select the **InteractableIcon** to create a new track.

Next, click the + to the **right** of the **InteractableIcon** and select **Transform** from the pop-up menu as shown below:

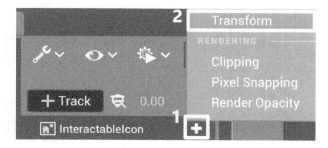

Now move the **Red Bar** on the Timeline to the position of **1** second as shown below:

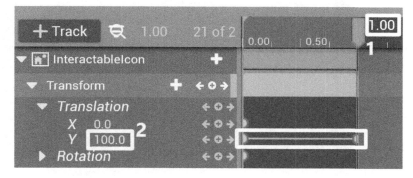

After expanding the **Transform** and **Translation**, as shown above, click on the **Y value** to edit and set the value to **100**, then press the **Enter** key. You'll see the keyframes generated in the Timeline panel.

So far the animation is complete, press the **Play** button on the **bottom** of the **Animations** tab to preview the animation. Finally, press **Compile** and **Save** to confirm all modifications and make sure no errors occurred.

The Horse Animation Blendspace and Blueprint

Before creating the Blueprint for the horse character, we have to create the Animation Blendspace and Blueprint as follows. Right-click in the Content Browser of the **Horses > Animations** folder and choose **Animation > Blend Space** from the context menu. Then in the **Pick Skeleton** panel, pick the **SKEL_Horse** to create the Blend Space, and then rename it to **BS_Horse**.

Double-click to open the **BS_Horse** as shown below:

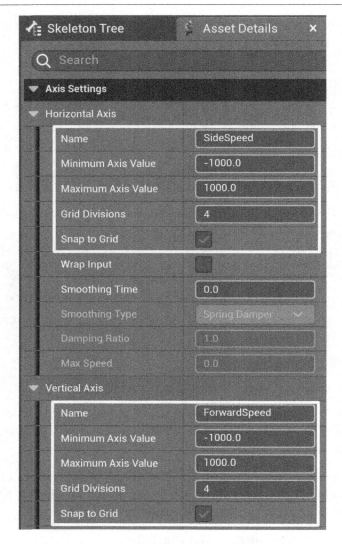

In the **Asset Details** panel, after renaming the **Horizontal** and **Vertical** Axis Names to **SideSpeed** and **ForwaredSpeed**, as shown above, set the **Minimum** and **Maximum** Axis Values to **-1000** and **1000** respectively, and **tick** the **Snap to Grid** checkboxes.

Continue to drag and drop the **Horse_Idle** and **Horse_Run** animations respectively into the grid as shown below:

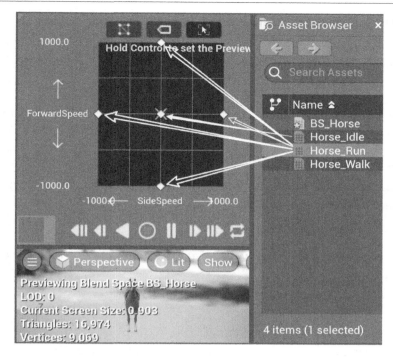

Finally, drag and drop the **Horse_Walk** animation into the grid as shown below:

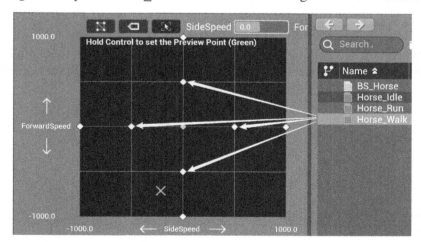

The HorseAnimInstance Class

Next, after selecting **Tools** > **New C++ Class…** from the main menu, choose the
RPGAnimInstance as the Parent Class, and in the next step, rename the class to
HorseAnimInstance and select the **Public/Animation** folder for the **Path** to generate
the C++ code.

Open the **HorseAnimInstance.h** header and add the following **bold** lines:

```
UCLASS()
class RPG_API UHorseAnimInstance : public URPGAnimInstance
{
  GENERATED_BODY()
public:
  virtual void NativeUpdateAnimation(float DeltaSeconds) override;
};
```

In the `public` section, we override the `NativeUpdateAnimation()` method.

Then add the following lines in the **HorseAnimInstance.cpp** file to implement the `NativeUpdateAnimation()` method:

```
#include "Characters/RPGCharacter.h"

void UHorseAnimInstance::NativeUpdateAnimation(float DeltaSeconds)
{
  // Call the parent's method
  Super::NativeUpdateAnimation(DeltaSeconds);

}
```

In the overridden method, the parent's `NativeUpdateAnimation()` method is called. Now build the project and back to Unreal Editor.

The Horse Animation Blueprint

After creating a folder called **Blueprints** in the **Horses** folder, right-click in the **Content Browser** of this folder and choose **Animation > Animation Blueprint** from the context menu. In the next step, select the **SKEL_Horse** as shown below:

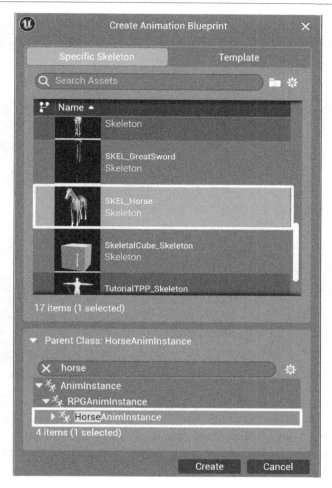

Then after expanding the **Parent Class**, find and select the **HorseAinmInstance** in the panel. Press the **Create** button to generate the **Animation Blueprint** and then rename it to **ABP_Horse**.

Continue to open the Blueprint and firstly, drag and drop the **BS_Horse** into the **AnimGraph** as shown below:

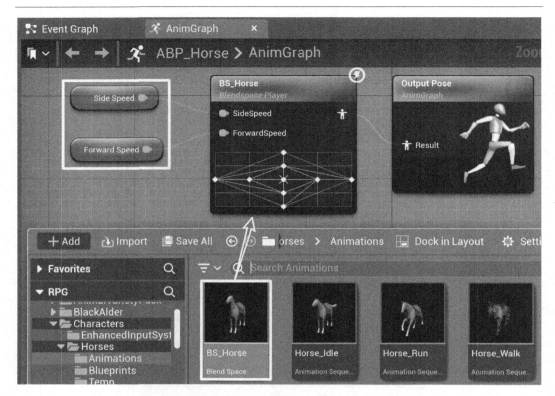

Then drag off from the **SideSpeed** pin and **ForwardSpeed** pin of the **BS_Horse** Node respectively and find and select **Get Side Speed** and **Get Forward Speed** from the list to create the **Side Speed** and **Forward Speed** Nodes as shown above. Lastly, after plugging the output of the BS_Horse Node into the **Result** pin of the **Output Pose** Node, press **Compile** and **Save** to confirm the modification.

The Interactable Interface Class

From the main menu, choose Tools > **New C++ Class...** and select **Unreal Interface** as the Parent Class. Next, after renaming the class to **Interactable**, select the **Public/Interfaces** folder for the **Path**. Finally, press the **Create Class** button to generate the Unreal Interface in Visual Studio.

Open the **Interactable.h** header and add the following **bold** lines:

```
...
UENUM()
enum EInteractableType
{
  Horse        UMETA(DisplayName = "Horse")
};
```

```
class RPG_API IInteractable
{
  GENERATED_BODY()

  ...
public:
  virtual EInteractableType GetInteractableType() = 0;
  virtual void ShowInteractText(bool visible, FString text = "") = 0;
  virtual void ShowInteractableIcon(bool visible,
                                    AActor* facingActor = NULL) = 0;
};
```

Before the **Interface** class, we declare an enum type EInteractableType to represent the types of interactable actors. In the Interface class, the GetInteractableType() method is to return the type of the interactable, and the ShowInteractText() and ShowInteractableIcon() methods are to show or hide the Interact text and the moving icon above the interactable, respectively.

The Horse Character Class

Back to Unreal Editor, choose Tools > **New C++ Class...** and select **RPGCharacter** as the Parent Class. Next, after renaming the class to **HorseCharacter**, select the **Public/Characters** folder for its **Path**. Finally, press the **Create Class** button to generate the class in Visual Studio.

Open the **HorseCharacter.h** header and add the following code in **bold**:

```
  ...
#include "Components/BoxComponent.h"
#include "Components/SceneComponent.h"
#include "Interfaces/Interactable.h"
#include "Components/WidgetComponent.h"
#include "HorseCharacter.generated.h"

UCLASS()
class RPG_API AHorseCharacter : public ARPGCharacter, public IInteractable
{
  GENERATED_BODY()
public:
  AHorseCharacter();

  UPROPERTY(VisibleAnywhere, Category = "Collider")
  UBoxComponent* BoxCollider;
  UPROPERTY(VisibleAnywhere, Category = "Dismount")
  USceneComponent* DismountRight;
  UPROPERTY(VisibleAnywhere, Category = "Dismount")
  USceneComponent* DismountLeft;
  UPROPERTY(VisibleAnywhere, Category = "Widget")
  UWidgetComponent* InteractText;
  UPROPERTY(VisibleAnywhere, Category = "Widget")
```

```
UWidgetComponent* InteractableIcon;
UPROPERTY(VisibleAnywhere, Category = "Interactable")
TEnumAsByte<EInteractableType> InteractableType;
UPROPERTY(VisibleAnywhere, Category = "Rider")
AActor* Rider;

UFUNCTION()
void OnBoxBeginOverlap(UPrimitiveComponent* OverlappedComp, AActor*
        OtherActor, UPrimitiveComponent* OtherComp, int32 OtherBodyIndex,
                        bool bFromSweep, const FHitResult& SweepResult);
UFUNCTION()
void OnBoxEndOverlap(UPrimitiveComponent* OverlappedComp, AActor*
        OtherActor, UPrimitiveComponent* OtherComp, int32 OtherBodyIndex);
virtual EInteractableType GetInteractableType() override;
virtual void ShowInteractText(bool visible, FString text = "") override;
virtual void ShowInteractableIcon(bool visible, AActor*
                                        facingActor = NULL) override;

virtual void Dismount(const FInputActionValue& value) override;
};
```

The BoxCollider property represents the **box** area in which the player can interact with the interactable actor. The DismountRight and DismountLeft **Scene** Components represent the **right** and **left** positions where the player will be located after dismounting from the horse. The InteractText, InteractableIcon, and InteractableType refer to the Interact text, icon, and type for the interactable, respectively. The Rider property refers to the Actor who is riding the horse. The GetInteractableType() method returns the Interact type,

The OnBoxBeginOverlap() and OnBoxEndOverlap() methods are delegates for the BoxCollider events, the ShowInteractText() and ShowInteractableIcon() methods are to show or hide the Interact text and icon, respectively. The overridden Dismount() method is to dismount the player from the horse.

Then open the **HorseCharacter.cpp** file and add the following lines:

```
#include "UI/Interaction/InteractTextWidget.h"
#include "UI/Interaction/InteractableIconWidget.h"
#include "Kismet/KismetMathLibrary.h"

AHorseCharacter::AHorseCharacter()
{
  BoxCollider =
            CreateDefaultSubobject<UBoxComponent>(TEXT("BoxComponent"));
  BoxCollider->SetupAttachment(RootComponent);
  DismountRight =
          CreateDefaultSubobject<USceneComponent>(TEXT("DismountRight"));
  DismountLeft =
          CreateDefaultSubobject<USceneComponent>(TEXT("DismountLeft"));
```

```
DismountLeft->SetupAttachment(RootComponent);
DismountRight->SetupAttachment(RootComponent);
InteractText =
        CreateDefaultSubobject<UWidgetComponent>(TEXT("InteractText"));
InteractText->SetupAttachment(RootComponent);
InteractableIcon =
      CreateDefaultSubobject<UWidgetComponent>(TEXT("InteractableIcon"));
InteractableIcon->SetupAttachment(RootComponent);
// Register the delegates
BoxCollider->OnComponentBeginOverlap.AddDynamic(this,
                                &AHorseCharacter::OnBoxBeginOverlap);
BoxCollider->OnComponentEndOverlap.AddDynamic(this,
                                  &AHorseCharacter::OnBoxEndOverlap);
}
```

In the constructor, after creating and attaching the components to the root component, we register the delegates for the **OnComponentBeginOverlap** and **OnComponentEndOverlap** events of the BoxCollider.

```
EInteractableType AHorseCharacter::GetInteractableType()
{
  return EInteractableType::Horse;
}
```

In the GetInteractableType() method, the Horse type is returned.

```
void AHorseCharacter::OnBoxBeginOverlap(UPrimitiveComponent*
      OverlappedComp, AActor* OtherActor, UPrimitiveComponent* OtherComp,
    int32 OtherBodyIndex, bool bFromSweep, const FHitResult& SweepResult)
{
  FString componentName;

  OtherComp->GetName(componentName);
  // Ignore the enemy lock box on the player
  if (componentName != "EnemyLockBox") {
    ARPGCharacter* player = Cast<ARPGCharacter>(OtherActor);
    // Also ignore the horse itself
    if (player && player != this)
    {
      player->InteractableActor = this;
      // Show the Interact text
      ShowInteractText(true);
    }
  }
}
```

When the player enters the box collider, the above OnBoxBeginOverlap() method is called, and in the method, after getting the colliding component's **name**, if it's not the name of the enemy lock box on the player, and the colliding Actor is also not the horse

itself, we set the player's current interactable actor to the horse character and **show** the
Interact text.

```
void AHorseCharacter::OnBoxEndOverlap(UPrimitiveComponent* OverlappedComp,
                     AActor* OtherActor, UPrimitiveComponent* OtherComp,
                                            int32 OtherBodyIndex)
{
  ARPGCharacter* player = Cast<ARPGCharacter>(OtherActor);

  if (player)
  {
    FString componentName;
    OtherComp->GetName(componentName);

    if (componentName != "EnemyLockBox") {
      player->InteractableActor = NULL;
      ShowInteractText(false);
    }
  }
}
```

When the player left the box collider, the above `OnBoxEndOverlap()` method is called,
and in the method, similarly after getting the colliding component's name, if it's not the
name of the enemy lock box, the player's current interactable actor is reset to NULL and
the Interact text is **hidden**.

```
void AHorseCharacter::ShowInteractText(bool visible, FString text)
{
  if (InteractText) {
    UInteractTextWidget* widget =
        Cast<UInteractTextWidget>(InteractText->GetUserWidgetObject());
    // If we have different text to show
    if (widget && text != "") {
      widget->InteractText->SetText(FText::FromString(text));
    }
    // Show or hide the Interact text
    InteractText->SetVisibility(visible);
    // If the Interact text is shown, hide the moving icon
    InteractableIcon->SetVisibility(!visible);
  }
}
```

In the `ShowInteractText()` method, after getting the widget, if the incoming text is **not**
a **null** string, which means that we have different text to show, then the `SetText()`
method is called to set the Interact text. Lastly, according to the incoming flag, we set
the visibility of the Interact text, and if it is shown, the moving interactable icon is
hidden.

```
void AHorseCharacter::ShowInteractableIcon(bool visible, AActor*
                                                       facingActor)
```

```
{
  if (InteractableIcon) {
    UInteractableIconWidget* interactableIconWidget =
      Cast<UInteractableIconWidget>(
                              InteractableIcon->GetUserWidgetObject());

    if (interactableIconWidget) {
      if (visible) {
        // Show the widget
        InteractableIcon->SetVisibility(true);
        interactableIconWidget->SetVisibility(ESlateVisibility::Visible);
        // Start playing the interactable animation
        interactableIconWidget->PlayMovingAnimation();
        // Rotate to face the player character
        if (facingActor) {
          FRotator rotation =
            UKismetMathLibrary::FindLookAtRotation(GetActorLocation(),
                                      facingActor->GetActorLocation());
          InteractableIcon->SetWorldRotation(rotation);
        }
      }
      else {  // Hide the widget
        interactableIconWidget->SetVisibility(ESlateVisibility::Hidden);
      }
    }
  }
}
```

In the `ShowInteractableIcon()` method, after setting the visibility of the interactable icon, if it is visible, we start playing the moving animation by calling the widget's `PlayMovingAnimation()` method. In the meantime, after obtaining the look at **rotation** from the horse to the player, the icon is **rotated toward** the player by calling its `SetWorldRotation()` method.

```
void AHorseCharacter::Dismount(const FInputActionValue& value)
{
  if (Rider) {
    ARPGCharacter* player = Cast<ARPGCharacter>(Rider);
    // Detach from the horse
    player->GetMesh()->
      DetachFromComponent(FDetachmentTransformRules::KeepWorldTransform);
    player->GetMesh()->AttachToComponent(player->GetRootComponent(),
                            FAttachmentTransformRules::KeepWorldTransform);
    // Reset to the original transform
    player->GetMesh()->SetRelativeTransform(player->OriginalTransform);
    // Place the player on the left side of the horse
    player->SetActorRelativeLocation(
                              DismountLeft->GetComponentLocation());
    // Stop the riding animation
    player->IsRiding = false;
    // Reset the horse stamina to the maximum
```

```
        Stats->SetStatValue("STA", Stats->GetStatValue("MaxSTA"));
        // Re-possess the player character (Unposses the horse automatically)
        AController* controller = GetController();
        controller->Possess(player);
        // Re-enable the collision detection
        BoxCollider->SetCollisionEnabled(ECollisionEnabled::QueryOnly);
        player->SetActorEnableCollision(true);
        // Reset the stamina bar to display the player's stamina
        player->UpdateStaminaUI(player->Stats->GetStatValue("STA"),
                                player->Stats->GetStatValue("MaxSTA"));
        // Restart the timer for regenerating the stamina
        player->RestartTimer();
    }
}
```

In the `Dismount()` method, if we have the rider actor, after getting the player, first its **Mesh** is **detached** from the horse character by calling its `DetachFromComponent()` method. Please note that here we have to choose an **FDetachmentTransformRules** type that is the **KeepWorldTransform**. Then the player's Mesh is **re-attached** to the root component by calling its **AttachToComponent()** method. Next, the **relative** transform of the Mesh is reset to the **original** transform before is attached to the horse.

Then we call the `SetActorRelativeLocation()` method to place the player on the **left** side of the horse at the position of the **DismountLeft** scene component. After dismounting from the horse, we reset the `IsRiding` flag to `false` to stop the **riding** animation followed by resetting the horse stamina to the maximum and **re-possessing** the player character by calling the controller's **Possess()** method. Next, we call the `SetCollisionEnabled()` method of the `BoxCollider` and `SetActorEnableCollision()` method of the player to **re-enable** the collision detection for the player character and the box collider.

Lastly, to reset the stamina bar for displaying the player's stamina, we call the `UpdateStaminaUI()` method to display the player's stamina and **restart** the timer for regenerating the player's stamina.

The code is not complete yet, let's continue to modify the RPGCharacter class as follows.

Interacting with the Horse Character

To interact with the Horse character, we have to modify the **RPGCharacter** class as follows. Open the **RPGCharacter.h** header, and add the following **bold** lines:

```
UCLASS()
class RPG_API ARPGCharacter : public ACharacter
{
    GENERATED_BODY()
```

```
public:
  // Sets default values for this character's properties
  ARPGCharacter();

  UPROPERTY(VisibleAnywhere, Category = "Riding")
  bool IsRiding = false;
  UPROPERTY(VisibleAnywhere, Category = "Riding")
  AActor* InteractableActor;
  UPROPERTY(VisibleAnywhere, Category = "Riding")
  FTransform OriginalTransform;
  ...
}
```

The IsRiding property represents whether the player is riding the horse, The
InteractableActor refers to the Actor whom the player is currently interacting with.
The OriginalTransform property is to store the player's **Transform** before mounting to
the horse. The Interact() method is the binding function to let the player interact with
an interactable actor.

Continue to open the **RPGCharacter.cpp** file, and after adding the following **includes**:

```
#include "Interfaces/Interactable.h"
#include "Characters/HorseCharacter.h"
```

Add the following **bold** lines in the **Interact()** binding method:

```
void ARPGCharacter::Interact(const FInputActionValue& value)
{
  if (InteractableActor) {
    IInteractable* interactable = Cast<IInteractable>(InteractableActor);

    if (interactable->GetInteractableType() == EInteractableType::Horse) {
      // Hide the Interact text and icon
      interactable->ShowInteractText(false);
      interactable->ShowInteractableIcon(false);
      // Get and save the current Transform
      OriginalTransform = GetMesh()->GetRelativeTransform();
      AHorseCharacter* horse = Cast<AHorseCharacter>(InteractableActor);
      // If the interactable is a horse
      if (horse) {
        FName mountSocket = TEXT("MountSocket");
        // The KeepRelativeTransform means relative to the horseback
        GetMesh()->AttachToComponent(horse->GetMesh(),
          FAttachmentTransformRules::KeepRelativeTransform, mountSocket);
        // Play the Sit animation
        IsRiding = true;
        horse->Rider = this;
        // Possess the horse
        AController* controller = GetController();
        controller->Possess(horse);
```

```
            // Disable the box collider of the horse
            horse->BoxCollider->
                        SetCollisionEnabled(ECollisionEnabled::NoCollision);
            // Note: Disable the player's collision detection, otherwise the
            //        camera will be blocked!
            SetActorEnableCollision(false);
            // Stop the timer for regenerating the stamina to stop updating
            // the stamina value
            ClearTimer();
            // Reset the stamina to the maximum
            Stats->SetStatValue("STA", Stats->GetStatValue("MaxSTA"));
            // Update the stamina bar to display the stamina of the horse
            UpdateStaminaUI(horse->Stats->GetStatValue("STA"),
                                    horse->Stats->GetStatValue("MaxSTA"));
        }
      }
    }
}
```

In the `Interact()` method, if currently, we have the interactable actor, after obtaining the `IInteractable` interface, if we are interacting with the horse, first hide the Interact text and icon, and after saving the current Transform of the player, if the interactable is a horse, we call the `AttachToComponent()` method to attach the player **Mesh** to the horseback on the specified **socket** and keep the **relative** transform.

Then the `IsRiding` flag is set to `true` to play the **Sit** animation and the player is assigned as the rider of the horse. Next, after **possessing** the horse character by calling the built-in **Possess()** function of the **Controller**, the horse box collider is **disabled** to prevent from interacting with the rider and the player's collision detection is also **disabled**; otherwise, the **camera** will be blocked.

Lastly, to update the stamina bar for the **horse** character, we first call the `ClearTimer()` method to stop the timer for regenerating the stamina, and thus stop updating the stamina value. Then, after resetting the player's stamina to the **maximum**, we call the `UpdateStaminaUI()` method to display the stamina of the **horse** character instead of the player.

Next, add the following **bold** lines in the **OnLockBoxBeginOverlap()** method:

```
void ARPGCharacter::OnLockBoxBeginOverlap(UPrimitiveComponent*
    OverlappedComp, AActor* OtherActor, UPrimitiveComponent* OtherComp,
    int32 OtherBodyIndex, bool bFromSweep, const FHitResult& SweepResult)
{
  IHealth* health = Cast<IHealth>(OtherActor);

  if (health && !health->IsDead()) {
    ...
  }
```

```
    // If we currently don't have any interactable actor
    if (!InteractableActor) {
      IInteractable* interactable = Cast<IInteractable>(OtherActor);
      // If it's interactable, show the moving icon
      if (interactable)
        interactable->ShowInteractableIcon(true, this);
    }
}
```

In the above code, when the enemy lock box is colliding with the **interactable**, if currently, we don't have any interactable actor, we try getting the **IInteractable** interface from the actor, and if the actor implements the interface, the ShowInteractableIcon() method is called to **show** the moving icon.

Then add the following **bold** lines in the **OnLockBoxEndOverlap()** method:

```
void ARPGCharacter::OnLockBoxEndOverlap(UPrimitiveComponent*
        OverlappedComp, AActor* OtherActor, UPrimitiveComponent* OtherComp,
                                          int32 OtherBodyIndex)
{
  ILock* target = Cast<ILock>(OtherActor);

  if (target)
  {
    ...
  }

  IInteractable* interactable = Cast<IInteractable>(OtherActor);
  // Hide the moving icon
  if (interactable)
    interactable->ShowInteractableIcon(false);
}
```

Similarly, when the interactable is **leaving** the enemy lock box, after getting the **IInteractable** interface, we hide the moving icon.

Next, to play the riding animation, continue to open the **RPGAnimInstance.h** header, and add the following **bold** lines in the class:

```
UCLASS()
class RPG_API URPGAnimInstance : public UAnimInstance
{
  GENERATED_BODY()
public:
  UPROPERTY(EditAnywhere, BlueprintReadWrite, Category = "Locomotion")
  bool IsRiding;
    ...
};
```

In the `public` section, the `IsRiding` property is declared to represent the status of riding a horse or not.

Finally, open the **RPGAnimInstance.cpp** file, and add the following **bold** lines in the `NativeUpdateAnimation()` method:

```cpp
void URPGAnimInstance::NativeUpdateAnimation(float DeltaSeconds)
{
  Super::NativeUpdateAnimation(DeltaSeconds);

  ARPGCharacter* owningActor = Cast<ARPGCharacter>(GetOwningActor());

  if (IsValid(owningActor))
  {
    float Speed = owningActor->GetVelocity().Size();

      ...
    IsFalling = owningActor->GetMovementComponent()->IsFalling();
    IsRiding = owningActor->IsRiding;
  }
}
```

In the method, after getting the status of riding a horse from the owning actor, it's assigned to the `IsRiding` property.

So far the horse character interacting code is complete, build the project and make sure no errors occurred.

Riding Animation Setup

Before setting up the Animation Blueprint, we need to download the horse riding animation. So go to the Mixamo website again, and after logging in, find and download the **Male Sitting Pose** animation under the **Animations** tab as shown below:

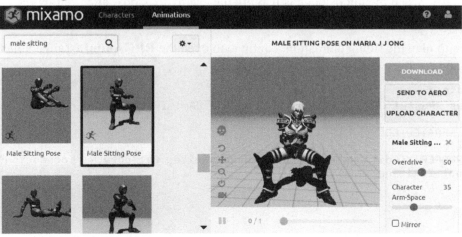

After adding the **root bone** to the FBX file using the mixamo converter in Blender, import the converted file into the Female > **Animations** folder in our project.

Next, let's continue to set up the riding animation in the Animation Blueprint. Open the **ABP_FemaleWarrior** Blueprint, and after opening the **Locomotion** tab, drag off from the **Idle/Run** state and add a new state called **Riding** as shown below:

Continue to double-click on the **Transition Rule** icon to open the tab as shown below:

After getting the **IsRiding** variable declared in the C++ code, drag off from the output of the node and plug it into the **Can Enter Transition** pin of the **Result** node as shown above.

Back to the **Locomotion** tab, drag off from the **Riding** state, and make a transition to the **Idle/Run** state as shown below:

Double-click on the **Transition Rule** icon to open the tab as shown below:

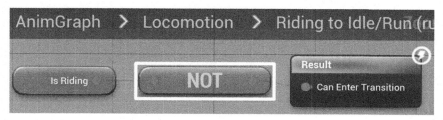

After getting the **IsRiding** variable, drag off from the output of the node and select the **NOT Boolean** under the **Math** > **Boolean** to create a **NOT** node as shown above. Then make a transition from the NOT node to the **Result** node.

Back to the **Locomotion** tab, double-click the **Riding** state to open the tab as shown below:

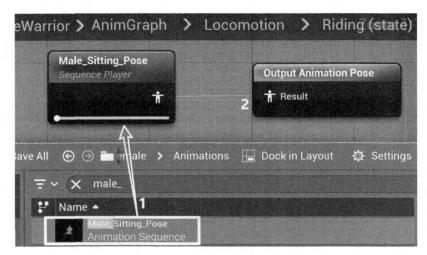

Then drag and drop the imported **Male_Sitting_Pose** animation into the state, as shown above, and make a transition from the **Male_Sitting_Pose** node to the **Output Animation Pose** node. Now press **Compile** and **Save** to confirm the modification.

The Mount Socket

Before creating the Blueprint for the Horse character, we have to create a **Socket** on the horse skeleton on which the player can be mounted. Open the **SKEL_Horse** in the Characters > **Horses** folder, and expand the **root** hierarchy until you see the **DEF-spine_004** bone as shown below:

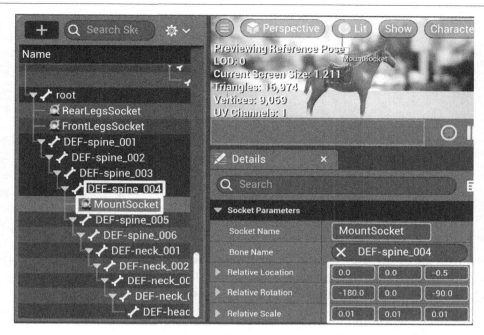

Right-click on the bone, and after selecting **Add Socket** from the context menu to create a Socket called **MountSocket**, modify the Socket's **Transform** parameters as shown above. Here we have to reset all the **Relative Scale** fields to **0.01** because the top **horse_rig** bone has a Scale of **100**.

The Horse Character Blueprint

Now it's time to create the Blueprint for the horse character. Right-click in the Content Browser of the **Horses** > **Blueprints** folder, choose **Blueprint Class** from the context menu, and then pick the **HorseCharacter** as the Parent Class to generate the Blueprint. After renaming it to **BP_Horse**, double-click to open the Blueprint in the editor as shown below:

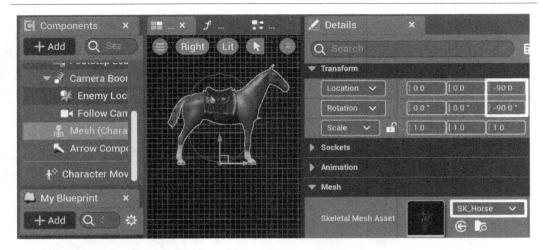

First, with the **Mesh** selected, after setting the **Skeletal Mesh** to the imported **SK_Horse** mesh, rotate the Mesh **-90** degrees to face the direction of the **Arrow Component** and then move it to inside the **Capsule** Component as shown above.

Next, expand the **Animation** section and set the **Anim Class** to the **ABP_Horse** Blueprint as shown below:

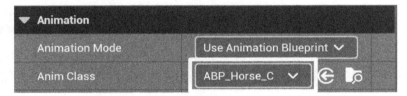

Continue to find and expand the **Collision** settings, as shown below, and make sure that the **Generate Overlap Events** checkbox is **unticked** because we'll use the **Box Collider** to generate the Overlay Events instead.

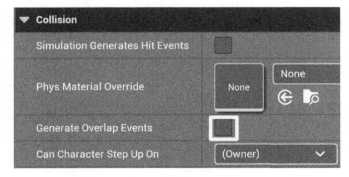

Next, with the **Box Collider** selected, and after moving it to the bottom of the Mesh, reset the **Box Extend** to as shown below:

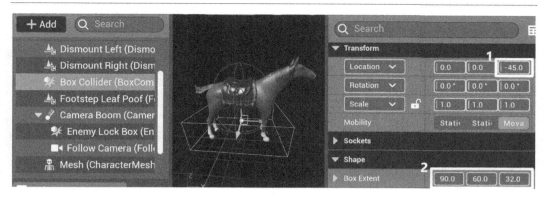

Continue to find and expand the **Collision** section, as shown below, and after **ticking** the **Generate Overlap Events**, reset the **Collision Presets** to **OverlayOnyPawn**.

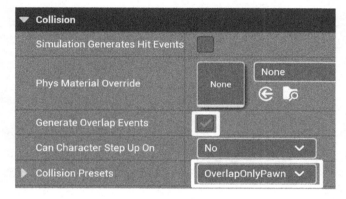

With the **Dismount Right** selected and move it to the **right** of the Mesh as shown below:

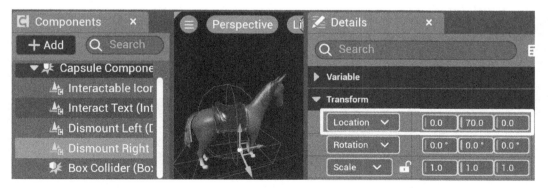

Next, with the **Dismount Left** selected, move it to the **left** of the Mesh as shown below:

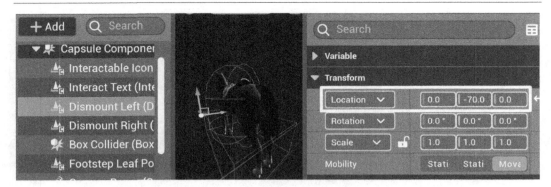

Continue to select the **Interact Text** and move it to **above** the horse as shown below:

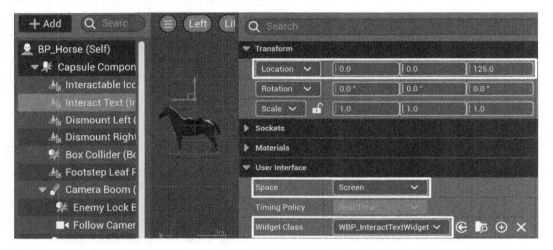

Then after expanding the **User Interface**, set the **Space** to **Screen** and **Widget Class** to the **WBP_InteractTextWidget** as shown above.

Next, find and expand the **Rendering** settings and **untick** the **Visible** checkbox as shown below:

Continue to find and expand the **Collision** section, **untick** the **Generate Overlap Events** checkbox, and set **Can Character Step Up On** to **No** as shown below:

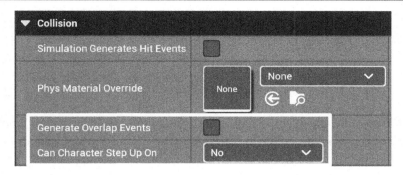

With the **Interactable Icon** selected, and after expanding the **User Interface** in the Details tab, set the **Widget Class** to the **WBP_InteractableIconWidget** as shown below:

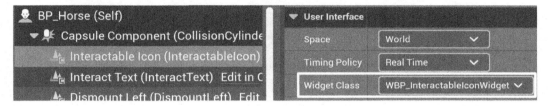

Please note that the **Space** is set to **World** here and we'll use C++ code to **rotate** it to face the player character. Continue to find and expand the **Rendering** settings, **untick** the **Visible** checkbox and in the **Collision** settings, **untick** the **Generate Overlap Events** checkbox, and also set **Can Character Step Up On** to **No**.

Next, with the **Capsule Component** selected and expand the **Collision** settings as shown below:

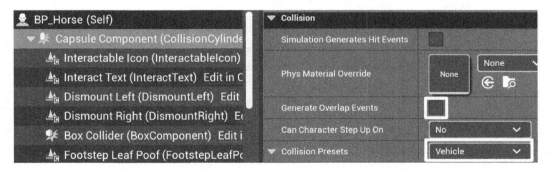

Untick the **Generate Overlap Events** checkbox and reset the **Collision Presets** to **Vehicle** as shown above. Continue to expand the **Shape** settings, and set the **Capsule Radius** to **60** as shown below:

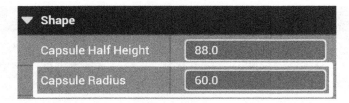

With the **Camera Boom** selected, find and expand the **Camera Settings**, and **untick** the **Inherit Yaw** checkbox, as shown below, because we'll control the **Yaw** of the Camera Boom in C++ independently.

Then, with the **BP_Horse** selected, find and expand the **Speed** settings, as shown below, and reset the **Walk** and **Run Speed** to **500** and **1000**, respectively.

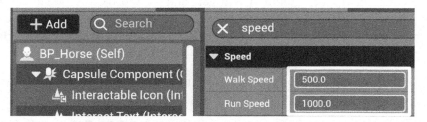

Continue to find and expand the **Stats** settings as shown below:

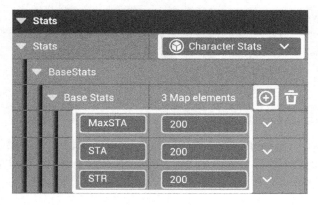

After clicking on the drop-down menu and selecting the **Character Stats**, press the +
button **three** times to add three new elements as shown above. Enter three **stamina**-
related **Stats**, namely the **MaxSTA**, **STA**, and **STR**, and set their values to all **200**.

Next, find and expand the **Pawn** settings, and **untick** the **Use Controller Rotation Pitch**
checkbox as shown below:

Creating the Input Action

Before testing the horse riding, we have to create an Input Action for the player to
dismount from the horse character. Inside the Content > **Input** folder, create a new
Input Action named **IA_Dismount** and then open the **IMC_Warrior** mapping context
asset, press the + next to the Mappings to add one more mapping as follows:

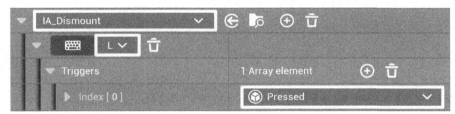

After selecting the **IA_Dismount** for the mapping, choose **Keyboard** > **L** key for the
action. Next, create a trigger and select **Pressed** from the dropdown.

Now back to the **BP_Horse** blueprint, search for the **Input** category in the Details panel,
and select the corresponding Input Actions for required fields including **Move**, **Jump**,
Zoom, **Look**, **Sprint**, and **Dismount** Actions as shown below:

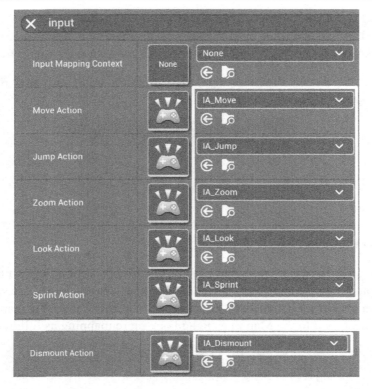

So far the code and settings for the Horse character are complete, press **Compile** and **Save** to confirm all modifications. Then drag and drop the finished **BP_Horse** Blueprint into the scene to create an instance of the Horse character.

Now press **Play** to run the game and move the player character toward the horse character in the scene. When the lock box collides with the horse character, the **Interactable Icon** will show up and the moving animation is playing as shown below on the **left**:

Continue to move the player toward the horse, when the character **collides** with the horse box collider, the **Interact Text** will appear as shown above on the **right**. After pressing the **E** key, the player will be mounted onto the back of the horse as shown below on the **left**:

In the meantime, you'll see the stamina bar is updated to display the stamina of the horse character instead of the player's. Finally, press the **L** key, and the player will be **dismounted** from the horseback as shown above on the above **right**, and the stamina bar is also updated to re-display the player's stamina.

5.7.3 Horse Full-Body IK

The new **Full-Body IK (FBIK)** is designed to act as a procedural adjustment tool within Control Rig, such as for ground alignment, or arm reaching behavior. The overall solver method is built on a **Position Based IK** framework, which enables faster rig performance, per-bone settings, preferred angles, squash and stretch, and more.

You must enable the **FullBodyIK** plugin. To do this, navigate in the Unreal Editor menu bar to **Edit > Plugins** and locate **FullBodyIK**. Ensure the plugin is **enabled** and restart the editor.

After enabling the FBIK plugin, we have to create an **IK Rig** asset for the Horse character and create controls as follows.

Horse IK Rig Setup

Right-click in the content browser of the **Horses** > **Animations** folder, and choose **Animation** > **Retargeting** > **IK Rig** from the context menu to create a new IK Rig as shown below:

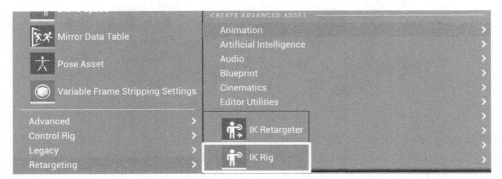

After re-naming the NewIKRig to **IKRig_Horse** as shown below:

Double-click to open it, and in the Details panel, pick the **SK_Horse** as the **Preview Skeletal Mesh**, as shown below:

Then, after pressing the **+Add New Solver** button in the **Solver Stack** panel, as shown below, select the **Full Body IK** to generate an IK Solver.

You'll see the "**Missing root bone**" message appears in the name of the **Full Body IK** solver as shown below:

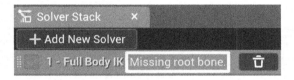

Next, with the **1 – Full Body IK** selected, find the **horse_rig** on the top of the hierarchy, and after **right**-clicking on it, select the **Set Root Bone on Selected Solver** option from the context menu as shown below:

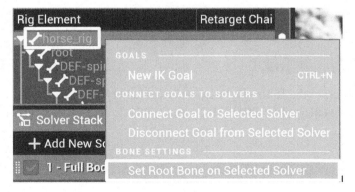

Continue to find and expand the **MCH-torso_parent** bone hierarchy, and after right-clicking on the **torso** bone, as shown below, select the **New IK Goal** option to generate an IK Goal for the bone. The purpose of the **IK Goal** here is to **fix** the bone at a certain position.

Then, with the generated **torso_Goal** selected, as shown below, after setting its **Z** position to **130**, press the Scale **Lock** icon. Reset the **X** Scale to **1** to resize the **Box** gizmo shown in the Viewport. Lastly, set the **Size Multiplier** to **2** to make the Goal **two** times bigger.

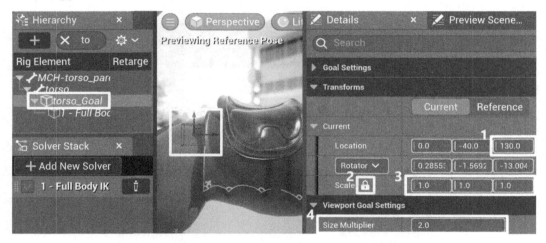

Continue to generate the following IK Goals for the **MCH-spine_002**, **spine_fk_002**, **spine_fk_001**, **tweak_spine_001**, **ORG-spine_001**, and **DEF-tail_001** bones as shown below:

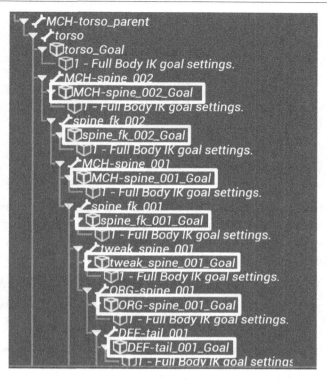

Then find and create the IK Goals for the **DEF-r_toe_L** and **DEF-r_toe_R** bones as shown below:

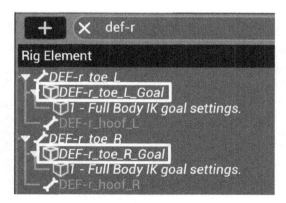

Continue to expand the MCH-spine_003 bone hierarchy, and after creating an IK Goal for the **ORG-shoulder_L** bone, as shown below, right-click on the **DEF-upper_arm_L** bone and select **Add Settings to Selected Bone** to generate the IK Goal settings for the bone.

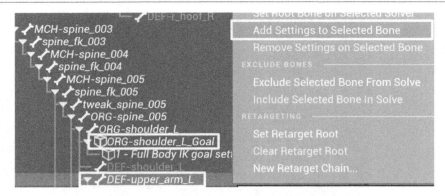

The **IK Goal settings** are to control the **Stiffness** and **Rotation Angles** of the bones. With the generated **Full Body IK bone settings** selected, and after expanding the **Preferred Angles** settings, **tick** the **Use Preferred Angles** checkbox and reset the **Preferred Angles** values as shown below:

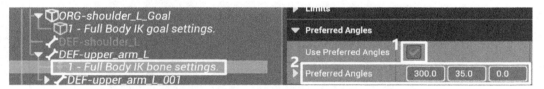

Continue to generate the following **IK Goal settings** for the **DEF-upper_arm_L_001**, **DEF-forearm_L**, **DEF-forearm_L_001**, **DEF-forefoot_L**, and **DEF-forefoot_L_001** bones as shown below:

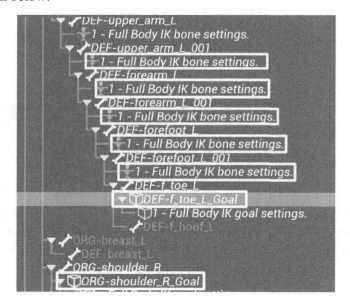

Then, as shown above, also create the **IK Goal** for the **DEF-f_toe_L** bone. For each IK Goal settings, **tick** its **Use Preferred Angles** checkbox in the **Details** panel. Their **Preferred Angles** values are listed as shown below:

IK Goal settings	Preferred Angles (X, Y, Z)
DEF-upper_arm_L_001 settings	**(-650, -20**, 0)
DEF-forearm_L settings	**(60**, 0, 0)
DEF-forearm_L_001 settings	**(85**, 0, 0)
DEF-forefoot_L settings	**(925**, 0, 0)
DEF-forefoot_L_001 settings	**(-140**, 0, 0)

So far we have finished the IK Goals and settings for the **Left** shoulder and its child's bones. Similarly, after expanding the **ORG-shoulder_R** bone hierarchy, create the IK Goals and settings for the **Right** shoulder and its child's bones. The IK Goals and settings should be the **same** for both the Left and Right shoulders.

Finally, to fix the positions of the **Neck**, **Head**, and **Skull** bones, after expanding the **MCH-spine_006** bone hierarchy, create the following IK Goals for the ORG-neck_001, ORG-neck_002, ORG-neck_003, ORG-neck_004, ORG-skull, and DEF-skull bones as shown below:

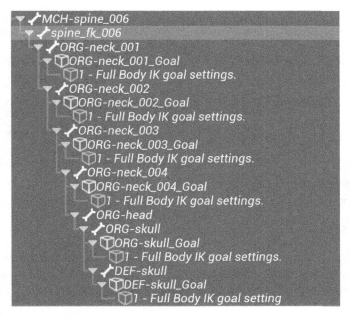

Legs IK Exposure and Previewing

After the IK Goals and settings are complete, it's time to preview the result as follows. With the **DEF-f_toe_R_Goal** selected, as shown below, and in the Details tab, after resetting its **Z** position to **40**, you'll see the **right** leg moves up as shown in the Viewport.

Because we'll change the **Z** position of the **DEF-f_toe_R_Goal** in C++ code, after expanding the **Exposure** settings, as shown above, **tick** the **Expose Position** checkbox.

Continue to select the **DEF-f_toe_L_Goal** and **tick** the **Expose Position** as shown below:

Similarly, with the **DEF-r_toe_L_Goal** and **DEF-r_toe_R_Goal** selected respectively, **tick** their **Expose Position** checkboxes as well in the Details tab. Finally, press **Save** to confirm all modifications.

IK Leg Sockets

After the IK Rig is ready, we have to create Sockets on the horse skeleton for calculating the **slope** of the ground and **Z offsets** for the legs IK as follows. Open the **SKEL_Horse** in the **Horses** folder, find and expand the **root** bone as shown below:

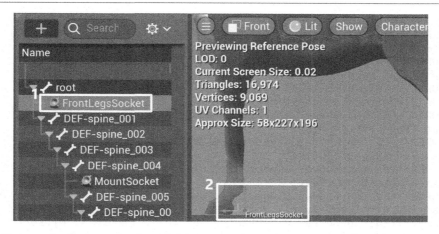

Right-click on the bone and select **Add Socket** from the context menu to create a Socket called **FrontLegsSocket** as shown above. Then, with the Socket selected, move it to under the **front legs** using the Gizmo in the Viewport.

Right-click on the **root** bone again and create another Socket called **RearLegsSocket** as shown below:

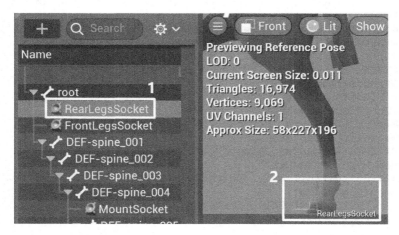

With the Socket selected, move it to under the **rear legs** in the Viewport as shown above. Finally, press **Save** to confirm the modification.

Implementing the Horse Legs IK in C++

Next, we are going to write the C++ code to implement the legs IK calculation. Back to Visual Studio, open the **HorseAnimInstance.h** header, and add the following **bold** lines:

```
UCLASS()
class RPG_API UHorseAnimInstance : public URPGAnimInstance
```

```
{
  GENERATED_BODY()
public:
  UPROPERTY(EditDefaultsOnly, Category = "Sockets")
  FName SlopeTraceStartSocket;
  UPROPERTY(EditDefaultsOnly, Category = "Sockets")
  FName SlopeTraceEndSocket;
  UPROPERTY(EditAnywhere, BlueprintReadWrite, Category = "Offsets")
  float FrontLeftLegOffset;
  UPROPERTY(EditAnywhere, BlueprintReadWrite, Category = "Offsets")
  float FrontRightLegOffset;
  UPROPERTY(EditAnywhere, BlueprintReadWrite, Category = "Offsets")
  float RearLeftLegOffset;
  UPROPERTY(EditAnywhere, BlueprintReadWrite, Category = "Offsets")
  float RearRightLegOffset;
  UPROPERTY(EditAnywhere, BlueprintReadWrite, Category = "Offsets")
  float TraceStartZOffset;
  UPROPERTY(EditAnywhere, BlueprintReadWrite, Category = "Rotator")
  float Pitch;
  UPROPERTY(EditAnywhere, BlueprintReadWrite, Category = "Rotator")
  float PitchMin = -35;
  UPROPERTY(EditAnywhere, BlueprintReadWrite, Category = "Rotator")
  float PitchMax = 35;
  UPROPERTY(EditAnywhere, BlueprintReadWrite, Category = "Offsets")
  float FrontLegsOffsetMax = 50;
  UPROPERTY(EditAnywhere, BlueprintReadWrite, Category = "Offsets")
  float RearLegsOffsetMax = 50;

  UPROPERTY(EditAnywhere, Category = "Sockets")
  FName FrontLeftLegSocket;
  UPROPERTY(EditAnywhere, Category = "Sockets")
  FName FrontRightLegSocket;
  UPROPERTY(EditAnywhere, Category = "Sockets")
  FName RearLeftLegSocket;
  UPROPERTY(EditAnywhere, Category = "Sockets")
  FName RearRightLegSocket;
  UPROPERTY(EditDefaultsOnly, Category = "Sockets")
  FName FrontLegsSocket;
  UPROPERTY(EditDefaultsOnly, Category = "Sockets")
  FName RearLegsSocket;

  bool TraceGround(FName socket, FVector& impactPoint,
                                    float startZOffset = 0);
  float CalculatePitch(float min, float max);

  virtual void NativeUpdateAnimation(float DeltaSeconds) override;
protected:
  virtual void NativeBeginPlay() override;
private:
  USkeletalMeshComponent* mesh;
};
```

The `SlopeTraceStartSocket` and `SlopeTraceEndSocket` properties represent the names of the **sockets** whose positions are used for the Line Trace. The `FrontLeftLegOffset`, `FrontRightLegOffset`, `RearLeftLegOffset`, and `RearRightLegOffset` properties are to store the **vertical offsets** of the legs IK, respectively. The `TraceStartZOffset` property is the **adjustment** value in the **Z** axis for the line trace starting position. The `Pitch` property represents the calculated **Pitch** value of the horse slope and the `PitchMin` and `PitchMax` properties are the **Minimum** and **Maximum** of the allowed slope Pitch values, respectively.

The `FrontLegsOffsetMax` and `RearLegsOffsetMax` properties represent the **Maxima** of the allowed front and rear legs IK offset values, respectively. The `FrontLeftLegSocket`, `FrontRightLegSocket`, `RearLeftLegSocket`, `RearRightLegSocket`, `FrontLegsSocket`, and `RearLegsSocket` properties represent the names of the sockets that their positions are used for the line trace starting positions.

The `TraceGround()` method is a help function that performs the line trace **vertically** from the specified socket location and finds the impact point on the ground. The `CalculatePitch()` method calculates the **Pitch** rotation value of the ground slope. In the `Protected` section, we override the **`NativeBeginPlay()`** method of the animation instance class. Lastly, the `mesh` property refers to the **horse** skeletal mesh.

Next, open the **HorseAnimInstance.cpp** file and add the following lines to implement the new methods:

```
#include "Kismet/KismetSystemLibrary.h"

void UHorseAnimInstance::NativeBeginPlay()
{
  AActor* owner = GetOwningActor();

  if (owner) {
    ARPGCharacter* horse = Cast<ARPGCharacter>(owner);

    if (horse) {
      mesh = horse->GetMesh();
      // Initialize the Pitch
      Pitch = CalculatePitch(PitchMin, PitchMax);
    }
  }
}
```

The `NativeBeginPlay()` method is called when the horse animation begins to play. In the method, after getting the horse mesh, we call the `CalculatePitch()` method to initialize the `Pitch` property.

```
bool UHorseAnimInstance::TraceGround(FName socket, FVector& impactPoint,
                                     float startZOffset)
```

```
{
  if (mesh) {
    FVector socketLocation = mesh->GetSocketLocation(socket);
    // Get the line trace start position with a Z offset
    FVector traceStart = socketLocation + FVector(0, 0, startZOffset);
    // The trace end position is 200cm below the start
    FVector traceEnd = socketLocation - FVector(0, 0, 200);

    FHitResult hitResult(ForceInit);
    TArray<AActor*> actorsToIgnore;
    actorsToIgnore.Add(GetOwningActor());
    // Perform the line trace and draw the debug trace per frame
    bool isHit = UKismetSystemLibrary::LineTraceSingle(GetWorld(),
                 traceStart, traceEnd, UEngineTypes::ConvertToTraceType(
                 ECC_WorldStatic), false, actorsToIgnore,
                     EDrawDebugTrace::ForOneFrame, hitResult, true,
                         FLinearColor::Red, FLinearColor::Blue, 1.0f);
    // If we hit something underneath
    if (isHit) {
      // Get the impact point position
      impactPoint = hitResult.ImpactPoint;
      return true;
    }
    else
      return false;
  }

  return false;
}
```

In the `TraceGround()` method, after getting the line trace **start** and **end** positions, we perform the line trace and draw the debug trace per frame. If we hit something underneath, get the **impact point** position from the hit result.

```
float UHorseAnimInstance::CalculatePitch(float min, float max)
{
  FVector startLocation, endLocation;
  // Perform the line traces to find the two positions on the ground
  bool isHitStart = TraceGround(SlopeTraceStartSocket, startLocation,
                                                                -70);
  bool isHitEnd = TraceGround(SlopeTraceEndSocket, endLocation, -50);

  if (isHitStart && isHitEnd) {
    // Get the vector in the X axis from the start to the end position
    FVector xAxis = startLocation - endLocation;
    // Build a rotation matrix given only an X axis and get the rotator
    FRotator rotator = FRotationMatrix::MakeFromX(xAxis).Rotator();
    // Check the limits for the Pitch
    if (rotator.Pitch > max)
      return max;
    else if (rotator.Pitch < min)
      return min;
```

```
        else
            return rotator.Pitch;
    }

    return 0;
}
```

In the `CalculatePitch()` method, after declaring two `FVector` variables to store the **start** and **end** ground positions for calculating the ground slope, we perform the line traces from the specified `SlopeTraceStartSocket` and `SlopeTraceEndSocket` sockets to obtain the two positions on the ground. Then, after getting the vector in the **X** axis from the **start** to the **end** position, we call the `MakeFromX()` method and pass in the vector to build a **rotation** matrix given only the **X axis vector** and get the **Rotator**. Lastly, after checking the limits for the rotator's **Pitch** value, the value is returned. The calculation is illustrated as shown below:

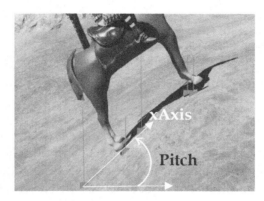

Finally, add the following **bold** lines in the `NativeUpdateAnimation()` method:

```
void UHorseAnimInstance::NativeUpdateAnimation(float DeltaSeconds)
{
    Super::NativeUpdateAnimation(DeltaSeconds);

    // Perform the calculation if not in a world being edited in the editor
    if (GetWorld()->WorldType != EWorldType::Editor) {
        // Only calculate the legs IK when is moving
        if ((SideSpeed != 0 || ForwardSpeed != 0) && mesh) {
            // Get the front legs socket's position
            FVector frontSocketLocation =
                                    mesh->GetSocketLocation(FrontLegsSocket);
            // Perform the ground trace and find the impact point's position
            FVector impactPoint;
            TraceGround(FrontLeftLegSocket, impactPoint, 35);
            // Find the front left leg's IK offset by the difference of the Z
            // positions
            FrontLeftLegOffset = impactPoint.Z - frontSocketLocation.Z;
            TraceGround(FrontRightLegSocket, impactPoint, 35);
```

```
        // Find the front right leg's IK offset
        FrontRightLegOffset = impactPoint.Z - frontSocketLocation.Z;
        // Check the limits
        if (FrontLeftLegOffset > FrontLegsOffsetMax)
          FrontLeftLegOffset = FrontLegsOffsetMax;
        if (FrontRightLegOffset > FrontLegsOffsetMax)
          FrontRightLegOffset = FrontLegsOffsetMax;
        // Find the rear legs IK offsets
        TraceGround(RearLeftLegSocket, impactPoint, 20);
        FVector rearSocketLocation = mesh->GetSocketLocation(
                                            RearLegsSocket);
        // Find the rear left leg's IK offset
        RearLeftLegOffset = impactPoint.Z - rearSocketLocation.Z;
        TraceGround(RearRightLegSocket, impactPoint, 20);
        // Find the rear right leg's IK offset
        RearRightLegOffset = impactPoint.Z - rearSocketLocation.Z;
        // Check the limits
        if (RearLeftLegOffset > RearLegsOffsetMax)
          RearLeftLegOffset = RearLegsOffsetMax;
        if (RearRightLegOffset > RearLegsOffsetMax)
          RearRightLegOffset = RearLegsOffsetMax;
        // Reset the Pitch before calculating the ground slope
        Pitch = 0;
        Pitch = CalculatePitch(PitchMin, PitchMax);
    }
  }
}
```

In the above code, we first determine whether or not a world **is being edited in the editor** and if the horse is moving, we calculate the legs IK as follows. First, after getting the **front** legs **socket's position**, the TraceGround() method is called to find the impact points on the ground from the **FrontLeftLegSocket** and **FrontRightLegSocket** sockets respectively and find the IK offsets of the **front left** and **right** legs respectively by calculating the difference between their **Z** positions. The following diagram illustrates the calculation:

After checking the limits of the above offsets, we repeat the same procedure for calculating offsets for the rear legs and also check the limits. Finally, before calculating the Pitch rotation for the horse, the **Pitch** property is reset to **0**.

Now build the project and make sure that no errors occurred. Then back to Unreal Editor and open the **ABP_Horse** Blueprint as shown below:

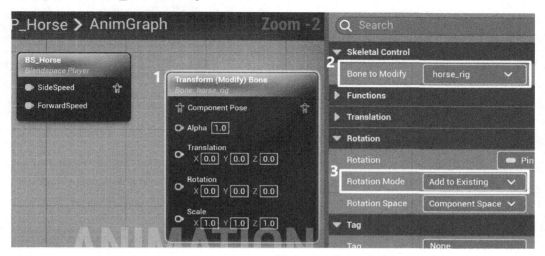

To change the **rotation** of the body of the Horse character according to the **slope** of the ground and avoid seeing the horse floating on the ground when walking on sloped terrains. First, create a **Transform (Modify) Bone** Node, as shown above, and set the **Bone to Modify** to the **horse_rig** bone and **Rotation Mode** to **Add to Existing** from the drop-down menus, respectively.

Then drag off from the **output** of the **Horse_BlendSpace** Node and plug into the **Component Pose** input pin of the **Transform Bone** Node. You'll see a **Local To Component** Node created automatically for us in between as shown below:

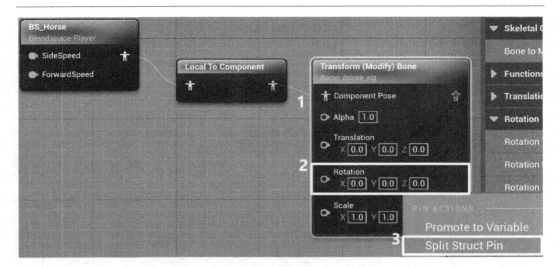

Next, right-click on the **Rotation** and select **Spilt Struct Pin** from the context menu as shown above. After the Struct Pin is split, right-click in the **AnimGraph** and select the **Get Pitch**, from the context menu, under the **Variables** > **Rotator** to get the **Pitch** variable as shown below:

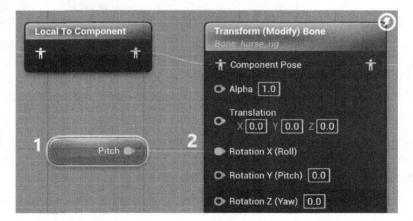

Continue to plug the output of the **Pitch** Node into the **Rotation X (Roll)** input pin as shown above.

To change the **Z** positions of the **IK Goals** of the Horse character according to the height of the terrain, create an **IK Rig** Node as shown below, and then set the **Rig Definition Asset** to the **IKRig_Horse** asset created before from the drop-down menu.

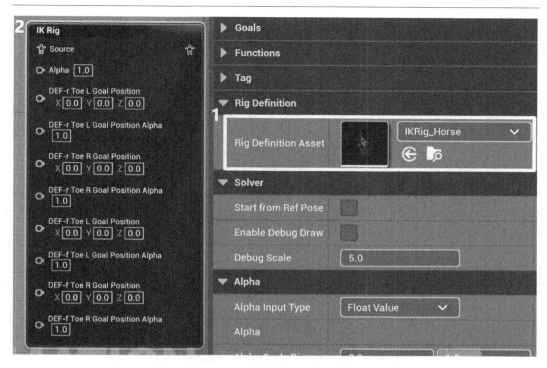

Then right-click on the **DEF-r Toe L Goal Position**, **DEF-r Toe R Goal Position**, **DEF-f Toe L Goal Position**, and **DEF-f Toe R Goal Position** respectively, and select **Spilt Struct Pin** to split the pins as shown below:

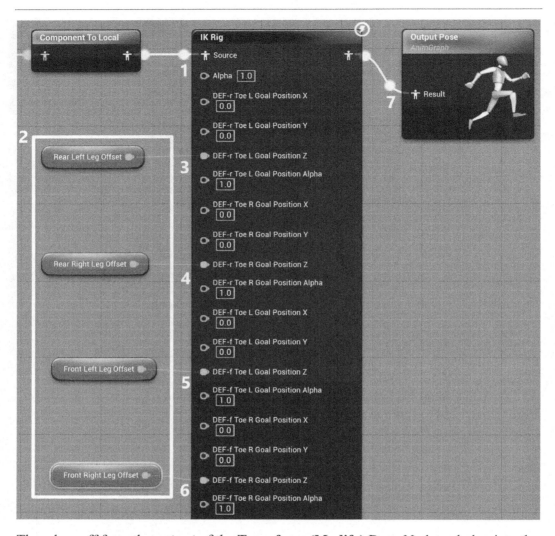

Then drag off from the **output** of the **Transform (Modify) Bone** Node and plug into the **Source** input pin of the **IK Rig** Node. Continue to get **Rear Left Leg Offset**, **Rear Right Leg Offset**, **Front Left Leg Offset**, and **Front Right Leg Offset** variables, as shown above, and plug the outputs of the **four** variable Nodes into the four **Position Z** input pins of the **IK Rig** Node, respectively.

Lastly, plug the output of the **IK Rig** Node into the **Result** pin of the **Output Pose** Node. So far the Horse IK setup is complete, press **Compile** and **Save** to confirm the modification, and then **close** the Blueprint.

Assigning the Socket Names

Re-open the **ABP_Horse** Blueprint, and in the **Details** panel, enter the following **socket** and **bone** names in the required fields under the **Sockets** section as shown below:

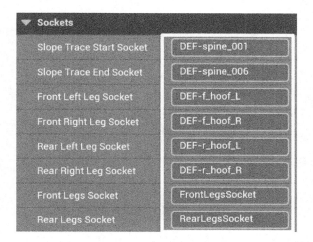

Then enter **50** in both **Front Legs Offset Max** and **Rear Legs Offset Max** fields respectively under the **Offsets** section as shown below:

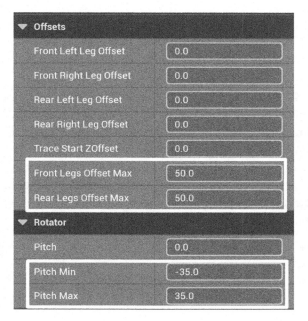

Finally, after entering **-35** and **35** for **Front Legs Offset Max** and **Rear Legs Offset Max** fields respectively under the **Rotator** section, as shown above, press **Save** to confirm the modification.

Now press **Play** to run the game, after the player character is mounted on the horseback, move the Horse character for a while and stop, you'll see the result as shown in the following two figures:

During horse moving, its body will be rotated to **align to** the slope of the terrain and after the horse stops, if its legs are stepping on higher ground, they will be moved up and bent.

5.8 Summary

Combat plays a key role in the fast-paced Action RPG design, this chapter explored how to implement this mechanism and Combos. First, the details of the design of a third person ARPG character and the camera controller were discussed. The topics about hit detection and damage of the melee weapon were also covered. Besides, we also demonstrated how to design and implement the automatic enemy locking mechanism. On the other hand, we introduced using animation notifications to integrate and play different sound effects on different landscape materials. Finally, the horse riding system was implemented using the latest **Full-Body IK** plug-in in UE5.

In the next chapter, we'll explore Visual Effects (VFX) design in ARPGs using the UE5 **Niagara** VFX System.

Exercises

5.1 Choose one of your favorite action RPGs, after exploring the character and camera control used in the game, modify the C++ code and Blueprints presented in this chapter to re-implement such mechanism.

5.2 Trace the C++ code for the great sword loading and the code for playing Combos, make sure that you fully understand the logic behind the algorithm.

5.3 Download more **Light** and **Heavy** melee attack animations for the great sword from the **Mixamo** website. After importing the animations into Unreal Editor, modify the **AM_GreatSwordSlash** Montage and the required C++ code used in this chapter to add the new animations into the Combos.

5.4 If you can find another horse skeletal mesh and its animations, for example, the **Horse Starter Kit** in the Unreal Marketplace. Follow the steps presented in the last section to create the **IK Rig** and finish the setup for the horse Full-Body IK. Then replace the horse model used in this chapter and re-run the game to explore what's the difference between using the one from the book's website and the new horse model.

5.5 Refer to the appendix section in this book and download horse gallop and walk sounds from the **mixkit** website. After importing them into the project, add **two** Anim Notify classes in C++ and then create two Blueprints derived from those classes. Open the HorseWalk and HorseRun animations respectively, and after adding the anim notify blueprints at their Notify tracks when the horse is stepping on the ground, add the Notify() overridden method and required properties in the C++ classes to store required sound cues. Then add code in the Notify() method to play the horse gallop and walk sounds.

5.6 We have demonstrated how to perform the sprint drain in the stamina system. So please implement the mechanism in C++ to drain the stamina when the player is doing the **double** or **multiple jumps**.

Visual Effects Design

Visual Effects (VFX) are another important feature that a player needs for an Action RPG. Magnificent VFX not only makes your game more immersing and interesting but makes the virtual world more realistic. In this chapter, we first introduce the **particle system** tool called **Niagara** in UE5, followed by implementing the most commonly used VFX in ARPGs, such as sword trails, shockwaves, and fireballs.

6.1 Niagara VFX System

Particle Systems can be used to simulate fuzzy phenomena like smoke or fire, which are difficult to reproduce using traditional rendering techniques. The Unreal Engine provides a tool called **Niagara** for us to create VFX using particle systems.

6.1.1 Niagara Overview

This section gives an overview of the Niagara VFX system in UE5. Niagara is Unreal Engine's next-generation VFX system. With Niagara, the technical artist can create additional functionality on their own, without the assistance of a programmer.

Core Niagara Components

In the Niagara VFX system, there are four core components: Systems, Emitters, Modules, and Parameters.

Systems

Niagara systems are containers for multiple emitters, all combined into one effect. For example, if you are making a **firework** effect, you might want multiple bursts in your firework. To do so you would create **multiple** emitters and place them all into a Niagara **system** called **Firework**. In the Niagara System Editor, you can modify or overwrite anything in the emitters or modules that are in the system. The **Timeline** panel in the System Editor shows which emitters are contained in the system and can be used to manage those emitters.

Emitters

Niagara emitters are containers for modules. They are single purpose, but they are also reusable. One unique thing about Niagara emitters is that you can create a simulation using the **module stack**, and then render that simulation multiple ways in the same emitter. Continuing our firework effect example, you could create one emitter that had a

sprite renderer for the spark, and a **ribbon renderer** for the stream of light following the spark.

Modules

Niagara modules are the base level of Niagara VFX. Modules are the equivalent of **UE4** Cascade's behaviors. Modules speak to common data, encapsulate behaviors, stack with other modules, and write functions. Modules are built using **High-Level Shading Language** (**HLSL**) but can be built visually in a Graph using nodes. You can create functions, include inputs, or write to a value or parameter map. You can even write HLSL code inline, using the **CustomHLSL** node in the Graph.

Parameters and Parameter Types

Parameters are an abstraction of data in a Niagara simulation. **Parameter types** are assigned to a parameter to define the data that the parameter represents. There are four types of parameters:

- ❖ **Primitive**: This type of parameter defines numeric data of varying precision and channel widths.
- ❖ **Enum**: This type of parameter defines a fixed set of named values and assumes one of the named values.
- ❖ **Struct**: This type of parameter defines a combined set of Primitive and Enum types.
- ❖ **Data Interfaces**: This type of parameter defines functions that provide data from external data sources. This can be data from other parts of UE5 or data from an outside application.

You can add a custom parameter module to an emitter by clicking the **Plus sign** icon (+) and selecting **Set new or existing parameter directly**. This adds a **Set Parameter** module to the stack. Click the **Plus sign** icon (+) on the **Set Parameter** module and select **Add Parameter** to set an existing parameter or **Create New Parameter** to set a new parameter.

Niagara Stack Model and Stack Groups

Particle simulation in Niagara operates as a **stack**—simulation flows from the top of the stack to the bottom, executing programmable code blocks called **modules** in order. Crucially, every module is assigned to a **group** that describes when the module is executed.

Templates and Wizards

When you first create a Niagara emitter or Niagara system, a dialog displays offering several options for what kind of emitter or system you want to create. One of these options is to choose a template. These templates are based on some **common base** effects and include various modules already. You can change any of the parameters in the template. You can add, modify or delete any of the modules. In a system template, you can also add, modify or delete any of the emitters. Templates are just there to jumpstart your creativity and give you something that you can work with immediately.

6.1.2 Niagara VFX Workflow

This section provides an overview of the Niagara VFX workflow and its core components.

Creating Emitters

When you create your emitters, you place modules in the stack that define how that effect will look, what actions it will take, and so on. In the **Emitter Spawn** group, place modules that define what will happen when the emitter first spawns. In the **Emitter Update** group, place modules that affect the emitter over time. In the **Particle Spawn** group, place modules that define what will happen when particles spawn from the emitter. In the **Particle Update** group, place modules that affect particles over time. In the **Event Handlers** group, you can create Generate events in one or more emitters that define certain data. Then you can create Listening events in other emitters which trigger a behavior in reaction to that generated event.

Creating Systems

Combine individual emitters into one system, which displays the entire visual effect you want to create. There are modules specific to systems, and some elements of the editor act differently when you are editing a system instead of an emitter. When you are editing a system in the Niagara Editor, you can change or override any modules in any emitter included in the system. You can also manage timing for the included emitters using the Niagara Editor's **Timeline** panel.

Creating a Module

When writing a module, there are many functions available for you to use:

- ❖ **Boolean** operators
- ❖ **Math** expressions
- ❖ **Trigonometry** expressions
- ❖ **Customized** functions

❖ **Nodes** that make boilerplate functions easier

Modules all use HLSL, and the logic flow is as follows:

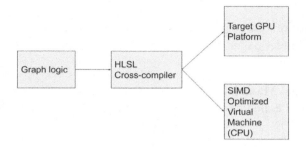

Remember that each module, emitter, and system you create uses resources. To conserve resources and improve performance, look through the modules already included in Niagara to see if you can accomplish your goal without creating a new module.

6.2 Niagara Quick Start

This Quick Start is designed to get you acquainted with creating visual effects (VFX) in Unreal Engine using Niagara. We will create a puff of leaves effect and attach it to the player character's footsteps so that the effect displays in an animation.

6.2.1 Project Setup

Before you start creating your Niagara effect, you need to set up your project with some basic materials and assets that you will be using in the rest of this section.

Creating a Mesh Shape

The first thing required for the effect is a leaf mesh shape and we are going to create a little puff of leaves that appears when your character runs. In your 3D modeling app, create a leaf shape, such as the one shown on the right:

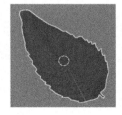

Next right click in the Content Browser of the **Content** folder and select **New Folder** from the context menu to create a folder called **Niagara**. Then open this folder and create a new folder inside called **3D_Assets** to store the leaf mesh. Finally, drag and drop your leaf model into the **3D_Assets** folder to import it to the project.

Creating a Material

Now we need to make a basic material to use for the leaf cloud and before doing so, first, create a new folder called **Materials** in the above **Niagara** folder. Then follow the following steps:

1. Right-click in the **Materials** folder and select **Material** from the context menu to create a Material called **M_MintLeaf**. Double-click to open it in the Material Editor.

2. With the **M_MintLeaf** node selected, as shown below, locate the **Material** section in the **Details** panel. Change the **Blend Mode** to **Masked**, as shown below, and check the box for **Two Sided**. Leave the other settings at their default.

3. Create a **Texture Sample** node. You can do this by holding **T** and clicking inside the Node Graph as shown below:

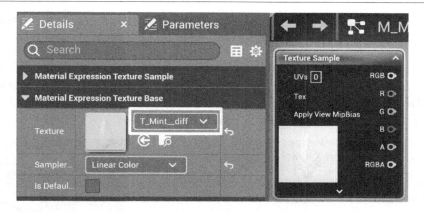

In the Details tab, locate the **Material Expression Texture Base** section, and change the **Texture** field to the **Diffuse** texture of the leaf mesh, here is the **T_Mint_diff** texture.

4.   Right-click on the graph and type "**particle**" in the **search** bar. Select **Particle Color** to add a Particle Color node. Then create a **Multiply** node by holding **M** and clicking inside the Node Graph.

Plug the **top** output of the Particle Color node into the **B** input on the **Multiply** Node, as shown below, similarly plug the top output of the **Texture Sample** node into the **A** input on the Multiply Node.

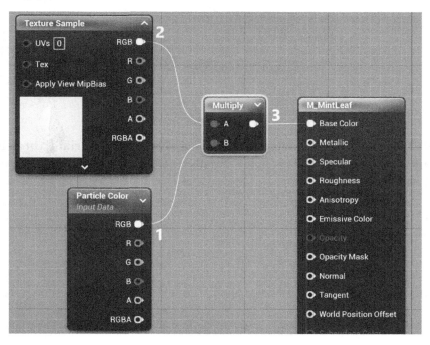

Next, plug the **output** of the Multiply Node into the **Base Color** input on the Main Material Node as shown above.

5. Create another **Texture Sample** node in the Node Graph, with the new Texture Sample node selected, locate the **Material Expression Texture Base** section in the **Details** panel. Click the dropdown, and type **Noise** in the search bar. Select the **T_Perlin_Noise_M** texture as shown below:

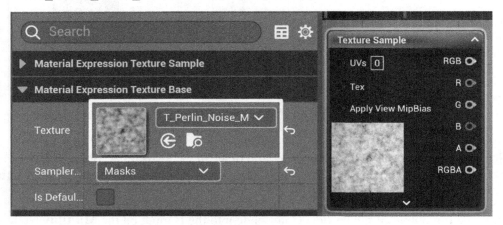

6. Right-click in the graph and type **dynamic** in the search bar, as shown below, then select **Dynamic Parameter** to add that node.

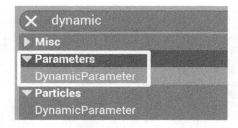

7. With the **Dynamic Parameter** node selected, locate the **Material Expression Dynamic Parameter** section in the **Details** panel. In **Array 0**, change the name to **Erode** as shown below:

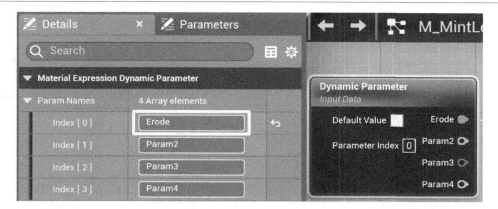

8. Right-click on the graph and type "**step**" in the search bar. Select **Value Step** to add that node as shown on the right:

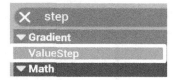

9. Drag off the **R** output of the **Noise** Texture Sample node and plug it into the **Gradient** input of the **Value Step** node. Drag off the **Erode** output of the **Dynamic Parameter** node, and plug it into the **Mask Offset Value** input of the Value Step node as shown below:

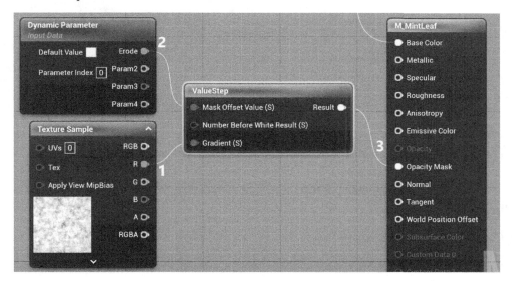

Drag off the **Results** output of the Value Step node and plug it into the **Opacity Mask** input of the main Material node as shown above.

10. From the **3D_Assets** folder in the **Content Browser**, drag and drop the **Normal Map** texture of the leaf mesh into the Node Graph as shown below:

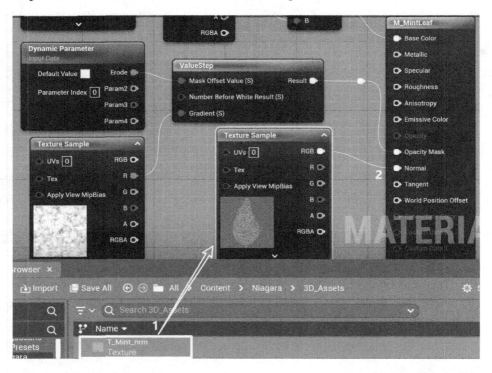

Then plug the **RGB** output of the Text Sample Node into the **Normal** input on the Main Material Node as shown above.

11. Click **Apply** and **Save**, then close the Material Editor.

6.2.2 Creating the Effect

Now that we have the mesh shape and basic material, it's time to create the Niagara effect.

Creating Systems and Emitters

Unlike in UE4 **Cascade**, Niagara emitters and systems are **independent**. The currently recommended workflow is to create a system from existing emitters or emitter templates.

First, create a **Niagara System** by right-clicking in the Content Browser of the **Niagara** folder, and from the context menu select **Niagara System**. The Niagara **Emitter Wizard** displays as shown below:

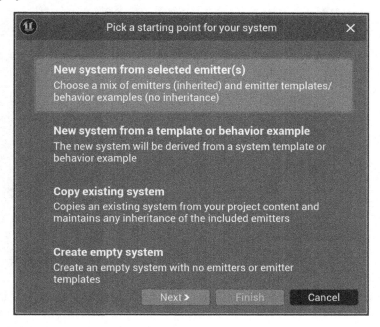

Select **New system from selected emitters**. Then click **Next**.

Under **Templates**, select **Simple Sprite Burst**. Click the **Plus sign** icon (+) to add the emitter to the list of emitters to add to the system. Then click **Finish** as shown below:

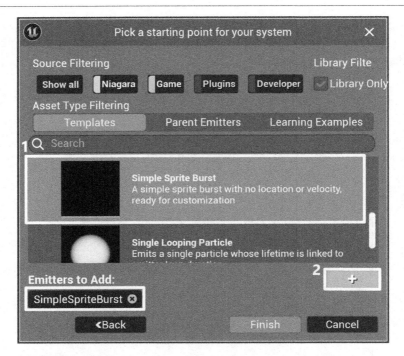

After naming the system **FXS_FootstepLeafPoof**, double-click to open it in the Niagara Editor.

The **emitter** instance in the new system has the default name of **SimpleSpriteBurst**. Click the **name** of the emitter instance in the **System Overview**, and the field will become **editable**. Name the emitter **FXE_LeafPoof** as shown below:

Until setting your mesh and material in the **Renderer**, you will not see anything in your preview. So in the **System Overview** tab, as shown below, select the **Sprite Renderer** under the **Render** section.

Click the **Trashcan** icon to **delete** the Sprite Renderer. Then click the **Plus sign** icon (+) to the right of **Render** and select **Mesh Renderer** from the list.

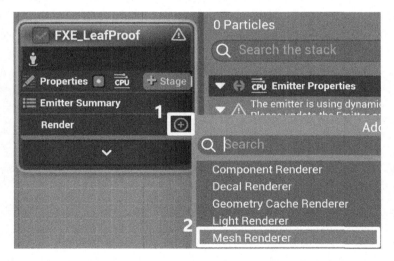

Then in the **Details** panel, click the dropdown next to **Index [0]** under the **Meshes** settings in the **Mesh Rendering** section, and select the imported **leaf mesh** in the **Project Setup** section as shown below:

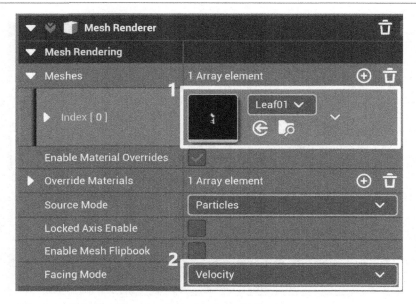

For **Facing Mode**, click the dropdown and select **Velocity**.

After clicking to **enable** the **Enable Material Overrides** setting, as shown below, the default is **0** Array elements. Click the **Plus sign** (+) icon to add an **Array element** and then click the dropdown next to **Explicit Material** and select the material we made in the **Project Setup** section.

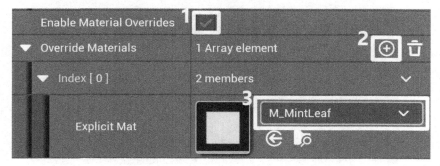

Now press **Save** to confirm the modification, and after completing this section, we have a Niagara system and an emitter instance, and you can drag the system from the Content Browser into the Level to preview it next to the Player Character. In the next part, we will edit the settings in the Niagara system to create the leaf cloud effect.

Note: When you make a particle effect, it is always a clever idea to drag your system to your level. This gives you a chance to see every change and edit in context.

6.2.3 Editing Module Settings

The Niagara Editor displays each emitter as a **stack**, with several groups of settings. We'll edit the modules in each group one at a time.

Emitter Update Settings

First, we are going to edit the modules in the **Emitter Update** group. These are behaviors that apply to the emitter, and that update **each frame**.

In the **System Overview**, click the **Emitter Update** group to open it in the **Selection** panel. Expand the **Emitter State** module. By default, the **Life Cycle Mode** should be set to **Self**. Change the **Emitter State** settings to the following values. This will give you a leaf poof that appears **once** and then **dissipates**.

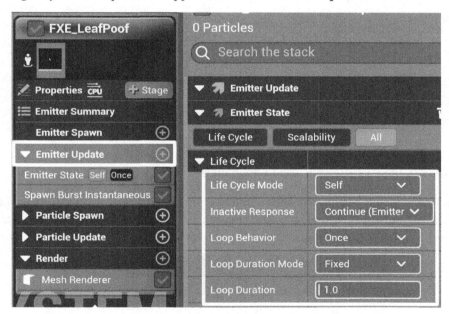

Expand the **Spawn Burst Instantaneous** module. Set the **Spawn Count** to **10**. A spawn count of **10** gives us a leaf cloud that is big enough to be visible, but small enough to be plausible.

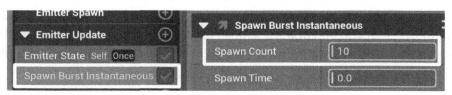

Particle Spawn Settings

Next, we'll edit the modules in the **Particle Spawn** group. These are behaviors that apply to particles when they **first spawn**.

In the **System Overview**, click the **Particle Spawn** group to open it in the **Selection** panel. Expand the **Initialize Particle** module. Under **Point Attributes**, select **Random** from the dropdown menu for the **Lifetime Mode**. This adds **Minimum** and **Maximum** fields to the Lifetime value, which will add some **variation** in **how long** each particle displays. Set the **Minimum** and **Maximum** fields to **0.4** and **0.6** respectively as shown below:

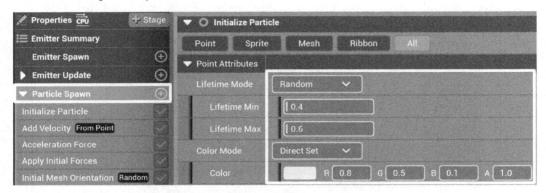

Then, after setting the **Color Mode** to **Direct Set**, as shown above, change the **Color** field to a **yellowish** color which makes the leaf looks rusty.

Continue to expand **Mesh Attributes** settings, locate the **Mesh Scale Mode** dropdown and select **Random Uniform**, as shown below. Then set the **Mesh Uniform Scale Min** and **Mesh Uniform Scale Max** values to **1.0** and **2.0**, respectively.

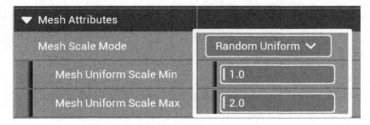

Click the **Plus sign** icon (+) for **Particle Spawn**, as shown below, select **Initial Mesh Orientation**. This contains **rotation** settings for our particle mesh, and we'll add some rotation to the shape, so it is **less uniform**. This will make the leaf cloud look a little more natural.

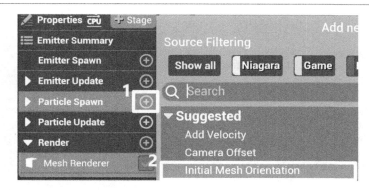

With the **Initial Mesh Orientation** module selected, under **Rotation** in the **Selection** panel, click to enable **Rotation**. Then click the **downward** arrow next to **Rotation** as shown below:

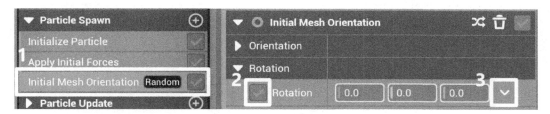

Enter **random** in the search bar, and select **Random Ranged Vector** as shown below. This will give a small amount of **random rotation** for the mesh.

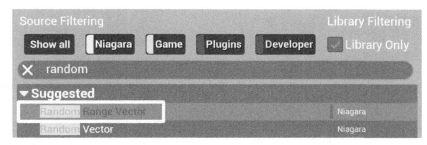

Leave the **Minimum** and **Maximum** values at their default as shown below:

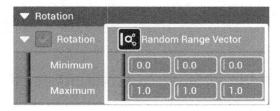

Click the **Plus sign** icon (+) again for **Particle Spawn** and select **Shape Location** as shown below:

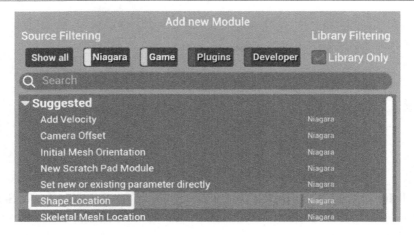

Then under the **Shape Location** section, after selecting **Cylinder** for the **Shape Primitive** field, as shown below. The Cylinder option constrains the spawning of particles to a cylinder shape. Because we want the leaf cloud to fly above the ground, change the **Cylinder Height** to **20** and the **Cylinder Radius** to **50**.

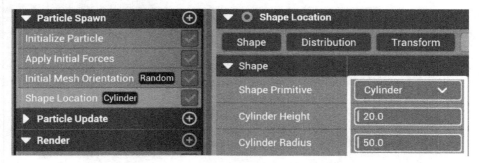

Click the **Plus sign** icon (+) for **Particle Spawn** and select **Add Velocity** as shown below:

Next, under the **Add Velocity** section, after selecting **From Point** for the **Velocity Mode** field, as shown below:

The **From Point** option makes the particles move out from a designated location at a designated speed. We use this so the leaf cloud particles start at the foot and move out from there.

Then set the **Velocity Speed** to **5** because we do not want the particles to spread too far, just enough to represent leaves that are disturbed by the runner's footsteps. That's why we use a relatively small number for the velocity speed.

Continue to click the **Plus sign** icon (+) for **Particle Spawn** and select **Forces > Acceleration Force**. We are going to use this to give the leaf cloud a small amount of **upward momentum**, so the leaf cloud spreads out and up from the footstep.

Note: An **error** displays after we add a velocity or force module because added modules are always positioned at the bottom of the group's stack. That positioning places them after the **Solve Forces** and **Velocity** module. Click **Fix issue** to resolve this error as shown below:

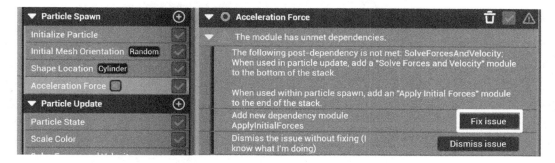

In the **Acceleration Force** module, set the **Acceleration** to X:0, Y:0, and Z:**200** as shown below:

Now the leaf cloud spreads out and up, but the upward momentum is a little too much. In the Particle **Update** step, you will add **drag** to slow down the upward momentum of the dust particles on each frame.

Particle Update Settings

Finally, we'll edit the settings in the **Particle Update** group. These behaviors are calculated on each particle in every frame.

Click the **Plus** sign icon (+) on the right of **Particle Update**, and select **Materials** > **Dynamic Material Parameters** as shown below:

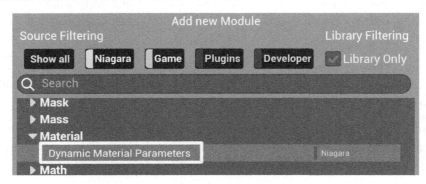

This is how we will connect to the **Erode** Dynamic Parameter in the Material. In the **Dynamic Material Parameters** module, you should see the **Erode** parameter we set up in our material. Click the **downward arrow** for Erode, as shown below:

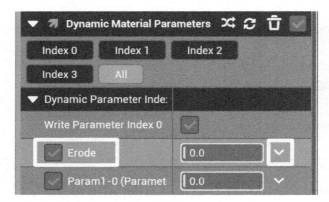

Select **Float from Curve** under **Suggested** as shown below:

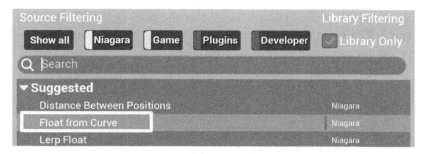

In the **curve editor**, click the **Drop Off** template to apply that style to the curve. This will make the material **fade out** over time.

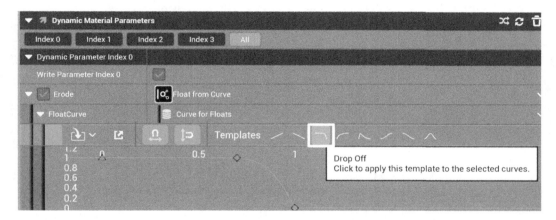

Continue to click the **Plus sign** icon (+) for **Particle Update** and select **Forces > Drag** as shown below:

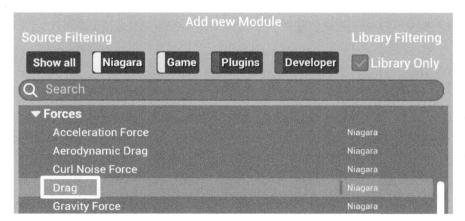

If any error occurs, click the **Fix issue** to resolve the error. In the **Drag** module, set the **Drag** to **12**. The **Drag** setting interacts with the acceleration force and keeps the leaf cloud's upward movement from seeming too unrealistic.

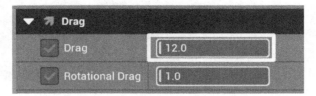

Lastly, with the **Scale Color** module selected, change the **Scale RGB** field under the **Scale Color** section to **X:5.0**, Y:1.0, and Z:1.0, as shown below:

The **X** setting value will **multiply** with the texture's **R** channel to make the leaf **redder** as you can see in the **Preview** panel.

Note: You can drag to reorder modules in the emitter node in the System Overview. However, you cannot reorder modules in the Selection panel.

6.2.4 Attaching Niagara Effects to the Character

Now we will add this effect to a character's run animation in C++. Because the Niagara system currently is a **plugin** for UE5, we have to modify the **project settings** in **Visual Studio**. Open the **RPG.Build.cs** file under the **Source** > **RPG** filter and add the following code shown in **bold**:

```
using UnrealBuildTool;

public class RPG : ModuleRules
{
  public RPG(ReadOnlyTargetRules Target) : base(Target)
  {
```

```
   PCHUsage = PCHUsageMode.UseExplicitOrSharedPCHs;

   PublicDependencyModuleNames.AddRange(new string[] { "Core",
                "CoreUObject", "Engine", "InputCore", "Niagara" });
   PrivateDependencyModuleNames.AddRange(new string[] {  });
      …
  }
}
```

The above code informs UE5 to include the **Niagara** module during compiling and building of our project. Now **save** the project and because the project settings are modified, we have to re-generate the Visual Studio Solution file as follows.

Generating Visual Studio Project Files

Close the Visual Studio and navigate to the project's location using Windows Explorer, then **right**-click the **RPG.uproject** file as shown below:

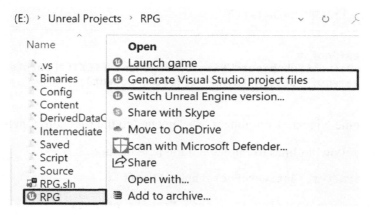

From the context menu, select **Generate Visual Studio project files** to re-generate the **RPG.sln** solution file. Now double-click the **RPG.sln** file to re-open the project in Visual Studio.

Activating Effects in C++

Open the **RPGCharacter.h** header, and add the following **bold** lines in the class:

```
UCLASS()
class RPG_API ARPGCharacter : public ACharacter
{
  GENERATED_BODY()

public:
  // Sets default values for this character's properties
  ARPGCharacter();
```

```
UPROPERTY(VisibleAnywhere, BlueprintReadOnly, Category = "Niagara")
class UNiagaraComponent* FootstepLeafPoof;

void ActivateFootstepLeafPoof();
    …
}
```

The `FootstepLeafPoof` is a **forward declared** property referring to the footstep leaf poof **NiagaraComponent**, and the `ActivateFootstepLeafPoof()` method is to **activate** the effects.

Continue to open the **RPGCharacter.cpp** file, and after adding the following **include** line:

```
#include "NiagaraComponent.h"
```

Add the following **bold** lines in the **constructor**:

```
ARPGCharacter::ARPGCharacter()
{
    …
  FootstepLeafPoof =
      CreateDefaultSubobject<UNiagaraComponent>(TEXT("FootstepLeafPoof"));
  FootstepLeafPoof->SetupAttachment(RootComponent);
}
```

After creating the Niagara Component, it's attached to the root component.

Then add the following lines to implement the new method:

```
void ARPGCharacter::ActivateFootstepLeafPoof()
{
  // Activate the footstep leaf poof Niagara effects
  if(FootstepLeafPoof)
    FootstepLeafPoof->Activate(true);
}
```

In the method, we call the built-in `Activate()` method of the NiagaraComponent and pass in `true` to **activate** the effects.

Note: If we didn't re-generate the Visual Studio project files in the previous step, an error says: **cannot open source file "NiagaraComponent.h"** will show up in the code editor.

Next, open the **FootstepAnimNotify.cpp** file, and add the following code shown in **bold**:

```
    …
#include "Characters/RPGCharacter.h"

void UFootstepAnimNotify::Notify(USkeletalMeshComponent* MeshComp,
```

```
                                      UAnimSequenceBase* Animation)
{
    ...

  if (Hit.PhysMaterial != NULL) {
    switch (Hit.PhysMaterial->SurfaceType.GetValue()) {
    case ESurfaceTypes::GrassDirt:
      // Play sound cue
      if (FootstepCues.Num()) {
        UGameplayStatics::PlaySoundAtLocation(GetWorld(),
                     FootstepCues[ESurfaceTypes::GrassDirt - 1],
                                   owner->GetActorLocation());
        // Get the character
        ARPGCharacter* player = Cast<ARPGCharacter>(owner);
        // Activate the effects
        if (player)
          player->ActivateFootstepLeafPoof();
      }
      break;
    case ESurfaceTypes::RockCliff:
      ...
    }
  }
}
```

After adding the include, in the `Notify()` method, after playing the stepping sound, we call the player's `ActivateFootstepLeafPoof()` method to **activate** the effects.

Assigning Effects in Blueprints

Now build the project and make sure that no errors occur. Back to Unreal Editor, open the **BP_FemaleWarrior** Blueprint, with the **Footstep Leaf Poof** selected as shown below:

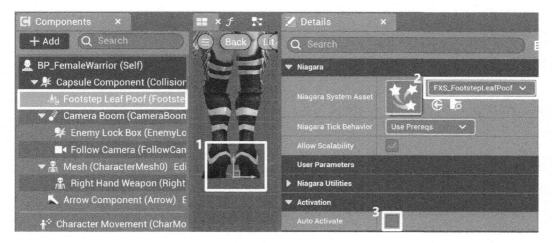

In the **Viewport**, move it to **under** the **feet** of the character, as shown above. Then, in the Details tab, find and in the **Niagara** section, select **FXS_FootstepLeafPoof** for the **Niagara System Asset** field. Lastly, **untick** the **Auto Activate** checkbox, because we'll activate the effect in C++ code. So far the Blueprint is complete, press **Compile** and **Save** to confirm the modification.

Now that the Niagara effect is attached to our character, press **Play** to run the game, after moving the player over the **GrassDirt** landscape layer, you'll see the leaf poof shows up as shown below:

If the effect does not look right to you, please adjust the various module settings until you like the look of the effect.

6.3 Special Effects for Action RPGs

After the Quick Start section, you already have a basic understanding of the Niagara system and its modules. This section will implement the most common and important Niagara effects in an ARPG.

6.3.1 Sword Trails

This section will discuss how to design and implement sword trails in Niagara.

Creating Sword Trail Textures

Create a texture called **T_SwordTrail_Fire.png** to represent the fire using any image creation tool like Photoshop as follows on the **left**:

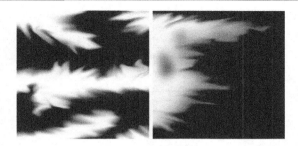

Then create another texture called **T_SwordTrail.png** to represent the sword trail as shown above on the **right**.

Now that the textures are ready, create a new folder called **Textures** in the **Niagara** folder to hold the sword trail textures. Drag and drop the above textures into the **Textures** folder to import them.

The Sword Trail Material

Right-click in the **Niagara** > **Materials** folder and select **Material** from the context menu to create a Material called **M_SwordTrail**. Double-click to open it in the Material Editor, and in the Details tab, set the **Blend Mode** and **Shading Model** fields to **Translucent** and **Unlit** respectively as shown below:

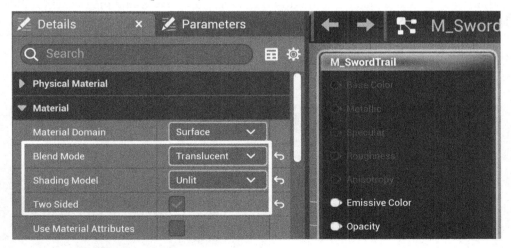

That's because the trail should be **transparent** and **unlit**. Also, **tick** the **Two Sided**, as shown above, to make the material two-sided such that we can see it from any side.

Next, create the following **Nodes** and make the **Transitions** between them in the Node Graph as shown below:

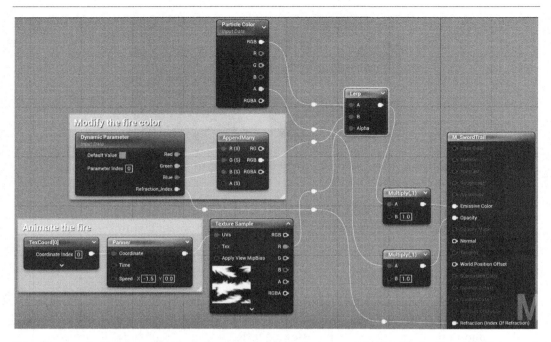

The **Dynamic Parameter** Node has **four** parameters, namely the **Red**, **Green**, **Blue**, and **Refraction_Index**, which are to modify the fire texture's color and the refraction index. Here the **AppendMany** Node is to make an **RGB** Vector using the three parameters, respectively. To blend the fire color and particle color, we use the **R** channel value of the fire texture as the **Linear Interpolant** (**Alpha**) input of the **Lerp** Node.

The **Dynamic Parameter** Node's settings are as follows:

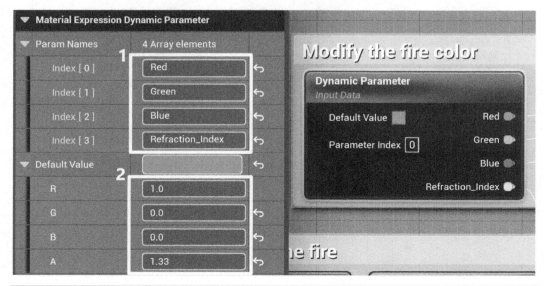

After entering the four names of the parameters respectively, change the values of the **R**, **G**, **B**, and **A** fields to **1**, 0, 0, and **1.33**, as shown above, which make the fire **red** and the 1.33 is the **water's** refraction index.

The **Panner** Node is to animate the fire texture and its settings are as shown below:

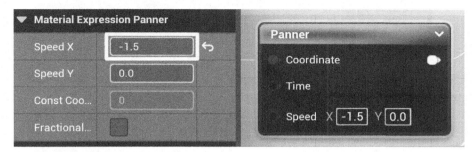

Set the **Speed X** to **-1.5** to make it pan to the **right**. Please note that the **Panner** Node needs a **TexCoord** Node for its **Coordinate** input.

Then add the following Nodes to the graph and make the **two** new transitions as shown below:

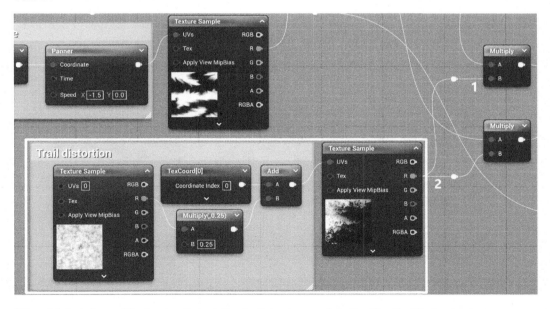

We add the above Nodes to distort the trail texture using the **Perlin Noise** texture (**T_Perlin_Noise_M**) in the **Starter Content** folder. The settings of the **TexCoord** Node in the **Trail distortion** part are as follows:

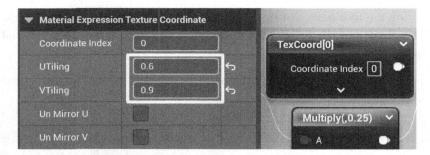

The **UTiling** and **VTiling** are set to **0.6** and **0.9** respectively to prevent the texture from repeating on the **U** and **V** axis. The **Multiply** Node settings are as follows:

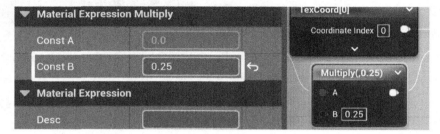

The **bigger** the value of the **Const B** the more distortion for the trail texture. Then add the nodes to animate the distortion and make a new transition as shown below:

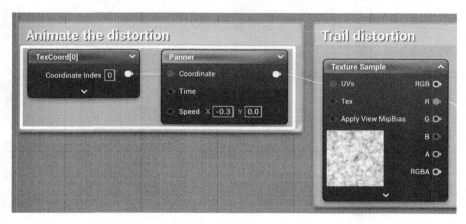

The new **Panner** Node's settings are as follows:

Lastly, we blend the fire color and trail color using the **Multiply** Node and also multiply the particle's **alpha** with the trail texture's **R** channel value to get the **Opacity** for the main material.

Next, add the following Nodes to the graph and make a new transition as shown below:

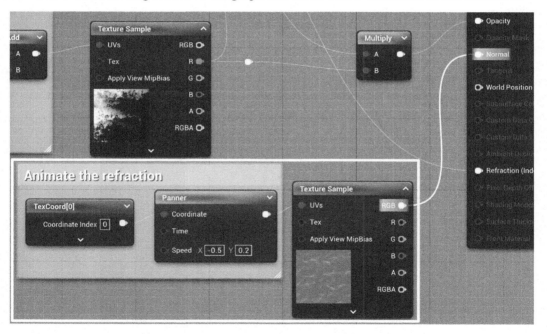

Because without the **Normal** map, we are **unable** to calculate the **Refraction**, here the water Normal Map (**T_Water_N**) in the Starter Content folder is used in the Texture Sample Node. Besides, the Panner Node makes the normal map panning to the right and thus changes the refraction frame by frame. Finally, plug the **RGB** output of the Texture Sample Node into the **Normal** input of the main material.

Now the material is complete, press **Save** to confirm the modification and you can preview the result in the **Viewport** in the upper-left corner as shown below:

Here you can see the distortion because of the refraction and the noise texture as shown above.

The Sword Trail Niagara System

After the material is ready, we'll create the Niagara system in this subsection. Right-click in the **RPG** > **Niagara** folder, select **Niagara System** from the context menu, and in the next step, choose **New system from** the **selected emitter(s)** and press **Next** as shown below:

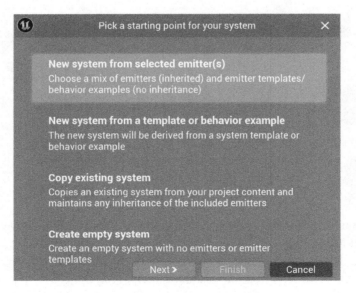

Next, pick the **Empty** emitter template, as shown below, and press the + button to add the Empty emitter.

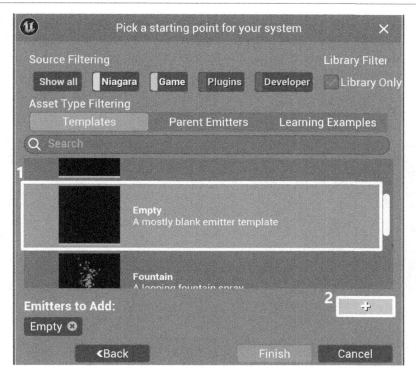

Now press the **Finish** button to create the Niagara system, rename it to
FXS_SwordTrail, and double-click to open it in the editor as shown below:

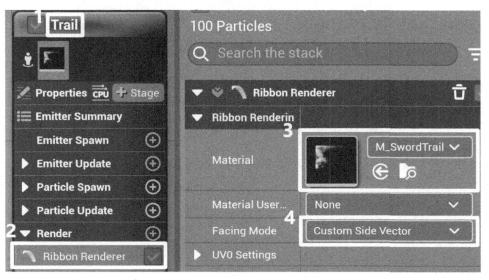

After renaming the emitter to **Trail**, as shown above, **delete** the original **Sprite Renderer** and add a **Ribbon Renderer** in the **Render** section. Then, in the **Details** tab, select the **M_SwordTrail** created before for the **Material** field under the **RIBBON RENDERING** section. Lastly, set the **Facing Mode** to **Custom Side Vector**.

Next, with the **Initialize Particle** module selected and select the **Point** tab as shown below:

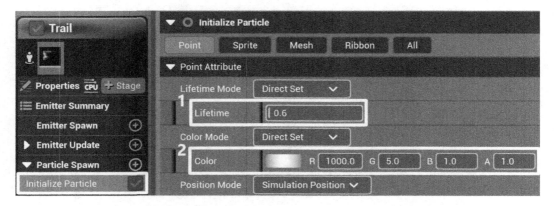

Set the **Lifetime** to **0.6** and the **Color** field as shown above. Continue to select the **Ribbon** tab, and after setting the **Ribbon Width Mode** to **Direct Set**, set the **Ribbon Width** to **100** as shown below:

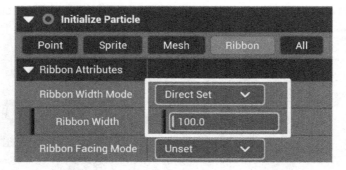

Continue to add a **Dynamic Material Parameters** module as shown below:

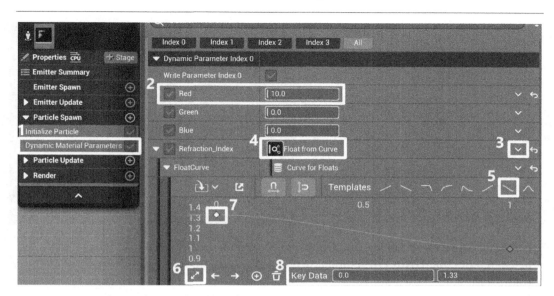

After setting the **Red** parameter to **10**, click the **downward arrow** for
Refraction_Index, and select **Float from Curve** for it. Then, after clicking the **Smooth
Ramp Down** template, press the **Zoom to fit all keys** icon to see all the keys. With the
first key selected on the curve, set the **Value** of the **Key Data** to **1.33** as shown above.

Lastly, select the **second** key, as shown below, and set its **Value** to **1** which means no
refraction at all after one second.

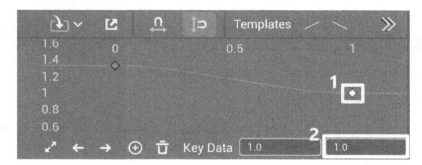

Continue to add a **Scale Ribbon Width** module under the **Particle Update** section as
shown below:

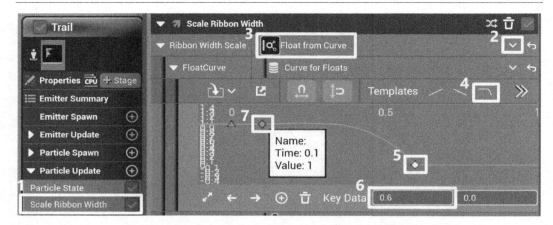

Click the **downward arrow** for **Ribbon Width Scale** and select **Float from Curve** for it. Then, click the **Drop Off** template which makes the ribbon width **shorter** for each frame until **0**, as shown above. With the **last** keyframe selected, set its **Time** to **0.6** in the **Key Data** field, lastly select the keyframe in the middle and set its **Time** and **Value** to **0.1** and **1**, respectively.

Then add a **Spawn Per Frame** module, under the **Emitter Update** section, to spawn the trail ribbons as shown below:

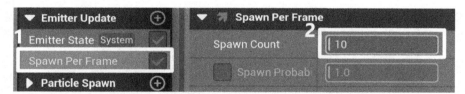

Set the **Spawn Count** to **10** which makes the effect more intense.

Creating the SCRATCH MODULE

To make the trail follows the sword rotation, we have to use the **SCRATCH MODULE** in the Niagara system. Press the **+** on the **Particle Spawn** and select **New Scratch Pad Module** as shown below:

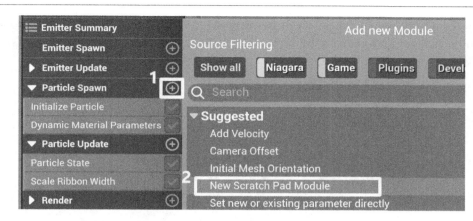

Then, as shown below, the **Scratch Pad** window will show up, change the module name to **Trail_Orientation**:

Continue to press the + button on the **Map Get** Node as shown below:

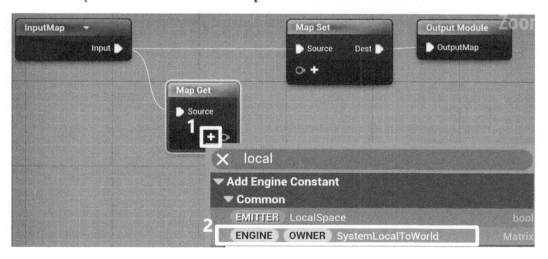

From the drop-down menu, select **SystemLocalToWorld** Parameter as shown above. Then press the + button again, in the search bar, type **vector,** and select **Vector,** as shown below, to add a Vector input.

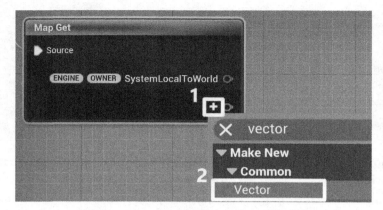

After changing the **Vector** name, under the **Module Inputs**, to **TrailFacing**, as shown below:

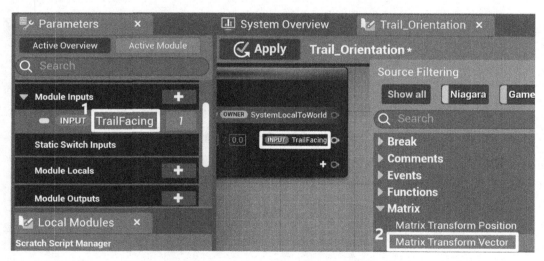

Drag off from the **SystemLocalToWorld** pin in the scratchpad, find and select the **Matrix Transform Vector** under the **Matrix** as shown above.

Next, plug the **TrailFacing** pin into the **V** input pin of the **Matrix Transform Vector** Node as shown below:

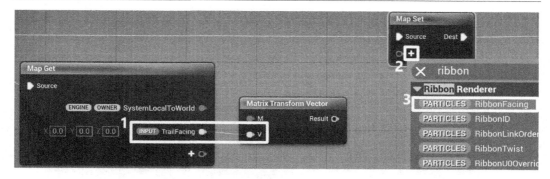

Then press the + button on the **Map Set** Node as shown above and select **RibbonFacing** from the drop-down menu.

Finally, plug the **Result** output pin into the **Ribbon Facing** input of the **Map Set** Node as shown below:

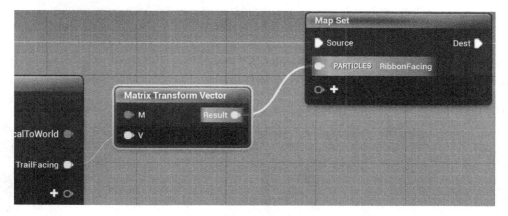

After pressing **Apply** to confirm the modification, back to the **Overview** tab, with the **Trail Orientation** module selected as shown below:

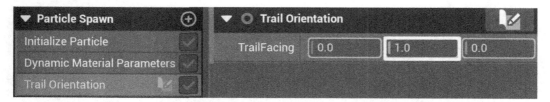

Change the **Y** field to **1**, as shown above, to align the edge of the trail to the **local Y-axis** of the Niagara system.

Sword Trail Particles

To make the sword trail more dramatic, we can add some particles along the trail. First, let's create the Material as follows. Right-click in the **Niagara** > **Materials** folder and select **Material** from the context menu to create a Material called **M_TrailParticle**. Then double-click to open the Material Graph as shown below:

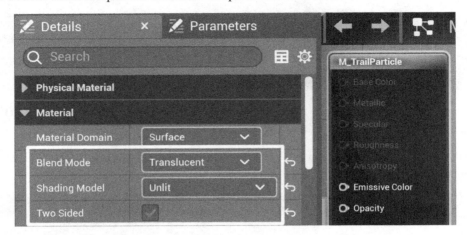

Set the **Blend Mode** and **Shading Model** to **Translucent** and **Unlit** respectively and also **tick** the **Two Sided** checkbox as shown above.

Then create the following Nodes and make the transitions as shown below:

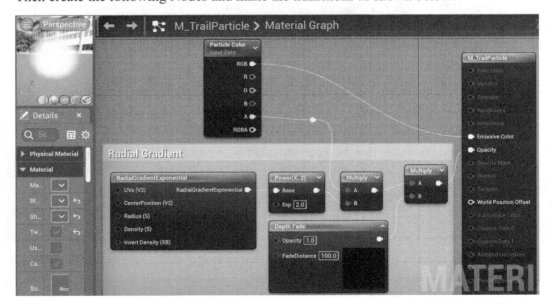

Here we use the **Particle** Color as the **Emissive** Color and use the **RadialGradientExponental** Node to generate a radial gradient for the material's **Opacity** as shown above. The **Power**, **Multiply**, and **Depth Fade** Nodes are to modify the strength of the fading. The result is shown in the Viewport tab.

The Sword Trail Particle Emitter

Now that the Material is ready, let's create another Emitter in the Niagara system. Back to the **System Overview** tab, right-click on the space and select **Add Emitter** as shown below:

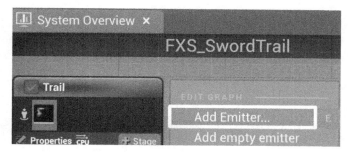

Then, in the next step, select the **Fountain** template as shown below:

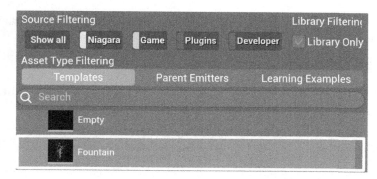

After changing the **name** of the **Emitter** to **Particle**, as shown below, with the **Sprite Renderer** selected, set its **Material** field to the **M_TrailParticle** created before.

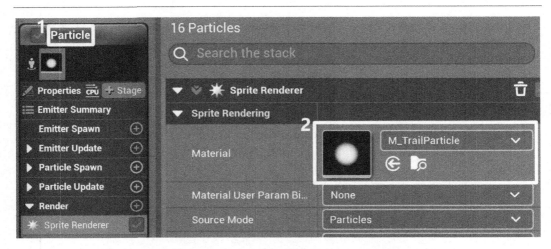

Then after **deleting** the **Gravity Force** module, add a **Vortex Force** module to put some **turbulence** to the particles as shown below:

Set its **Vortex Force Amount** to **100** as shown above. Next, select the **Add Velocity In Cone** module, and set its **Velocity Mode** to **From Point** as shown below:

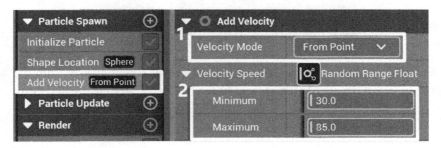

Then modify the **Minimum** and **Maximum** to **30** and **85** respectively as shown above. Next, modify the **Sphere Radius** of the **Shape Location** module to **1** as shown below:

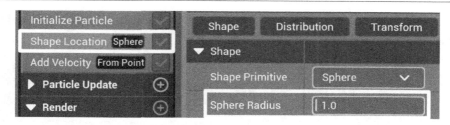

With the **Initialize Particle** module selected, change its **Lifetime Min** and **Max** fields to **0.8** and **1.75** respectively as shown below:

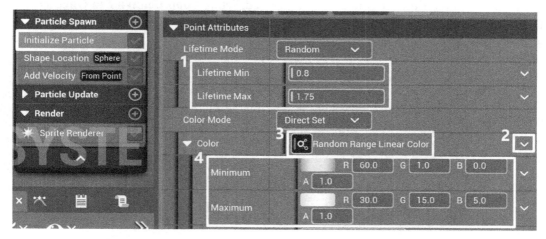

Then press the **downward** arrow, and after selecting **Random Range Linear Color** for the **Color** field, modify the **Minimum** and **Maximum** values as shown above.

With the **Scale Color** module selected, as shown below, set its **R** field of the **Scale RGB** to **17**.

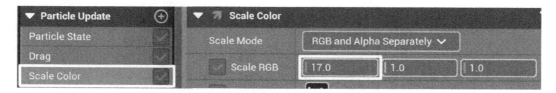

Next, modify the **Drag** value of the **Drag** module to **1** to slow down the particles as shown below:

Continue to modify the **SpawnRate** value of the **Spawn Rate** module to **20** as shown below:

Finally, with the **Emitter State** module selected, set its **Loop Behavior** to **Once** as shown below:

You can preview the result in the Viewport, as shown below, then press **Save** to confirm the modification.

Attaching the Sword Trail Niagara System

Now that the sword trail Niagara system is complete, we'll add the system to the great sword Blueprint and before doing so, let's modify the C++ code as follows. Open the **SwordEquipmentComponent.h** header in Visual Studio and add the following **bold** lines:

```
UCLASS()
class RPG_API USwordEquipmentComponent : public UEquipmentComponent
{
  GENERATED_BODY()

public:
  UPROPERTY(EditAnywhere, Category = "Niagara")
  class UNiagaraSystem* SwordTrailFXS;

  void ActivateSwordTrail(bool activate);
  virtual void BeginPlay() override;
private:
  class UNiagaraComponent* SwordTrailNiagaraComp;
};
```

In the `public` section, the `SwordTrailFXS` property refers to the Niagara System, and the `ActivateSwordTrail()` method is to activate the sword trail. The `SwordTrailNiagaraComp`, declared in the `private` section, refers to the Niagara Component that we will create in the `BeginPlay()` method.

Then open the **SwordEquipmentComponent.cpp** file, and add the following lines to implement the `ActivateSwordTrail()` method:

```
#include "NiagaraFunctionLibrary.h"
#include "NiagaraComponent.h"

void USwordEquipmentComponent::ActivateSwordTrail(bool activate)
{
  if (SwordTrailNiagaraComp) {
    if (activate)  // Activate the trail Niagara system
      SwordTrailNiagaraComp->Activate();
    else           // Deactivate the trail
      SwordTrailNiagaraComp->Deactivate();
  }
}
```

In the method, according to the incoming flag, we call the `Activate()` or `Deactivate()` methods to **activate** or **deactivate** the sword trail, respectively.

Lastly, add the following **bold** lines in the `BeginPlay()` to spawn the Niagara System and attach it to the sword trail socket.

```
void USwordEquipmentComponent::BeginPlay()
{
  Super::BeginPlay();

  if (SwordTrailFXS) {
    // Spawn the FX at the mesh's SwordTrail socket
    SwordTrailNiagaraComp =
```

```
        UNiagaraFunctionLibrary::SpawnSystemAttached(SwordTrailFXS, this,
                        "SwordTrailSocket", FVector(0.f), FRotator(0.f),
                    EAttachLocation::Type::KeepRelativeOffset, false, false);
    }
}
```

Then open the **WarriorCharacter.h** header and add the following **bold** line in the class:

```
class RPG_API AWarriorCharacter : public ARPGCharacter
{
    GENERATED_BODY()
public:
    AWarriorCharacter();

    void ActivateSwordTrail(bool activate);
        ...
}
```

The `ActivateSwordTrail()` method is to activate the sword trail when the sword attack Montage is playing.

Continue to open the **WarriorCharacter.cpp** file, and add the following lines to implement the method:

```
#include "Inventory/SwordEquipmentComponent.h"

void AWarriorCharacter::ActivateSwordTrail(bool activate)
{
    if (RightHandWeapon)
        RightHandWeapon->ActivateSwordTrail(activate);
}
```

In the method, we call the `ActivateSwordTrail()` method of the sword equipment component to activate or deactivate the sword trail.

Next, open the **SwordAnimNotifyState.h** header, and add the following **bold** lines in the class:

```
UCLASS()
class RPG_API USwordAnimNotifyState : public UAnimNotifyState
{
    GENERATED_BODY()
public:
    virtual void NotifyBegin(USkeletalMeshComponent*
        MeshComp, UAnimSequenceBase* Animation, float TotalDuration) override;
        ...
};
```

We override the **NotifyBegin()** method to play the sword trail when the attack Montage **starts** playing.

Continue to open the **SwordAnimNotifyState.cpp** file, and add the following lines to implement the **NotifyBegin()** method:

```
void USwordAnimNotifyState::NotifyBegin(USkeletalMeshComponent* MeshComp,
                        UAnimSequenceBase* Animation, float TotalDuration)
{
  AWarriorCharacter* warrior = Cast<AWarriorCharacter>(
                                            MeshComp->GetOwner());
  // Activate the sword trail
  if (warrior)
  {
    warrior->ActivateSwordTrail(true);
  }
}
```

In the method, after getting the warrior character, we call its ActivateSwordTrail() method and pass in **true** to **activate** the sword trail.

Finally, add the following **bold** lines in the **NotifyEnd()** method:

```
void USwordAnimNotifyState::NotifyEnd(USkeletalMeshComponent* MeshComp,
                                    UAnimSequenceBase* Animation)
{
  AWarriorCharacter* warrior = Cast<AWarriorCharacter>(
                                            MeshComp->GetOwner());

  if (warrior)
  {
    // Deactivate the sword trail
    warrior->ActivateSwordTrail(false);
    // If we have the next Combo to play
    if (warrior->NextComboType != EComboTypes::Empty) {
      FText sectionName;
      …
    }
  }
}
```

In the method, when the attack Montage **stops** playing, the sword trail is **deactivated.**

Now build the project and make sure that no errors occurred. Back to Unreal Editor, open the **BP_FemaleWarrior** Blueprint as shown below:

Then, with the **RightHandWeapon** selected in the Components tab, set the **Sword Trail FXS** field to the **FXS_SwordTrail** Niagara system created before.

Creating the Sword Trail Socket

Finally, open the **SK_GreatSword** Skeletal Mesh, and with the **GreatSword** selected in the **Skeletal Tree** panel as shown below:

Press the + button to add a new socket named **SwordTrailSocket**, and then in the **Viewport**, move the socket to the **blade** of the great sword.

Now press **Compile** and **Save** to confirm all modifications, then press **Play** to run the game. After clicking the mouse button to play the attack Montage, you'll see the sword trail and particles as shown below:

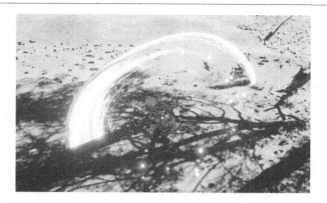

6.3.2 The Impact Effect and Shockwaves

In this section, we'll implement the sword impact effect and its shockwaves. First, let's create the required textures.

Impact Effect and Shockwave Textures

Use any image creation tools to create the following **T_Shockwave**, **T_Hit_Sprite_White_Rings**, and **T_Hit_Sprite_White_Smoke** textures for the impact shockwave and smoke effects:

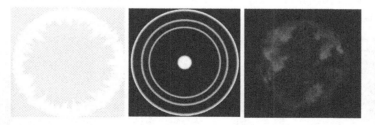

The **right** figure above is for the smoke effect. Also, prepare the following **T_RippleNormalMap Normal Map** texture for the Shockwave effect:

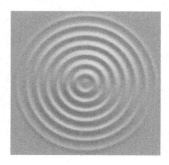

To create the above map, you can find any single ripple image and use the Normal Map creation tool to generate the texture. After the textures are ready, drag and drop them into the Niagara > **Textures** folder in the project.

Impact and Shockwave Materials

Right-click in the Niagara > **Materials** folder and select **Material** from the context menu to create a new material called **M_Shockwave**. Then open the material in the editor as shown below:

Set the **Blend Mode** and **Shading Model** to **translucent** and **Unlit**, as shown above, also **tick** the **Two Sided** checkbox. Then add the following Nodes and make the transitions as follows:

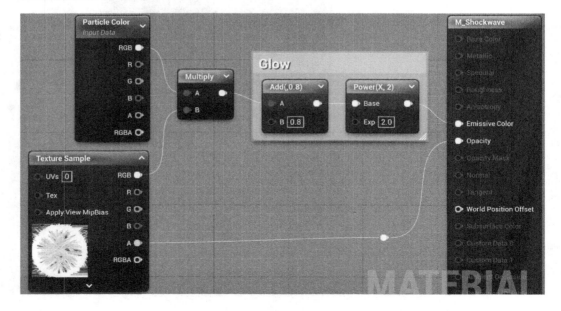

In the above nodes, after multiplying the particle color and the shockwave texture color, we use **Add** and **Power** Nodes to make the color glow and the output is plugged into the **Emissive** Color as shown above. Lastly, plug the **A** output of the texture sample into the **Opacity** of the main material.

Continue to create another material called **M_ShockwaveDistortion** in the Materials folder. After setting the **Blend Mode** and **Shading Model** to **translucent** and **Unlit**, and **ticking** the **Two Sided** checkbox of the main material node, add the following Nodes and make the transitions as follows:

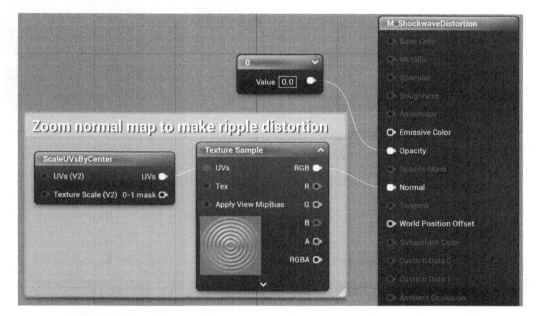

The **ScaleUVsByCenter** node here is to zoom the ripple normal map and the **Opacity** of the main material is set to **0**, which makes the material **transparent**.

Continue to add the following nodes and then plug the result of the Lerp node into the **Refraction** pin of the main material node as follows:

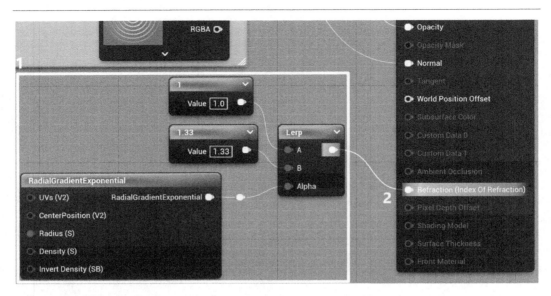

The **RadialGradientExpontential** node (function) procedurally generates gradients to add to our material, eliminating the need for textures and saving memory.

The **RadialGradientExpontential** output is plugged into the **Linear Lerp** Node's **Alpha** input to lerp between two constants, **1.0** and **1.33**, which are the refraction indexes of the **air** and **water**, respectively. The purpose is to make a **circular** shape of refraction.

Lastly, add a **Dynamic Parameter** Node and make the transitions as follows:

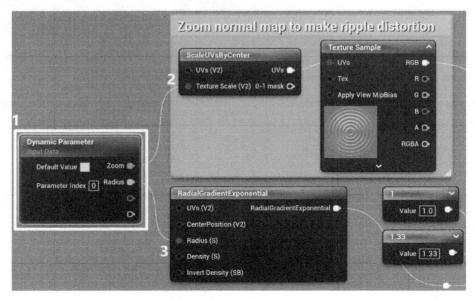

The settings of the **Dynamic Parameter** Node are as follows:

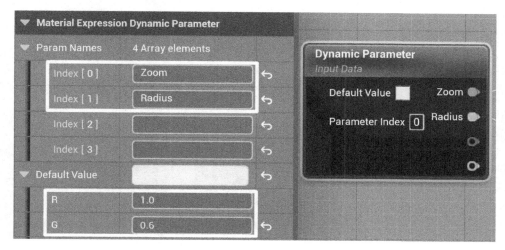

The **Zoom** parameter is to control the zoom of the Normal Map to make ripple distortion effects with the **ScaleUVsByCenter** Node. The **Radius** parameter is to control the **Radius** of the **RadialGradientExpontential** Node and its value is set to **0.6**.

Now press **Apply** and **Save** to confirm the modification and you can see the result in the Viewport as shown below:

Next, we'll create the material for the texture of the ring as follows. Right-click in the **Materials** folder again and select Material from the context menu to create a new material called **M_Rings**. After setting the **Blend Mode** and **Shading Model** to **translucent** and **Unlit**, and **ticking** the **Two Sided** checkbox of the main material node, add the following Nodes and make the transitions as follows:

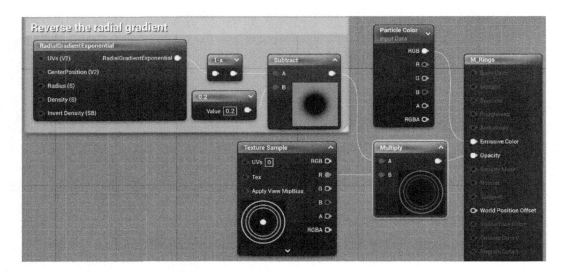

To make the ring **fade** from outside to its center, the output of the **RadialGradientExponential** Node is plugged into the **1-x** Node to achieve this effect, the constant **0.2** is to adjust the radius of the **black** area around the center as shown in the **Subtract** Node. Then, after multiplying the gradient and texture color, we plug the output into the **Opacity** of the main material node.

Lastly, let's create the material for the texture of the smoke as follows. Right-click in the **Materials** folder again and select Material from the context menu to create a new material called **M_Smoke**.

After setting the **Blend Mode** and **Shading Model** to **translucent** and **Unlit**, and **ticking** the **Two Sided** checkbox of the main material node, add the following Nodes and make the transitions as shown below:

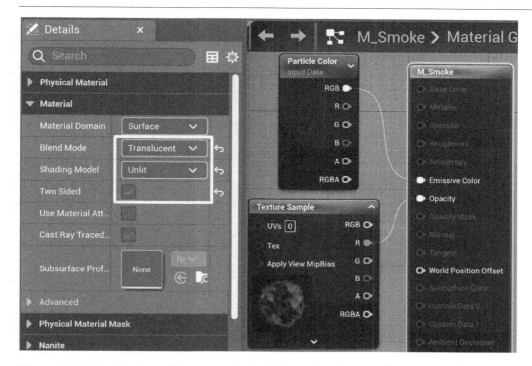

The material is simple and because the background of the smoke texture is **black**, we plug the **R** output into the **Opacity** of the main material node and use **Particle** Color as the **Emissive** Color.

Creating the Impact Niagara System

Now that all the materials are complete, it's time to create the Niagara system for the sword impact and shockwaves as follows. Right-click in the **Niagara** folder and select **Niagara System** from the context menu, then press **Next** to continue and in the next step, pick the **OmniDirectional Burst** Template as shown below:

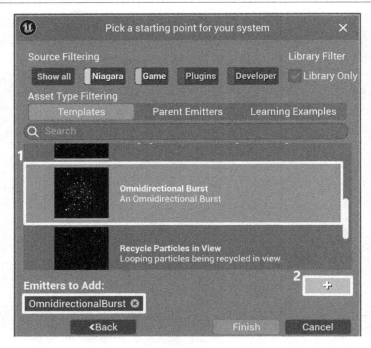

After pressing the + button to add the Emitter, press **Finish** to create the system and rename it to **FXS_Impact**. Double-click to open it in the Niagara editor as shown below:

Because we'll create the **Ash** particles first, after renaming the Emitter's name to **Ash**, as shown above, with the **Sprite Renderer** module selected, set its **Material** to the **M_TrailParticle** created before.

Next, press the + icon on the **Particle Spawn** to add a **Curl Noise Force** module as shown below:

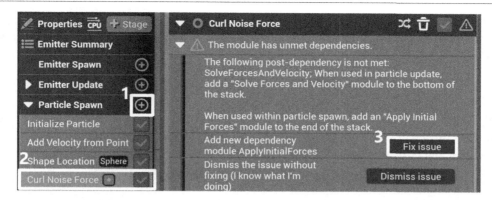

Press the **Fix issue** button and the **Apply Initial Forces** module will be generated for us to fix the issue.

Then modify the settings of the modules as follows. First, with the **Spawn Burst Instantaneous** module selected, set its **Spawn Count** field to **100** as shown below:

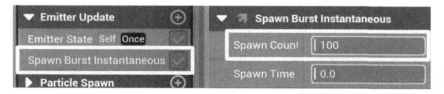

Next, with the **Initialize Particle** module selected, set its **Lifetime Min** and **Max** fields to **0.8** and **1.75** respectively as shown below:

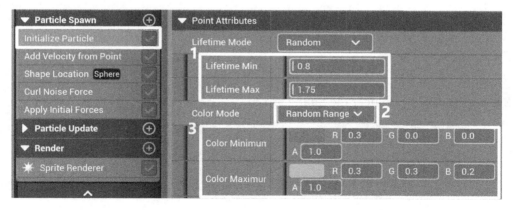

After setting the **Color Mode** to **Random Range**, set the **Color Minimum** and **Maximum** values as shown above.

With the **Add Velocity From Point** module selected, set the **Minimum** and **Maximum** fields under the **Velocity Speed** to **20** and **280** respectively as shown below:

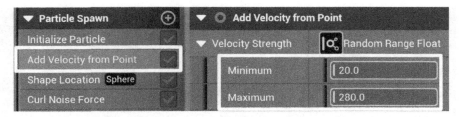

Continue to select the **Curl Noise Force** module, as shown below, and set its **Noise Strength** and **Noise Frequency** to **10** and **1.6** respectively:

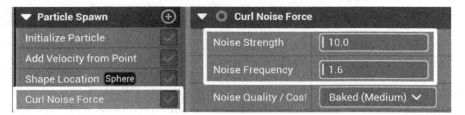

Then, with the **Gravity Force** module selected, as shown below, press the **downward arrow** to the right of the **Gravity** as shown below:

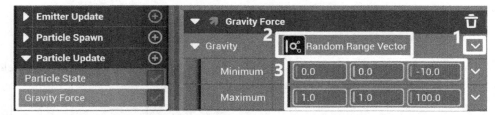

After selecting the **Random Range Vector** for it, set the **Minimum** and **Maximum** fields as shown above.

Continue to select the **Shape Location Sphere** module, as shown below, and set the **Sphere Radius** field under the **Shape** to **120**.

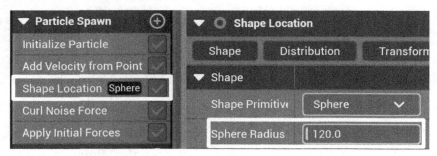

Finally, with the **Scale Color** module selected, as shown below:

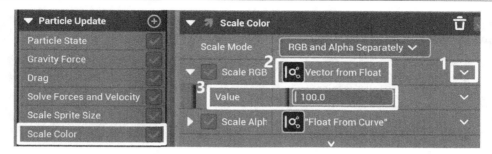

Press the **downward arrow** to the right of the **Scale RGB**, as shown above, select **Vector from Float** for it, then set the **Value** to **100**.

Now press **Compile** and **Save** to confirm the modification and the result can be previewed in the Viewport as shown on the right:

Next, we'll create the Emitter for the **Sparks** particles, which is similar to the **Ash** Emitter, so with the **Ash Emitter** selected, press **Ctrl + C** to copy the Emitter and then **Ctrl + V** to duplicate a copy of it. After renaming it to **Sparks** as shown on the right:

Delete the **Shape Location Sphere** and **Curl Noise Force** modules under the **Particle Spawn** section, then continue to delete the **Gravity Force** and **Drag** modules under the **Particle Update** section. That's because we want the sparks shooting from the center point without any turbulence and gravity.

Then reset the settings of the modules as follows. First, set the **Spawn Count** of the **Spawn Burst Instantaneous** module to **50** as shown below:

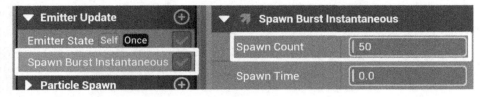

Next, with the **Initialize Particle** module selected, after clicking the **Point** tab, set its **Lifetime Min** and **Max** fields to **1.0** and **1.7** respectively as shown below:

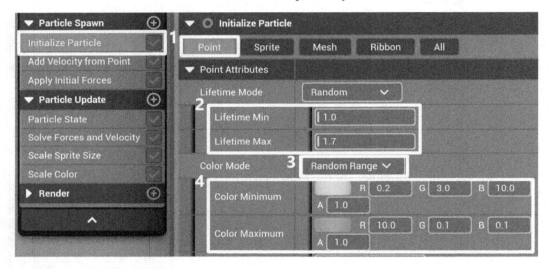

Then reset the **Color Minimum** and **Maximum** values as shown above. Continue to click the **Sprite** tab, and after resetting the **Sprite Size Mode** to **Random Non-Uniform**, set the **Sprite Size Min** and **Max** values as shown below:

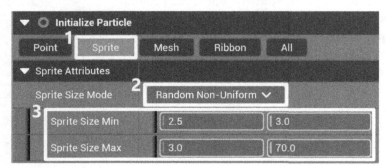

Please note that here we use the **Non**-Uniform Size Mode to **elongate** the sprite in the **Y** direction.

With the **Add Velocity From Point** module selected, after pressing the **reset** icon to the right, under the **Add Velocity from Point**, you'll see the **Velocity Strength** field, as shown below, set its value to **100**.

Continue to select the **Scale Sprite Size** module and after pressing the **downward arrow** to the right of the **Scale Factor**, as shown below, select **Random Range Vector 2D** for it.

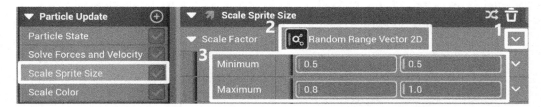

Then set the **Minimum** and **Maximum** values as shown above. Finally, with the **Sprite Renderer** module selected as shown below:

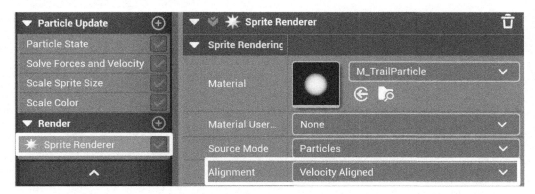

Reset the **Alignment** to **Velocity Aligned** as shown above. This step is required because we want the **length** of the sparks particle to get **elongated** in the direction of the velocity.

Now press **Save** to confirm the modification and you can preview the result in the Viewport as shown below:

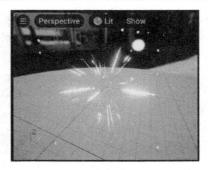

Here the sparks are shooting from the center of a sphere shape like rays as shown above.

Next, we'll create the Emitter for the **Shockwave** particle. With the **Sparks** Emitter selected, press **Ctrl + C** on the keyboard and then **Ctrl + V** to duplicate a copy of it. After renaming it to **Shockwave** as shown below:

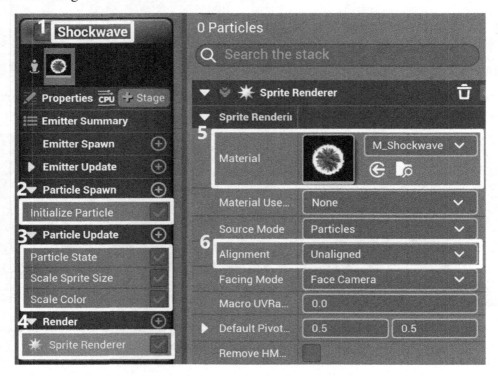

Delete the **Add Velocity from Point** and **Apply Initial Force** modules under the Particle **Spawn** section, then continue to delete the **Solve Forces and Velocity** module under the Particle **Update** section. That's because we don't need any Forces and Velocity-related modules for the shockwave.

With the **Sprite Renderer** module selected, after setting its **Material** to the **M_Shockwave**, as shown above, reset the **Alignment** to **Unaligned**.

Next, we need to reset the settings of the modules as follows. First, set the **Spawn Count** of the **Spawn Burst Instantaneous** module to **1** as shown below:

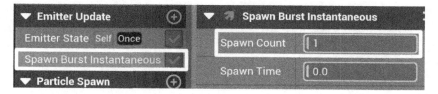

Then with the **Initialize Particle** module selected, reset its **Lifetime Min** and **Max** fields to **0.5** and **1.5** respectively as shown below:

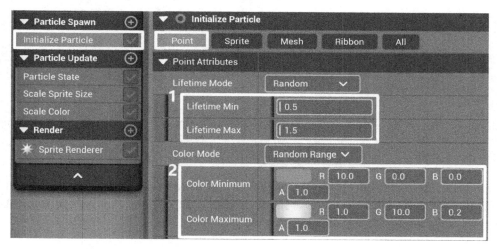

Reset the **Color Minimum** and **Maximum** values as shown above. Continue to click the **Sprite** tab, and after resetting the **Sprite Size Mode** to **Uniform**, set the **Uniform Sprite Size** value to **300** as shown below:

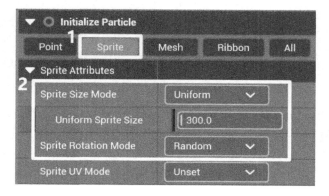

Because we want the circular shockwave to **rotate** as well, set the **Sprite Rotation Mode** to **Random** as shown above.

Continue to select the **Scale Sprite Size** module as shown below:

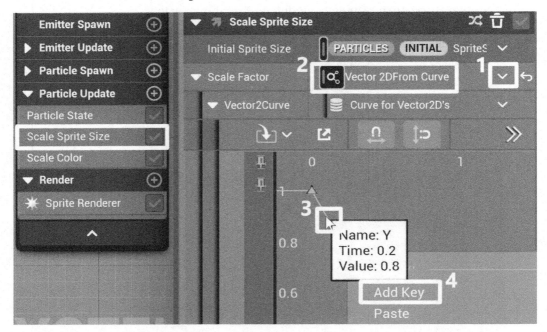

After selecting the **Vector 2Dfrom Curve** for the **Scale Factor**, move the mouse cursor over the line at time **0.2** position, as shown above, right-click on the line and select **Add Key** to add a keyframe as follows:

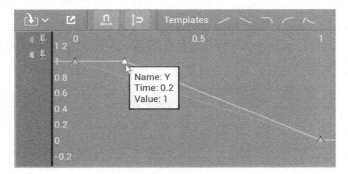

Then, with the keyframe selected, set its Key Data **value** to **1** as shown above. Continue to select the **first** keyframe, as shown below, and set its Key Data **value** to **0**.

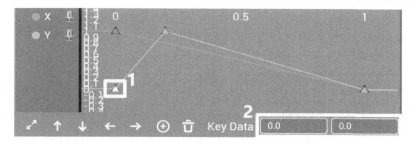

Repeat the same steps for the **X (red)** line, and the result is both the **X** and **Y** have the same curve, as shown below:

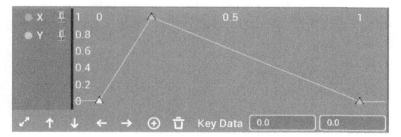

Lastly, with the **Scale Color** module selected, and after pressing the **downward arrow** to the right of the **Scale RGB**, select **Random Range Vector** for it as shown below:

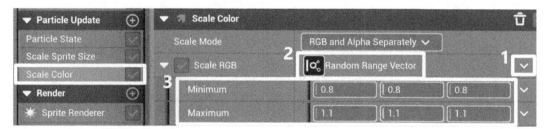

Then set the **Minimum** and **Maximum** values as shown above. After pressing **Save** to confirm the modification, you can preview the result in the Viewport as shown below:

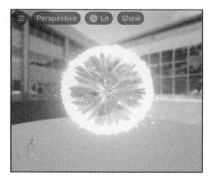

Next, we'll create the Emitter for the shockwave rings effects and re-use the **Shockwave** Emitter. So after duplicating a copy of the Shockwave Emitter, rename it to **Shockwave_Rings** as shown below:

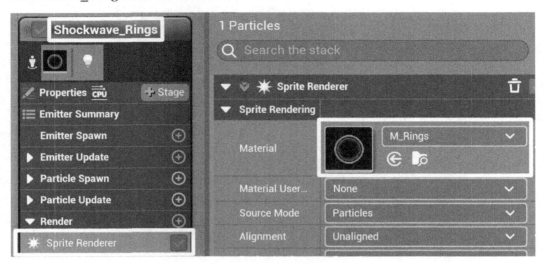

With the **Sprite Renderer** selected, set its **Material** to the **M_Rings** created before as shown above. Then after selecting the **Initialize Particle** module, reset the **Lifetime Min** and **Max** values to **0.5** and **1**, which is overall **shorter** than the shockwave's particle, as shown below:

Then reset the **Uniform Sprite Size** to **230**, which is **smaller** than the shockwave's particle as shown below:

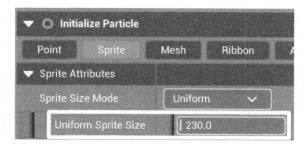

Lastly, with the **Scale Color** selected, after resetting the **Scale Mode** to **RGB and Alpha Separately** as shown below:

Set the **Scale RGB** values, as shown above, to make the rings **redder**. The result is shown on the right:

Next, we'll create the Emitter for the **Smoke** effects and re-use the **Shockwave** Emitter. So after duplicating a copy of the Shockwave Emitter, rename it to **Smoke** as shown below:

With the **Sprite Renderer** selected, set its **Material** to the **M_Smoke** created before as shown above. Then, with the **Initialize Particle** module selected, reset the **Lifetime Min** and **Max** values to **1.6** and **1.8**, as shown below:

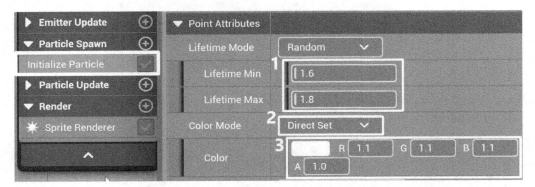

After resetting the **Color Mode** to **Direct Set**, set the **Color** values as shown above.

Then reset the **Uniform Sprite Size** to **400**, which is **larger** than the shockwave's particle as shown below:

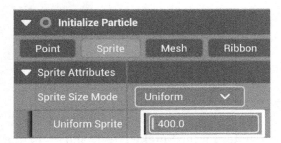

Continue to select the **Scale Sprite Size** module and reset the curve as shown below:

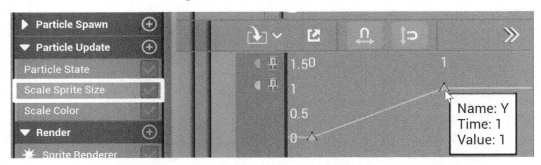

The **Key Data** for the **first** and **second** keyframes are Time: **0**, Value: **0**, and Time: **1**, Value: **1**, respectively.

Lastly, with the **Scale Color** selected, reset the **Scale Mode** and **RGB** values to their defaults as shown below:

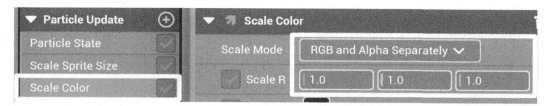

Now press **Save** to confirm the modification and the result is shown on the right:

Finally, we'll copy the **Smoke** Emitter to create the **Shockwave Distortion** effects. So after duplicating a copy of the **Smoke** Emitter, rename it to **Shockwave_Distortion** as shown below:

After **deleting** the **Scale Color** module, because the **heat** distortion is **transparent** and does **not** need any color, add a **Dynamic Material Parameters** module in the Particle

Update section as shown above. With the **Sprite Renderer** selected, reset its **Material** to **M_ShockwaveDistortion**.

Next, reset the settings for the modules as follows. First, reset the **Lifetime Min** and **Max** values to **1** and **1.3** respectively as shown below:

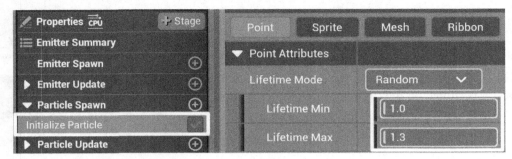

Then **reduce** the **Uniform Sprite Size** to **240** as shown below:

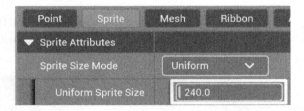

Continue to select the **Scale Sprite Size** module, and with the **second** keyframe selected, reset the **Key Data** of both **X** and **Y** axes to Time: **0.4**, Value: 1 as shown below:

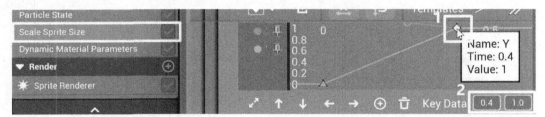

Now press **Compile** and **Save** to confirm all modifications. So far the impact and shockwave effects are complete, in the next section, we'll play the effects in C++ during the combat.

Playing the Impact Effect and Shockwaves

Back to Visual Studio and after opening the **SwordEquipmentComponent.h** header, add the following **bold** lines:

```
UCLASS()
class RPG_API USwordEquipmentComponent : public UEquipmentComponent
```

```
{
  GENERATED_BODY()

public:
  UPROPERTY(EditDefaultsOnly, BlueprintReadWrite, Category = "Niagara")
  class UNiagaraSystem* ImpactFXS;

  void SpawnImpactFX(FVector location);
  ...
};
```

The `ImpactFXS` property refers to the Niagara System that stores the sword impact and shockwave effects. The `SpawnImpactFX()` method is to spawn the Niagara System at the passed in location.

Next, open the **SwordEquipmentComponent.cpp** file and add the following lines to implement the `SpawnImpactFX()` method:

```
void USwordEquipmentComponent::SpawnImpactFX(FVector location)
{
  // Spawn the Niagara System at the location
  if(ImpactFXS)
    UNiagaraFunctionLibrary::SpawnSystemAtLocation(GetWorld(), ImpactFXS,
                              location, FRotator(0), FVector(1), true);
}
```

In the method, we call the built-in `SpawnSystemAtLocation()` method to spawn the Niagara System at the impact point.

Finally, open the **SwordDamageAnimNotifyState**.cpp file, add the following **bold** lines in the **NotifyTick()** method:

```
void USwordDamageAnimNotifyState::NotifyTick(USkeletalMeshComponent*
            MeshComp, UAnimSequenceBase* Animation, float FrameDeltaTime)
{
  ...

    if (isHit)
    {
      for (const FHitResult HitResult : HitArray) {
        // Get the IHealth interface
        IHealth* health = Cast<IHealth>(HitResult.GetActor());
        // If the target implements the IHealth and is not dead
        if (health && !health->IsDead()) {
          // Obtain the hit bone's name from the result
          FName boneName = HitResult.BoneName;
          // Play the impact VFX at the impact point
          warrior->RightHandWeapon->SpawnImpactFX(HitResult.ImpactPoint);

          // Only apply damage if has Stats
```

```
ASword* greatSword = Cast<ASword>(warrior->RightHandWeapon
                                        ->equipment);
    ...
}
    ...
}
```

In this method, when the sword is hitting the actor, we **spawn** the effects at the impact point.

After building the project, make sure that no errors occurred and back to Unreal Editor.

Assigning the Impact and Shockwaves Niagara System

Open the **BP_FemaleWarrior** Blueprint, and with the **RightHandWeapon** selected as shown below:

Set the **Impact FXS** field to the **FXS_Impact** Niagara System just created.

After pressing **Compile** and **Save**, press **Play** to run the game. Move the player character toward the wolf enemy, click the mouse button to attack, and you'll see the impact and shockwave effects playing at the location of impact as shown below:

6.3.3 Fireballs

In this section, we'll continue to design and implement the popular fireball effect using Niagara.

Fireball Textures

To create the fireball effect, we need to prepare the following trail texture called **T_FireballTrail**.

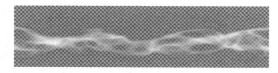

The size is **1024** by **256,** and the background is **transparent**. Then import the texture into the Niagara > **Textures** folder.

Fireball Materials

Right-click in the Niagara > **Materials** folder, then select **Material** from the context menu to create a new material called **M_Fire** for the fire animation. Double-click to open it in the Node Graph editor, and after setting the main material node to **Translucent** and **Unlit**, add the following nodes and make transitions as shown below:

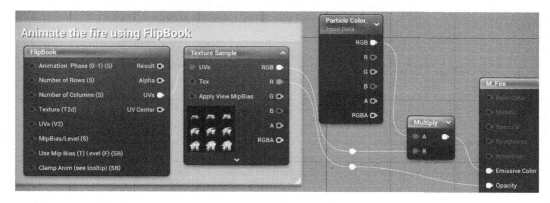

In this Material**,** we use the **FlipBook** Node to render a Flipbook Animation, which requires a flipbook texture called **T_Fire_SubUV** in the **StarterContent** > **Textures** folder as follows:

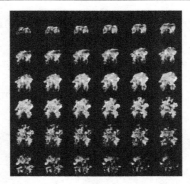

It consisted of a series of fire textures arranged in six rows and six columns. The **FlipBook** Node needs the **Number of Rows** and **Number of Columns** inputs to separate the texture into a series of smaller images. Then its **UVs** output pin is plugged into the **UVs** input of the Texture Sample Node to play the fire animation. You can preview the animation in the Viewport by right-clicking on the Texture Sample Node and selecting **Start Previewing Node** as shown below:

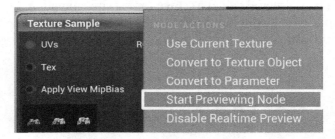

Then, after multiplying the color of the fire texture with the Particle color, the **RGB** output is used as the **Emissive** Color and the **R** channel output is plugged into the **Opacity** of the main material node to make the background transparent.

To animate the refraction, we copy-and-paste the nodes from the previous **M_SwordTrail** Material and make transitions as shown below:

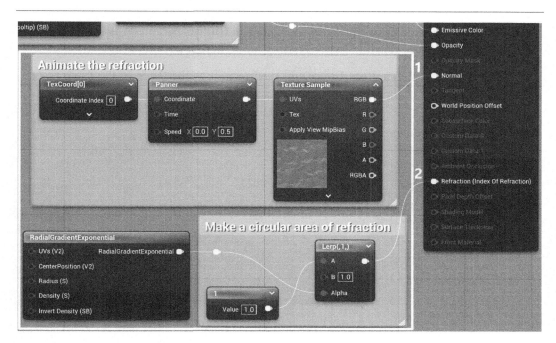

To make a **circular** area of refraction instead of a square, we add a
RadialGradientExponential Node and use its output as the **Alpha** of the **Lerp** Node to
linearly lerp between **1** and **1.33**. In other words, outside the circular area, there is no
fraction at all.

Then add a **Dynamic Parameter** Node and make transitions as shown below. Its
settings are as follows:

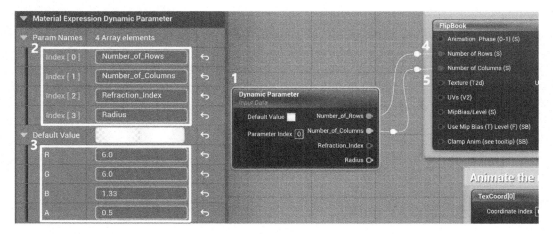

The first and second parameters are the numbers of the **rows** and **columns** in the
flipbook texture, there are both **6** in this case. The **Refraction_Index** parameter means

the refraction index of the water which is **1.33**. The **Radius** parameter is for the **RadialGradientExponential** Node's **Radius** input, here it's set to **0.5**.

Lastly, connect the **Refraction_Index** and **Radius** pins to the **B** pin of the **Lerp** node and the **Radius** pin of the **RadialGradientExponential** node respectively, as shown below:

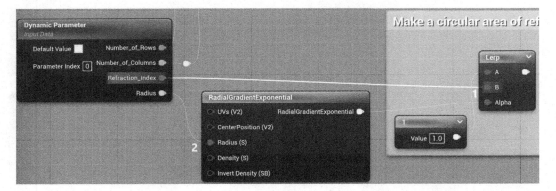

The result can be previewed in the Viewport on the right:

Next, we'll create the Material for the smoke effects. Right-click again in the Niagara > **Materials** folder, then select **Material** from the context menu to create a new material called **M_FireballSmoke**. Double-click to open it in the Node Graph editor, and after setting the main material node to **Translucent** and **Unlit**, add the following nodes and make transitions as shown below:

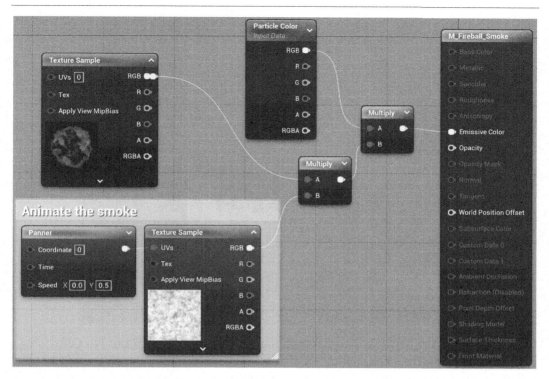

In this material, we use a **Panner** Node to animate the **Noise** texture, then multiply the **RGB** output with the smoke texture color to make a distortion. Finally, the result is multiplied with the **Particle** color again to become the **Emissive** Color as shown above.

Lastly, we'll create the Material for the fireball trails. Right-click again in the Niagara > **Materials** folder, then select **Material** from the context menu to create a new material called **M_FireballTrail**. Double-click to open it in the Node Graph editor, and after setting the main material node to **Translucent** and **Unlit**, add the following nodes and make transitions as shown below:

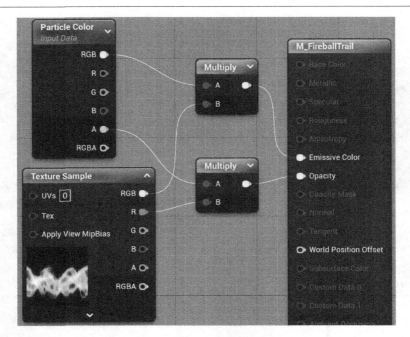

The **RGB** output of the **Texture Sample** node is multiplied with the **Particle** color to become the **Emissive** Color, and the **R** channel output is multiplied with the **Alpha (A)** of the **Particle** Color and the result is used as the **Opacity** input as shown above.

To animate the distortion, we copy-and-paste the nodes from the previous **M_SwordTrail** Material and the result is plugged into the **UVs** of the trail Texture Sample node as shown below:

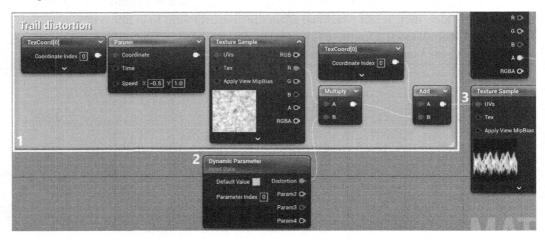

The **Dynamic Parameter** node's settings are as follows:

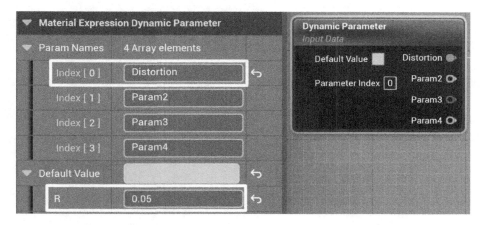

The **Distortion** parameter is set to **0.05**, as shown above, and to stretch the trail horizontally, we set the second **TexCoord** Node's **UTiling** to **2.5** as shown below:

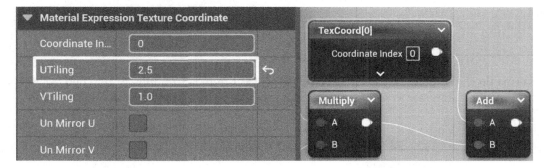

After pressing **Save** to confirm the modification, preview the material in the Viewport as shown on the right:

So far all the materials are complete and let's create the Niagara system in the next section.

The Fireball Niagara System

Right-click in the **Niagara** folder and choose **Niagara System** from the context menu, then press **Next** to continue, and in the next step, after selecting the **Simple Sprite Burst** Template as shown below:

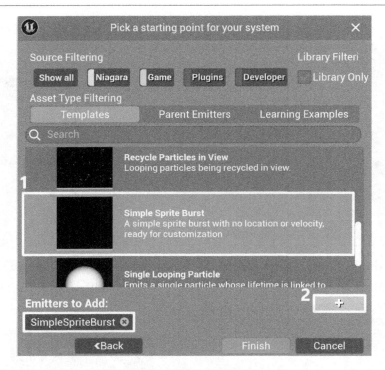

Press the + button to add the **SimpleSpriteBurst** Emitter. Continue to find and select the **Fountain** Template, as shown below, and press the + button again to add a **Fountain** Emitter.

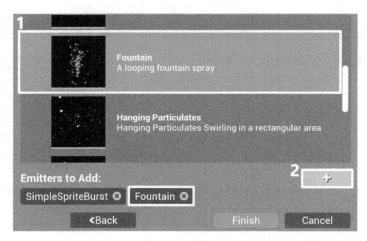

Now press **Finish** to create the system and rename it to **FXS_Fireball**. Then double-click it to open the **System Overview** panel as shown below:

After renaming the **SimpleSpriteBurst** Emitter to **Fire**, as shown above, with the **Sprite Renderer** selected, set its **Material** to the **M_Fire** Material.

Next, with the **Emitter State** selected, set the **Loop Behavior** to **Infinite**, because we want the fire to play forever, and set **Loop Duration** to **0.1** as shown below:

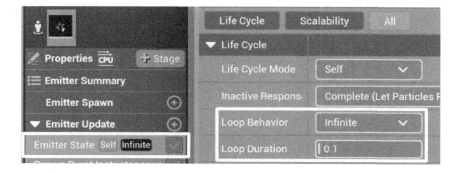

Then, after selecting the **Spawn Burst Instantaneous** module, set the **Spawn Count** to **2** as shown below:

Continue to select the **Initialize Particle** module, and reset the **Lifetime Min** and **Max** values to **0.2** and **0.35** respectively as shown below:

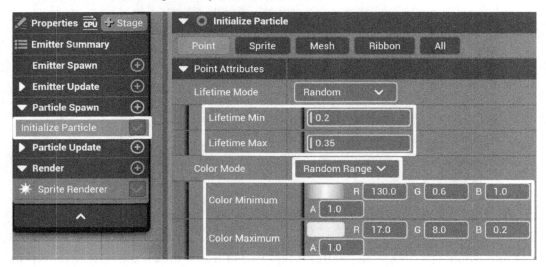

After resetting the **Color Mode** to **Random Range**, set the **Color Minimum** and **Maximum** values as shown above.

Next, set the **Uniform Sprite Size** to **165** and **Sprite Rotation Mode** to **Random** as shown below:

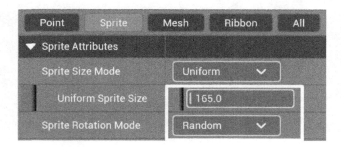

So far the fire Emitter is ready, let's continue to set up the smoke Emitter as follows. First, after renaming the **Fountain** Emitter to **Smoke** as shown below:

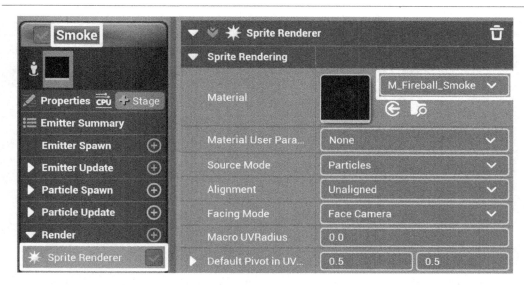

Set the **Material** of the **Sprite Renderer** module to the **M_Fireball_Smoke** Material as shown above.

With the **Emitter State** selected, set **Loop Duration** to **0.01** as shown below:

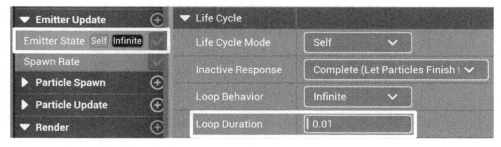

Then, with the **Spawn Rate** selected, set its **SpawnRate** to **200** as shown below:

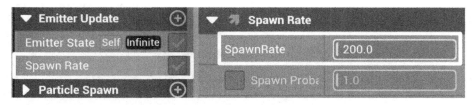

Continue to select the **Initialize Particle** module, after resetting the **Lifetime Min** and **Max** values to **0.2** and **0.7** respectively as shown below:

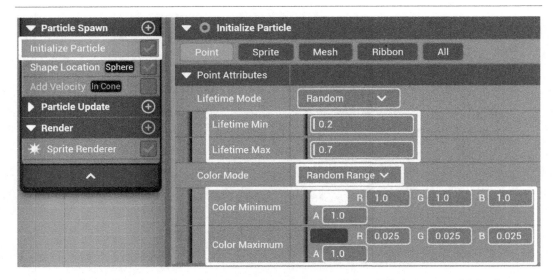

Reset the **Color Mode** to **Random Range** and set the **Color Minimum** and **Maximum** values as shown above. Next, after setting the **Sprite Size Mode** to **Random Uniform**, as shown below, set the **Uniform Sprite Size Min** and **Max** values to **65** and **90**, respectively.

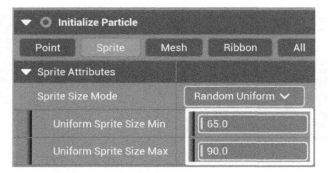

With the **Shape Location** module selected, after setting the **Sphere Radius** to **45**, **untick** the **Add Velocity** checkbox as shown below:

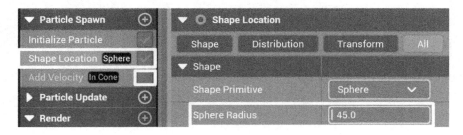

Lastly, after adding a **Curl Noise Force** module in the Particle **Update** section, set the **Noise Strength** and **Frequency** to **80** and **15** respectively as shown below:

Also **untick** the **Drag** and **Gravity Force** modules, as shown above, because we don't need any force for the smoke effects.

So far the fire and smoke effects are complete, press **Compile** and **Save** to confirm the modification. The result is as shown on the right in the Viewport.

Next, we'll create the spark particles for our fireball and re-use the Emitter created from the previous Niagara system. Find and open the **FXS_SwordTrail** Niagara system and with the **Particle** Emitter selected, press **Ctrl + C** to copy the Emitter. Then back to the **FXS_Fireball** System Overview panel, after pressing **Ctrl + P** to duplicate the Emitter as shown below:

After renaming the Emitter to **Sparks,** with the **Sprite Renderer** selected, set its **Material** to the **M_Radial_Gradient** Material from the **StarterContent** folder.

Then reset the settings of the modules as follows. First, with the **Emitter State** selected, after resetting the **Loop Behavior** to **Infinite,** set the **Loop Duration** to **2** as shown below:

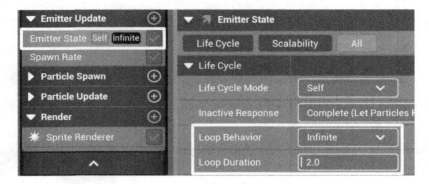

Next, with the **Spawn Rate** selected, set its **SpawnRate** to **120** as shown below:

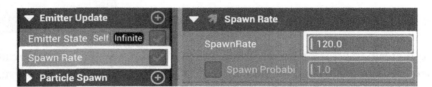

Continue to select the **Initialize Particle** module, after resetting the **Color Mode** to **Random Range,** set the **Color Minimum** and **Maximum** values as shown below:

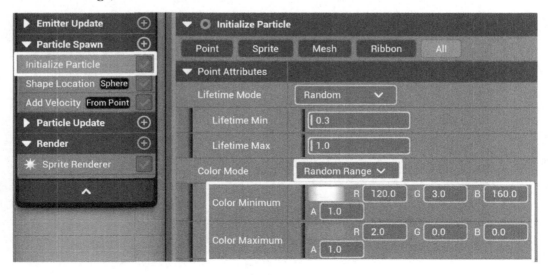

With the **Shape Location** module selected, set the **Sphere Radius** to **65** as shown below:

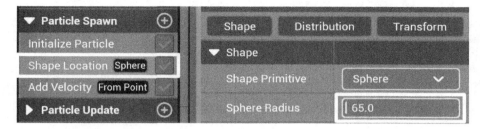

Lastly, with the **Scale Color** selected, set the **Scale RGB** values as shown below:

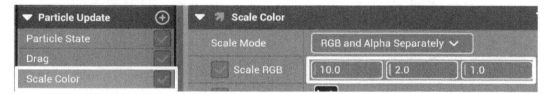

So far the sparks effect is complete, after pressing **Save** to confirm the modification, the result is as shown below:

Finally, we'll create the trail effect for the fireball and re-use the trail Emitter from the **FXS_SwordTrail** Niagara system. Copy-and-paste the **Trail** Emitter of the **FXS_SwordTrail** into the **FXS_Fireball** System Overview panel, then rename it back to **Trail** as shown below:

Next, with the **Ribbon Renderer** selected, and after resetting its **Material** to the **M_FireballTrail**, as shown above, set the **Ribbon Shape** to **Multi Plane** and **Multi Plane Count** to **3**, which make the ribbon more dramatic.

Continue to select the **Initialize Particle** module as shown below:

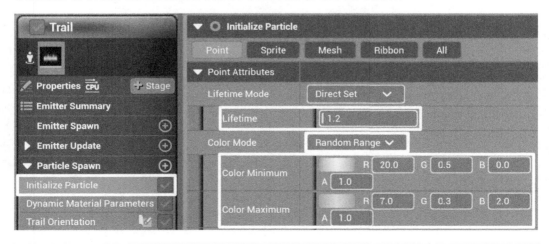

After resetting the **Lifetime** to **1.2** and the **Color Mode** to **Random Range**, set the **Color Minimum** and **Maximum** values as shown above. Then reset the **Ribbon Width** to **100** as shown below:

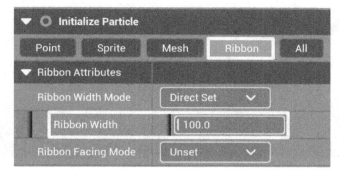

With the **Dynamic Material Parameters** selected, set the **Distortion** parameter to **0.05** as shown below:

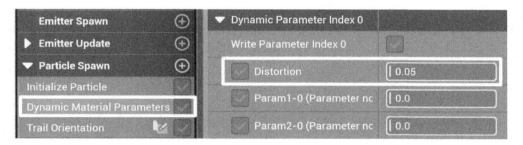

Lastly, add a **Curl Noise Force** module in the **Particle Update** section as shown below:

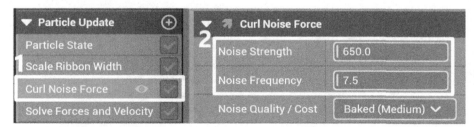

Then set the **Noise Strength** and **Frequency** to **650** and **7.5** as shown above. We add this module to make the trail a little curl.

Now press **Compile** and **Save** to confirm all modifications, then drag and drop the **FXS_Fireball** Niagara system from the folder into the scene, after moving it using the mouse, you'll see the fireball with the trail as shown below:

6.3.4 The Mesh Disintegration Effect

This section will implement the disintegration effect of the enemy mesh after being hit by a fireball. We'll also cover how to reuse and modify the script from the Niagara module to implement our modules.

The Disintegration Niagara System

First, let's create a Niagara System called **FXS_Disintegration** in the **Niagara** folder with the **Empty** Emitter template. Then open it in the editor as shown below:

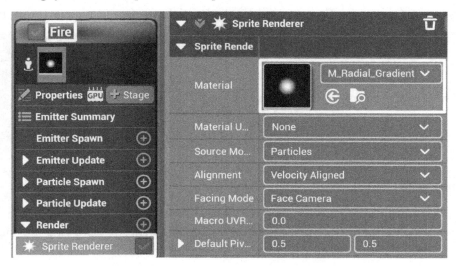

After renaming the Emitter to **Fire**, with the **Sprite Renderer** selected, set its **Material** to the **M_Radial_Gradient** Material from the **StarterContent** folder.

Then add a **Spawn Rate** module in the Emitter **Update** section and an **Initialize Mesh Reproduction Sprite** module in the **Particle Spawn** section respectively as shown below:

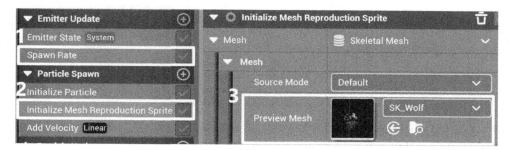

With the **Initialize Mesh Reproduction Sprite** selected, set the **Preview Mesh** field to the **SK_Wolf** skeletal mesh as shown above. This module aims to spawn the particles on the **surface** of the skeletal mesh.

Because we'll spawn lots of particles for the disintegration fire, with the **Properties** selected, as shown below:

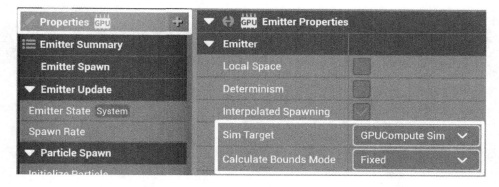

After setting the **Sim Target** to **GPUCompute Sim**, as shown above, select **Fixed** for the **Calculate Bounds Mode** field to fix the error that appeared. Now select the **Spawn Rate** module as shown below:

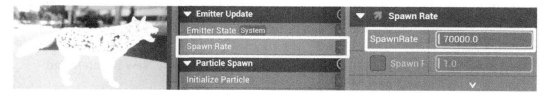

After setting the **SpawnRate** to a large value, such as **70000** as shown above, you'll see the particles spawned on the surface of the wolf mesh.

Continue to add a **Kill Particles in Volumn** in the Particle **Update** section as shown below:

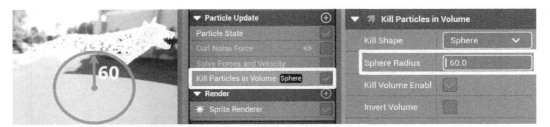

Set the **Sphere Radius** to **60** and the particles spawned in the range of the sphere will be killed as shown above in the Viewport.

Next, double-click the **Kill Particles in Volume** module to open its script in the **Node Graph** tab as shown below:

That's because we'll re-use the existing Niagara script and modify it to become our module later. Then, with **all** the Nodes in the **Node Graph** selected press **Ctrl + C** on the keyboard to copy the Nodes.

Next press the **+** to the right of the **Particle Update** and choose **New Scratch Pad Module** from the **Add new Module** panel as shown below:

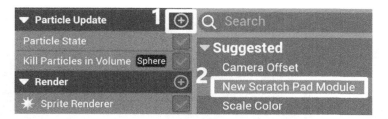

Then the **Scratch Pad** will open, as shown below:

After renaming the module to **KillParticlesInSphere**, as shown above, **delete** the three Nodes. Then press **Ctrl + V** on the keyboard to paste the Nodes to the Scratch Pad as shown below:

Continue to find the last **Map Set** Node, as shown above, and plug its **Dest** output into the **OutputMap** pin of the **Output Module**. Now press **Apply** to confirm the modification.

Then back to the **System Overview** tab, after **unticking** the **Kill Particles in Volume**, as shown below, to **disable** the module.

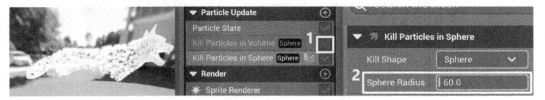

Next, with the **Kill Particles in Sphere** selected, as shown above, reset the **Sphere Radius** to **60** and you'll see the same result as shown in the Viewport.

Continue to press + on the **Particle Update** and select the **Kill Particles in Sphere** from the **Add new Module** panel as shown below:

Because we already have the same module, Niagara System will add a **001** suffix to the module name as shown above. Then reset its **Sphere Radius** to **70** and **tick** the **Invert Volume** as shown below:

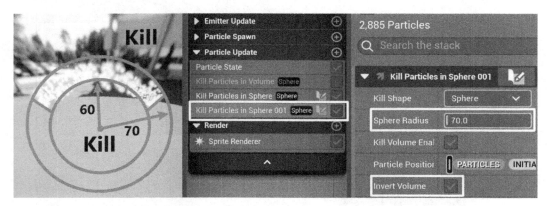

Now you'll see the particles only spawn in the **arc** shape area as shown above. That's because the bigger sphere volume is **inverted** such that the particles **outside** the bigger sphere are killed as well.

Continue to add an **Add Velocity** module in the Particle **Spawn** section and a **Curl Noise Force** module in the Particle **Update** section respectively as shown below:

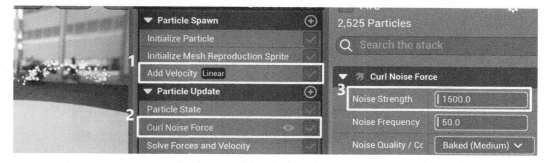

Then, with the **Curl Noise Force** module selected, set the **Noise Strength** to a **huge value** such as **1500** above, but you'll see the particles seem **not** disturbed at all as shown in the Viewport. To solve this issue, we have to modify the script in the **Kill Particles in Sphere** module as follows.

Next, double-click the **Kill Particles in Sphere** module to open the **Scratch Pad** as shown below:

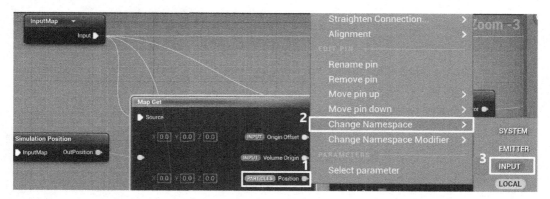

Find the first **Map Set** Node, as shown above, and after **right**-clicking on the **Particle Position** pin, select **Change Namespace** > **INPUT** to change its **Namespace** to **INPUT** as shown below:

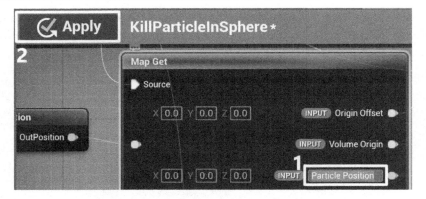

Continue to change its name to **Particle Position**, as shown above, and press **Apply** to confirm the modification.

Then switch back to the **System Overview** tab, and you'll see the **Particle Position** Input field appears in the **Selection** tab as shown below:

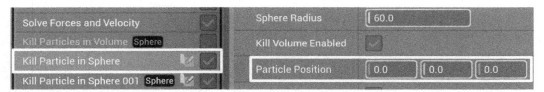

Now we can apply the **Curl Noise Force** to the particles by changing the new **Particle Position** Input as follows:

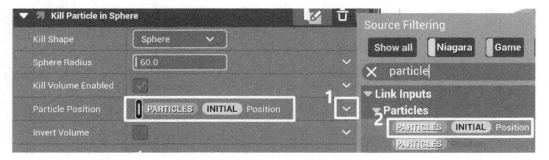

Press the **downward** arrow to the right of the **Particle Position**, as shown above, and select **PARTICLES INITIAL Position** for it.

Repeat the same step for the **second** Kill Particles in Sphere module, as shown below, you'll see the particles now **move upward** because they are affected by the **Add Velocity** module in which an **upward (Z)** velocity is applied.

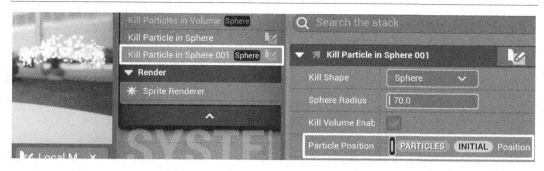

Continue to select the **Curl Noise Force** module, and reset its **Noise Strength** to a **smaller** value such as **500** below:

Because the curl noise force is applied now, the particles are disturbed a lot as shown in the Viewport.

Lastly, the other settings for the modules are as follows. With the **Initialize Particle** selected, after resetting the **Lifetime** to **0.35** and **Color Mode** to **Random Range** as shown below:

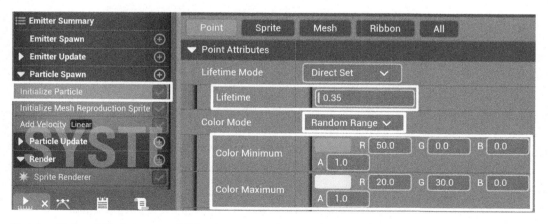

Set the **Color Minimum** and **Maximum** as shown above. Finally, we have to convert some properties of the **Kill Particles in the Sphere** module to become **User parameters** for setting their values in C++ code.

With the **Kill Particles in the Sphere** module selected, after pressing the **downward** arrow to the right of **Sphere Radius**, as shown below, select **Read from new User parameter** for it.

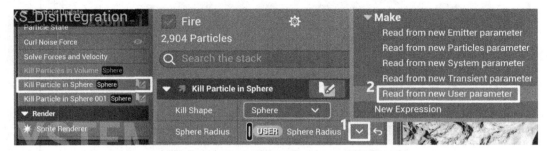

Similarly, after pressing the **downward** arrow to the right of **Origin Offset** and selecting **Read from new User parameter** for it, Niagara will create a new User parameter called **Origin Offset** as shown below:

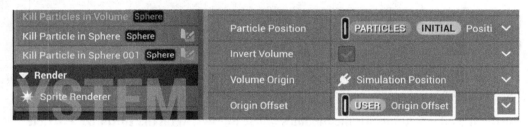

Then, in the **User Parameters** panel, as shown below:

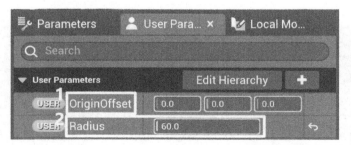

You'll see the two User Parameters, right-click on them and **rename** their names to **OriginOffset** and **Radius** respectively, as shown above, reset the **Radius** parameter back to **60**.

Next, press the + button to the right of **User Parameters** and select **float** under **Common**, as shown below, to create a new parameter.

After renaming the new parameter to **Edge**, as shown below, reset its value to **15**.

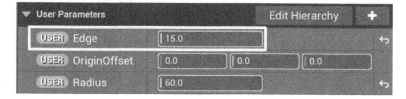

Continue to select the **Kill Particles in the Sphere 001** module, after pressing the **downward** arrow to the right of **Sphere Radius**, as shown below, select **Add Float** under **Dynamic Inputs** for it.

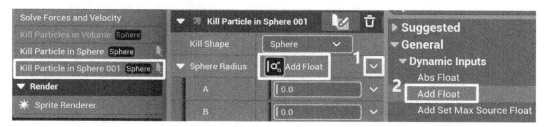

Then **two** floats (**A** and **B**) will appear under the **Sphere Radius** as shown above.

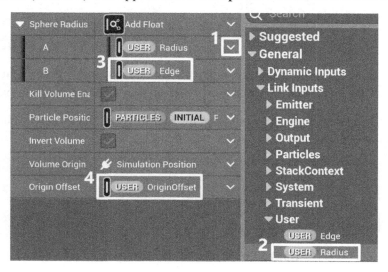

Press the downward arrow to the right of **A**, select the **Radius** User parameter as shown above under the **User**. Similarly, select the **Edge** User parameter for the **B**. The result is that we can **dynamically** set the Sphere Radius value in C++ code by changing the values of the two User parameters.

Lastly, select the **OriginOffset** User parameter for the **Origin Offset** field, as shown above, and the settings for the **Fire** Emitter is complete. The result is shown on the right in the Viewport:

In the next step, we'll re-use the **Fire** Emitter to create the **Ash** particles. **Duplicate** a copy of the **Fire** Emitter and rename it to **Ash** as shown below:

After selecting the **Sprite Renderer**, reset its **Material** to the **M_Fire** created before, as shown above, because we need the **heat distortion** feature from that material.

Next, with the **Spawn Rate** selected, reset the **SpawnRate** to a **smaller** value such as **50000** as shown below:

Continue to select the **Initialize Particle** module as shown below:

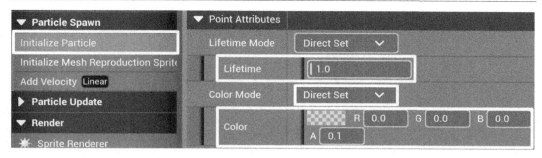

After resetting the **Lifetime** to **1** and **Color Mode** to **Direct Set** respectively, set the **Color** values as shown above. Finally, reset the **Uniform Sprite Size Min** and **Max** values as shown below:

Now press **Compile** and **Save** to confirm the modification. The result is shown in the Viewport as shown on the right:

So far the Niagara system for the disintegration effects is complete, in the next step, we'll modify the wolf's materials to disintegrate the mesh as follows.

The Disintegration Material

Find the **Materials** folder under the **AnimalVarietyPack** > **Wolf** folder as shown below:

In the content browser, you'll see the **M_Wolf** and **M_WolfFur** Materials. With them selected, right-click and select **Duplicate** from the context menu to duplicate two new materials. Then modify their names to **M_Wolf_Radial_Disintegration** and **M_WolfFur_Radial_Disintegration** respectively as shown above.

Then open the **M_Wolf_Radial_Disintegration** Material in the **Material Graph** and with the **main Material Node** selected as shown below:

After resetting the **Blend Mode** to **Masked**, as shown above, the **Opacity Mask** pin will be **enabled**.

Next, after adding the **SphereMask** and **LocalPosition** Nodes to the Graph as shown below:

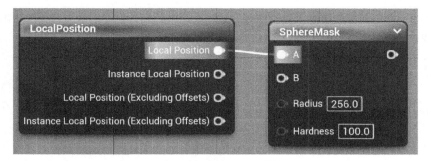

Plug the **Local Position** output of the LocalPositiom Node into the **A** pin of the **SphereMask** Node as shown above. Because the **SphereMask** Node needs the **Radius** and **Hardness** inputs and we'll set their values in C++ code, create a **Const** node and then right-click on it as shown below:

Select **Convert to Parameter** to convert the constant node to a **Parameter** node, as shown below, then after renaming it to **Radius**, set the **Default Value** to **60** and plug its output pin into the **Radius** pin of the **SphereMask** node.

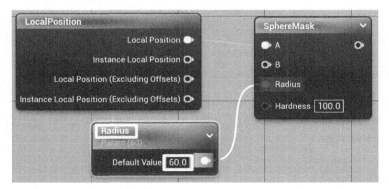

Next, **duplicate** the **Radius** Parameter node to a new node, rename it to **Hardness** as shown below:

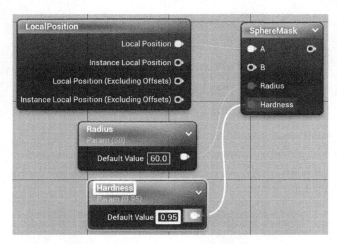

Reset its **Default Value** to **0.95** and plug its output pin into the **Hardness** pin of the **SphereMask** node.

UE5 provides the **Material Parameter Collection** asset for us to store global parameters. Right-click in the **Wolf** > **Materials** folder under the **AnimalVarietyPack**, select **Materials** > **Material Parameter Collection**, as shown below, to create a Material Parameter Collection, and then rename it to **MPC_Disintegration**.

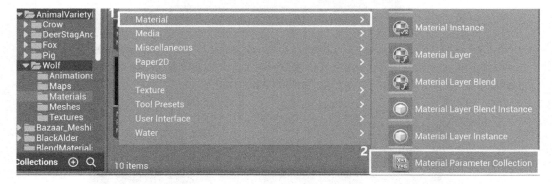

Then double-click the **MPC_Disintegration** to open it in the editor, press + to the right of **Vector Parameters** to create **one** parameter as shown below, and then **rename** the parameter to **Location**.

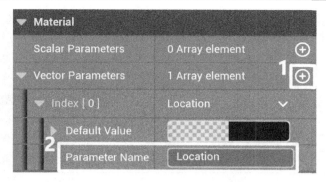

Now that the settings for the parameters are complete, back to the **Material Graph** tab, drag and drop the **MPC_Disintegration** asset into the Graph as shown below:

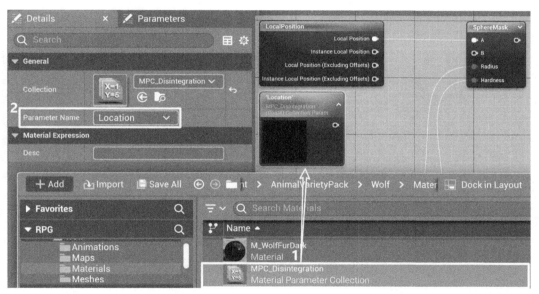

A new Node named **None** will be created for us and, with the Node selected, set its **Parameter Name** to **Location** from the drop-down menu, as shown above, you'll see the Node's name is changed to **Location**.

Next, drag off the output pin of the **Location** Node, as shown below, and select the **ComponentMask** under the **Math** to create a **Mask** Node.

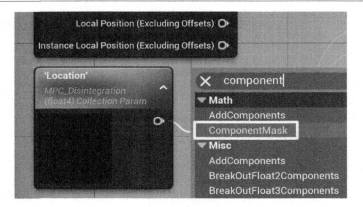

Then, with the **Mask** Node selected, **tick** the checkbox of the **B** field in the **Details** tab, as shown below, then plug the output of the Mask Node into the **B** input pin of the **SphereMask** Node.

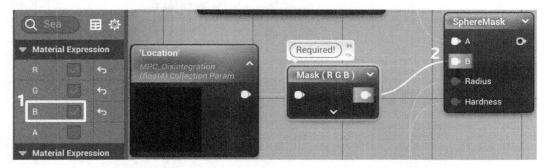

Please note that the Mask is **required**; otherwise, an error will occur if we plug the **Location** output into the B pin of SphereMask Node directly.

Now you can right-click on the **SphereMask** Node to **preview** the sphere mask in the Viewport as shown below:

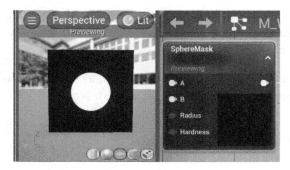

To preview the result using the wolf mesh, find the **SK_Wolf** Skeletal Mesh in the **Wolf** > **Meshes** folder as shown below:

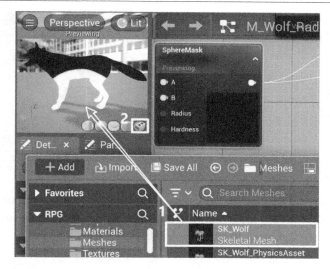

Drag and drop it into the Viewport and press the **Mesh** icon at the **lower-right** corner to use the wolf mesh for previewing. As shown above, the **black** part will be masked, which means that part will be **invisible**. But in our case, we want the **white** part to be eroded and thus invisible. So drag off the output pin of the SphereMask Node, enter **1-** in the search bar as shown below:

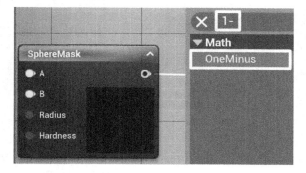

Select the **OneMinus** to create a **1-x** node, then right-click on the node and start previewing in the Viewport, you'll find that now the four legs of the wolf are masked as shown below:

Lastly, plug the output of the **1-x** Node into the **Opacity Mask** input of the main material Node. Now press **Apply** and **Save** to confirm all modifications, and in the Viewport, you'll see the masked part is **invisible** as shown below:

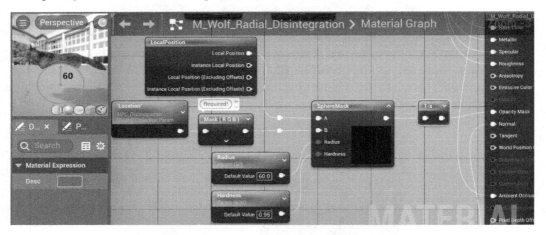

Making the Glow Edge

To make the fire-burning edge around the eroded mesh, we can use the **3ColorBlend** Node to achieve this purpose as follows. First, add a **3ColorBlend** Node to the Graph as shown below:

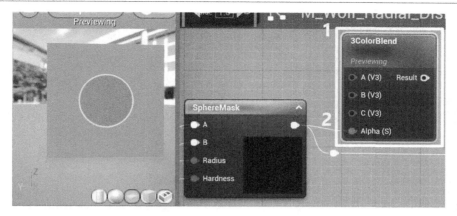

Then drag off the output of the **SphereMask** and plug it into the **Alpha** input as shown above. Start previewing the **3ColorBlend** Node in the Viewport, you can see a **blue** circle with a **green** outline and **red** around the circle. That's because the **A**, **B**, and **C** inputs of the 3ColorBlend Node represent **Red**, **Green**, and **Blue** colors respectively by default.

To only keep the outlined ring, drag off the **A** pin of the **3ColorBlend** and add a **Const** Node as shown below:

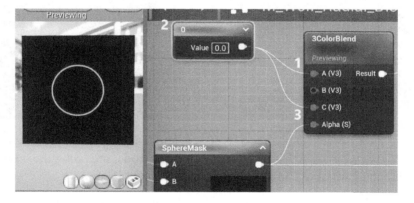

Continue to drag off the output of the Const Node and plug into the **C** input of the **3ColorBlend**, which makes the **Red** and **Blue** inputs all **0**, and as shown in the Viewport, both regions become **black** now.

Next, drag off the **B** pin of the **3ColorBlend** and add another **Const** Node as shown below:

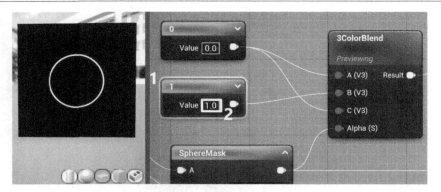

After resetting its **Value** to **1**, as shown above, the ring now becomes **white**. Finally, to make the eroded edge glows and change color, after adding a **Multiply** Node, drag off the **A** pin of the Node and add a **Const4Vector** Node as shown below:

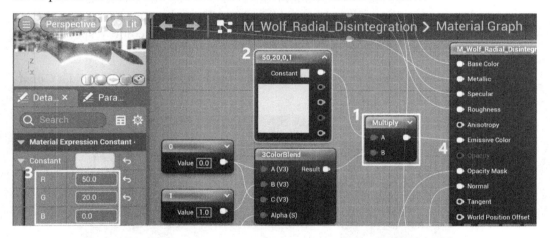

After setting its **R**, **G**, and **B** channels to **50**, **20**, and **0** as shown above, plug the **Result** of the **3ColorBlend** into the **B** input of the **Multiply** Node, then plug the output of the Multiply into the **Emissive Color** input of the main material node.

Now stop previewing the 3ColorBlend Node, and after switching to the **mesh** preview mode, you'll see the eroded edge glows as shown in the Viewport.

So far the disintegration material for the wolf mesh is complete, press **Apply** and **Save** to confirm the modification, and the **modified** Node Graph is shown below:

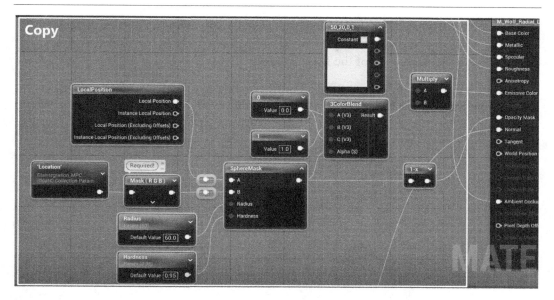

Because we'll re-use the new nodes in the next step, with all the new nodes selected, as shown above, then press **Ctrl + C** to copy the nodes.

The Fur Disintegration Material

The **SK_Wolf** skeletal mesh has two Materials, one for the mesh and another one for the **fur**. In this subsection, we'll continue to modify the **M_WolfFur_Radial_Disintegration** Material created before. Double-click the **M_WolfFur_Radial_Disintegration** to open the Material Graph as shown below:

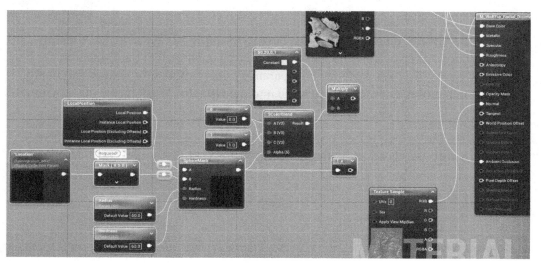

Press **Ctrl + V** to paste the copied nodes into the Graph, as shown above, and because the main Material Node is already **Masked**, the **Opacity Mask** is **enabled** and is connected to the **A** channel of the **Base Texture**.

Then, after plugging the output of the **Multiply** Node into the **Emissive Color** of the **main** material node as shown below:

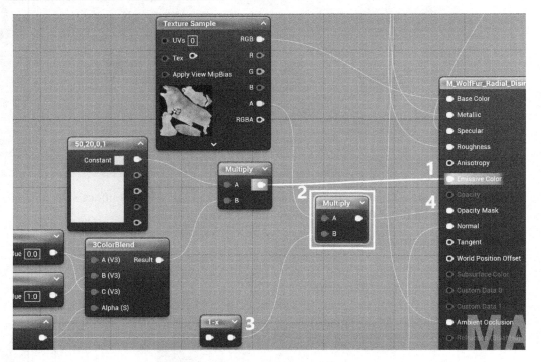

Drag off from the **A** output of the **Base Texture Sample** Node and add a **Multiply** Node, as shown above, then plug the output of the **1-x** Node into the **B** input of the new **Multiply** Node. This will keep the transparency of the original fur texture and finally, plug the output of the new Multiply Node into the **Opacity Mask** of the main material node.

So far all the integration material settings for the Wolf enemy are complete, and after pressing **Apply** and **Save**, open the **SK_Wolf** Skeletal Mesh in the **Wolf > Meshes** folder as shown below:

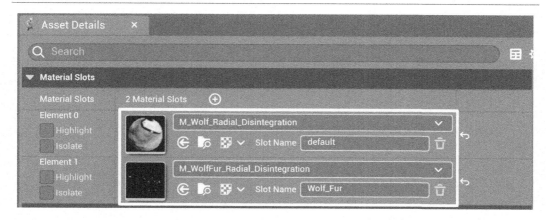

After resetting the two **Material Elements** to the **M_Wolf_Radial_Disintegration** and **M_WolfFur_Radial_Disintegration** respectively as shown above, press **Save** to confirm the modification.

6.3.5 Mesh Disintegration in C++

In this section, we'll play the disintegration effect in C++ when the wolf enemy is dying with the UE5 built-in **Timeline** mechanism. First, back to Visual Studio and open the **Enemy.h** header, add the following **bold** lines:

```
...
#include "NiagaraComponent.h"
#include "Components/TimelineComponent.h"
#include "Enemy.generated.h"

UCLASS()
class RPG_API AEnemy : public ANPC, public IHealth, public ILock
{
  GENERATED_BODY()
public:
  AEnemy();

  UPROPERTY(VisibleAnywhere, BlueprintReadOnly, Category = "Niagara")
  UNiagaraComponent* DisintegrationFX;
  UFUNCTION()
  virtual void TimelineProgress(float value);
  void ActivateDisintegration(bool activate,
                                FVector location = FVector(0,0,0));

  ...

protected:
  FTimeline CurveFTimeline;
```

```
UPROPERTY(EditAnywhere, BlueprintReadOnly, Category = "Timeline")
UCurveFloat* CurveFloat;
UPROPERTY(EditAnywhere, BlueprintReadOnly, Category = "Timeline")
float EndDisintegrationRadius;
UPROPERTY(EditAnywhere, BlueprintReadOnly, Category =
                                    "MaterialParameter")
FString RadiusParameterName;

virtual void BeginPlay() override;
virtual void Tick(float DeltaTime) override;
private:
  bool isDead = false;
};
```

Because we are going to use the **Niagara** and **Timeline Component** classes, the `TimelineComponent.h`, and `NiagaraComponent.h` headers have to be included.

In the `public` section, the `DisintegrationFX` property refers to the disintegration effect. The `TimelineProgress()` method is a **delegate** that will be bound to the `FTimeline` variable `CurveFTimeline` below. The `ActivateDisintegration()` method is to activate or deactivate the effect.

In the `protected` section, the `CurveFTimeline` represents a timeline, and the `CurveFloat` property refers to the **curve** of `float` values, and we can edit the curve later in the editor. The `EndDisintegrationRadius` property represents the **largest** value of the **Radius** parameter of the effect.

The `RadiusParameterName` property is to store the **name** of the material's **Radius** parameter. Lastly, we also override the `BeginPlay()` and `Tick()` methods.

Then open the **Enemy.cpp** file and add the following **bold** lines in the **constructor** to create the Niagara Component and attach it to the **Mesh** of the enemy.

```
AEnemy::AEnemy()
{
    …

  DisintegrationFX =
      CreateDefaultSubobject<UNiagaraComponent>(TEXT("DisintegrationFX"));
  DisintegrationFX->SetupAttachment(GetMesh());
}
```

Continue to add the following lines to implement the new methods:

```
void AEnemy::BeginPlay()
{
  Super::BeginPlay();
```

```
    if (CurveFloat) {
      // Declare the function to handle timeline float track
      FOnTimelineFloat timelineProgress;
      // Bind the TimelineProgress method
      timelineProgress.BindUFunction(this, FName("TimelineProgress"));
      // Add the float curve to the timeline and connect it to the
      // timeline's interpolation function
      CurveFTimeline.AddInterpFloat(CurveFloat, timelineProgress);
      // Set not to loop
      CurveFTimeline.SetLooping(false);
    }
}
```

In the BeginPlay() method, after declaring a **FOnTimelineFloat** function to handle the timeline **float** track, we bind the TimelineProgress() method to the function by calling its **BindUFunction()** method and passing in the **name** of the method. Then the AddInterpFloat() method is called to add the **float curve** to the timeline and connect it to the interpolation function of the timeline. Lastly, set the timeline to **not looping**.

```
void AEnemy::ActivateDisintegration(bool activate, FVector location)
{
  if (activate) {
    if (DisintegrationFX)
      DisintegrationFX->Activate(true);
    // Start playing the timeline
    CurveFTimeline.PlayFromStart();
  }
  else {
    if (DisintegrationFX)
      DisintegrationFX->Deactivate();
  }
}
```

In the ActivateDisintegration() method, if the incoming flag is true, meaning that to **activate** the effect, we call the Activate() method of the effect to activate it and then the timeline's PlayFromStart() function is called to start playing the timeline from the beginning. On the other hand, if the incoming flag is false, meaning to **deactivate** the effect, then the Deactivate() method is called to deactivate it.

```
void AEnemy::TimelineProgress(float value)
{
  // To be implemented by the child classes.
}
```

The TimelineProgress() method is the **interpolation** function (delegate) of the timeline, and it will be implemented in the **Wolf** child class.

```
void AEnemy::Tick(float DeltaTime)
{
```

```
  Super::Tick(DeltaTime);

  // Advance the timeline
  CurveFTimeline.TickTimeline(DeltaTime);
}
```

In the overridden `Tick()` method, we call the **`TickTimeline()`** method of the timeline and pass in the `DeltaTime` to advance the timeline.

Finally, add the following **bold** lines in the **`PlayDeathMontage()`** method to **activate** the disintegration effect when the enemy is dying.

```
void AEnemy::PlayDeathMontage()
{
  if (DeathMontages.Num() != 0)
  {
    // Activate the disintegration effect
    ActivateDisintegration(true);
    // Get a random integer from 0 to the array size minus one
    int num = FMath::RandRange(0, DeathMontages.Num() - 1);
    // Play the Montage
    PlayAnimMontage(DeathMontages[num]);
  }
}
```

Next, we continue to implement the `TimelineProgress()` method, open the **Wolf.h** header, and add the following **bold** lines:

```
UCLASS()
class RPG_API AWolf : public AEnemy
{
  GENERATED_BODY()

public:
  AWolf();

  virtual void TimelineProgress(float value) override;
  virtual void BeginPlay() override;
private:
  UMaterialInterface* meshMaterial;
  UMaterialInterface* furMaterial;
  UMaterialInstanceDynamic* meshDynamicMaterial;
  UMaterialInstanceDynamic* furDynamicMaterial;
};
```

In the `Public` section, we declare and override the **`TimelineProgress()`** and `BeginPlay()` methods.

In the `Private` section, we declare two **`UMaterialInterface`** pointers that refer to the **two** material elements of the wolf skeletal mesh, respectively. The two

UMaterialInstanceDynamic pointers refer to the **Dynamic Material Instances** created during the runtime.

Open the **Wolf.cpp** file, and add the following lines to implement the methods:

```
void AWolf::BeginPlay()
{
  Super::BeginPlay();

  USkeletalMeshComponent* wolfMesh = GetMesh();
  // Get the materials
  TArray<UMaterialInterface*> matInterfaces = wolfMesh->GetMaterials();
  // The first material is for the mesh
  meshMaterial = matInterfaces[0];
  // Create the dynamic material instance
  meshDynamicMaterial = UMaterialInstanceDynamic::Create(meshMaterial,
                                                     this);
  // Replace the original material
  wolfMesh->SetMaterial(0, meshDynamicMaterial); // Slot 0 is for the mesh
  // The second material is for the fur
  furMaterial = matInterfaces[1];
  furDynamicMaterial = UMaterialInstanceDynamic::Create(furMaterial,
                                                     this);
  wolfMesh->SetMaterial(1, furDynamicMaterial);  // Slot 1 is for the fur
}
```

In the `BeginPlay()` method, after getting the wolf skeletal mesh component and the two materials, we call the built-in `Create()` method of the `UMaterialInstanceDynamic` to create a **Dynamic** Material Instance for the mesh and fur, respectively. Then the `SetMaterial()` method of the skeletal mesh component is called to **replace** the original materials with the new dynamic material instances, respectively. Please note that this is required; otherwise, we are unable to reset the material parameters during the runtime.

```
void AWolf::TimelineProgress(float value)
{
  if (DisintegrationFX) {
    if (value >= EndDisintegrationRadius)
      ActivateDisintegration(false);
    else {
      // Set the Niagara System's Radius parameter
      if(DisintegrationFX)
        DisintegrationFX->SetVariableFloat(RadiusParameterName, value);
      // Also set the Material's Radius parameter and here we
      // have to use the FName of the parameter
      if(meshDynamicMaterial)
        meshDynamicMaterial->
             SetScalarParameterValue(FName(RadiusParameterName), value);
      if (furDynamicMaterial)
        furDynamicMaterial->
             SetScalarParameterValue(FName(RadiusParameterName), value);
```

```
      }
    }
}
```

In the `TimelineProgress()` method, if the incoming value is greater than or equal to the `EndDisintegrationRadius` property, then we **stop** the disintegration effect. Otherwise, the `SetVariableFloat()` and `SetScalarParameterValue()` methods are called respectively to set the **Radius** parameters of the Niagara System and Material.

Now build the project and make sure that no errors occurred. So far all the C++ code for the effect is complete, and in the next step, let's create the **Curve** asset for the timeline and finish up the settings of the enemy Blueprint.

The Timeline Curve

Because we'll use a **Curve** to control the Material Parameters, back to Unreal Editor and create a folder called **Curves** in the **Content** folder. Then right-click in the Content Browser of the Curves folder, and select **Miscellaneous** > **Curve** from the context menu, the following **Pick Curve Class** panel will appear:

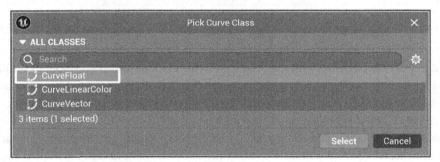

Select the **CurveFloat** and press the **Select** button to create the asset for editing the curve. After changing its name to **RadiusCurve**, double-click to open the **Curve Editor** as shown below:

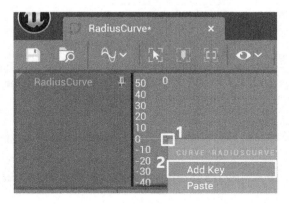

Zoon in the grid using the mouse wheel until you can see the time **0** at the top, then **right**-click on the **horizontal** axis at **Time: 0**, **Value: 0** position, as shown above, and continue to select **Add Key** to add a **key** at that position as shown below:

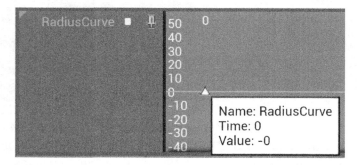

Next, add another key at **Time: 5**, **Value: 0** position as shown below:

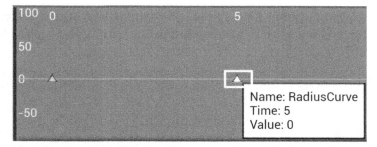

Lastly, with the **second** key selected, after setting its **Value** to **100**, as shown below:

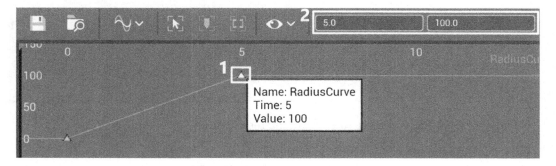

Now press **Save** to confirm the modification, then open the **BP_Wolf** Blueprint as shown below:

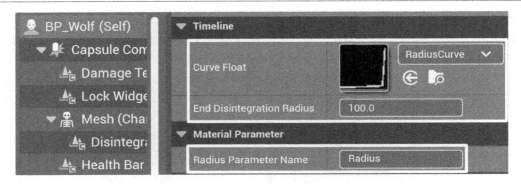

After expanding the **Timeline** and **Material Parameter**, set **Cure Float** to the **RadiusCurve** just created and **End Disintegration Radius** to **100**, which means that, when the value of the **Radius** parameter is 100, the disintegration **stops**. Continue to set the name of the **Radius** parameter to **Radius** as shown above.

Next, with the **Disintegration FX** selected, after setting the **Niagara System Asset** to the **FXS_Disintegration** Niagara system, **untick** the **Auto Activate** checkbox as shown below:

Now press **Compile** and **Save** to confirm the modification.

Before testing the effects, we have to reset the values of the **Radius** parameters in the disintegration materials. So open the **M_Wolf_Radial_Disintegration** and **M_WolfFur_Radial_Disintegration** materials respectively, and reset the **Default Value** of the **Radius** parameters to **0** as shown below:

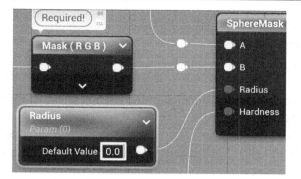

Now press **Play** to run the game, after attacking the wolf enemy and when the dying animation is playing, the disintegration effects will play as shown on the right:

6.3.6 Enemy Destruction and Resurrection

After the enemy is disintegrated, it has to be removed from the scene, and if it's a respawnable actor, we have to respawn it again in the scene. In this section, we'll implement the destruction and resurrection of the enemy character after being attacked.

Back to Visual Studio, after opening the **Enemy.h** header, add the following **bold** lines in the class:

```
UCLASS()
class RPG_API AEnemy : public ANPC, public IHealth, public ILock
{
  GENERATED_BODY()
public:
  AEnemy();

  UPROPERTY(EditDefaultsOnly, BlueprintReadOnly, Category = "Respawn")
  TSubclassOf<AEnemy> EnemyClass;
  UPROPERTY(EditDefaultsOnly, BlueprintReadOnly, Category = "Respawn")
```

```
    bool Respawnable = true;
    FVector CalculateRespawnLocation();
    virtual void Respawn();
    ...
};
```

The `EnemyClass` property refers to the enemy's **Blueprint** class and the `Respawnable` bool property represents whether the enemy is respawnable. The `CalculateRespawnLocation()` method is to calculate and return the enemy respawn location and the **virtual** function `Respawn()` is to respawn the enemy.

Then open the **Enemy.cpp** file and add the following lines to implement the new methods:

```cpp
FVector AEnemy::CalculateRespawnLocation()
{
  // Get the enemy's current location
  FVector center = GetActorLocation();
  // Initialize the respawn position using the Z position of the center
  FVector respawnPos(0, 0, center.Z);
  // Get the radius and angle randomly in the polar coordinate system
  float radius = FMath::RandRange(300.0, 1350.0);
  float angle = FMath::RandRange(0.0, 360.0);
  // Convert the polar coordinate to a respawn position
  respawnPos.X = center.X + radius * FMath::Cos(angle);
  respawnPos.Y = center.Y + radius * FMath::Sin(angle);
  // Prepare the line trace strat and end position vectors
  FVector traceStart = FVector(respawnPos.X, respawnPos.Y,
                                              respawnPos.Z + 200);
  FVector traceEnd = FVector(respawnPos.X, respawnPos.Y,
                                              respawnPos.Z - 200);
  FHitResult hitResult(ForceInit);

  TArray<AActor*> actorsToIgnore;
  actorsToIgnore.Add(this);
  // Perform the line trace
  bool isHit = UKismetSystemLibrary::LineTraceSingle(GetWorld(),
          traceStart, traceEnd,
              UEngineTypes::ConvertToTraceType(ECC_WorldStatic),
      false, actorsToIgnore, EDrawDebugTrace::Persistent, hitResult, true,
                          FLinearColor::Red, FLinearColor::Blue, 1.0f);

  if (isHit)
    // Add an offset to the impact point at the Z axis
    return hitResult.ImpactPoint + FVector(0, 0, 10);
  else
    return center;
}

void AEnemy::Respawn()
{
```

```
    // No implementation in this virtual function, the derived class will
    // re-implement this method
}
```

In the `CalculateRespawnLocation()` method, the enemy's current location is obtained first and used as the **center** of a circular respawn area, then a vector variable `respawnPos` is declared and initialized using the center's **Z** position. Next, we obtain the **radius** and **angle** values randomly in the **polar** coordinate system. Then the polar coordinate is converted to a respawn position and the conversion is illustrated in the figure below:

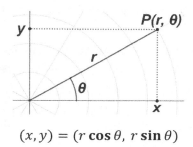

$$(x, y) = (r \cos \theta,\ r \sin \theta)$$

The x and y coordinates of the respawn position are obtained using the **trigonometric ratio** as shown above.

Please note that we are unable to use the converted location for respawning the enemy directly, that's because this location may be **underneath** the landscape. The solution here is to do a line trace and find an appropriate respawn position right above the landscape whose Collision **Object Type** is set to **WorldStatic**. So after using the current respawn location to obtain the trace start and end points, the line trace is performed and if we hit something, an offset is added to the impact point at the **Z** axis which will get a new location that is right **above** the terrain, and finally, it's returned as the enemy respawn location.

In the `Respawn()` method, we **do not** provide any implementation because different enemies may have different ways to respawn.

Continue to open the **Wolf.h** header and add the following **bold** line in the class:

```
UCLASS()
class RPG_API AWolf : public AEnemy
{
  GENERATED_BODY()

public:
  AWolf();

  void Respawn() override;
    …
```

```
};
```

The overridden `Respawn()` method is to implement the respawn of the Wolf enemy character.

Finally, open the **Wolf.cpp** file and add the following lines to implement the `Respawn()` method as follows:

```
void AWolf::Respawn()
{
  FVector respawnLocation = CalculateRespawnLocation();
  Destroy();

  GetWorld()->SpawnActor<AWolf>(EnemyClass, respawnLocation, FRotator());
}
```

In the `Respawn()` method, after calling the inherited `CalculateRespawnLocation()` method to obtain a respawn location, we destroy the character and then call the built-in `SpawnActor()` method and pass in the Blueprint class and the respawn location to respawn the wolf character in the scene.

Next, add the following **bold** lines in the `TimelineProgress()` method as follows:

```
void AWolf::TimelineProgress(float value)
{
  // Set Radius parameters for Niagara and Material
  if (DisintegrationFX) {
    if (value >= EndDisintegrationRadius) {
      ActivateDisintegration(false);
      // Detroy the enemy if it's not respawnable
      if(!Respawnable)
        Destroy();
      else
        Respawn();
    }
    else {
      …
    }
  }
}
```

In the `TimelineProgress()` method, after the enemy is disintegrated, if it's respawnable, we call the `Respawn()` method to respawn the enemy.

After building the project, back to Unreal Editor and press **Play** to run the game, after the wolf is attacked and disintegrated, it'll be removed from the scene first and then respawned inside a **circular** area centered at the original location.

6.3.7 Fireball Projectiles

As the fireball Niagara system is ready, in the last section of this book, we'll implement the fireball projectile in C++ as follows. Because casting fireballs can be categorized as a **spell**, let's create the base class called **Spell** for the fireball projectile first.

Press **Tools** > **New C++ Class…** from the main menu and in the next step, choose **Actor** as the Parent Class, then press the **Next** button to continue.

After changing the class name to **Spell**, add "**Public/Spells**" to the **Path** as shown below:

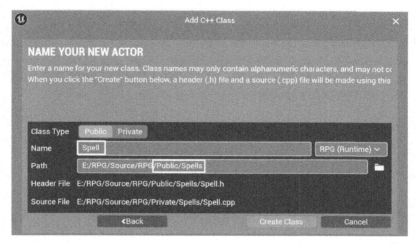

Press **Create Class** to generate the class in Visual Studio. Open the **Spell.h** header and add the following **bold** lines:

```
#include "CoreMinimal.h"
#include "GameFramework/Actor.h"
#include "Stats/WeaponStats.h"
#include "Spell.generated.h"

UCLASS()
class RPG_API ASpell : public AActor
{
  GENERATED_BODY()

public:
  // Sets default values for this actor's properties
  ASpell();

protected:
  // Called when the game starts or when spawned
```

```
    virtual void BeginPlay() override;

public:
    // Called every frame
    virtual void Tick(float DeltaTime) override;
    UPROPERTY(Instanced, EditAnywhere, Category = "Stats")
    UWeaponStats* Stats;
};
```

In the `public` section, we add a **Stats** property for the Spell class.

Now build the project and make sure that no errors occurred, next we are going to create the `Fireball` class.

The Fireball Class

Back to Unreal Editor, press **Tools** > **New C++ Class...** again from the main menu, and next choose the `Spell` as the Parent Class, then press the **Next** button to continue. In the next step, after renaming the class to **Fireball** and selecting the **Public/Spells** folder for the **Path**, press the **Create Class** button to generate the class.

Open the **Fireball.h** header and add the following **bold** lines:

```
#include "CoreMinimal.h"
#include "Spell.h"
#include "Components/SphereComponent.h"
#include "NiagaraComponent.h"
#include "NiagaraFunctionLibrary.h"
#include "GameFramework/ProjectileMovementComponent.h"
#include "Fireball.generated.h"

UCLASS()
class RPG_API AFireball : public ASpell
{
    GENERATED_BODY()
public:
    AFireball();

    UPROPERTY(EditAnywhere, BlueprintReadOnly, Category = "SphereCollider")
    USphereComponent* SphereCollider;
    UPROPERTY(EditAnywhere, BlueprintReadOnly, Category = "Niagara")
    UNiagaraComponent* FireballFX;
    UPROPERTY(EditAnywhere, BlueprintReadOnly, Category = "Projectile")
    UProjectileMovementComponent* ProjectileMovement;

    UFUNCTION()
    void OnSphereColliderBeginOverlap(UPrimitiveComponent* OverlappedComp,
                AActor* OtherActor, UPrimitiveComponent* OtherComp, int32
            OtherBodyIndex, bool bFromSweep, const FHitResult& SweepResult);
};
```

In the `public` section, after declaring the constructor, we declare a **SphereComponent** property `SphereCollider` to represent the sphere collider. The `FireballFX` property refers to the fireball effect and the `ProjectileMovement` property refers to the **Movement Component** that is used to move the fireball projectile. Lastly, the `OnSphereColliderBeginOverlap()` method is a delegate for the sphere collider's begin overlay event.

Next, add the following lines in the **Fireball.cpp** file to implement the **constructor** and the **OnBoxColliderBeginOverlap()** method:

```cpp
#include "Interfaces/Health.h"
#include "Stats/DiceRoll.h"

AFireball::AFireball()
{
  if (!RootComponent)
  {
    // Create the RootComponent which is a SceneComponent
    RootComponent = CreateDefaultSubobject<USceneComponent>(
                                    TEXT("ProjectileSceneComponent"));
  }

  if (!SphereCollider)
  {
    // Create the sphere component as the collider
    SphereCollider =
        CreateDefaultSubobject<USphereComponent>(TEXT("SphereComponent"));
    // Set the RootComponent to be the collision component
    // Note: We are making the Sphere Collider a RootComponent since the
    //       simulation will drive it!
    RootComponent = SphereCollider;
  }

  if (!ProjectileMovement)
  {
    // Use the Projectile Movement Component to drive the fireball
    // projectile's movement
    ProjectileMovement =
        CreateDefaultSubobject<UProjectileMovementComponent>(
                                    TEXT("ProjectileMovementComponent"));
    // Set the sphere collider as the updated component
    ProjectileMovement->SetUpdatedComponent(SphereCollider);
    // No initial speed and gravity
    ProjectileMovement->InitialSpeed = 0;
    ProjectileMovement->ProjectileGravityScale = 0;
  }

  FireballFX =
    CreateDefaultSubobject<UNiagaraComponent>(FName("NiagaraComponent"));
  FireballFX->SetupAttachment(RootComponent);
```

```
    // Register the delegate
    SphereCollider->OnComponentBeginOverlap.AddDynamic(this,
                                   &AFireball::OnSphereColliderBeginOverlap);
}
```

In the constructor, after creating the RootComponent and SphereComponent, we set the RootComponent to be the collider by assigning the **Sphere Collider** to it. Here we are making the `SphereCollider` a `RootComponent` since the simulation will drive it!

Then after creating the **Projectile Movement Component** to drive the fireball projectile's movement, we call the `SetUpdatedComponent()` of the component to set the **sphere collider** as the **updated component**, and also set no initial speed and no gravity for the movement component. Lastly, after creating the fireball Niagara component and attaching it to the RootComponent, the `OnSphereColliderBeginOverlap()` method below is assigned as the delegate of the collider's `OnComponentBeginOverlap` event.

```
void AFireball::OnSphereColliderBeginOverlap(UPrimitiveComponent*
    OverlappedComp, AActor* OtherActor, UPrimitiveComponent* OtherComp,
    int32 OtherBodyIndex, bool bFromSweep, const FHitResult& SweepResult)
{
  if (OtherActor != Owner && OtherActor->GetOwner() != Owner) {
    // Get the IHealth interface
    IHealth* health = Cast<IHealth>(OtherActor);
    // If implementing the IHealth and is not dead, apply the damage
    if (health && !health->IsDead()) {
      if(Stats)
        health->ApplyDamage(Stats->AttackPower->Roll(), Owner);
    }

    // Destroy the fireball
    this->Destroy();
  }
}
```

In the `OnSphereColliderBeginOverlap()` delegate function, after try getting the `IHealth` interface, if the hit actor implements the `IHealth` and is not dead, we apply the damage and pass in the fireball's **Attack Power** as the damage value. Finally, we call the `Destroy()` method to destroy the fireball and remove it from the scene.

Now build the project and make sure that no errors occur, then go back to Unreal Editor.

Fireball Stats

Before creating the **Fireball** Blueprint, let's create the **Stats** for it. First, create a new folder called **Spells** in the **Characters** folder. Then right-click in the Content Browser of the **Spells** folder, and choose **Blueprint Class** from the context menu, then in the **Pick Parent Class** window, find and select the **DiceRoll** class. After pressing the **Select** button to create the Blueprint, rename it to **BP_FireballDamage**.

Next, double-click the Blueprint to open it in the editor, and reset the **Modifier** field to a **large** value such as **1000** in our case, as shown below:

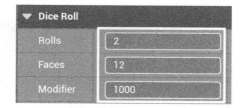

Also, set the **Rolls** and **Faces** to **2** and **12**, respectively. Now press **Compile** and **Save** to confirm the modification.

The Fireball Projectile Blueprint

Next, right-click in the **Spells** folder again, and choose **Blueprint Class** from the context menu. Then in the **Pick Parent Class** window, find and select the **Fireball** class under the **Spell**, and press the **Select** button to create the Blueprint. After renaming it to **BP_Fireball**, double-click to open it in the editor.

With the **Fireball FX** selected in the **Components** panel, set its **Niagara System Asset** field to **FXS_Fireball** as shown below:

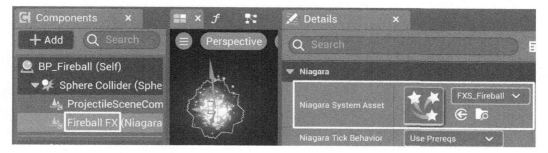

Next, select the **Sphere Collider** and set its **Sphere Radius** field to **50**, which makes the Sphere Collider **bigger**, as shown below:

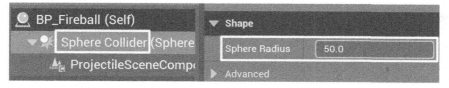

Fireball Collision Setup

To prevent the fireball projectile from being blocked by the great sword, with the **Sphere Collider** selected, continue to find and expand the **Collision** settings as shown below:

After setting the **Collision Presets** to **Custom...**, set the **Collision Responses** of the **WorldDynamic** and **Pawn** fields to **Ignore** and **Overlap** as shown above.

Projectile Movement and Fireball Stats Setup

Continue to select the **Projectile Movement** as shown below, find and expand the **Projectile** settings, and reset the **Max Speed** to **0** because we'll use the **X** Velocity later as the fireball projectile's speed.

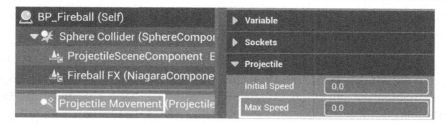

Then expand the **Velocity** settings and set the **X** Velocity to **3000** as shown below:

Lastly, with the **BP_Fireball** selected, expand the **Stats** section as shown below:

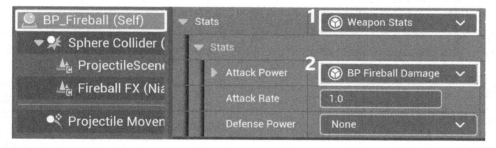

After selecting the **Weapon Stats** for the **Stats** field, select the **BP_FireballDamage** for the **Attack Power** as shown above. Now press **Compile** and **Save** to confirm the modification.

The Cast Fireball Montage Setup

To cast the fireball, we need a magic cast animation, so go to the **Mixamo** website again, and after login in, enter "**magic**" in the **search bar** as shown below:

Find the **STANDING 2H MAGIC AREA ATTACK 02** animation, as shown above, then press the **DOWNLOAD** button to download the animation **without** skin.

After converting the animation to have the **root** bone in **Blender**, back to Unreal Editor and import the animation into the **Warriors** > **Female** > **Animations** folder. Then right-click on the imported animation sequence and choose **Create** > **Create AnimMontage** from the context menu to create a Montage called **AM_CastFireball**.

Casting Fireball Projectiles in C++

To cast fireballs in C++, open the **WarriorCharacter.h** header and add the following **bold** lines:

```
#include "CoreMinimal.h"
#include "RPGCharacter.h"
#include "Animation/SwordAnimNotifyState.h"
#include "Spells/Fireball.h"
#include "WarriorCharacter.generated.h"
    ...
UCLASS()
class RPG_API AWarriorCharacter : public ARPGCharacter
{
    GENERATED_BODY()
public:
    AWarriorCharacter();

    virtual void PlayCastFireballMontage(const FInputActionValue& value)
                                                            override;

    void CastFireball();
        ...

protected:
    AFireball* fireball;
    UPROPERTY(EditDefaultsOnly, BlueprintReadOnly, Category = "Fireball")
    TSubclassOf<AFireball> FireballClass;
    UPROPERTY(EditDefaultsOnly, BlueprintReadOnly, Category = "Montages")
    UAnimMontage* CastFireballMontage;
    UPROPERTY(EditDefaultsOnly, BlueprintReadOnly, Category = "Fireball")
    float FireballLifeSpan;
};
```

In the `public` section, the **overridden** `PlayCastFireballMontage()` method is to play the cast fireball Montage, and the `CastFireball()` method is to cast the fireball projectile.

In the `protected` section, the `fireball` refers to the `Fireball` instance created at run-time and the `FireballClass` property represents the `Fireball` **Blueprint** class. The `CastFireballMontage` property refers to the cast fireball Montage. The `FireballLifeSpan` property is the **life span** of the fireball projectile.

Next, open the **WarriorCharacter.cpp** file and add the following lines to implement the **two** new methods:

```
void AWarriorCharacter::PlayCastFireballMontage(const FInputActionValue&
                                                                value)
{
  if (IsValid(CastFireballMontage))
    PlayAnimMontage(CastFireballMontage);
}

void AWarriorCharacter::CastFireball()
{
  // Get the fireball socket location
  FVector FireballSocketLocation =
                        GetMesh()->GetSocketLocation("FireballSocket");

  FActorSpawnParameters spawnParams;
  // Set the owner of the projectile
  spawnParams.Owner = this;
  // The Pawn that is responsible for damage done by the spawned Actor
  spawnParams.Instigator = this;
  // Spawn the fireball projectile
  fireball = GetWorld()->SpawnActor<AFireball>(FireballClass,
              FireballSocketLocation, GetActorRotation(), spawnParams);

  if (fireball) {
    // Set the life span
    fireball->SetLifeSpan(FireballLifeSpan);
  }
}
```

In the `PlayCastFireballMontage()` method, we call the `PlayAnimMontage()` method to play the Montage.

In the `CastFireball()` method, after getting the fireball socket location, we declare a `FActorSpawnParameters` object and set the projectile's **Owner** and **Instigator** to the warrior character through the object. Then we call the `SpawnActor()` method and pass in the Blueprint class to spawn the fireball projectile from the socket location on the warrior. Lastly, the fireball's life span is set to the value of the `FireballLifeSpan` property.

Now build the project, back to Unreal Editor, and open the **BP_FemaleWarrior** Blueprint as shown below:

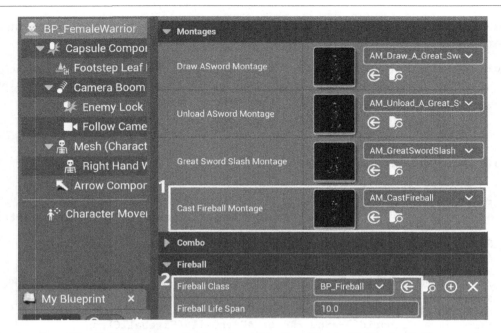

Set the **Cast Fireball Montage** field to the **AM_CastFireball**, **Fireball Class** to the **BP_Fireball**, and **Fireball Life Span** to **10** as shown above.

The Fireball AnimNotify

Next, let's create an **AnimNotify** in C++ for the cast fireball Montage. From the main menu, choose **Tools > New C++ Class…** and in the next step, pick **AnimNotify** as the Parent Class. Next, after renaming it to **FireballAnimNotify** as shown below, select the **Public/Animation** folder for the **Path**.

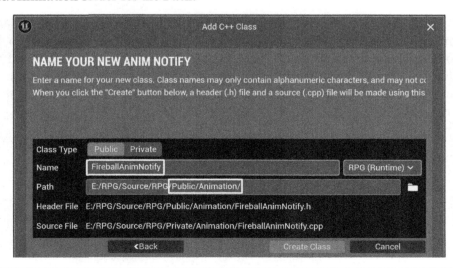

Press the **Create Class** button to generate the class in Visual Studio. Open the **FireballAnimNotify.h** header and add the following **bold** lines in the class:

```
UCLASS()
class RPG_API UFireballAnimNotify : public UAnimNotify
{
  GENERATED_BODY()
public:
  virtual void Notify(USkeletalMeshComponent* MeshComp,
                           UAnimSequenceBase* Animation) override;
};
```

In the `public` section, we override the built-in `Notify()` method.

Next, add the following lines in the **FireballAnimNotify.cpp** file to implement the **Notify()** method:

```
#include "Characters/WarriorCharacter.h"

void UFireballAnimNotify::Notify(USkeletalMeshComponent* MeshComp,
                           UAnimSequenceBase* Animation)
{
  AWarriorCharacter* warrior = Cast<AWarriorCharacter>(
                           MeshComp->GetOwner());

  if (warrior) {
    warrior->CastFireball();
  }
}
```

In the method, after getting the warrior character, we call its `CastFireball()` method to cast the fireball projectile.

Now build the project and go back to Unreal Editor, open the **AM_CastFireball** in the editor as shown below:

After pausing the animation preview, move the **red bar** on the Timeline to frame **50**, as shown above, then right-click on the **first (1)** track under the **Notifies**. Next, select **Add Notify... > Fireball Anim Notify** from the context menu and panel to create an Anim Notify on the vertical line. Now press **Save** to confirm the modification.

Creating the Fireball Socket

Continue to open the **SKEL_FemaleWarrior** in the **Warriors** > **Female** folder, and after expanding the bone hierarchy, find the **LeftHandMiddle1** bone as shown below:

Right-click on the bone and choose **Add Socket** to create a Socket called **FireballSocket** as shown above. Then press **Save** to confirm the modification.

Adding the Input Action

Finally, inside the Content > **Input** folder, right-click and select **Input** > **Input Action** to create an Input Action named **IA_CastFireball**. Then open the **IMC_Warrior** Mapping Context, add a new mapping and select **IA_CastFireball** as shown below:

Continue to select **Keyboard** > **3** for the mapping, and then after creating a trigger, select **Pressed** from the dropdown menu.

Now that the code and settings are all complete, press **Play** to run the game. After pressing the **3** key on the keyboard, the cast fireball Montage will be played and followed by the fireball projectile shooting from the socket on the character's palm. The results are as shown in the following two figures:

The left figure shows the fireball being cast and the right figure shows the damage done by the fireball hitting the enemy.

6.4 Summary

The **Niagara VFX System** is the primary tool to do visual effects (VFX) inside UE5. In this chapter, we provided an Overview and a Quick Start guide to get you up and running. After the Quick Start, we designed and implemented the common VFX in the ARPGs including the impact and shockwave effects, the disintegration effect, and fireballs. We also demonstrated how to play the Niagara VFX and cast fireballs in the C++ code.

After six chapters about the Basics, Combat, and VFX design, you already have a solid foundation to explore further topics in ARPG design. In the second volume of this book, we are going to cover advanced UE5 topics including **Artificial Intelligence (AI)**, **RPG User Interface** design, **Dialogues** and **Quests**, **Character Customization**, **Inventory** and **Shops**. Looking forward to seeing you soon, good luck!

Exercises

6.1 Currently, the leaf poof effect only is played when the player is stepping on the **DirtGrass** physical material. Use the knowledge you learned from this chapter to design a Niagara effect and modify the related C++ code to play the effect when the player is stepping on the **RockCliff** material.

6.2 Find a free sound from the Internet or the Epic Marketplace and, after importing it into Unreal Editor, add the C++ code to our project to play the sound when the player is casting the fireball.

6.3 In this chapter, we respawned the enemy character in a circular area after it's dead. Please re-implement the respawn, but this time respawn the enemy character in a **rectangular** area instead of the circular area.

A.1 How to Avoid Crashing the Unreal Editor

Unreal Editor crashing usually is a headache for beginners to programming in UE5 C++. In this section, the author provides two important tricks and outlines the mistakes that beginners tender to overlook and cause the Editor to crash as follows:

1. **Always Check the Nullptr**

   The first and **most common** mistake when writing C++ and crashing the Unreal Editor is forgetting to check the **null pointer** (`nullptr` or `NULL`). This mistake maybe not be an issue in other game engines such as the **Unity** game engine that uses C# as the script language. But always remember that checking null pointers is a **required** and **good** practice! That is because null pointers not only cause the Unreal Editor to crash but make the project difficult to debug especially in a large game project no matter which game engine you use.

   Unreal Engine also provides the `IsValid()` function in C++ and Blueprint to check if an object is non-null and not marked ready for being garbage collected during the next garbage collection cycle. So if the Unreal Editor crashes for no reason, please double check if you forget to check **null pointers** or forget to assign values or Blueprint classes to **properties** declared in C++.

2. **Check If in Unreal Editor**

   Another common issue that causes the Unreal Editor to crash is forgetting to check if we are in Unreal Editor. For example, if we are adding an Anim Notify to the animation sequence or montage, but some pointers maybe not be initialized yet during editing and this will also crash the Editor. So to prevent this issue, you can always check if the `WorldType` of the global `UWorld` top-level object equals the `EWorldType::Editor` type to determine if you are currently in the Unreal Editor as demonstrated in the C++ code of this book.

A.2 Online References and Resources

Some useful online references and resources are provided in this section including tutorials and articles.

A.2.1 Video Tutorials

There are several old useful UE4 and new UE 5 tutorials on YouTube channels worth mentioning in this subsection and they are categorized as follows:

Real World Landscape Creation

Importing Real World Heightmaps into Unreal Engine by C:\Insert Name Here, https://www.youtube.com/watch?v=kEgijZUKMGc&t=354s.

Realistic Landscape Materials

Unreal Engine Landscape Master Material Tutorial by Unreal Sensei, https://www.youtube.com/watch?v=3hmRN8bXMM0&t=1693s.

UE4: Fix Landscape Texture Tiling with This UE4 Macro/Micro Variation Technique by WorldofLevelDesign, https://www.youtube.com/watch?v=zUyl2MbcKuE.

Combo Animation System

Tutorial: Advanced combo animation system by LeafBranchGames, https://www.youtube.com/watch?v=UI7mjCLknws.

Horse Riding and Legs IK

Unreal Horse Riding by CodeLikeMe, https://www.youtube.com/watch?v=qVDEefZT__8&t=263s.

Unreal Leg IK by CodeLikeMe, https://www.youtube.com/watch?v=kK9rQzbSzio&list=RDCMUClb6Jh9EBV7a_Nm52 Ipll_Q&index=2.

Visual Effects

UE4 VFX For Games: Realistic Fireball Projectile by JangaFX VFX Software & Tutorials at https://www.youtube.com/watch?v=6Lk3SL44A6o&t=74s.

Some textures used in the impact effect are from the following **Unity** tutorial:

Create Hit Impact Effect - Unity Game tutorial by Game Dev University, https://www.youtube.com/watch?v=rB7yA2P8xT8&t=1s.

UE5 Tutorials

TerreSculptor to Unreal Engine 5 Landscape by Demenzun Media, https://www.youtube.com/watch?v=EVNrYPwYfMM.

UE5 World Partition by Demenzun Media, https://www.youtube.com/watch?v=fDgKV3SjDTI&t=558s.

Foot IK Tutorial in Unreal Engine 5 with Custom Character by UNF Games, https://www.youtube.com/watch?v=lfU3p80EjQE&t=5889s.

Sword Trail Effect by Rimaye, https://www.youtube.com/c/RimayeAssetsandTutorialsNIAGARA.

Sword Trail in UE5 Niagara Tutorial by CGHOW, https://www.youtube.com/watch?v=XnZS-ycyNPU&t=927s.

Disintegration in UE5 Niagara Tutorial by CGHOW, https://www.youtube.com/watch?v=4dYg4bvf4Rc&t=546s.

A.2.2 Modern C++ in Visual Studio

The Microsoft online C++ language documentation, at https://docs.microsoft.com/en-us/cpp/cpp/?view=msvc-170, provides documents and tutorials for learning to use C++ and the C++ standard library.

A.2.3 UE5 Online Document

The **Unreal Engine 5 Document** at https://docs.unrealengine.com/5.0/en-US/ has complete resources for learning to use UE5. If you are new to Unreal Engine then the online document here is the first place you have to visit.

A.2.4 Unreal Engine Forums

The Unreal Engine forums at https://forums.unrealengine.com/ is an invaluable knowledge base and you can usually find solutions to common Unreal C++ issues from here.

A.3 Online Art Assets and Tools

The free art assets used in this book can be downloaded from the Author's website and the Epic Games Marketplace, or the following websites.

A.3.1 Online Free Assets

Melee Weapons

Heavy Full Metal Sword by Lokomotto, https://www.turbosquid.com/3d-models/sword-remake---3d-model-1309370.

Horse Models

Low-poly horse for games by lespol, https://www.turbosquid.com/3d-models/free-low--horse-3d-model/810753.

Sounds

Free Game Sound Effects from mixkit.co, https://mixkit.co/free-sound-effects/game/.

A.3.2 Free Art Creation Tools

Image Creation and Editing

Photopea, free Photoshop-like image creation, and editing tool, at https://www.photopea.com/.

Normal Map Creation Tools

NORMALMAP ONLINE at https://cpetry.github.io/NormalMap-Online/.

Index

#define Directives.......... 56

& operator...................... 44

&& operator................... 43

^ operator 44

| operator 44

| | operator.................... 43

~ operator...................... 44

<< operator.................... 44

2D unit vectors............. 134

3D unit vector.............. 134

A

access level..................... 45

Access Modifer

private......................... 38

Access Modifier

protected.................... 62

public 38

static 38

Access Modifiers............. 67

Activating Effects in C++
.... 485

Adding A Root Bone to
Mixamo Animations....... 212

Adding Animation
Sequences to a Montage
.... 305

Adding Camera
Components in C++ 224

Adding the Enhanced Input
Module 251

Anim Graph Setup for
Montages...................... 310

Animal Variety Pack....198

Animating the Horse ...407

Animation Blueprints for
Player Characters 233

AnimInstance 231

Asset Compatibility 10

Assigning Effects in
Blueprints.....................487

Assigning Physical
Materials........................396

Assigning Stats in the
Blueprint 279

Assigning the Impact and
Shockwaves Niagara
System 534

Assigning the RPGHUD in
the Project Settings 293

Assigning the Socket
Names.............................458

Associating Animation
and Character Blueprints
....242

Asymmetry 328

Attaching the Great
Sword 363

Attaching the Sword Trail
Niagara System 506

Auto Activate checkbox
................................488, 582

Auto Landscape Material
....187

Automatic Horse Rigging
....404

B

base stats........271, 273, 275

Blender Rigify Animbox
Addon........................... 403

Block scope.................... 38

Blueprints for Enemies 352

Blueprints for the Great
Sword........................... 342

Boolean Type 35

Bottom Toolbar............. 19

break keyword....47, 49, 50

by reference................... 45

by value 45

C

C++ Variable Scope....... 38

Calling Functions across
the C++ and Blueprint
Boundary 124

Cascade......................... 472

case label section........... 47

cast operator () 37

Casting Fireball Projectiles
in C++ 594

Character Data Types ... 35

Class

constructor 63

destructor 64

inheritance34, 66, 67, 71,
76

interface..................... 34

overloading............... 71

overriding 71

polymorphism 34

Static Members 69

this keyword 66

Class Naming Prefixes 133

Class Wizard 118

classification 66, 78

Collision Presets.. 435, 437, 592

combo 315

condition section.............48

Constant Shifts 328

Content Drawer 7

Content Drawer / Content Browser 15

Core Niagara Components 464

Creating a Module........466

Creating an Attack Montage 304

Creating an Epic Games Account 3

Creating Emitters..........466

Creating Heightmaps from Real-World Data. 148

Creating Light and Sky 147

Creating Physical Materials 395

Creating Player Starts 266

Creating RPG Character Class 222

Creating Sphere Trace Sockets...........................345

Creating States and Conduits 235

Creating Systems 466

Creating Systems and Emitters........................472

Creating the CharacterStats Class.... 273

Creating the GameMode Blueprint 265

Creating the Input Mapping Context...........................246

Creating the Montage from an Animation Sequence........................308

Creating the SCRATCH MODULE 498

Creating the StatsModifier Class...............................276

Creating the Warrior Class in C++ 225

Creating Warrior Characters from Mixamo 195

Critical hits....................329

cross product 136

C-style string.............40, 41

D

Damage Text Blueprint and Animation..............386

dangling pointer...........143

Data Layers for World Partition............................7

decision-making structures........................46

Declaring pointers..........50

default case label...........48

Defining and Using Templates........................57

delegate assignment.......42

Derived Stats................271

Desktop development with C++ 11

Details Panel 17

Development Platform Changes 10

Dissecting the Third Person Character 131

Distance-based Texture Blending........................179

dot product...................134

Download and Install the Epic Games Launcher 2

Dynamic Parameter Node 490, 515, 537, 540

dynamically sized........139

E

Emitter Update Settings 477

Emitter Wizard 473

Enabling Root Motions .. 215

Enemy Lock Collision Box Setup 383

Enemy Montage Setup 361

Enemy Stats Setup....... 360

enumeration 36

Error List and Output Window 29

escape sequence............40

Exception

catch keyword 85

throw keyword..........87

exception handler..........85

explicit type conversions 37

Exporting the Horse Skeletal Mesh 406

Exporting the Horse Walk Animation....................408

Extending a C++ Class via Blueprints 122

F

Finishing up Character
Blueprint Settings 262

Fireball Collision Setup591

Fireball Materials 535

Fireball Stats 590

Fireball Textures 535

first-in, first-out 96

Fixing Landscape Texture
Repetition...................... 172

FlipBook Node 535, 536

footstep sound playing393

G

garbage collection130, 131,
140, 141, 142, 143, 144, 602

Generating Visual Studio
Project Files................... 485

generic programming.... 57

GUI 299

H

Has-A 84

Health Bar Setup........... 359

heap 50

horizontal displacement
.... 134

Horse IK Rig Setup 442

How C++ Works............. 26

How to Make an RPG . 270

How to Use Abstract
Classes and Interfaces ... 84

HUD 290

I

IK Leg Sockets 448

Impact and Shockwave
Materials....................... 512

Impact Effect and
Shockwave Textures 511

Implementing the Sprint
Drain 294

implicit conversions.......37

Importing Animations.....214

Importing Megascans
Textures.......................... 158

Importing Mixamo
Characters 196

Importing the Height Map
File.................................. 156

initializer.......................... 48

Input Actions . 10, 243, 244,
246, 251, 325, 439

Input Mapping Contexts
.... 10, 243, 246

Installing Blender............210

Installing Unreal Engine 5
.... 3

Integer Type Modifiers..34

Interactable Icon and Text
Widgets 409

Interacting with the Horse
Character 426

Is-A...................................84

iterator.............................. 48

L

Landscape Materials 161

Landscape Textures Tiling
.... 170

last-in, first-out 97

Launching Unreal Engine
.... 4

Layered Blend Per Bone
Setup 313

Legs IK Exposure and
Previewing 447

Level Viewport 14

Loading and Unloading
Landscape Cells 157

Lock Interface........378, 379

Locomotion Animations
.... 205

logical operations 43

Lumen Global
Illumination and
Reflections 6

M

magnitude (length)...... 134

Main Toolbar.................. 18

Making a Property Show
up in the Editor............. 120

Making Height Map using
TerreSculptor 151

Maps and GameMode Setup
.... 265

match expression........... 47

Material Parameter
Collection........566, 576, 582

Matrix Transform Vector
Node.............................. 500

Megascans Trees.......... 200

Melee Weapons.............. 605

memory leak 63

Method Overloading 74

Mixamo Converter Plug-in
.... 210

Mixamo Rootbaker......... 212

Modifiers 275

Module scope................. 38

Montage Slots 309

Multiple Inheritance 80, 82

multithreaded programming 100

N

Naming C++ Variables . 37

Nanite Virtualized Geometry 6

nested structures............ 47

Noise-based Texture Blending....................... 175

normalized................... 136

NORMALMAP ONLINE 605

Numeric Types......... 34, 35

O

object-oriented design .. 62, 66, 84

Object-Oriented Programming ...... See OOP

OOP 34, 100

Outliner........................... 16

P

Painting Foliage 189

Parameterized Constructors 65

Particle Spawn Settings 478

Particle Systems 464

Particle Update Settings 482

Perlin Noise 179, 491

Photopea 605

Physical Surfaces.......... 394

Playing Combos in C++ 319

Playing Damage Text Animation in C++ 390

Playing the Impact Effect and Shockwaves...........532

polar coordinate system 585

Previewing Blend Spaces 219

Procedure scope 38

Projectile Movement and Fireball Stats Setup.......592

pure virtual member function 78

Q

Quadruped Fantasy Creatures 199

Quaternion 133

Quixel Bridge...8, 158, 159, 190

Quixel Bridge Integration8

R

RadialGradientExponentia l Node 516, 537, 538

raw pointer......................63

Regenerating the Skeleton from Mesh.......................213

Riding Animation Setup 430

role-playing video game 146

Rotating the Player toward the Enemy........384

Runtime Lifecycle...........130

S

Sample Poses 217

Secret Stats 273

Setting Defaults in the Constructor................... 122

Setting up the Damage Text Widget.................. 392

Sidebar Tabs 7

simple data types........... 34

smart pointers 143

Sounds........................... 605

Stamina .271, 280, 282, 287, 288, 289, 290, 293, 294

StaminaBar UI Blueprint 283

String Concatenation..... 41

string literal 40

structured programming 62

Sword and Fairy 7 222

Sword Trail Particle Emitter 503

Sword Trail Particles... 501

Sword Trail Textures... 488

Sword-Playing Animations 208

SystemLocalToWorld.. 500

SystemLocalToWorld Parameter 500

T

TCHAR 138

TerreSculptor 149

The #undef directive..... 56

the auto keyword 38

the Blend Settings........ 314

The C++ Build Process in Visual Studio.................. 27

The Cast Fireball Montage Setup 593

the const keyword 39

The DamageTextWidget
Class 385

the DiceRoll class 329

The Disintegration
Material 563

The Disintegration
Niagara System 552

The do Statement 50

The Enemy Class 347

The EnemyAnimInstance
Class 351

The Female Warrior
Blueprint 228

The Fireball AnimNotify
.... 596

The Fireball class 588

The Fireball Niagara
System 541

The Fireball Projectile
Blueprint 591

the Fireball Socket 598

the Footstep AnimNotify
Blueprint 401

The for Statement 48

The Fur Disintegration
Material 573

the HealthBar UI
Blueprint 300

The Horse Animation
Blendspace and Blueprint
.... 415

The Horse Animation
Blueprint 418

The Horse Character
Blueprint 433

The Horse Character Class
.... 421

the Horse Legs IK in C++
.... 449

The HorseAnimInstance
Class 417

The if Statement 46

The IHealth Interface
Class 340

the Impact Niagara
System 517

The Interactable Interface
Class 420

The Item Class 332

the member access
operator 63

The Mount Socket 432

The NPC Class 346

the RPGHUD Blueprint
.... 292

The RPGHUD Class 290

The StaminaBarWidget
Class 280

The switch Statement 47

The Sword Trail Material
.... 489

The Sword Trail Niagara
System 494

the ternary operator 57

The Timeline Curve 580

the typename keyword . 58

The Weapon Class 334

The WeaponStats Class 332

The while Statement 49

The Wolf Class 350

The World Partition Cell
Size 193

Thread Synchronization 89

type conversions 37

type-safe 37

U

UE5 Migration Guide 8

unit vector 134

Unreal C++ Variable
Declaration 38

Unreal Engine forums. 604

Unreal Motion Graphics UI
Designer 280

Unreal Objects (UObject)
.... 129

Updated User Interface .. 7

USGS Earth Explorer .. 149

Using Animation
Notifications 316

Using the Enhanced Input
System for Interaction 243

V

Vector 133

Version-Specific
Conversion Notes 9

vertical displacement .. 134

virtual function 78

Visual Studio

   Installer 11

   integrated development
     environment 2

   script debugging 31

Visual Studio debugger 28,
29

Visual Studio Debugging
Toolbar 28

Visual Studio IDE

   Code Editor 23

   Options Window 24

   Solution Explorer 24

Visual Studio Toolbar

   Comment 26

   Create a new project . 25

Save all files 25

Save the current file ... 25

Uncomment 26

Windows Debugger .. 25

Volumetric Cloud 148

W

Weapon Mounting and
Unloading Montage Setup
.... 371

What Stats Should a Game
Have? 272

What's new in UE5 5

World Partition for Large,
Open Environments 6

Made in the USA
Las Vegas, NV
19 June 2024